Ariane de Waal
Theatre on Terror

CDE Studies

Edited by
Martin Middeke

Volume 27

Ariane de Waal

Theatre on Terror

Subject Positions in British Drama

DE GRUYTER

Zugl.: Bochum, Univ., Diss., 2016

ISBN 978-3-11-063524-9
e-ISBN (PDF) 978-3-11-051708-8
e-ISBN (EPUB) 978-3-11-051543-5
ISSN 2194-9069

Library of Congress Cataloging-in-Publication Data
A CIP catalog record for this book has been applied for at the Library of Congress.

Bibliographic information published by the Deutsche Nationalbibliothek
The Deutsche Nationalbibliothek lists this publication in the Deutsche Nationalbibliografie; detailed bibliographic data are available on the Internet at http://dnb.dnb.de.

© 2018 Walter de Gruyter GmbH, Berlin/Boston
This volume is text- and page-identical with the hardback published in 2017.
Printing and binding: CPI books GmbH, Leck

♾ Printed on acid-free paper
Printed in Germany

www.degruyter.com

Contents

Acknowledgements —— VII

1 Introduction —— 1

2 Theoretical Framework —— 15
2.1   Discursive Formations —— 15
2.2   Theatre in/as Discourse —— 20
2.3   De/Constructing the Subject —— 24
2.4   Theorising Subject Positions —— 33
2.5   Performing Subject Positions —— 41

3 Home-Front Plays: Subject Positions in the British Terror City —— 48
3.1   Patriot Subjects, Terrorist Suspects —— 50
3.2   British Muslim Subjectivities —— 74
3.3   Articulations of Citizenship —— 92
3.4   (Un)Grieving Femininities —— 118
3.5   Traumatised Masculinities —— 138

4 Front-Line Plays: Positioning 'Self', 'Other', and Other Selves in Iraq and Afghanistan —— 161
4.1   Determining the Enemy Positions —— 163
4.2   Appropriating Afghan Femininities —— 186
4.3   Neoliberal War Agents —— 203
4.4   Reporting Front-Line Deaths —— 224
4.5   Military Masculinities —— 244

5 Conclusion —— 265

Works Cited —— 271
   Primary Literature —— 271
   Secondary Literature —— 272

General Index —— 291

Index of Plays —— 296

Acknowledgements

This monograph is a slightly revised version of my PhD thesis, which was handed in at Ruhr University Bochum in December 2015. The German Society for Contemporary Theatre and Drama in English distinguished this work with the CDE Award in 2016. I am very grateful to CDE for this distinction and for the inclusion of my work in the *CDE Studies* series. Special thanks are due to CDE's vibrant PhD community, to Anja Müller and Eckart Voigts for organising the London theatre excursions, and to Martin Middeke and Clare Wallace for hosting the postgraduate forum.

My sincerest thanks go to my supervisors: I would like to express my immense gratitude to Anette Pankratz for her diligent, thorough, and kind criticism of my work, her penchant for irony, and for encouraging me to keep interrogating my own interpretations; I am also extremely grateful to Roland Weidle for his detailed and valuable annotations and his ongoing support.

Many colleagues and friends have been thoughtful interlocutors during my completion of this project and most helpful proofreaders of the manuscript in its various stages. I am especially grateful to Anna Billmann and Gareth Wheeler for their careful corrections and to Marcel Hartwig, Jim Reynolds, Mark Schmitt, and Claus-Ulrich Viol for offering crucial suggestions when most needed.

The doctoral project on which this book is based was funded by the German National Academic Foundation from 2013–2016. Besides their financial support, I am particularly thankful for having been given the opportunity to participate in engaging doctoral seminars and summer schools.

This project moved forward in no small measure thanks to my research stay with Queen Mary, University of London, in 2014. I am much indebted to the insightful and inspiring conversations I have had with the research students and staff of the Drama Department. I especially wish to thank Catherine Silverstone for invigorating discussions about trauma and performance.

I would also like to express my gratitude to the playwrights who kindly discussed their work with me: Tim Crouch, Chris Goode, Dennis Kelly, Mark Ravenhill, Atiha Sen Gupta, and Simon Stephens.

Very heartfelt thanks travel to the Niederrhein region, to my parents Hildegund and Jürgen, my brothers Sebastian and Simon, and my incredible nieces Leia and Lia Marie. Last, but never least, I thank my dearest friends, who have given me the kindest, craziest, and most loving support I could have wished for: many thanks to my London Fellows, especially to Felipe and Verity, and the warmest 'thank you' to Martina, Seetha-Linda, and Vincent for holding down the home front in Bochum with and for me.

Copyright Acknowledgements

Earlier versions of material used in chapters three and four appeared in the following articles, reprinted with permission from the publishers:

de Waal, Ariane. "'Do Not Run on the Platforms ... If You Look a Bit Foreign': De/Constructing the Travelling Terrorist Assemblage." *Liminalities: A Journal of Performance Studies*, vol. 12, no. 5, 2016, pp. 1–17.
—. "Staging Wounded Soldiers: The Affects and Effects of Post-Traumatic Theatre." *Performance Paradigm*, no. 11, 2015, pp. 16–31.
—. "(Sub)Versions of the Them/Us Dichotomy in Iraq War Drama." *Journal of Contemporary Drama in English*, vol. 2, no. 1, 2014, pp. 131–144.

1 Introduction

All research on the 'war on terror' is characterised by a constitutive incompleteness.[1] The images and documents that comprise the 'war on terror' archive have undergone processes of redaction and erasure, and even the most abundant visual records, like the footage of the falling twin towers or the Abu Ghraib torture photographs, obliterate traces of the violence committed in secret prisons or drone strikes. Due to its essential formlessness, it is impossible to determine with any certitude or objectivity what this war encompasses or where it ends. Whenever it seemed that the (British) 'war on terror' might be drawing to a close – when the UK government decided to stop using this terminology around 2006,[2] the last British troops were withdrawn from Afghanistan in 2014, or the last British resident was released from Guantánamo Bay in 2015 – the war machine subtly shifted gear. Marked by indefinite detention and an incalculable threat, this global conflict appears to prolong itself endlessly in relation to the inexhaustible resources of (counter-)terrorism and "the spectral infinity of its enemy" (Butler, *Precarious Life* 34). In a moment of intense uncertainty surrounding the means, ends, and limits of (countering) terrorism, this study approaches the recent theatres of war through theatrical stagings of terror and examines British drama written within and against the current contours of conflict.

Scholars and critics have attributed an important cultural and educational function to political theatre after 9/11: it has been dubbed "a necessity rather than an optional extra" (Billington, *State* 392), and performances have been likened to crash courses (Cull, "Staging" 125), "designed to enlighten us" (Sierz, *Rewriting* 85). Despite – or perhaps rather because of – the well-established critical view of "a general resurgence of political theatre [...] in the wake of 9/11" (Reinelt, "Toward" 81),[3] just what it is that makes this theatre 'political' is not always submitted to critical scrutiny. On the one hand, there is an observable tendency

---

[1] Citing Joseph Pugliese's claim that the obliteration of evidence and omission of information in the 'war on terror' context produces a *"constitutively incomplete"* scholarship, Rustom Bharucha contends that "[t]he future of researching terror [...] is as challenging as trying to predict how one can begin to assess its material opacity" (186).
[2] In late 2006 the Foreign Office advised cabinet ministers and diplomats to no longer refer to the 'war on terror'. However, media outlets like the *Sun* refused to "scrap" the terminology (*Sun* 8), and usage of the phrase persisted regardless, if sometimes in a slightly modified form.
[3] The notion that the upsurge of political theatre in the UK should be attributed to 9/11 and particularly the controversy surrounding the Iraq war was first expressed by theatre critics such as Jasper Rees (17) and Kate Kellaway (5) and subsequently advocated by, amongst others, scholars Chris Megson (369) and Stephen Bottoms (57).

DOI 10.1515/9783110517088-001

to revert to what Baz Kershaw has called "the unhelpful idea that 'all theatre is political'" (*Radical* 63),[4] an assumption which deflects attention from the kind of political imagination that a particular performance engenders. On the other hand, appraisals of theatre after 9/11 all too often take its resistant stance for granted; in pitting it "against media hegemony", this position tends to champion theatre as the more ethical, critical, and honest alternative to the "false objectivity and speculations of minutia-driven reportage" (Colleran 10). Scholarship that is attentive to post-9/11 theatre's (lack of) political potential has mainly focused on two areas of enquiry: one strand of research centres upon documentary and especially verbatim theatre, a genre that has been perceived to deliver the "most incisive critique" (Megson 370); the other strand foregrounds experimental performance or approaches terror(ism) "through the lens of performance" (Bharucha 30). In contrast, the politics of text-based theatre and, in particular, non-documentary drama have not been the subject of comparable scholarly consideration. As a consequence, a wide range of British new writing in response to the 'war on terror' has been critically neglected. This book seeks to redress this imbalance by offering an extensive investigation into British drama after 9/11 and a systematic examination of its politics.

In order to (re)politicise the discourse on post-9/11 theatre, this study will introduce a concept from poststructuralist political theory, the notion of subject positions, into the discussion of the plays. Based on Michel Foucault's theorisation of discursive formations, Ernesto Laclau and Chantal Mouffe have established "the existence in each individual of multiple subject positions corresponding both to the different social relations in which the individual is inserted and to the discourses that constitute these relations" (Mouffe, "Hegemony" 90). Since the 'war on terror' can be defined as a "type of discursive formation" in the Foucauldian sense (Hodges 5), it can be seen to provide a range of subject positions to which individuals become attached, but which they can also refuse to inhabit. Broadly speaking, this discursive system, hierarchically structured by national(ist), racial, religious, gendered, classed, and sexual dynamics, makes available such partially fixed subject (and object) positions as the "benevolent, civilised and moral masculinity of the West and the backward, barbaric, oppressive, deviant masculinity of the 'brown man', the 'free' Western woman and the oppressed, subjugated Muslim woman" (Khalid 20). This raises the question how theatrical events that specifically address the 'war on terror' relate to the constitution of subjectivities within the discursive field.

---

[4] See, for instance, the very first sentence of Amelia Howe Kritzer's study *Political Theatre in Post-Thatcher Britain* (2008): "In a sense, all theatre is political" (1).

Taking seriously Foucault's claim that "[t]here is not, on the one side, a discourse of power, and opposite it, another discourse that runs counter to it" (*History*, vol. 1, 101), the present study seeks to overcome conceptions of a dominant 'war on terror' discourse that could be challenged by the oppositional discourses articulated in drama.[5] Instead, it treats theatre as one surface of emergence in the discursive formation surrounding (counter-)terrorism and war, as a site of cultural production that participates in a discursive field of force where progressive, conservative, and resistant elements converge and coexist. Between and beyond the binary poles of subversion versus containment, the negotiation of subject positions in post-9/11 drama at times reinforces the logics of correlation and division that Foucault identifies at work in the discursive formation and at other times disrupts, interrupts, or obstructs the system of dispersion. In positing theatre 'on', rather than 'against', terror, it is my aim to problematise critical assumptions regarding theatre's "well-established tradition of opposition" (Delgado and Svich 7).[6] I propose that theatre events which engage with the discursive regimes of war and terrorism (plays on/about terror, in a topical sense) not only combat hegemonic representations (plays that launch an attack on/against the war, in an oppositional sense) but also often work to replicate them – like the 'war on terror', this 'theatre on terror' may set out with good intentions (i.e. an agenda of dissent) but ultimately falls back on the dichotomous structures, hierarchical valuations, or universalising images that sustain the war agenda.

Although both the discursive regime of the 'war on terror' and the subject positions it generates have been fruitfully analysed from the perspectives of discourse analysis (Hodges), gender studies (Hunt and Rygiel), geography and geopolitics (Gregory and Pred; Ingram and Dodds), media and cultural studies (Lewis; Hutnyk), and critical race and sexuality studies (Puar; Bhattacharyya), these various and intriguing contributions have not yet been systematically applied to the study of drama. Apart from a number of articles on individual plays, more comprehensive studies of British theatre's engagement with the 'war on terror' started to emerge around 2011. As hinted above, existing scholarship in this field has tended to either focus on discussions of verbatim theatre or combine an analysis of experimental or protest performance with the application of a per-

---

5 For examples of this line of argument, see Lane (61–78); Colleran (10); Tomlin (118).
6 The oppositional impetus is reflected, for instance, in the formation of the Theatres against War initiative in the US in 2002 or UK theatres' active contribution to the anti-war protests in 2003. This stance is subtly satirised in Tim Crouch's play *The Author* (2009), where an actor revels in her memories about "the day the theatre marched against the war", which ends with the singing, costumed protesters "walking over the photograph of the dead girl" used as a banner (28–29).

formance studies lens to politics and terrorism. The majority of previous studies apply comparative approaches by considering plays from various locations, especially British and American productions. Moreover, most studies do not adhere to a post-9/11 time frame but include plays that address such diverse conflicts as the Troubles in Northern Ireland, the wars in former Yugoslavia, the First Gulf War, civil wars in Africa, or the conflict in Israel and the Palestinian territories. A brief overview of significant research with one or several of these emphases will serve to highlight the gaps in existing scholarship.

There is a general agreement among commentators that the resurgence in documentary forms, particularly on the London stage, can be linked to 9/11 and its aftermath (Brady 27). In view of the seeming prevalence of verbatim plays engaging with the 'war on terror', Stephen Bottoms remarks that "[m]ere dramatic fiction has apparently been seen as an inadequate response to the current global situation" (57). While 'mere fiction' may appear insufficient to counter the 'fictional' evidence produced by politicians to make their case for the Iraq invasion, verbatim theatre is commonly appraised for "respond[ing] to a perceived democratic deficit in the wider political culture" (Megson 370). The premise that verbatim theatre is particularly well suited to challenge the official version of events has spawned a number of investigations into the relationship between documentary plays and the wider 'war on terror' discourse, which lay crucial groundwork for this study. Yet the 'stage time' given to documentary responses does not always seem justified. Even though this project also had to negotiate the difficulties that come with delineating a corpus of plays that is still evolving, I would argue that the claim that documentary drama is particularly representative of British theatre in the long 'war on terror' decade cannot be sustained. While the immense popularity of verbatim theatre may be linked to the post-9/11 moment, the number of (partly) documentary responses to the 'war on terror' is still, by far, eclipsed by non-documentary material. Hence, one of the aims of this book can already be specified as redressing the disproportionate emphasis placed upon verbatim theatre by giving a greater focus to 'conventional' drama.[7]

Another cluster of existing research takes an interest in performance in the 'war on terror' and the 'war on terror' as performance. This two-tier approach is usually based on the hypothesis that the arena of politics has become increas-

---

[7] Conventional drama can, in this context, perhaps best be defined as adhering to what Hans-Thies Lehmann calls "the essential form semantics of drama", i.e. "the embodiment of characters or allegorical figures through actors; [...] a high degree of abstraction of world representation [...]; the representation of political, moral and religious issues of social life [...]; a progressive action even in the case of extensive de-dramatization", etc. (48–49).

ingly theatricalised, a development seen as particularly evident in the context of the 'war on terror', as issues of staging, timing, and visibility have been key to this "war of images" (Mitchell 3). Proponents of performance studies were quick to point out after 9/11 that "the idea of performance [...] [is] critical to any understanding of our present situation" (Bell 7). A notable study that uses the tools and methods of this discipline to analyse the 'present situation' is Sara Brady's *Performance, Politics, and the War on Terror* (2012). Brady productively maps the political arena after 9/11 as a platform for competing performances, struggling to maintain or contest "a status quo established in the process" (19). Another seminal publication in this field is Rustom Bharucha's *Terror and Performance* (2014). Tracing the everyday manifestations of (counter-)terrorism across diverse locations as unscripted performances, Bharucha excavates a density and diversity of performative acts, rituals, registers, and energies, and he persuasively makes the case for "a much wider understanding of 'performance' [as] inextricably linked to [...] negotiations of terror in the public sphere" (19–20). Within the strand of scholarship that centres on performance, Jenny Hughes's research is the most directly relevant to the subject of this study, not least due to her sustained focus on British theatre and culture. In *Performance in a Time of Terror* (2011), she analyses the various ways in which performance makes use of, refuses, and interrupts the visual and discursive regimes of war.

It is worth noting that there are scholars who do focus on text-based theatre; book-length studies include Jeanne Colleran's *Theatre and War: Theatrical Responses since 1991* (2012), Julia Boll's *The New War Plays: From Kane to Harris* (2013), and Sara Soncini's *Forms of Conflict: Contemporary Wars on the British Stage* (2015). As can be gathered from the subtitles of the first two books, these authors extend the time frame of their analyses well into the 1990s and hence focus not on the war(s) of the first decade of the 21st century but more broadly on "plays informed by [the] New Wars" (Boll 7) or, rather vaguely, "plays [...] written in direct response to the emergent New World Order" (Colleran 6). In addition, none of these studies are exclusively about British drama,[8] and they are driven primarily by questions of representation, revising and revisiting definitions of war drama, mimesis, theatre of testimony and witnessing in the light of mass media spectatorship and 'new wars' theory. The first anthology to deal exclusively with post-9/11 theatre, *Political and Protest Theater after 9/11* (2012), edited by Jenny Spencer, also looks at British and American perform-

---

8 Even though Soncini centrally addresses the British stage, Tony Kushner's *Homebody/Kabul*, which was written before 9/11 and premiered at New York Theatre Workshop in 2001, is among the texts that figure most prominently in her analysis.

ances alongside each other but makes a crucial case for considering the particular time frame of the 'war on terror'. Based on the tenet that political theatre has to be situated "within the sociohistorical context that provides the targets of protest and makes the politics legible", Spencer insists that the "wars on terror produced a radically different sociohistorical context in both the United States and Britain" (Editor's Introduction 1). She notes the spectacular nature of the terrorist attacks, heightened patriotic and nationalist sensibilities, and increased securitisation among the most significant components of the post-9/11 landscape. The volume emphatically highlights the significance of developing the concept of post-9/11 theatre as a category in its own right.

As a result of the scholarly emphasis on performance and verbatim plays, a wide range of British new writing that is responsive to the 'war on terror' has been critically neglected; this encompasses plays about the wars in Iraq, such as Jonathan Holmes's *Fallujah* (2004) or Adam Brace's *Stovepipe* (2008), and Afghanistan, such as DC Moore's *The Empire* (2010) or Morgan Lloyd Malcolm's *Belongings* (2011), as well as pieces that deal with the changed position of British Muslims in society, such as Alia Bano's *Shades* (2009) or Atiha Sen Gupta's *What Fatima Did...* (2009) – all of which will be discussed in detail in the following chapters. Even though a number of previous studies acknowledge the relevance of analysing the interconnections between sociopolitical context and theatrical events, the prevalence of comparative perspectives comes at the expense of a thorough interrogation of UK-based contexts. Moreover, the scholarly attention given to various earlier conflicts – while doubtlessly disclosing historical developments, precedents, and palimpsests relevant to the current contours of conflict – has tended to impede a comprehensive investigation of the relationship between the discursive field of the 'war on terror' and the theatrical events situated within and against it. Why do these research gaps matter?

First, the tendency to overlook conventional drama is problematic, for it suggests that the theatre is incapable of responding to the challenges of terrorism and the attendant securitisation and curtailing of civil rights witnessed in Western societies. Some voices in performance studies have indeed encouraged such a view, as evident from John Bell's article "Performance Studies in an Age of Terror" (2003):

> the idea of performance offers concepts, means of analysis, and methods of action which can help us figure out where we are and what we ought to do – certainly better than concepts of [...] 'drama' and 'theatre', which seem to be, consciously or unconsciously, now scrupulously estranged from the things of import that happen around us. (7)

Soon after the start of the Iraq war, British theatre criticism was to implicitly contradict Bell by celebrating political theatre's re-engagement with 'real' events. Kate Kellaway's oft-cited observation of "a remarkable moment for political theatre. Not only have 9/11, the Iraq war and the Bush administration energised playwrights, the acoustic has never been so good" (5) is indicative of this trend and was soon echoed in academic literature. With the benefit of critical hindsight, theatre events taking place in established institutions cannot easily be dismissed as 'estranged from the things of import'. Writing over ten years after Bell's provocation, Bharucha has decisively rejected the notion "that only the language of 'performance' [...] can legitimately address the terror of our times" (22–23). Despite his own emphasis on performative dynamics, Bharucha warns against "rul[ing] out the lurking presence and interruptive power of the languages and concepts of theatre in making sense of the diverse 'performances' of terror" (23).

What concerns me about the available scholarship on post-9/11 drama is that this 'interruptive power' all too often tends to be taken for granted. Implicit in the critical celebration of British theatre's (re)turn to politics is an assumption that any play which explicitly addresses the issue of (counter-)terrorism or the wars in Iraq and Afghanistan is per se political. In other words, the subject matter becomes confounded with a play's status as political, in spite of the fact that theatre, as Walter A. Davis has suggested, "need never directly address a political topic in order to be political in the deepest sense, by making it impossible for us to experience the world the way we previously did" (18). Even if Davis's demand may be slightly overstepping the mark, the generic labelling of post-9/11 plays as political does not stand up to scrutiny if one situates the political, as Mouffe proposes, on the ontological level that "concerns the very way in which society is symbolically instituted" ("Agonistic Public Spaces" 95). An overt theatrical engagement with events that are certainly highly political can still leave the symbolic order of society intact, or, to put it with Jacques Rancière, do nothing to reconfigure the "distribution of the sensible", that system of sense experience which sustains social divisions and partitions (*Politics* 7). I partly share James Harding's concern that "9/11 has pushed the discourse of our discipline back toward a conventional, indeed reactionary, understanding of the interrelation of politics, theatre, and performance" (20), in connection with a retreat from Kershaw's reinterpretation of political theatre as radical performance. In taking up Harding's call to "excavate the ideological in the theatres we study" (21), I propose to scrutinise the political potential of post-9/11 plays by reading them within and against the discursive formation of the 'war on terror'.

Second, the marginalisation of non-documentary drama results in a canonisation of a limited set of plays that is, in reality, not representative of the British theatre scene after 9/11. So far, (semi-)documentary pieces such as David Hare's *Stuff Happens* (2004), Victoria Brittain and Gillian Slovo's *Guantanamo: 'Honor Bound to Defend Freedom'* (2004), and Robin Soans's *Talking to Terrorists* (2005) have been among the most widely discussed. While there is thus a host of interpretations of these texts, crucial points of connection to dramatic fiction remain unexplored, despite the fact that previous research has directly encouraged a more comprehensive interrogation of fictional plays. Hughes's study suggests that non-documentary drama may, in some cases, be better suited to formulate a critique of the panic-ridden sensibilities and political schematising inaugurated by 9/11. Based on her finding that "political theatre stimulated by the war on terror has drawn on the uncertain affectivity of the voice to dramatise a crisis of democracy", Hughes concludes that "the fictional plays [...] exploit these failures more critically than the verbatim plays" (*Performance* 122). Hence, it seems that the critical picture of post-9/11 theatre can be enriched and illuminated by extending the discussion of dramatic fiction.

Third, the tendency to cover plays that respond to a range of crises, particularly the conflicts of the 1990s, leaves the specific 'war on terror' context somewhat under-researched. The relevance of limiting the time frame to the long decade after 9/11 consists in, on the one hand, coming to terms with a distinct group of dramatic works and, on the other hand, accounting for sweeping social, political, and cultural changes that started to affect British society in 2001 and reverberate in the plays produced after this date. As regards the former aspect, Jenny Spencer establishes the discontinuities between British new writing before and after the Iraq invasion as manifest in the shift from in-yer-face theatre that is political in a more abstract sense to issue-based theatre that explicitly seeks engagement with current events (Editor's Introduction 3). Similarly, David Edgar argues for regarding "post-9/11 theatre [as] a fifth act", situated after the concern with class issues in the 1950s and 60s, with post-war British history in the 70s, with the politics of identity and feminism in the 80s, and superseding the in-yer-face theatre of the 90s (111).[9]

Undoubtedly, then, not only the form and aesthetics but also the thematic concerns of post-9/11 plays can be differentiated from previous phases of new writing. In the body of playtexts responding to the 'war on terror', there is a distinct engagement with the changes in British society and culture. To briefly summarise here what will be considered in detail throughout my discussion of the

---

[9] This is not to suggest that Edgar's version of theatre historiography is authoritative; there are evidently competing (and necessarily simplifying) attempts at periodisation, as Janelle Reinelt cautions ("Selective Affinities" 306–307). These reservations notwithstanding, Reinelt similarly notes a (re)turn to "explicitly topical themes" (312).

plays, the global 'war on terror' has entailed profound consequences for the UK in at least three interconnected areas: the effect of counter-terrorism legislation and securitisation on social and urban infrastructures, civil liberties, and forms of citizenship; the impact of an emerging culture of suspicion on the social position of British Muslims; changing assessments of community and tolerance in the wake of fierce debates surrounding immigration, integration, and multiculturalism.[10] First of all, the attacks of 9/11 and 7/7 have engendered heightened security measures in the UK, led to broadened definitions of terrorism, new anti-terrorism legislation, and a significant increase in arrests (Hewitt 33–42). As a second aspect, and partly as a result, the status of British Muslims, disproportionately targeted by security measures, has changed perceptibly. Tariq Modood points out that the "politics of being Muslim in Britain [...] has, inevitably, come to be dominated by 9/11 and its aftermath" (199), and he connects this primarily to the role played by the security state. Finally, Paul Gilroy foregrounds one of the central sociocultural changes when he argues that "the neo-imperial and unending 'war on terror' [...] has decisively altered the ways that multicultural society is understood and evaluated" ("Multiculture" 432). Nira Yuval-Davis expands on this point by explaining that 9/11 has fuelled not only claims about the "death of multiculturalism" but also led to a redefinition of diversity "in multi-faith rather than multi-cultural terms" ("Intersectionality, Citizenship" 572, n. 1). Politicians' attempts to distance the UK from the term 'war on terror' did nothing to counteract the continuing impact and direction of these social, cultural, and policy changes.

Fourth, the prevailing view that American and British productions should be discussed alongside each other – "since these two nations were the principal partners in [the Iraq and Afghan] conflicts", as Colleran argues (6) – comes at the expense of a detailed exploration of the British 'war on terror' context. Echoing Colleran, Spencer's editorial comment, "the closeness of the relationship between the U.S. and the U.K. governments and artists [...] made the inclusion of both British and American examples [...] important" (Editor's Introduction 3), similarly raises the question whether political alliances should be seen to justify critical choices regarding the text corpus for analysis. Apart from the benefit of concentrating on one sociopolitical context, the sheer number of British respons-

---

[10] Supplementing this sketch of sociopolitical changes, Richard Jackson lists the following areas to illustrate the ramifications of the 'war on terror' in international relations and domestic politics: "Its impacts can be clearly seen in security, policing, foreign policy, the legislative process, immigration, banking, travel, the media, race relations, popular culture, education, health and sport" (3).

es to the 'war on terror' warrants a more sustained focus on productions in the UK. Hughes has been one of the few scholars to pursue such an exclusive emphasis in an extensive study.[11] She refers to her prioritisation of British performances as "stimulated by a desire to explore the local and global interconnections prevalent in one site's response to global conflict" (*Performance* 32). As evident from her work, such a focus indeed facilitates a more exhaustive exploration of the ways in which theatre has represented (and possibly also affected) the UK's position in the globalised field of the 'war on terror'.

This book addresses the identified research gaps by offering an extensive examination of a wide range of British, and primarily English, drama in response to the 'war on terror', informed by cultural studies, cultural theory, and poststructuralism. In order to redress the marginalisation of conventional drama, the focus will be on new writing – in Aleks Sierz's working definition, "plays written in a distinctive and original voice which deal with contemporary issues" (*Rewriting* 63). The study deliberately draws on a broad array of playtexts, from the well-known to the little-known, although the emphasis is doubtlessly placed on bringing critical attention to plays that have been largely overlooked. The corpus for analysis was organised according to three criteria for inclusion: (1) plays that directly and specifically deal with the (British) 'war on terror', that is, post-9/11 counter-terrorism measures, the 2005 London bombings, the military interventions in Iraq and Afghanistan, or the sociohistorical impact and political consequences of the wars; (2) plays that were either first produced in the UK or, if first produced elsewhere, still framed as specifically British responses;[12] (3) published plays that were performed for larger audiences, at 'mainstream' theatrical venues. This latter decision is as much due to practical considerations connected to my location outside the UK as it is motivated by a conviction that "mainstream practices are useful in drawing critical attention to the institution as a site of production of cultural knowledge", as Fiona Wilkie suggests (89). The time frame from which the corpus is drawn is bookended by the beginning of the Iraq war in 2003, as notable British responses began to emerge after that date,[13] and the withdrawal of British troops from Afghanistan in 2014.

---

11 Another publication in this area is forthcoming at the time of writing: Clare Finburgh's *Watching War on the Twenty-First-Century Stage: Spectacles of Conflict* (Bloomsbury Methuen Drama, 2017).
12 A notable example discussed in this book is Simon Stephens's *Pornography*, which was first produced at Schauspielhannover in Germany in 2007 and staged at the Tricycle Theatre in 2009.
13 Although it is thus the Iraq invasion, rather than 9/11, which marks the beginning of the time frame, I throughout use the term *post-9/11* instead of *post-war drama*. Alan Read refers to the "context of post-war drama" (230), which he dates from the toppling of Saddam Hussein's statue

By laying the focus on the figuration of subject positions in drama, my aim is to contribute both to a critical assessment of theatre's relationship to the 'war on terror' and to the methodological development of a theory of subject positioning in performance. At this point, it is useful to recapitulate (and slightly revise) Erika Fischer-Lichte's oft-cited claim that the theatre is centrally concerned with the staging of identity by retracing the recent shift in theatre and performance studies towards (re)conceptualising the subject.[14] This terminological move echoes developments in sociology, where scholars have increasingly come to question the heuristic and analytical value of the notion of identity (Anthias 492), charging the concept for being both too ambiguous and essentialist to serve as an adequate tool for social analysis (Brubaker and Cooper 2). In line with these critiques, one can detect in the discourse of theatre and performance studies a turn towards interrogating the precarious constitution of the subject (Kreuder et al. 11). In the introduction to their anthology *Performance, Identity, and the Neo-Political Subject* (2013), Matthew Causey and Fintan Walsh formulate the challenge to move beyond (the politics of) identity in theatre, performance, and cultural studies. This important volume discusses how what they tentatively call 'the neo-political subject' – i.e. a malleable, resistant, "post-identitarian" subject (11) – might be constituted both theoretically and theatrically. Taking up Causey and Walsh's call "to think about the subject of theatre and performance afresh" (1), I draw on the poststructuralist vocabulary of subject positions to develop a critical apparatus that allows for conceiving of a historically and politically instituted subject, whose multiple position-takings directly correlate to the discursive field of sociality and provide the basis for resistant practices. Although scholars in cultural studies, sociology, and discursive psychology have, for some time now, been exploring the concept of subject positions to solve the conceptual problems of essentialised identities and the impasse of identity politics (Chang; Brummett and Bowers; Edley), systematic attempts to make the idea of subject positions viable for a discussion of theatre are rare. So far, these have mainly been confined to the study of postcolonial theatre and monodrama (Lo; Tompkins) or (auto-)biographical and solo performance (Heddon; Pakis), although these forms are by no means the only sites where multiple, con-

---

on 9 April 2003. Yet, because of the difficulties in determining the actual start and end of the Iraq war, let alone the terminology with which to refer to this protracted conflict, I find such a phrase problematic and opt for *post-9/11* as a temporal marker.
14 Fischer-Lichte's survey of the history of European theatre and drama is premised on changing tenets of identity; she argues that "[i]n theatre it is *always* a question of (in structural terms) the creation of identity [...], it is *always* a matter of certain aspects and factors which allow someone to say 'I'" (*History* 2).

tradictory, or alternative subject positions are enacted. By facilitating a dialogue between these areas of research, this study aims to contribute to the search for alternative models of subject construction. As I hope to show, it is by giving embodiment to and situating subjectivities in the particular (geo)political, cultural, and social context of the British 'war on terror' that theatre becomes an exemplary site through which to examine the potential and limits of subject formation at this historical juncture.

This book seeks to go one step further than previous studies that make the case for theatre's "ability to discern different discursive formations at work" (Colleran 7). I will argue that theatre does not merely 'discern' discursive formations but engages in a far more complex relationship with them. Theatre does not simply re-present an external social reality, but actively and self-reflexively participates in the formation of 'war on terror' discourses. "Whether or not theatre of the real has a singular ability to change reality outside the theatre", as Carol Martin writes of productions that claim a specific relationship with 'the real', "it does contribute to formulating what we understand as reality" (120). Martin's assessment is reflected in Reinelt's argument, with regard to theatre's relationship to public events: "When theatre can put forth a unique, aesthetic means of understanding or interpreting the world, it takes its place with other forms of public discourse as actively 'making' culture" ("Toward" 81). Reinelt's emphasis on theatre as a form of public discourse is important. While much recent discussion has revolved around "apparitions of the real" in theatre and performance (Tomlin 13), this study tracks the ways in which post-9/11 theatre enters into conversation with the discourse – rather than the historical or social realities – of the 'war on terror'. One of my central claims is that theatre has to be situated at once as a reflection and a part of the discursive formation, which raises the crucial issue of how it 'takes its place' in relation to the construction and contestation of subject positions in the discursive fields of war and (counter-)terrorism.

In order to interrogate this relationship, the study addresses the following research questions: (1) Which racial, gendered, sexual, religious, and class-specific subject positions are (re)produced in theatrical responses to the 'war on terror', and how do these relate to the system of dispersion operative in the discursive field?; (2) Which interferences and hierarchies between subjects are established, and what is their function within the plays and in culture at large?; (3) What are the dramatic modalities and limits of subject constitution with regard to the cultural formations arising from the 'war on terror'? The overarching aim that links these strands of enquiry is an assessment of British theatre's role and potential in post-9/11 culture. Defining subject positions as theatrically (re)produced locations on vectors of race, gender, sexuality, religion, and class, I apply an intersectional approach that accounts for the interdependencies of and shifting hierarchies between these social categories. Building primarily on the theories of Foucault, Laclau/Mouffe, and Judith Butler, a methodology for analysing the negotiation of subject positions in drama will be developed. Neither adhering strictly to a literary nor theatre studies approach, this study combines textual analysis of the plays with a consideration of the interrelations between the semiotic and the performative, to draw on Fischer-Lichte's terminology. In order to account for the manifold meanings that staging adds and generates, the reading of the playtexts will be partly complemented by performance analysis, drawing on reviews and, whenever possible, on video materials, original interviews with playwrights/practitioners,[15] or my own attendance of productions.

Theoretical assumptions will be elaborated in detail in chapter two, which is centrally concerned with reviewing theories of discursive formations, the subject, and subject positions. This chapter aims at creating a methodological toolkit to examine theatre's role in/as discourse and the construction and negotiation of subject positions in drama. As evident from the spatial coordinates implicit in the term *subject position*, the poststructuralist self that is conjured up by this terminology is invariably a located one, and a multiply situated one at that. In line with the conceptualisation of the subject in terms of positionality, as a question of location in a discursive social field, the ensuing analysis chapters follow a spatial trajectory. The conviction underlying this arrangement is that, just as the subject, the theatre is inherently site-specific, in the sense evoked by Una Chaudhuri, as systematically interrogating the "politics of location" (251). The terrain of contemporary subjectivities will be charted in two principal sections, each of which is arranged around a cluster of war plays. Chapter three is situated closest to 'home', focusing on the impact of war and (counter-)terrorism on the British 'terror city'. Revolving around what will be conceived as home-front plays, it focuses on the subject positions that are constructed and contested within the domestic and (sub)urban settings that begin to be affected by the discursive regime of the 'war on terror'. Chapter four follows diverse subjects to the shifting battlefields in Iraq and Afghanistan. The analysis of front-line plays centres on figurations of racialised masculinities and femininities along and across the lines dividing 'self' and 'other', heteronormative and queer, heroic and victimised subjectivities.

---

[15] Specifically, the book draws on interviews I conducted with Chris Goode, Dennis Kelly, Mark Ravenhill, Atiha Sen Gupta, and Simon Stephens, which took place in London and Hamburg in 2014; original quotations from these interviews have been included with reference to "personal communication" in the following chapters.

The division of the analysis part into 'home' and 'front' sections is not designed to endorse these traditional wartime binaries but, rather, to facilitate tracing the multiple acts of border-crossing of fluid, uncontainable subjectivities situated neither 'here' nor 'there'. What emerges throughout the analysis is, therefore, not a dichotomy but a dialectics of home and front, which bears enormous relevance for the mutually implicated subject positions negotiated within and beyond these territories. In order to duly consider the subjects produced in the "zone of indistinction" that is constitutive of contemporary configurations of power (Diken and Laustsen 293), the neat structural division between home-front and front-line plays will be interrupted by discussions of plays that are situated in-between, whose setting transcends geopolitical boundaries or conveys a sense of spatial indeterminacy. Inspired by Gilles Deleuze and Félix Guattari's terminology, these boundary-defying sections will be announced as "lines of flight" (161), a concept that promises to capture those deterritorialising movements which systematically disrupt the clear demarcation of 'home' and 'front' territories and subjectivities.

2 Theoretical Framework

2.1 Discursive Formations

The collapse of the World Trade Center towers in New York, shackled detainees in orange jumpsuits wearing blacked-out ski goggles, surgical masks, and industrial earmuffs at Guantánamo Bay, the 'hooded man' standing on a cardboard box in Abu Ghraib prison with electrical wires attached to his hands, the wrecked red double-decker bus in Tavistock Square, London – the iconic images that have shaped (Western) perceptions of the 'war on terror' bear witness to destruction and mutilation. Yet, despite their undeniably real material and traumatic impact, the fact that these temporally and spatially dispersed incidents can be enumerated in a seemingly coherent series testifies to the broader discursive framework that conditions their emergence. Regardless of the question what 'really' happened on 11 September 2001 or on 7 July 2005, the heavily mediatised and incessantly discussed events have become intelligible to a Western public through the discourse that classifies them as elements in the 'war on terror'. In order to theorise the genesis and impact of this discursive regime, scholars in such fields as political theory (Neal), critical discourse analysis (Hodges), and cultural studies (J. Kelly) have drawn on Foucault's term *discursive formation*. Given Foucault's own occasional vagueness regarding the concept and the at times imprecise manner of its application in some of these studies, this chapter is concerned with a detailed examination of the terminology before considering theatre's role in/as discourse.

Foucault first offered a definition of the terms *discourse* and *discursive formation* in the work written to outline his method, *The Archaeology of Knowledge* (1969). Approaching, as he describes, the "raw" material of "a population of events in the space of discourse", Foucault formulates the question central to the archaeological project: "how is it that one particular statement appeared rather than another?" (*Archaeology* 29–30). The enquiry into the historical conditions of the emergence of statements is designed to overcome the problematic assumptions of such unquestioned continuities as the *oeuvre*, the *spirit* of a certain period, or *tradition*. Dispensing with these unities, as Foucault suggests, sets free a "vast field", which is "made up of the totality of all effective statements (whether spoken or written), in their dispersion as events" (29). The archaeological study seeks to excavate this field by dissecting the appearance, coexistence, succession, and transformation of statements (and the concomitant exclusion of other statements), by determining the "interplay of relations within it and outside it" (32). In the chapter on "Discursive Formations", Foucault suggests four hypotheses concerning the unity of statements – reference to the same object, equal manner and form, usage of coherent concepts, and permanence of themes (*Archaeology* 35–39) – which he successively rejects. Instead of well-defined objects, he discovers "series full of gaps"; heterogeneous formulations instead of a "normative type of statement"; contradictory rather than logically connected concepts; instead of a common thematic, "various strategic possibilities that permit the activation of incompatible themes" (41). This leads him to shift his focus altogether from unity to dispersion. The emphasis on a regular, systematic type of dissemination is central to Foucault's working definition of discursive formations:

> Whenever one can describe, between a number of statements, such a system of dispersion, whenever, between objects, types of statement, concepts, or thematic choices, one can define a regularity (an order, correlations, positions and functionings, transformations), we will say [...] that we are dealing with a *discursive formation*. (41)

A discursive formation, then, does not emerge around a static set of objects, statements, concepts, or themes; rather, it is "a distribution of gaps, voids, absences, limits, divisions" (134). The fact that it establishes correlations between seemingly disparate and sometimes contradictory elements would explain the possibility of speaking of a series of events in the 'war on terror', even when they are hardly linked by a common thematic. For example, whereas the fall of the twin towers was immediately understood as a blow to the perceived impermeability of the United States and its borders, the photographs of the prisoner abuse at Abu Ghraib prison could be read as testifying precisely to a fleeting "moment of omnipotence" (McClintock 72). These events are not simply the reverse sides of the coin of warfare (attack/counter-attack), but their emergence and interpretation is subject to the rules of formation that determine the perception of 9/11 as a tragedy to be "loudly mourned" – with an "iconography of the dead" preserving a public resting place for each loss – whereas the lives abused and obliterated at Abu Ghraib vanish into the gaps and voids of the system of dispersion (Butler, *Frames* 24).

The fairly explicit definition in *The Archaeology of Knowledge* notwithstanding, Foucault does not always rigorously distinguish between the terms *discursive formation* and *discourse*. While it becomes clear that discourse, as the smaller unit, is encompassed by the discursive formation, both entities can be disassembled to reveal groups of statements (*Archaeology* 129–131). Even if the two terms cannot be neatly separated from each other, what can be ascertained is a difference in emphasis: while a discourse is constituted by statements, the discursive formation regulates their relations; the latter is "the law of such a series", its "principle of dispersion and redistribution" (121). Speaking of *discursive formations* thus draws attention to the rules that govern which statements are included or excluded in a discourse, how and when statements (dis)appear, how they correlate, etc. The discursive formation is defined by the relative unity of these rules. Another way of conceptualising the relation between discourse and the discursive formation, then, is to see the latter as the totality of discourses that are subject to the same regularities of dispersion (see Reisigl 89). In this manner, the discursive formation of the 'war on terror' could be seen to organise the circulation of complementary and contradictory discourses, such as the 'clash of civilisations' thesis, the discourses of freedom, democracy, and liberation, of fundamentalism versus secularism, of militarisation versus pacifism, or of security versus civil liberties.

Due to the operation of the rules of formation, the enunciative options in a given discursive field are always limited. In fact, as Foucault somewhat polemically states, "there are, in total, relatively few things that are said" (*Archaeology* 134). There is always a lack that is correlative with and constitutive of the field. While it is not the task of an archaeological analysis to "give voice to the silence" or describe a statement by "rediscovering the unsaid whose place it occupies" (134–135), the central question of why one statement appears rather than another signals the method's sensitivity to principles of exclusion. It is precisely because *"everything* is never said" (134) – or more accurately, because everything cannot be said – that the discursive formation effectively regulates what counts as truth at particular sociohistorical junctures. As Foucault has famously put it in a 1980 interview:

> Each society has its régime of truth, its 'general politics' of truth: that is, the types of discourse which it accepts and makes function as true; the mechanisms and instances which enable one to distinguish true and false statements, the means by which each is sanctioned; [...] the status of those who are charged with saying what counts as true. ("Truth" 131)

Consequently, the discursive formation delimits what is knowable, sayable, and conceivable about a certain object in a society at a given time. It is on this basis that the 'war on terror' has been discussed as a discursive formation. Adam Hodges, for instance, specifies that "the Bush 'War on Terror' Narrative is a type of discursive formation that sustains a *regime of truth*. It places boundaries around what can meaningfully be said and understood about the subject" (5). It is significant to underscore here that discourse does not simply determine ways of speaking or thinking about an object that always already pre-exists it, but discourses are, as Foucault insists, "practices that systematically form the objects of which they speak" (*Archaeology* 54). Although the events of 11 September 2001 doubtlessly took place, it is their immediate discursivation that made them intelligible as a terrorist attack, rather than, say, an illegal or criminal act.[1] In this sense, the moments alluded to at the beginning of the chapter cannot be witnessed as pre- or extra-discursive events; "the 'impression'", as Jacques Derrida says of 9/11, "cannot be dissociated [...] from everything that also and first of all formed, produced, and made it possible" (qtd. in Borradori 88). When Derrida stresses that the 'impression' of the event is instantly 'formed', he is referring to what Foucault theorises as the formative power of discourse. The 'war on terror' discourse is not merely a reflection of (or on) certain events, but an ordering system that gives form to them in the first place.

Even if there is a strong constructionist component to this understanding of discourse, the discursive formation does depend on material conditions, including economic, juridical, social, and technological relations (Foucault, *Archaeology* 49–50). As Foucault specifies, the discursive emergence of an object depends profoundly on what he calls *primary relations:* "Discursive practices [...] take shape in technical ensembles, in institutions, in behavioral schemes, in types of transmission and dissemination, in pedagogical forms that both impose and maintain them" ("Will to Knowledge" 12). While this differentiation can be helpful, a neat distinction between discursive and non-discursive practices is not tenable, for "no object is given outside every discursive condition of emergence", as Laclau and Mouffe hold (107). The interdependence of discursive and material elements indicates that one would be wrong to infer from the constructionist aspect of discourse that social agents could intentionally, by mobilising a certain way of speaking about an object, manipulate reality. From a Foucauldian perspective, this is the first misunderstanding that characterises many studies into the 'war on terror' discourse. As Hodges's above-cited reference to the 'Bush "War on Terror" Narrative' indicates, George W. Bush and Tony Blair are often seen as the authors, or initiators, of such a discourse. This notion also forms the starting point of Richard Jackson's study, *Writing the War on Terrorism* (2005): "Through a carefully constructed public discourse, officials have created a new social reality where terrorism threatens to destroy everything that ordinary people hold dear" (1). Jackson's notion that the ideologues of a 'war on terror' have successfully spun a narrative, composed of a "set of words, assumptions, metaphors, grammatical forms, myths and forms of knowledge", in order to "achieve a number of key political goals" (2), is in-

---

[1] Brady raises the noteworthy question: "What [...] would have happened if the perpetrators had been portrayed as 'criminals' instead of 'terrorists'? A reality constructed not around a criminal justice reaction but a military one so quickly set in that it is difficult to even contemplate what a legal prosecution might have looked like" (5).

compatible with a Foucauldian approach. Whereas, for Foucault, certain discourses may well have an "author function", the subject – for all its speaking, thinking, writing, and scheming – can never be the "originator" of discourse, but remains a "variable and complex function" of it ("What" 211, 221). *Discourse* refers to an "anonymous field", not an intentionally scripted configuration of statements, within whose boundaries subjects speak and act (Foucault, *Archaeology* 137). Accordingly, any reference to an *a priori* subjectivity that orchestrates discourse would have to be rejected.

Another frequent misconception relates to the understanding that discourses engage in some kind of hegemonic contestation, with dominant discourses seeking to suppress oppositional, dissonant, or counter-discourses. This may generally be a fruitful approach to discourse analysis, but it is irreconcilable with Foucault's theorisation. As has been outlined above, the interplay of relations within a discursive formation is not limited to the combination of compatible statements, which could then be countered from a position located somewhere outside this terrain. Instead, discourse itself constitutes "a field of strategic possibilities", within which "opposed strategies" as well as "irreconcilable interests" are dispersed (Foucault, *Archaeology* 40). In the first volume of *The History of Sexuality* (1976), Foucault explicitly rejects the dichotomy of dominant versus counter-discourse:

> we must not imagine a world of discourse divided between accepted discourse and excluded discourse, or between the dominant discourse and the dominated one; but as a multiplicity of discursive elements that can come into play [...]. Discourses are not once and for all subservient to power or raised up against it, any more than silences are. [...] There is not, on the one side, a discourse of power, and opposite it, another discourse that runs counter to it. (100–101)

This explication has particular pertinence not only for my reading of the 'war on terror' discourse but also for a discussion of the potentialities of political theatre with regard to strategies of resistance, to which I will turn in the following section. As this passage cautions, the 'war on terror' cannot be understood as an 'accepted' or 'dominant' discourse that could be challenged by a 'discourse that runs counter to it'.

Yet this kind of reasoning is characteristic of studies that apply Foucault's terminology to the 'war on terror'. Jackson, for instance, implicitly (and, I would assume, unwittingly) inverts Foucault's dictum: "Discourses are an exercise of power; that is, they try to become dominant [...] by discrediting alternative or rival discourses" (19). Especially the notion that the 'war on terror' discourse discredits dissonant voices is frequently encountered. John Kelly, in his analysis of the interplay of remembrance, militarisation, and the heroisation of soldiers in popular cultural activities, seeks to demonstrate the hegemonic tendencies of the 'war on terror' discourse in the UK. His argument that the operation of the discursive formation "enables counter-hegemonic views to be symbolically annihilated" (724) proves equally untenable within a Foucauldian framework. Hodges is more in line with Foucault's terminology when he writes that discourse provides the "regime from within which [both] supporters and critics of the Bush administration have operated" (5). It is hence more accurate to state that dissenting voices are subject to the same rules of formation within the enunciative field of the 'war on terror'. This is not to suggest that there is no hierarchy of statements; Foucault does point out "the variants and different effects – according to who is speaking, his position of power, the institutional context" (*History*, vol. 1, 100). Yet one must be careful to resist the framing of protest or dissent as counter-discursive, at least if one wants to retain a Foucauldian perspective. While there is certainly the possibility of formulating counter-arguments, oppositional views do not run counter to discourse as such. This is the case because the discursive formation regulates the emergence and relation of elements, not their immediate content. The 'war on terror' discourse prescribes 'sayable' statements not by providing a set of reiterable catchphrases and sound bites but insofar as it determines the divisions, links, series, or distances between statements. This is the combinatory logic of discourse that Butler implies when she writes that the "binarism [...] in which only two positions are possible – 'Either you're with us or you're with the terrorists' – makes it untenable to hold a position in which one opposes both and queries the terms in which the opposition is framed" (*Precarious Life* 2).

2.2 Theatre in/as Discourse

What is theatre's role with regard to the discursive formation of the 'war on terror'? In the Foucauldian framework proposed here, the view that theatre has some unique "ability to discern different discursive formations at work and identify their rhetorical stance and implicit arguments" (Colleran 7) cannot be sustained. First of all, the discursive formation is not marked by a unified 'rhetorical stance'; as has been outlined, it determines the correlation of discursive elements, rather than a particular line of argument. Second, this study does not project theatre into a detached vantage point from which the discursive regime could be assessed. While particular plays may doubtlessly be critical of many of the arguments that gained traction in the 'war on terror' context, their own discourse depends on the rules of formation that delimit the discursive field. In other words, theatrical events have to be situated within – not outside of, or opposed to – the discursive formation of the 'war on terror'. This perspective does not necessarily entail a pessimistic verdict on theatre's critical potential, as I will show by drawing on Kershaw's idea of radical performance.

Without using a Foucauldian terminology, Kershaw is nonetheless interested in "theatre's relationship with the wider social order, in all its discursive and institutional complexity" (*Politics* 2). The premise with which he approaches performance is "that the micro-level of individual shows and the macro-level of the socio-political order might somehow productively interact" (1). Kershaw's description of the interplay between theatrical events and the social order chimes with Hodges's approach to political speeches in the 'war on terror' context with the "aim [...] to illuminate the connection between microlevel discursive action and macrolevel cultural understandings" (4). Might not the theatrical event be seen as producing another kind of micro-level articulation that can be situated with a view to the macro-level discursive formation? Kershaw sets up distinct criteria for an evaluation of whether or not performance can "achieve efficacy in a particular historical context" (*Politics* 3). Building on Philip Auslander's claim that performance is necessarily implicated in cultural formations, he infers that "the politics of post-modern performance [...] must be one of resistance from within the dominant" (*Radical* 70). Translated into the terminology used in this study, theatre cannot be placed outside discursive formations but can only unfold its resistant potential from within them. Kershaw, however, goes on to problematise Auslander's notion of resistance as too "reactive" (74). In its stead, he proposes to conceive of "performative negotiation and exchange that can, under certain circumstances, constitute a radical inflection of dominant discourses" (86). Although the notion of 'dominant' discourses is, strictly speaking, not tenable in the theoretical framework applied here, Kershaw's idea of the 'inflection' of discourse is nevertheless productive.

Rather than countering 'war on terror' discourse, what drama might do is inflect its order, elements, correlations, rules, and positions; that is, performance might employ the enunciative modalities within this discursive field in a modulated form, with a subtle shift in gesture, pitch, volume, tone, mood, or voice. Where Kershaw's postulate would have to be slightly revised is his claim that radical performances "are not only resistant to dominant ideologies, but [...] sometimes transgressive, even transcendent, of ideology itself" (*Radical* 18). In respect of Foucault's explication of the workings of discourse, I will adhere to a terminology of resistance/inflection, rather than transgression/transcendence. A pertinent concern regarding the foreclosure of transcendence is raised by both Auslander and Kershaw. "The key political problem [...] becomes", for Kershaw: "how can performance, in being always already implicated in the dominant, avoid replicating the values of the dominant?" (70). Auslander suggests that the co-optation of artistic practices can be averted if they self-reflexively deconstruct their own means of representation (31). The strategies he traces in performance, such as problematisation of character and text or reflection of a massmediated, "alienated self-in-alterity" (171), are, however, not entirely applicable to the field of post-9/11 drama reviewed in this study, which can be characterised precisely as the type of issue-based theatre that Auslander's examples seek to overcome. I therefore turn to Hughes's conceptual framework, for she has usefully revisited the question of co-optation with a view to theatre events that explicitly address the 'war on terror'. Citing Kershaw's concern with the need to display dominant values without replicating them, she proposes

> the term 'critical mimesis' to explore this simultaneous mirroring and refusal of hegemonic values in performance. Critical mimesis is a term that responds to the urgent demand for an interruption of the atrophic, petrified projections of self and other mobilised by the mimetic excesses of a system in crisis. (*Performance* 18)

In advocating the notion of critical mimesis,[2] Hughes implicitly gestures towards the replacement of transgressive by resistant, and at times even conservative, tactics. This becomes evident as she points out a shift in the focus of political art: "Whereas artists have asked 'how can we change the world?', performance in a time of terror has responded to a different imperative", namely, "'how can we live here?'" (190). This change in orientation is manifest, according to Hughes, in the turn towards questions of survival and resilience (i.e. the conservation, rather than transformation, of life). Liz Tomlin similarly detects in theatre and performance around the turn of the century a shift "to a resistant politics that [...] seeks [...] to expose the workings of the [capitalist] spectacle from within" (31).

If these analyses are correct, then where and how precisely can the critical, or the resistant, be located in theatrical events that are situated within discursive formations? Two elements of Hughes's framework have particular pertinence for my analysis: the first is her thesis of the 'simultaneous mirroring and refusal of hegemonic values'; the second is her emphasis on "performance's relationship with waste and wasted life" (*Performance* 33). These notions crucially resonate

---

[2] Throughout this study, I follow Hughes's understanding of (critical) mimesis as extending beyond questions of imitation and reflection. Building on Michael Taussig, Hughes proposes a conception of mimesis "as a material practice that makes and unmakes bodies and worlds", which encompasses those dimensions of performance that are often understood as nonmimetic ("performance's excess, affect, potentiated signification"), for these are "profoundly mimetic of the upheavals and uncertainties of a time of terror" (*Performance* 14, 26).

with Foucault's theorisation of the possibility of resistance. First, if theatre can be situated in the discursive field in terms of a critical mimesis – that is, a reflection and concomitant refusal of the divisions, correlations, and dispersions within this regime – this could help readdress the question of resistance without reverting to such notions as 'oppositional' or 'counter-discourse'. To be sure, the idea that the enunciative modalities within a given discursive formation can be exploited for the sake of subversion is not incongruous with a Foucauldian viewpoint. As Foucault notes regarding the emergence of the discourse on homosexuality in the 19th century, "it also made possible the formation of a 'reverse' discourse: homosexuality began to speak in its own behalf, [...] often in the same vocabulary, using the same categories by which it was medically disqualified" (*History*, vol. 1, 101). The notion of a 'reverse' discourse seems compatible with identifying in performance the potential to expose the workings of the discursive regime of which it partakes in order to illustrate "the effects of power peculiar to the play of statements" (Foucault, "Truth" 113). In this sense, the simultaneity of mirroring and refusal could be grasped by means of Peggy Phelan's idea of "mak[ing] counterfeit the currency of our representational economy" (164). Many of the plays examined in this study circulate the vocabulary, the combinatory logic and distances of 'war on terror' discourse with a critical inflection, thus permitting reflection on the "tactical productivity" of statements (Foucault, *History*, vol. 1, 102).

Second, the turn to 'waste and wasted life' in performance ties in with what Foucault refers to as the "insurrection of subjugated knowledges" (*'Society'* 7). Although, as has been discussed, Foucault rules out the notion that the archaeological project uncovers the 'unsaid' that the rules of formation prevent from emerging, a level of critical reflexivity regarding the gaps and absences in a given discourse can nevertheless be achieved. Significant in this respect is Foucault's definition of "subjugated knowledges" as the buried historical contents excavated by the archaeological project and, in a broader sense, as "a whole series of knowledges that have been disqualified", including "nonconceptual", "insufficiently elaborated", "naive", or "hierarchically inferior knowledges" (7). These differential types of knowledge can be posited against the hierarchies of official discourse. This is probably the closest Foucault comes to formulating the possibility of something resembling a counter-discourse. The (re)activation of what Foucault calls – pace Deleuze – "minor" knowledges as a tactics of "struggle" (10) could be seen in evidence in theatrical strategies that turn to waste. The insurrection of subjugated knowledges, discarded objects, and minor subjects will be traced in a number of plays which can be seen to rebuild the 'war on terror' archive (see especially chapter four).

One final remark on the way in which this study approaches – or rather, how it does not approach – theatrical discourse is in order. As will be apparent from my repeated insistence on a Foucauldian perspective, theatre is treated as one surface of emergence amongst others in the discursive formation of the 'war on terror'. While it is important to acknowledge that stage discourse generically differs from the modalities of enunciation of, say, political speeches or media reports – most crucially, dramatic discourse is reproduced, or "*represented* discourse" (Issacharoff 9) – I am not primarily interested in the specificities of its speech situation.[3] Such work has been undertaken from the perspective of theatre semiotics in the tradition of Keir Elam and Patrice Pavis; notable studies are Issacharoff's *Discourse as Performance* (1985) and Vimala Herman's *Dramatic Discourse* (1995). My approach foregrounds an aspect that is, at best, marginal to these authors. For Issacharoff, one of the three ways in which dramatic discourse works is "referentially […]: stage discourse places events in relation to the 'real' world outside the theater" (3). Herman similarly hints at drama's "complex relation to the world of existing human affairs" (8). If not the empirical, then the discursive reality of the 'war on terror' serves as a constant frame of reference for the plays that are discussed in this study. Theatre will be regarded as one of the cultural spaces where this discourse operates, is effectuated, mediated, and critically inflected. The focus is, accordingly, not so much on theatre's unique dialogic or discursive modalities but on its relationship to extra-theatrical discursive events. In order to interrogate this complex relationship, the analysis of individual plays will be consistently contextualised with a view to the discursive elements circulating in relation to the subject position examined in each chapter.

2.3 De/Constructing the Subject

The poststructuralist understanding of subject positions that informs this study is characterised by two conceptual departures: from the unitary, rational, autonomous subject of classical philosophy and from essentialist notions of identity. The first departure has replaced "the self-identical subject capable of critical reflection" with "the situated and contingent subject of postmodernity" (Elliott 100). The second has reconfigured identity as incomplete and never "fully con-

---

[3] To Michael Issacharoff's designation of dramatic discourse as represented, one would have to add its split nature, as it is simultaneously addressed "*intra-scenically* (i.e. at the interlocutors in the play) and *extra-scenically* at the theatron" (Lehmann 127); see also Manfred Pfister's differentiation between the internal and external communication system (2–4).

stituted" (Laclau and Mouffe 110–111), as "fragmented and fractured" (Hall, "Introduction" 4), or dismissed the term altogether as "both overinclusive and underinclusive" (Chang 690). Born out of these deconstructive manoeuvres is the notion of the precarious, relational, incomplete subject that is dispersed across disparate and often contradictory positions. Whereas "humanist conceptions of the subject tend to assume a substantive person" (Butler, *Gender Trouble* 14), the poststructuralist subject is not a substance but a form, to be filled by historically, socially, and culturally specific contents. Even if the accounts of the subject on which this study is based – most notably the theorisations of Foucault, Butler, and Laclau/Mouffe – offer significant reworkings of Louis Althusser's position, his reconceptualisation of the subject as the effect of ideology provides a substantial foundation for these subsequent developments of a theory of the subject as 'subject-ed'. For this reason, and because I will draw on the concept of interpellation at various points in this study, his account provides a suitable point of departure.

In "Ideology and Ideological State Apparatuses" (1971), Althusser envisages the way in which individuals are turned into subjects in his influential, if controversial, scene of interpellation:

> ideology 'acts' or 'functions' in such a way that it 'recruits' subjects among the individuals (it recruits them all), or 'transforms' the individuals into subjects (it transforms them all) by that very precise operation which I have called *interpellation* or hailing, and which can be imagined along the lines of the most commonplace everyday police (or other) hailing: 'Hey, you there!' [...] Assuming that the theoretical scene I have imagined takes place in the street, the hailed individual will turn around. By this mere one-hundred-and-eighty-degree physical conversion, he becomes a *subject*. (118)

The caller hails the anonymous individual into the position of the subject, simply by addressing 'you there'. By responding to the call and accepting the address as constitutive, the hailed individual is invariably inserted into ideology. The reason for the effectiveness of interpellation lies in the individual's recognition of him- or herself as a subject, engendered by the realisation that "'it was *really him* who was hailed' (and not someone else)" (118). In consequence of (mis)recognising itself in this address by the 'other', the subject 'freely' submits to its subjection. Evidently, the becoming of the subject can, as has been pointed out by abundant critiques (see Montag 55–56), never be that simple. Yet it is important to bear in mind that the scenario of interpellation is metaphorical, a "theoretical theatre" (Althusser 118), designed to exemplify the workings of ideology. Althusser emphasises that the temporal sequence in which he presents the events merely serves the illustration; in fact, "individuals are always-already interpellated by ideology as subjects" (119). Hence, Butler concludes that, if "the scene is exemplary and allegorical, [...] it never needs to happen for its effectivity to be presumed" (*Psychic Life* 106).

Nevertheless, it is precisely the theatrical quality of the scene that signals its relevance for an analysis of subject construction in drama. Althusser explicitly pursues the theatrical analogy: "the 'actors' in this *mise en scène* of interpellation, and their respective roles, are reflected in the very structure of all ideology" (120). This remark indicates that, as much as the theatre serves as the vehicle for the metaphor, the concept of interpellation can in turn be transferred to the theatrical context. The dramatic text characteristically abounds in scenes of address. One way of linking the micro-level theatrical event to the macro-level discourse is hence to conceive of scenically enacted 'hailing' and response as a transaction that connects figures to the outside discursive framework. Peter Buse's approach to Trevor Griffiths's *Comedians* (1975) as a "drama of contested interpellation" (100) exemplarily demonstrates the validity of the concept in drama analysis. Beyond its relevance for describing the ideologically charged interaction between characters, the critical currency of the terminology also pertains to the spectators' relation to the theatrical representation. As Buse contends, "all theatrical performance 'hails' its audience" (101). Reading the way in which an audience is addressed in terms of an "interpellative invitation" (Reinelt qtd. in Harvie 245) has become something of a critical commonplace. Any approximation of the subject position into which spectators are presumably inserted is, however, inherently problematic – a point to which I will return in the following section.

It is particularly Althusser's rejection of an originary, *a priori* subjectivity that can be seen as formative for subsequent poststructuralist understandings of the subject. In spite of Foucault's rejection of the concept of ideology in particular and the Marxist framework more generally, he shares with Althusser this insistence on the subject as "an effect, not a cause of the conflictual processes of ideology or power" (Montag 59). Although Foucault replaces ideological interpellation with "discursive productivity", his subject is still historically instituted; it is "initiated through a primary submission to power" (Butler, *Psychic Life* 2).[4] For Foucault, the production of the subject essentially takes two different forms, which correspond to an often attested conceptual shift in his work: from the genealogical analyses of disciplinary power to the hermeneutics and technologies

---

[4] This is not to suggest that the constitution of the subject can be reduced to either discursive or power relations; Foucault elsewhere describes how "multiple bodies, forces, energies, matters, desires, thoughts, and so on are gradually, progressively, actually and materially constituted as subjects" ('*Society*' 28). Still, as has been accurately summarised, "Foucault's interest is in showing *the extent to which* subjects are the effects of discourses or power" (M. Kelly 89).

of the self (Rayner 121–123). In the second volume of *The History of Sexuality* (1984), Foucault comments on his change of perspective from discourse via power to "the practices by which individuals were led to focus their attention on themselves, to decipher, recognize, and acknowledge themselves as subjects" (5). These practices, which constitute the "relationship of self with self and the forming of oneself as a subject" (6), have to be differentiated from discursive and disciplinary modes of subject formation. Foucault's turn towards "techniques of the self" ("About the Beginning" 203) has frequently been read as a corrective to his earlier studies (Lemke 203). I would hold against this argument that there exists a productive friction, rather than contradiction, between the two modes of subject constitution charted in Foucault's work. As this tension will be central to my analysis, it merits deeper examination.

As Foucault makes clear in "The Subject and Power" (1982), the "form of power which makes individuals subjects" hinges on "two meanings of the word 'subject': subject to someone else by control and dependence; and tied to his own identity by conscience or self-knowledge" (781). The two forms of subject formation alluded to here can be differentiated by means of the terms *subjection* (*assujettissement*) and *subjectivation* (sometimes translated as *subjectification*), as Mark Kelly helpfully clarifies (87–88). Whereas *subjection* mainly refers to becoming subject in the first sense evoked by Foucault, 'subject to someone else by control', subject to discourse and knowledge, *subjectivation* – a neologism coined in Foucault's later work – refers to the predominantly active process of assuming subjectivity and self-consciousness, "the way a human being turns himself into a subject" (Foucault, "Subject" 778). The neat separation between the two terms is not altogether tenable when read against Foucault's various versions and revisions of subject construction. In particular, Kelly's claim that "subjectivation […] only refers to our constitution as subjects in one sense, namely the active one" (88) would seem to be contradicted by Foucault's emphasis on the interdependencies of both modes. As Foucault insists, not only do "technologies of domination […] have recourse to processes by which the individual acts upon himself", but the techniques of the self are, in turn, "integrated into structures of coercion" ("About the Beginning" 203). Rather than seeing subjectivation as a purely active "matter of self-relation" (Kelly 99), then, it would make more sense to read it, as Béatrice Han does, in terms of a "tension between activity and passivity", where the self-constitution of the subject remains dependent on "the unmasterable 'outside' constituted by […] power relations" (172).

It is my view that the ambiguity between subjection and subjectivation should be seen more in terms of a productive irresolution than a terminological indistinction.[5] The fact that these processes are intricately affiliated should not render a differentiation between them obsolete. For the sake of terminological clarity, I will in the following use the terms *subjection* and *subjectivation* to emphasise either processes of subjugation or of self-formation; *subject formation* or *constitution* will be reserved for the general processes of becoming subject, as pertaining to either of these modes. In order to briefly summarise the distinction at stake here: the term *subjection* foregrounds the way in which power works on and thereby produces the subject, whether by means of coercive practices or disciplinary methods that subjugate 'docile' bodies or by producing a knowable, definable, classifiable subject in discursive regimes; *subjectivation*, in contrast, draws attention to the subject's power to work on itself, to find out (and find ways to express) the truth about itself, to modulate a self-relation that becomes decisive in its interaction with both itself and others. Emphasising how the latter processes are restricted by available schemes of intelligibility, or how subjugation depends on the subject's implementation of classificatory schemes, is not the same as suggesting that the two modes are too embroiled to be differentiated.

In the immediate context of the 'war on terror', one could identify strategies of subjection in the workings of media, parliamentary, and legal discourse, in the disciplinary apparatus instated at prisons abroad or in the extraordinary detention practices used against terror suspects at home. When studying these modes of subjugation, the focus is on the production of the subject in relation to the particular power/knowledge nexus that sustains the 'war on terror'. These discursive and disciplinary processes of subjection are complemented by culturally instituted forms of subjectivation. The technologies of the self that are specific to the 'war on terror' comprise participation, via call-in radio shows, public debates, or casual conversations, in the incessant introspection into 'our' values and way of life, through which the subject forms itself in relation to its access to and possession of 'freedom' and 'democracy'. They are in evidence in any practice designed to "declare aloud and intelligibly the truth about oneself" (Foucault, "About the Beginning" 201), whether in the confessions of former 'Islamic State' fighters who have returned to the UK, in the speech acts whereby 'good' Muslims disassociate themselves from their fellow (mis)believers with 'terrorist' inclinations or in those whereby a 'good' citizen disengages from the Iraq war by carrying a "Not in My Name" banner, in the act of expressing an

---

5 Han states a common critical position when she refers to a "fundamental ambivalence" arising from Foucault's opacity regarding the difference between these concepts (172).

impossible identification with the victims of the 2015 Charlie Hebdo attack via the Twitter hashtag "#JeSuisCharlie", in all those testimonies of where 'I' was, what 'I' did, thought, and felt on 9/11 or 7/7.[6] In response to the discursive and disciplinary framework of the 'war on terror', subjects are not only constituted as objects of knowledge but also acquire specific understandings about themselves.

Emphasising the complex interplay between processes of subjugation and techniques of self-formation helps counter the argument that there is no possibility of agency in Foucault's conception of the subject. In this context, Linda Martín Alcoff speaks of the "neo-determinism" of the subject in poststructuralist theory, which "erase[s] any room for maneuver by the individual within a social discourse or set of institutions" ("Cultural Feminism" 415, 417). This line of critique is echoed by Stuart Hall, who accuses Foucault of constructing "certain 'empty' discursive subject positions [...] which individuals seem to occupy in an unproblematic fashion" ("Introduction" 10). I would hold that these criticisms, while certainly not unjustified, are based on a somewhat one-sided reading of the earlier works and largely overlook Foucault's "ethical turn" towards subjectivation and self-care (Rayner 123). In response to the charge that there exists no notion of resistance in his work, Foucault had always insisted that his understanding of flexible power relations corresponds to the conception of a "free" subject, able to manipulate and resist them – otherwise, one would be looking at "states of domination" (*History*, vol. 2, 292). In his late work, Foucault locates the possibility of resistance explicitly in the techniques of the self, writing that, if "the self is nothing else than the historical correlation of the technology built in our history", then "the problem is to change those technologies" ("About the Beginning" 222–223).

In his comprehensive account of the genesis of the modern subject, cultural theorist Andreas Reckwitz captures the tension between subjugation and subjectivation in terms of the double structure of the "*subiectum*" (10), who is both subject(ed) to a particular formation of discourses and practices and models itself as an expressive, reflexive subject in response to social rules and cultural codes. Most important in this context is Reckwitz's emphasis on the cultural criteria of intelligible subjectivity, the specific normative patterns that are formed in particular historical moments and stipulate a set of (dis)positions, competencies, affective schemes, and interpretive frameworks (10–11). His study lays fundamental groundwork for an attempt to capture the modalities and limits of subject

---

[6] The emergence of the '9/11 story' exemplifies these new technologies of the self (see Butler, *Precarious Life* 5).

formation in the 'war on terror' context. The essential terminology he offers for a cultural theory perspective on the subject can briefly be introduced by way of reviewing what he refers to as the five elements of the cultural transformation of the subject in modernity.[7] While outlining these, I will translate his original terms into English (rendered in italics) in order to arrive at a terminological toolkit that can be used in this study.

First, Reckwitz stresses the necessary plurality of *subject orders* (15), which are temporally coexistent and discontinuous. The identity of a subject order is established through a logic of exclusion; it is constructed against the differentially marked figures of *anti-subjects* (16). Pace Derrida and Laclau/Mouffe, these anti-subjects can be read as forming the constitutive outside that stabilises and, at the same time, destabilises the subject. Second, *subject forms* (16) are constructed in dependence on social discourses and consolidated in everyday practices that sustain culturally dominant form of subjectivity. Third, *hegemonic subject cultures* (17), that is, subject forms which seek to become institutionalised, are consistently challenged and complemented by minoritarian movements that produce alternative versions of subjectivity. Reckwitz's emphasis on scrutinising the cultural spaces where new *subject codes* (19) are initiated especially bears upon an analysis of drama. Fourth, subject cultures are always marked by friction, contradiction, and heterogeneity, resulting in a *cultural logic of hybridity* (19). Fifth and lastly, subject cultures have to be understood as *intertextual constellations* (19–20), meaning that they combine historically malleable cultural codes; for instance, traces of former subject cultures can be newly applied and cited in new subject forms.

With his emphasis on the cultural codes that determine what counts as an intelligible subject, Reckwitz clearly owes much to Butler's account of subject formation. Across her works, Butler has continuously scrutinised the norms that delimit recognisable versions of subjectivity.[8] It is in particular her consideration of the "exclusionary conceptions of who is normatively human", of "what counts as a livable life and a grievable death" (*Precarious Life* xiv–xv), in the context of the ethical turn associated with her essay collections *Precarious*

---

7 Reckwitz's central argument about the development of the modern subject from the respectable bourgeois subject of the 18th and 19th centuries, via the extroverted 'employee subject' of the mid-20th century, to the postmodern creative consumer subject of the 1980s is only marginal to the theoretical considerations offered here and will therefore not be discussed at any length.
8 See, for instance, Butler's definition of "gender intelligibility" in *Gender Trouble* (1990): "'persons' only become intelligible through becoming gendered in conformity with recognizable standards. […] 'Intelligible' genders are those which in some sense institute and maintain relations of coherence and continuity among sex, gender, sexual practice, and desire" (22–23).

Life (2004) and *Frames of War* (2009), that is invaluable to my analysis. Butler theorises the impact of the discursive regime of the 'war on terror' in terms of the creation, circulation, and distribution of 'frames of war'. Modes of subject constitution are intricately connected to these acts of framing, which "variably constitute and de-constitute personhood" (Butler, *Frames* xii). Butler is especially interested in the subject's refusal to adopt a position that is complicit with war. The potential for resistance is traced in two strategies, which resonate with the previously identified theatrical tactics of critical mimesis or turn to waste. First, the constant redistribution of frames bears an inherent risk for their stability, as "reproduction becomes the site where a politically consequential break is possible" (24). The circulation of the frame conditions its contingency; as with Butler's theory of performativity, its permanent reiteration opens up gaps in the normative framework in which, through the activation of alternative affects or ethical responses, resistant subjectivities could be formed. Second, through its selection, organisation, and structuring of the field of war, the frame systematically shuts out alternative options that could be reanimated by artistic and political strategies:

> the frame is [...] always keeping something out, always de-realizing and de-legitimating alternative versions of reality, discarded negatives of the official version [...], it is busily making a rubbish heap whose animated debris provides the potential resources for resistance. (xiii)

Most significantly, the frame shuts out the precarious conditions of those 'shadow-lives', or 'non-lives', whose subjecthood cannot be registered according to the conceptions that delimit the normatively human (xxix). Throughout her essay collections, Butler approaches an ethics that allows for apprehending these discarded lives such that the exclusionary norms of recognisability could be challenged.

Since Butler's studies will be revisited across the following chapters, I will emphasise just two further aspects of her earlier work that usefully supplement the account of the subject that has been approached via Althusser, Foucault, and Reckwitz. In *The Psychic Life of Power* (1997), Butler offers a compelling response to the question frequently raised in connection with Althusser's theory: why would individuals submit to their interpellation? Even if Althusser implies that there may be 'bad' subjects who do not "work all right 'all by themselves', i.e. by ideology" (123), there is no consistent consideration in his texts of what it is that the subject hopes to gain by accepting the assignation of subjectivity. Butler supplies this missing link: she argues that the psychic life of the subject, its desires and affects, needs to enter into the picture in order to explain why it forms a "passionate attachment" (*Psychic Life* 129) to its mode of existence. Crucially, the subject is willing to (mis)recognise itself in the hail "because it promises identity" (108). Affect theory in the wake of Butler's study provides a useful idiom to track "the investments and incoherence of [...] subjectification in relation to the world's disheveled [...] dynamics", as Lauren Berlant puts it (53). *Incoherence* is a key term here: whereas its affective disposition can nudge the subject towards cooperation with the "discursive demand to inhabit a coherent identity", the psyche is also precisely the locus where such a "regularization" can be resisted (Butler, *Psychic Life* 86). After all, the attachment to a given identity is never consummate; psychic energies always "exceed" the demand (86).

The subject's ability to contest imposed norms is the second aspect of Butler's work that I would like to stress here. In her theory of performativity, which conceives of the subject as constituted through performative reiteration (i.e. the repetition of rule-governed discourses), Butler famously locates agency "within the possibility of a variation on that repetition" (*Gender Trouble* 198). Although this subject is still a socially constructed, historically instituted one that has to incessantly 'repeat' normative discourses in order to become intelligible, it retains some agency with regard to the way in which it reiterates its discursive positions.[9] Therefore, Butler raises the crucial question for an analysis of the cultural reproduction of identities: "What kind of subversive repetition might call into question the regulatory practice of identity itself?" (44). She locates the potential for (gender) transformation and subversion "in the possibility of a failure to repeat, a de-formity, or a parodic repetition" (192). In other words, the reiteration of subject codes in incongruous settings, such as the "replication of heterosexual constructs in non-heterosexual frames" (43), exposes the constructedness of all identities. Accordingly, processes of subjectivation can contest the norms of intelligibility by means of subversive reiteration, rather than transgression, of cultural codes and practices. Butler is here, again, touching on a point that has particular resonance for analysing theatrical strategies of discursive inflection. Her conception of parodic repetition provides an additional perspective for approaching a critical mimesis of subject constitution in drama.

---

9 Admittedly, this position in Butler's work is not without contradictions. Geoff Boucher, in a relatively comprehensive critique, points out that it is not clear how Butler, despite conceiving of the subject as discursively produced, still implies some kind of pre-discursive intentionality that allows for the subject to choose between positions or decide on how to perform its reiterations (115–122). This rather phenomenological assumption contrasts strongly with her constructionist account.

2.4 Theorising Subject Positions

When Foucault, Butler, or Reckwitz write about the subject as a variable function of discourse, as an effect of the performative reiteration of cultural scripts, or as a bearer of different dispositions and practices, they are all hinting at the subject's dispersion across various positions. The poststructuralist subject is not only historically situated, but its diverse identifications are also a question of social location. In *The Archaeology of Knowledge*, Foucault states that discursive formations regulate "the various positions that [a subject] can occupy or be given when making a discourse" (60). Discourse, in short, configures the "possible position of speaking subjects" (137). This is why statements should "no longer be situated in relation to a sovereign subjectivity" (e.g. as effectuated by Bush/Blair), but with regard to the instantiation of a "speaking subjectivity" (137). The notion of subject positions that Foucault develops in elaborating his archaeological method is closely related to what Deleuze and Guattari conceptualise as the "subject of enunciation" (the speaking subject), which recoils into the "subject of the statement" (the spoken subject) (129). Bound by the rules of formation, the subject that wishes to come into enunciation cannot simply make any type of statement. Examining the internal and external procedures of discursive control, Foucault stresses that not everyone has equal access to or status within a discourse; he refers to the "rarefaction" and the "privileged or exclusive right" of speaking subjects, who must obey the "rules of a discursive 'policing'" ("Order" 52, 61–62).

This conception of speaking positions has become highly influential in feminist and postcolonial thought. As Alcoff summarises,

> there is a growing recognition that where one speaks from affects the meaning and truth of what one says, and thus that one cannot assume an ability to […] transcend one's location. In other words, a speaker's location […] has an epistemically significant impact on that speaker's claims and can serve either to authorize or disauthorize one's speech. ("Problem" 6–7)

Regarding legitimation, the acquisition of a speaking position seems to depend primarily on processes of subjection: the grids of the discursive field regulate, as Butler puts it, "what will and will not count as a viable speaking subject" (*Precarious Life* xix). If a subject that wishes to come into enunciation does not obtain access to such speaking positions, there is little room for manoeuvre, even if one concedes that the mere act of making a statement could potentially inaugurate a new position. At one end of a spectrum of speaking subjectivities, one would thus find positions that disable the articulation of publicly audible statements. With regard to these silent/silenced positions, Alcoff raises the crucial question of whether "speaking for others [is] ever a valid practice" ("Problem" 7) – an issue that obviously pertains to the theatre. In this context, Gayatri Chakravorty Spivak's seminal article "Can the Subaltern Speak?" (1988) is of vital significance. Spivak's problematisation of the location of the subaltern woman offers a crucial corrective to the largely Eurocentric and androcentric poststructuralist perspective. The position of the subaltern woman who, as Spivak has famously put it, "cannot be heard or read", who "cannot speak" (104), is displaced and appropriated by the subject who effortlessly assumes a viable speaking position.

Beyond aspects of subjection in the instantiation of a (non-)speaking position, Alcoff's discussion also subtly shifts the emphasis to questions surrounding subjectivation: "in speaking for myself, I am also representing myself in a certain way, as occupying a specific subject-position [...]. In speaking for myself, I (momentarily) create my self" ("Problem" 10). The formative processes at work in 'speaking for myself' indicate that speaking positions are to be located at the intersection of processes of subjection and subjectivation. The position from which a subject speaks may be restricted by discourse, but, in assuming this position, the subject also fashions its self. It is essential not to revert to a deterministic understanding of the suturing of subjects to particular enunciatory positions. As Butler contends, "it is not the case that a 'subject-position' preexists the enunciation that it occasions, for certain kinds of enunciations dismantle the very 'subject-positions' by which they are ostensibly enabled" (*Bodies* 114). Despite binding the subject to the rules of formation, a speaking position may thus also hold the possibility of resistance. The conceptual closeness between the subject who speaks and the subject who fashions itself may already be implicit in Foucault's reference to the "formation of subjective positions" as one of the four central manners in which the discursive formation operates and should be analysed (*Archaeology* 130).

I suggest that the term *subjective position* can serve as a more general descriptor in those cases where the subject's acquisition of a location in discourse gives rise to or is facilitated by techniques of self-formation (e.g. speaking for, reflecting on, or writing about oneself). The subjective position can thus be differentiated from what could be designated as an *object position*, which is assigned to an individual in the classifying practices of discourse and the subjugation of 'docile' bodies. The distribution of object positions operates through the "objectivizing of the subject in [...] 'dividing practices'" (e.g. "the mad and the sane, the sick and the healthy" [Foucault, "Subject" 777–778]). The aforementioned assumption of a silent/silenced position is one salient example of the "creation of an object position for people", which involves "suppression [...] of voice, literal and figurative" (Brummett and Bowers 127). In contrast to being interpellated into an object position, one turns oneself into a subject by performatively occupying subjective positions:

> You do not have the same type of relationship to yourself when you constitute yourself as a political subject who goes to vote or speaks at a meeting and when you are seeking to fulfill your desires in a sexual relationship. Undoubtedly there are relationships and interferences between these different forms of the subject; but we are not dealing with the same type of subject. In each case, [...] one establishes a different type of relationship to oneself. (Foucault, "Ethics" 290)

A subjective position is acquired as the subject moulds its relationship to itself in the various social, political, or sexual practices evoked by Foucault. As Reckwitz writes with regard to postmodern culture, for example, the individual takes up subjective positions in correlation with the aesthetic code of 'self-creation' and the economic code of market-oriented choice and consumption (26). In each case, the subjective position is forged through participation in specific social practices and is bound up with a set of contingent dispositions, that is, a complex of behavioural scripts, interpretive knowledges, affective schemes, and motivations.

In addition to the aspects of (non-)speaking and subjective/object positions, the work on subject positions that has been pursued in cultural studies distils a third dimension from Foucault's work. Drawing attention to Foucault's extended discussion of Diego Velasquez's painting *Las Meninas* (1656), in which Foucault identifies "an ideal point in relation to what is represented" (*Order* 15), Hall infers that "discourse also produces a *place for the subject* (i.e. the reader or viewer [...])"; discourses, in other words, "construct subject-positions, from which they alone make sense" ("Work" 56). Evidently, Hall's reading of Foucault here is somewhat one-sided, for Foucault, in fact, draws attention to the convergence of a number of lines of sight, rather than suggesting that there is only one spectatorial viewpoint inscribed into representation. Yet it may be worth staying with Hall's argument for a while and trace its further development in the field of cultural studies. Barry Brummett and Detine Bowers define a subject position as "a stance, role, or perspective one takes in relationship to a text so as to read or engage the text" (118). They discern three types of positioning:

> First, a reader might take an *identified* subject position. This reader finds characters, themes, or images in the text with which he or she identifies, or desires to identify. [...] Second, the reader might take an *implied* subject position. Here, the reader does not identify with a character or image in the text, but is nevertheless called to and constructed as a subject in order to read it. [...] Third, the reader might take a *subversive* subject position, in which a subjectivity is assumed that is at odds with, and often directly opposed to, the call of the text. (118–119)

Brummett and Bowers's differentiation between identified, implied, and subversive subject positions is partly reminiscent of Hall's typology of the decoding process of televisual discourse, in which the viewer assumes a dominant-hegemonic, negotiated, or oppositional position ("Encoding" 101–103). Although this terminology can be fruitfully applied to the theatrical situation, as will be elaborated in the following section, the problematic assumptions underlying any approach to spectatorial positions are evident. An obvious concern pertains to the question of how such processes of positioning could be measured with regard to specific theatre events, and to what extent, if at all, this would assist in analysis. Furthermore, the reliance on an equivalence between the subject positions offered in (dramatic) discourse and the ones occupied in the reception process cannot be sustained. Paul Smith voices this concern when he insists that "there is a distinction to be made between the subject-position prescribed by a text and the actual human agent" (34). Although he does not reject the view that texts construct subject positions, Smith cautions against inferring from these "*preferred* positions" the subject positions occupied by recipients, which are "actually constructed in a dependency upon discursive formations", not singular texts (34, 39) – or, one might add, individual performances.

In any case, the assumption of a particular subject position is only ever temporary and precarious, as Laclau and Mouffe's comprehensive discussion of subject positions from a political theory perspective has demonstrated. In their seminal work *Hegemony and Socialist Strategy* (1985), they conceive of individuals as "[s]ocial actors" who "occupy differential positions within the discourses that constitute the social fabric" (xiii). The discursive formation regulates the dispersion of these locations by establishing systems of difference and equivalence which posit each subject position in an arbitrary and contingent relation to another (106–107, 115). While their framework is evidently indebted to *The Archaeology of Knowledge*, Laclau and Mouffe begin to differentiate their conception from Foucault's when they introduce the psychoanalytical notion of overdetermination into their analysis, based on Althusser's adaptation of Freudian terminology. By transposing psychoanalytical categories into a political theory perspective, Laclau/Mouffe pave the way for reconceiving Jacques Lacan's universal 'split subject' as a historically malleable product of contradictory sociocultural codes (Reckwitz 84). Since the central impetus behind *Hegemony and Socialist Strategy* is the reworking of Marxist approaches to an essentialised working-class subject, Laclau and Mouffe primarily address "the difficulties of the working class in constituting itself as a historical subject", which they trace back to the "fragmentation of its positionalities" and the "overdetermination of some entities by others" (105). Social agents do not solely occupy a class position, for instance, but are inscribed into multiple discourses and relations. Depending on the subject's locus in a particular historical configuration, one of these positions will symbolically overdetermine the others, such as the working-class position in class conflict.

What is more, each subject position is in itself overdetermined, as it is open to conflicting constructions. Never amounting to a stable, permanent identity, subjectivity can thus only be "precariously and provisionally [...] sutured at the intersection of various discourses" (Mouffe, "Hegemony" 90). Drawing on Lacan's *"points de capiton"*, Laclau and Mouffe call these temporary fixations *"nodal points"* (112). As partial and tenuous arrests of meaning in a discursive field that is inherently in flux, nodal points temporarily halt the signifying chain which establishes shifting relations of equivalence and difference between subject positions, producing such privileged entities as 'Man', 'the proletariat', and so on (117). It is, however, vital to note that the subject's diverse positions can never "be fixed in a closed system of differences" due to the open and fluid character of the social (115); also, the constitutive outside against which subjectivity is constructed continues to destabilise the point of suture. The central term to describe the provisional fixation or dislocation of differential positions is *articulation*, which Laclau and Mouffe define as "any practice establishing a relation among elements such that their identity is modified" (105). As an example, they refer to "a series of subject positions which were accepted as *legitimate differences* in the hegemonic formation corresponding to the Welfare State" but were subsequently "expelled from the field of social positivity and constructed as negativity", as "parasites on social security (Mrs Thatcher's 'scroungers')" (176). In the manner delineated here, hegemonic articulatory practices constantly seek to displace "the frontier of the social" (176) by relegating new anti-subjects beyond the boundaries of the social field. In this vein, the prevalent critiques of multiculturalism in the UK in the wake of 9/11 could be read in the context of attempts to dislocate the 'legitimate differences' of a multi-faith community. Thus, a liberal democratic society increasingly comes to define itself against 'extremists' and 'fundamentalists', whereas, in the 1990s, the radicalisation of Muslim militants in the UK had gone largely unnoticed, or even been tolerated (J. Burke 41–44). This shifting of the social frontier is bound up with the temporary fixation of the interplay between multiple subject positions – for instance, those of young male British Muslims – which become sutured at the nodal point of faith.

Articulatory practices are, however, also essential to form alliances and build politically progressive movements. Radical democratic struggles, for Laclau and Mouffe, crucially depend on "the expansion of chains of equivalence", that is, on the equivalential articulation between different kinds of struggle (182–183). Building on Laclau and Mouffe's framework, Hall has fruitfully extended the notion of articulation to denote the way in which subjects "fashion, stylize, produce and 'perform' [their] positions" in relation to the discursive formation "or are in a constant, agonistic process of struggling with, resisting, negotiating, and accommodating the normative or regulative rules" ("Introduction" 13–14). Hall's gesture towards the divergent ways in which subjects 'perform' their positions – ranging from an adoption to a dismissal of subject codes – signals that the conceptual flexibility of subject positions helps extenuate some of the deterministic tendencies in poststructuralist thought. "The place of [...] resistance has", as Paul Smith puts it succinctly, "to be glimpsed somewhere in the interstices of the subject-positions which are offered in any social formation. More precisely, resistance must be regarded as the by-product of contradictions in and among subject-positions" (25).

Laclau/Mouffe's notion of nodal points emerging at intersecting social grids partly prefigures the concept of intersectionality, developed in feminist and antiracist scholarship from the late 1980s onwards. Legal scholar Kimberlé Crenshaw originally coined the term *intersectionality* in order to redress the failure of legal doctrine to account for "the multi-dimensionality of Black women's experience" (383). Her work became immensely influential in promoting an intersectional approach to identity, whose remit now stretches far beyond the legal discipline and has become detached from the singular focus on black women. The central image of this approach replaces the static differences of identity politics with an emblem of positionality, namely, that of a crossroads:

> Intersectionality is what occurs when a woman from a minority group [...] tries to navigate the main crossing in the city. [...] The main highway is 'racism road'. One cross street can be Colonialism, then Patriarchy Street. [...] She has to deal not only with one form of oppression but with all forms, those named as road signs, which link together to make a [...] many layered blanket of oppression. (Crenshaw qtd. in Yuval-Davis, "Intersectionality and Feminist Politics" 196)

Though offering an evocative view of the multiplicity of marginalisation, Crenshaw's image contains various conceptual problems. Katharina Walgenbach has criticised the crossroads model for failing to effectively conceptualise the interdependency of the vectors of discrimination, which potentially remain separate before and after the point of junction (49). She proposes the term *interdependent categories* in order to think of the effects of oppression as emerging not only between, but also and consistently within categories (23–24). I would contend that, despite valid criticism of the image, the concept of intersectionality does not preclude a view of variously interlocking, mutually constitutive categories. The difficulties inherent in the imagery of the crossroads might be solved by a change of metaphor, by replacing the single point of intersection with, say, "a series of nomadic lines of interconnection", as Rosi Braidotti suggests (*Transpositions* 57). If one abandons the additive image of the junction, it becomes possible to conceive of intersectionality "as a three-dimensional relationship, a matrix, in which all these identities are constituents of the others" (Garner 47).

The intersectional approach serves as a productive framework for theorising the subject's multiple, interlocking positionalities in racial, gendered, sexual, class, and other hierarchies. Although intersectional scholarship has predominantly concentrated "on the particular positions of multiply marginalized subjects", as Jennifer Nash summarises, the concept can effectively be extended to a general theory of the subject (9–10). This study is responsive to Nash's demand to take into account how "positions of dominance and subordination work in complex and intersecting ways" and, accordingly, "to theorize an array of subject experience(s)" (10). As Yuval-Davis points out, only an analysis of both disadvantaged and privileged subject positions "expands the arena of intersectionality to a major analytical tool" ("Intersectionality and Feminist Politics" 201). In accordance with these insights, I conceive of subject positions as interdependently constituted at various intersections of social categories, in a complex interplay of privilege and oppression.

A further academic route that the concept of subject positions has taken is that of discursive psychology, the final area of study to be reviewed here. In this field, a narrower conception of discourse applies, and subject positions "can be defined quite simply as 'locations' within a conversation" (Edley 210). As John Shotter clarifies (following Rom Harré), these "'locations' [...] specify a set of rights and duties, privileges and obligations, as to who may speak to whom and in what manner" (102). What distinguishes the conception of subject positions as loci in conversations from the poststructuralist account of speaking subjectivity is a stronger focus on processual and context-specific subject formation. The poststructuralist speaking position, "as a structurally defined place in the symbolic", here receives a more pragmatic turn towards the dynamics of concrete social episodes (Angermüller 2994). Hence, an individual occupies sequential subject positions in specific conversational scenarios: "the use of such pronouns as 'I' (and 'you')" is seen as "index[ing] *momentary* status locations" in the structural grid of conversation (Shotter 100). Depending on its conversational involvements, the subject thus occupies a series of temporary and shifting positions.

One significant publication that can loosely be associated with this field is Bronwyn Davies and Rom Harré's "Positioning: The Discursive Production of Selves" (1990). Writing from backgrounds in sociology and psychology respectively, Davies and Harré propose the category of subject positions in order to move beyond psychological conceptions of the self and sociological conceptions of the role (47).[10] The terminology they develop for analysing the positioning of speakers in conversations can suitably be applied to dramatic discourse:

> There can be interactive positioning in which what one person says positions another. And there can be reflexive positioning in which one positions oneself. However, it would be a mistake to assume that, in either case, positioning is necessarily intentional. (48)

As regards interactive positioning, Davies and Harré describe how, in the course of a conversation, speakers provide subject positions for one another, which often take the form of complementary positions revolving around shared interpretations and cultural codes. The "choosing subject" can take up or refuse the positions offered, occupy multiple/contradictory positions within one conversation, or negotiate new positions (52–53). To this differentiation one could add Reckwitz's classification of the social practices that are shaped by and give shape to subject codes: he distinguishes between intersubjective (e.g. conversations), interobjective (activities involving objects),[11] and self-referential practices (acting on oneself, i.e. technologies of the self) (38). These discursive tactics of positioning can very well be ascribed to the interaction between characters on stage or between performers and spectators, the staged interaction with props or self-referential monologic acts, as will be elaborated in the next section.

Five interconnected aspects emerge from this theorisation of subject positions. First, subject positions are discursive locations; as (non-)speaking positions, they are linked to a set of enunciative modalities that regulate the emergence and legitimacy of statements to be made from that position. Second, discursive formations are structured by grids of classification that produce subject positions in accordance with forms of knowledge. Here, object positions can be differentiated from the subjective positions that a social agent fashions and performs by modulating a self-relation in interaction with these codes. Third, subject positions are positions of reception/decoding that texts, or discourses, offer to the viewer, reader, or spectator. There is considerable room for the individual subject to negotiate or refuse preferred positions, which can nevertheless

---

[10] The theoretical position according to which social agents take on certain roles (e.g. sex roles) has to be rejected for its positing of a subject who internalises a universal norm (see Carrigan et al. for a critical perspective), rather than occupying dispersed positions in relation to contingent, culturally constituted subject codes.

[11] The process of subject formation in relation to physical objects, whether materially present or imagined, is illustrated in the intriguing examples offered by Deleuze and Guattari: "The point of subjectification can be anything [...]. For anorexics, food plays this role [...]. A dress, an article of underwear, a shoe are points of subjectification for a fetishist. So is a faciality trait for someone in love" (129).

be analytically approximated. Fourth, social agents always occupy multiple, intersectional, and often contradictory subject positions. The overdetermination operating among positions temporarily produces privileged nodal points, or subject forms, but subject positions can never be fully sutured. The subject retains some agency and potential for resistance by articulating between its positions and the discursive formation. Fifth, and lastly, subject positions are loci that speakers avail themselves of and make available to each other in conversations. Although these positions are regulated by discursive formations, cultural codes and scripts, individuals exert some choice in relation to their positioning. All five aspects are relevant to my analysis of the theatrical negotiation of subject positions.

2.5 Performing Subject Positions

The poststructuralist dispersion of the subject across multiple positions had diverse reverberations in aesthetic developments and new dramaturgies from the 1970s onwards. Attendant upon the 'death' of the unitary subject may have been, as Elinor Fuchs suggests, *The Death of Character* (1996). The turn away from the ontological certainty and stable identity of theatrical character is, as Fuchs emphasises, by no means a direct result of poststructuralist theorising – she conceives of the 'death of character' as beginning with the symbolist movement in the 1890s (29–30). Arguing that "'character' as a term of dramatic art can never be independent of contemporary constructions of subjectivity" (8), Fuchs nevertheless considers the impact of poststructuralist deconstructions of the self-sufficient subject on the "aversion" to notions of autonomous character evident in the work of postmodern practitioners (9–10). Deirdre Heddon makes a similar point, in *Autobiography and Performance* (2008), when she argues that the revision of identity as "multiple and constructed" is "reflected in a number of related shifts in the characterisation of the performer" (81). Gerda Poschmann and Hans-Thies Lehmann are among those who have contributed most substantially to theorising the dissolution of autonomous character. Lehmann's *Postdramatic Theatre* (1999) examines an array of substitute entities that have ostensibly come to replace character in the type of ceremonial, self-reflexive, non-text-based theatre evoked in the title;[12] among these are "juxtaposed 'language sur-

---

[12] According to Lehmann's definition, "staged text" in postdramatic theatre "is merely a component with equal rights in gestic, musical, visual, etc., total composition" (46).

faces' (*Sprachflächen*)", "incomprehensible emblems", "de-psychologized speaking machines", or "live, trembling human sculpture[s]" (18, 79, 115, 165).

While these studies doubtlessly capture notable developments away from fictive figures and individuated characters, I am entirely in accord with Cristina Delgado-García's critique of the somewhat premature dismissal of the term *character* (xi). There is a question to be raised about the conceptual benefits of the verdict on the 'death of character'. If, as these scholars acknowledge, the notion of character crucially depends on contemporary constructions of subjectivity, should not the concept be adapted to accommodate the "multiple and provisional selves" (Heddon 81) that appear in performance? Perhaps the critical aporia here consists in what Delgado-García diagnoses as "a marked lack of consensus regarding what theatrical character is, to which notions of reality or subjectivity it is entitled to relate" (45). Looking at characters on stage that are experienced in terms of "indistinctiveness, hybridity, or fragmentation" (18), Delgado-García suggests that if such 'dividuated' figures have superseded the liberal-humanist conception of the person as distinct, unique, and individual, the concept of theatrical character might have to be expanded accordingly. I find her proposal to read character as "any figuration of subjectivity in theatre, regardless of how individuated or, conversely, how unmarked its contours might be" (14) immensely productive.

This study is, however, not so much motivated by an imperative to (re)think character so as to include radically fragmented subjectivities; rather, it seeks to contribute to these debates by developing a progressive notion of subject positions in order to proffer a politically salient discussion of theatrical character that reaches beyond formal and aesthetic concerns. While building on these recent problematisations, this study asks how the proclaimed move "towards a post-identitarian subject" (Causey and Walsh 11) can be reconciled, and possibly reassessed, with a view to plays that still invest in relatively stable, self-contained characters. The challenge here is to adapt a critical apparatus that is deeply conversant with the dissolution of the subject in postdramatic and experimental forms to the seemingly hostile terrain of conventional drama, without reneging on the gains made in theatre/performance studies and poststructuralist theory. Even in productions where actors 'impersonate' figures instead of offering their "presence on stage for contemplation" (Lehmann 135), it does not automatically follow that one is dealing with a restitution of the fantasy of the whole, singular subject. And although an acting style which invites identification with a character instead of exposing it may reinforce the analogy between character and subject, the subject thus represented is not necessarily a coherent or unified one.

Most significantly, if one conceives of the subject as the occupant of disparate subject positions, then these are neither equivalent to nor fully commensurable with theatrical character. While a performer may (re)present the dispersed subject positions of one character, different actors can enact one subject position that is distributed across a set of characters, or the differential positions inhabited by one character can be emphasised by multiple casting. In addition, the theatrical negotiation of subject positions is by no means restricted to the level of character, for spectators are positioned in relation to characters, actors, and the performance more generally. And there is the question of subject positions appearing where characters do not, that is, the theatrical representation of subject constitution beyond embodiment, which occurs in the interstices between the mimetic and diegetic space, or between the stage and the auditorium. The conceptual difference between the categories of character and subject positions can perhaps best be grasped as a difference in scale. Timothy Clark's influential ecocritical essay on "Derangements of Scale" (2012) provides a valuable model for the application of scales to (literary) texts. He proposes three different scale readings: the first, personal scale centres purely on the characters represented; the second scale connects the figures and their relationships to the national, cultural, and historical context in which they are embedded; the third scale 'zooms out' of the narrative in an even broader sense, leaving characters behind in a way that dislodges human agency, making people appear like objects or things. Evidently, Clark drafts this third move in an attempt to develop ecocritical readings beyond anthropocentrism, but I would suggest that his idea of reading at the third scale can be applied to the negotiation of subject positions in drama. Applying the third scale to the subject(s) represented on stage means 'zooming out' of the level of character such that particular subject positions can be abstracted from the theatrical representation and seen in relation to the larger discursive formation, reaching beyond questions of individuality, personality, or identity.

The aspect of character that is most relevant to this study is, accordingly, what Chaudhuri refers to as its connection "to the 'outside', that is to the actual socio-cultural world of the audience" (97) – with the slight conceptual shift that this world is here theorised as a discursive field, rather than a historical and social reality. Key to scrutinising this relation without running the risk of heralding a somewhat naive analogy is, as Berlant suggests, "not to see what happens to aesthetically mediated *characters* as equivalent to what happens to people but to see that in the affective *scenarios* of [literary] works [...] we can discern claims about the situation of contemporary life" (9). The subject constituted on, off, or in-between stage (and auditorium) cannot be seen as a construction that only bears relevance to the as-if world of the play. Subject positions are not hermetically enclosed in the dramatic cosmos but constantly refer back to the discursive formations and forms of knowledge that condition their emergence. This study is only interested in the representation of character, then, insofar as it articulates between the world of the stage and the larger discourses involved.

My analysis of how this plays out in performance is guided by the five aspects of subject positions elaborated in the previous section. I will conclude this theory chapter by discussing how these aspects pertain to the theatrical context. Regarding the first area of (non-)speaking positions, its most obvious point of application relates to the manner in which dramatic characters or entities claim a particular speaking space, or fail to do so, and what the modalities of their becoming subjects of enunciation are. I am operating on the thesis that the negotiation of locations in stage discourse bears relevance for and is reflective of the dispersion of viable speaking positions in the discursive formation. As is evident from the discussion above, an analysis of these positions has to pay as much attention to the performing subject of articulation as to the "silenced presences" which it speaks to, and sometimes speaks for (Lo 126). The dramatic construction of silenced positions can be connected to a critique of the rarefaction of speaking positions – as will be argued with regard to plays that engage with subaltern Afghan women, for example – or to a dramaturgical search for ways of mediating the 'unmarked' dimension of subjectivity that Phelan evokes, with the aim to protect (dramatic) subjects from the visual and sonic regimes of the 'war on terror'. Phelan's interrogation of the political value that might lie in remaining unmarked, in not being "reproduced within the ideology of the visible" (1) – and audible, one should add – informs my analysis of subject positions that are located off stage.

The differentiation between subjective and object positions provides a rich resource in virtually all the chapters. As I will argue throughout, numerous plays in the 'war on terror' context situate subjects at the junction of active processes of self-formation and disciplinary modes of objectification, often foregrounding the restrictions that discursive regimes impose on the horizon of viable subjectivation. The limits of self-formation are as much instituted in the relation between the fictive world of the play and the discursive 'outside' as they are realised in the relationship between performers/characters and the audience. As Fischer-Lichte's concept of the autopoietic feedback loop implies, subject constitution in performance can only function through the active investment of the spectator. Fischer-Lichte outlines how "all participants always act both as subjects *and* objects. They co-determine the entire process, stimulating new performative turns while also being determined by the turns effected by others" (*Transformative Power* 172). Due to this mutual determination, there are no entirely autonomous subjects who "fashion themselves independently of others and external directives" (164). Hence, it appears that the interaction between subjectivation and subjection is continuously replayed as a fundamental register of aesthetic experience, for any act of self-formation is inherently dependent on the spectators' willingness to confer subjectivity.

Closely connected to this is the aspect of preferred positions. The multiplicity of these is, again, intrinsic to the theatrical decoding process: "Theatre, by virtue of its very symbiotic nature, proffers multiple ways of reading, or [...] multiple subject positions within a single discourse at any one point in time", as Jacqueline Lo asserts (125). In spite of the inherent plurality of these positions, the analytical act of determining an "idealized audience", as Auslander maintains, can serve "to reveal a political *potential* within the work, a potential that is not always realized in the work's interaction with every audience" (30). Such an analysis differs markedly from phenomenological approaches to reception that rest, as Elin Diamond has criticised, on a conception of the "coherent subject/spectator while asserting 'universal and enduring' conditions that undergird the humanity of the object (character)" (408). In the context of recent theorisations of spectatorship, Maaike Bleeker and Isis Germano have advocated a theory of positioning that could be seen to meet Diamond's demand to historicise and politicise (the limits of) identification. They propose an analysis that excavates the ideological positions implied by modes of staging, "both in concrete embodied space and with regard to the ways in which our perceptions of things include attitudes toward them: assumptions, expectations, beliefs, desires, and fears" (365). Echoing the notion of preferred positions proposed here, Bleeker and Germano are adamant to distinguish between "an implied position [...] and that of an actual spectator" (365). In other words, there is substantial room for spectators to negotiate their individual response.

This is where Laclau/Mouffe's concept of overdetermination comes in, if taken to indicate the excess of meaning, the overflow of discursivity, which perpetually subverts the tenuously acquired subject positions of performer, character, or spectator. Theatre is an exemplary site to explore the possibility of resistance arising from tensions between subject positions in the 'war on terror' discourse, as it generically relies on a heterogeneous collision of acoustic, visual, and linguistic codes of subject formation. As Heddon writes of autobiographical performance, and as could be ascribed to theatre more generally, performance exposes not only the "multiplicity of the performing subject, but also the multiplicity of discourses that work to forge subjects" (39). While drama can draw on this plurality as a political resource, there is evidently also a strong pull towards reduction and simplification. With respect to the stakes of verbatim theatre, for instance, Heddon remarks that the people interviewed for these productions might feel their varied positions reduced to an "extract" (135). The fixation of contingent subject positions or the foregrounding of a singular position in a particular character may, in fact, be bound up with the form semantics of drama. If the "core of drama was the human subject in conflict, in a 'dramatic collision' (Hegel)", then theatre "essentially constituted the self through an intersubjective relationship with the antagonist", as Lehmann contends (154). Hence, the consolidation of subject positions might be more characteristic of dramatic theatre than an exploration of the fluid potential of overdetermination or unfixity. Nevertheless, as my analysis will evince, even formally and aesthetically conventional plays situate characters in-between contradictory positions in order to reflect how the ideal of a self-identical, unified subject eludes the conflicting demands imposed by 'war on terror' discourses.

Finally, the idiom of positioning developed to describe the processual subject formation at work in negotiating loci in conversations provides a useful terminology for an analysis of dialogic or monologic subject constitution. Although the discussion here to some degree overlaps with an examination of the theatrical negotiation of speaking positions, the concept of discursive positioning calls for a greater focus on the shifting dynamics and interferences between subject positions as well as the attendant hierarchies. Linda Kintz's analysis, in *The Subject's Tragedy* (1992), throws into sharp relief that the subject in/of performance is an invariably mobile, mutable one. As her study demonstrates, the language developed in discursive psychology can serve to describe the continuous negotiation of subject positions in performance. Kintz defines dramatic subject positions as tenuous acquisitions of "a discursive 'I' dependent on a 'you'", that is, as essentially unstable, "thetic" reinstatements of identity (137). Within (and sometimes beyond) the boundaries of the cultural scripts that determine intelligible subjectivity, figures reflexively and interactively assume 'thetic' positions vis-à-vis the 'other' (whether imagined, embodied on stage, or sitting in the auditorium).

By way of concluding this theoretical chapter, I propose that a third strategy of political theatre can be added to the hitherto discussed tactics of critical mimesis/reverse discourse and turn to waste/minor knowledges. This study locates theatre's resistant potential, its ability to critically inflect 'war on terror' discourse, primarily in the figuration, negotiation, and dislocation of subject positions. While there may be no such thing as a counter-discourse pitted against the dominant discourse of the 'war on terror' – an imagined confrontational scenario in which theatre always emerges as the challenger to the manipulations of politicians and the media – there is nevertheless the potential for unfixing nodal points and deconstructing or reassembling the intelligible subject forms instituted in the field of war. Although dramatised subject positions are necessarily anchored in the discursive field, productive fissures can be produced between contradictory positions that derive from various discourses or within singular positions that cannot be fully sutured. In addition, the figuration of differentially valued positions critically reflects on the volatile social territory of unstable hierarchies and privileges. Since spectators are inevitably implicated as those who confer or deny subjectivity, the theatre is a particularly potent site to permit reflection on the acquisition and contestation of subject positions in the 'war on terror'.

3 Home-Front Plays: Subject Positions in the British Terror City

In view of the bombings on the London transport network, the police shooting of a Brazilian immigrant on the tube, the stationing of tanks and troops at Heathrow Airport, attacks on as well as raids of urban mosques and Muslim homes, it is not always easy to sustain Giorgio Agamben's dictum that "[t]oday it is not the city but rather the camp that is the fundamental biopolitical paradigm of the West" (*Homo Sacer* 181). In spite of the continuing significance of the camp in present (geo)political contexts, critics have more recently pointed to the status of urban environments as "the battlegrounds of the future", insisting that "we need to treat cities [...] as the primary unit of analysis" (Kilcullen 38). With the 2001 attacks in New York and Washington, the train blasts in Madrid in 2004, the 2005 London bombings, the terror attacks in central Paris in 2015 and in Brussels in 2016, Western cities have become battlegrounds in the 'war on terror' with real material consequences. Beyond the immediate impact of these attacks, biopolitical imperatives submit subjects to policing, racial profiling, and interpellation into an ideology of fear and suspicion that tangibly affects their movements and habit(ation)s in urban space. Perhaps, as the central site in mobile societies of control and surveillance, as a zone of exception and indeterminacy, "the city is [itself] becoming an indistinct space: a camp" (Diken and Laustsen 298). Scholars have variously come to characterise citizens' altered modes of living and experiences in the 'terror city' in terms of "a new urban vulnerability" (Gray and Wyly 330) or "a new landscape of urban fear" (Seidler 1).

The imaginary geographies that configure the urban as vulnerable provide an attendant series of subject positions for those inhabiting the city, which are mainly, but not exclusively, structured by racialised hierarchies. In this regard, Joseph Pugliese charts how "[t]he civic spaces of the city become spaces of uncivil danger, fraught with racialised taunts, repeated security checks and harassment, and the possibility of both symbolic and physical violence" (24). At the same time, both those who are privileged and those disadvantaged by vectors of race and ethnicity are hailed into efforts of policing and surveillance, continuously incited to be watchful and vigilant – although subjects positioned at the higher end of racial/class hierarchies will rarely find themselves at the receiving end of suspicion. By means of warnings to passengers to keep their belongings with them at all times, to report any suspicious behaviour or unattended luggage – in short, by what Cindi Katz has termed "banal terrorism", the "everyday, routinized, barely noticed reminders of terror" (350) – citizens are continuously interpellated into the "contemporary western 'community of anxiety'" (G. Nash

99). In this environment, subjects are under permanent pressure "to perform – or else", as Jon McKenzie's famous dictum goes (120). Diana Taylor echoes this notion when she writes:

> we are all required [...] to undergo ritual acts of surveillance by showing our IDs, submitting to searches, taking off our shoes, reacting to color-coded alerts, and having our phones tapped. We perform terror every day; we incorporate it. (1893)

The affects, anxieties, and pre-emptive measures related to the terrorist threat extend all the way into the supposedly private sphere of the home, which acquires a synecdochic relationship with the 'homeland' as a space that needs to be monitored, defended, and secured. Engin Isin, who argues that current manifestations of governmentality both institute and rely on a form of neurotic subjectivity, asserts that "the home [has] emerged as a major security concern" and describes how the "neurotic citizen [...] invests in the production of a stable home in the service of his homeland" (230–231). Just as the fortification of national boundaries is reproduced at the level of (sub)urban and domestic space in the guise of bunkering, fortressing, and the gating of communities (Katz 353), the home itself may serve as a model for national security discourses that revolve around the protection of the 'nation home'. In the course of these concerted efforts at fortification, "the nation-state is implicitly or explicitly redesignated as a 'home front', a battle line behind which the civilian populace is mobilized as a supporting arm of the military" (Tyler 59).

This chapter analyses how British plays negotiate subjectivity within and against this 'landscape of urban fear'. The intention behind this focus on the home-front setting is not to cement the necessarily fluid boundaries between 'home' and 'front' but to acknowledge the ways in which these are continuously traversed, for instance, by news coverage, letters and emails sent from the front, or soldiers' video clips viewed by communities at home (Acton 177; Youngs 926). In drama, it is the figure of the returning veteran that most palpably connects the front line with the home front, and many plays further deny a strict separation by having alternate settings or including flashbacks to the front in what is predominantly a domestic setting. Yet focusing on the negotiation of subject positions at home is a fruitful way to throw into relief the plays' various engagements with the discourses and practices surrounding urban militarisation and securitisation, policing and surveillance, multiculturalism and cohabitation, citizenship and exclusion.

In a sense, the imbrications of home and front may already be implicit in the term *home front*, as captured by Gillian Youngs's definition:

the 'new home front' in the war on terror has multiple dimensions to it. Just as it refers to links between 'home' (as in national or domestic) and the 'front' (as in the military spheres of action in Iraq and Afghanistan), it also refers literally to the home front, with terrorist attacks and continuing threats of them in the UK, importantly from home-grown as well as internationally networked terrorists. (925)

In the plays analysed in this chapter, the home front features in both senses of the word. While multiple links between home and front are forged in these pieces, all of them are also, and perhaps primarily, interested in the effects of the 'war on terror' on individuals and communities in the UK. The home, both as domestic place and as iconic of national space, emerges as a contested locus, where subjects are positioned by and position themselves in relation to discourses surrounding belonging, anxiety, and security. The topographical and tropological links between subject constitution and the discourse/practice formation that is aptly (if problematically) labelled by the US administration's neologism *Homeland Security* will serve as a persistent focal point throughout this enquiry. In particular, this chapter will investigate (1) dramatic (de)constructions of the terrorist-versus-patriot opposition; (2) the negotiation of British Muslim subjectivities against the backdrop of tense community relations; (3) articulations of post-9/11 citizenship with a view to privatised and individualised modes; (4) (re-)enactments and refusals of female grief in relation to rituals of commemoration; (5) the positioning of masculinities within and beyond a post-traumatic frame in response to the violent events associated with war and terrorism.

3.1 Patriot Subjects, Terrorist Suspects

Two of the most overdetermined subject positions in the discourses surrounding the security of the home front are those of the 'terrorist' and the 'patriot'. The discursive formation of the 'war on terror' institutes a grid of classification that configures these positions as polar opposites. The dividing practices that create this particular dispersion can be described as processes of proxy and direct exclusion (see Richardson 152). In the first manoeuvre, the terrorist is discursively excluded from the semantic positions of *citizen* and *patriot* because of a perceived lack of the characteristics pertaining to these. In the second, the terrorist is excluded precisely because of his/her perceived characteristics, which are in turn defined in sharp contradistinction to the citizen/patriot. These discursive processes tie in with the material threat of legal exclusion, as terrorists, or terrorist suspects, can become exempt from citizenship.[1] In terms of the semantic-ideological opposition, an Orientalist discourse posits the terrorist as the underside of the patriot along the vectors of gender, race, sexuality, pathology, and corporeality (Alexander 235–236). As Andrea Nachtigall's discourse analysis of gendered representations of the 'war on terror' has unearthed, there are four discursive frames that mark the Islamic terrorist as Oriental 'other': lack of rationality; abnormal sexuality; adherence to archaic values of masculinity, warfare, and honour; misogyny (314). Against this characterisation, the Western 'self' is constituted in relation to sanity/rationality, a 'healthy' (hetero)sexuality, moderate masculinity, and liberal values concerning women (319). Notions of proper/appropriate sexuality are particularly pertinent in this regard, as foregrounded in the work of Jasbir Puar and Amit Rai, who hold that the construction of the terrorist as sexually perverted "invites an aggressive heterosexual patriotism" (117).

While this remark suggests that the discursive construction of the patriotic citizen operates within a heteronormative framework, Puar has in her subsequent study put forward the thesis that the exclusion of 'perverse' terrorist bodies from the national project has partly invited the participation of queer 'native' citizens. In *Terrorist Assemblages* (2007), Puar charts a discursive shift that allows for homosexual subjects to fashion themselves as belonging to the imperialist nation in formerly unavailable ways. This inclusion of queer white bodies depends on the concomitant racialisation and exclusion of the 'other': "The emergence and sanctioning of queer subjecthood is a historical shift condoned only through a parallel process of demarcation from populations targeted for segregation, disposal, or death" (Puar xii). Adopting Lisa Duggan's notion of homonormativity, Puar develops the concept of homonationalism, which rests on a differentiation of queer patriot bodies from non-national terrorists and terrorist look-alikes. As Puar's reading of the ascription of sexual deviancy to terrorist bodies in the Abu Ghraib torture acts, in popular representations of Osama bin Laden, or in the hate crimes committed against Sikh populations in the US demonstrates, the "failed and perverse, [...] emasculated bodies" of could-be terrorists are "metonymically tied to all sorts of pathologies of the mind and body – homosexuality, incest, pedophilia" (xxiii). Although I find Puar's argument persuasive, I partly concur with Bharucha's critique of her schema insofar as it does not seem to apply to, for instance, the London bombers, because it fails to engage "with the heteronormative 'ordinariness' of such terrorist perso-

---

[1] In the UK, this has factually become possible in the context of post-9/11 legislation with the Immigration, Asylum and Nationality Act 2005 (Kundnani 39).

nae, even at the level of masquerade" (82). This caveat notwithstanding, Puar's framework can usefully be extended to describe the larger discursive mechanisms that produce the terrorist in contradistinction to the patriot, and vice versa. In conjoining the 'perverse' terrorist with 'properly' national bodies, Puar's analysis importantly illuminates the "production of imbricated normative patriot and terrorist corporealities that cohere against and through each other" (xxiv). Most crucially in the context of this chapter, Puar discloses the convergence of terrorist and patriot subjects as "not distant, oppositional entities, but 'close cousins'" (38). I am particularly interested in the way in which a dismantling of the distance between these positions can work towards destabilising a discursive framework that supports the violent expulsion of "those people deemed to display the signifiers of real or 'dormant' terrorists" (Graham, "Cities" 273).

The distribution of antagonistic terrorist/patriot positions is clearly in evidence in (counter-)terrorism discourses and cultural representations on the British home front. The dependence of patriotic subject formation on the terrorist as anti-subject can be illustrated by the notion of suspect communities, a concept that was originally coined by Paddy Hillyard in reference to the Troubles in Northern Ireland. In the post-9/11 and post-7/7 context in the UK, numerous scholars have argued that British Muslims have been discursively framed as the new suspect community. Christina Pantazis and Simon Pemberton, for instance, attribute this shift to changes in legislation as well as political and academic discourses (649–650). Pointing to the emphasis in British counter-terrorism practices on pre-emptive measures and community policing, manifest in an increased number of raids, stops and searches, arrests, and detentions (all targeted at suspected Muslim terrorists), they hold that "the demarcation of a specific social group as a suspect community arguably serves to generate fear of this social group amongst a wider society" (661). Thus, the positioning of British Muslims as terrorist suspects is tied to the construction of an anxious national subject, imbued with the "'permission to hate' these groups" (661). The work pursued by Mary Hickman and her collaborators on the shift from the Irish to the Muslim suspect community similarly highlights the role of the national subject in the project of "suspectification" (Hickman et al. 10). Their study importantly traces the close collusion of the discourses of the 'enemy within' and of 'community responsibility', which effectively leads to the community taking over the security services' task to "tackle terrorism" (17).

The insertion of British citizens into a patriotic community has operated through a number of public initiatives. Among these was a nation-wide "counter-terror publicity campaign" launched by the Metropolitan Police in 2010 (BBC News, "Police"), based in part on the distribution of posters instructing travellers at airports and train stations or residents of social housing estates on how to detect potential terrorists (under the headline "Terrorism: If You Suspect It, Report It").[2] Another poster issued by the City of London Police addressed commuters in numerous Underground stations in 2014 with the slogan: "We love rush hour. It gives us 300,000 extra pairs of eyes". The priming techniques that find application in these representations encourage viewers to train their gaze on "the 'next terrorist' in the midst of safety", as Sara Upstone writes of the post-9/11 climate of suspicion (35). Evident in these campaigns is the fantasy of installing an all-seeing panoptic gaze by effectively recruiting citizens into what Jonathan Burnett calls "the police 'family' (i.e. all those who carry out policing or quasi-policing functions)" (14). This interpellative invitation is clearly linked to mechanisms of subjection that hail citizens into the position of the patriot, rather than the development of patriotic affiliations as a matter of self-relation. And yet the recruitment of patriotic subjects crucially depends on attendant processes of subjective introspection, as Gilroy's comment on the rise of authoritarian modes of belonging in the wake of 9/11 indicates:

> State-sponsored patriotism and ethnic absolutism are resurgent [...], but the work involved in knowing oneself and understanding the traditional defining norms of one's own official culture is not as easy as it might have been in the past. Technology, deindustrialisation, consumerism, loneliness and the fracturing of family forms have changed [...] national culture as much or even more than immigration ever did. ("'Where'" 267)

As becomes apparent here, the subject's quest of self-knowledge is vital to the overall patriotic project. In parallel, one could argue that, although primarily a question of the objectivising mechanisms of discourse and the use of disciplinary power, those interpellated into the position of could-be terrorists similarly dispose of a limited range of subjectivising practices in order to declare/confess the truth about themselves.

If, as has been argued, the successful acquisition of a particular subject position depends both on cultural codes of intelligibility and, in the theatre event, on spectatorial recognition, then the performative (dis)identification of the 'next terrorist' becomes a significant resource. A number of plays seem to tap into its resistant potential, often adhering to what could here preliminarily be called a critical mimesis of the rise of suspicion and patriotism. Among these is Ali Taylor's *Overspill*, first performed at the Churchill Theatre in Bromley in 2008, which centres upon a multicultural trio of young men, whose streetwise dispositions,

---

[2] A wide distribution of these posters across London could still be observed in 2015; some of the templates can be viewed on the Metropolitan Police website.

mixed ethnic backgrounds, and slightly belligerent behaviour renders them terrorist suspects as soon as bombs begin to explode in the town centre. Dennis Kelly's play *After the End*, which premiered at the Bush Theatre in London in 2005, has a male character lock his female love interest into a nuclear fallout shelter, acting on the claim that terrorist bomb blasts wrecked the city. The exploitation of the patriotic subject position offered up by 'war on terror' discourse as a kind of false pretext in order to pursue private initiatives is also the subject of Kelly's *Osama the Hero* (2005), which will be considered at length in this chapter, preceded by a discussion of Henry Adam's *The People Next Door* (2003). My analysis of these plays proceeds on the thesis that, if (counter-)terrorism discourse regulates the distance and opposition between the positions of patriot and terrorist, theatrical inflections of the discursive regime consist in destabilising this fixation of nodal points, as Puar does, by inverting these positions or uncovering the ways in which they are, in fact, mutually constitutive.

Terrorist Clones, Patriot Clowns: Henry Adam's *The People Next Door*

Strategies of dismantling the terrorist-patriot opposition are central to Henry Adam's *The People Next Door*, which premiered at the Traverse Theatre in Edinburgh in 2003 and transferred to the Theatre Royal Stratford East for a London run in the same year. Adam's play was one of the earliest pieces of new writing that responded directly to the impact of 9/11 and the 'war on terror' on British society. While set on a generic British housing estate, the play – as an example of "Scottish playwriting" and in the context of its Edinburgh production – also bears particular resonance for post-devolutionary discussions of Scottish identity, as Trish Reid has demonstrated (192–196). *The People Next Door* can be seen as an exemplary home-front play in that it illustrates the replication of global conflicts in a local setting, by zooming in onto the "neighborhood scale", which, in the 21st-century terror city, has presumably become marked by "the divided allegiances of faith, ethnicity, nation, and generation" (Gray and Wyly 336). As a "multicultural farce" (Südkamp 165) – or what could be labelled a comedy of "neighbour terrorism" (a term originally referring to acts of violence committed by radicalised UK citizens [Moran 29]) – Adam's play offers a satirical look at the culture of suspicion and community policing, pivoting on the clownish figures of could-be terrorist and would-be patriot.

The emergence of post-9/11 discourse is metonymically represented by the entrance of policeman Phil on stage. The character personifies the power/knowledge nexus associated with the 'war on terror', which is necessarily given a comic inflection due to the clownesque style of performance implied in the stage directions: "PHIL *is lean and fit and cocky, his wide-boy swagger screaming 'top-dog' at anyone who cares to listen*" (Adam 6).³ All the subjects in the scenic space are positioned, and need to position themselves, within this discursive field as soon as Phil has made his entrance. This applies specifically to Nigel, the protagonist. The stage directions describe him as "*a big lanky man of mixed, indeterminate race*" (3), and the ambiguity concerning his ethnic (self-)identification is reflected in Nigel's first speech on stage, which takes place before the policeman's entrance. The opening scene, in which Nigel interacts with his mirror image, is a prime example of Reckwitz's interobjective subjectivation. In an ironic variation on the Lacanian mirror-stage situation, Nigel (mis)recognises himself as a racialised subject in the interaction with the prop:

> My name is Salif. Salif, bwa. That' my name. Salif. That' an African name, bwa, Moslem name. Salif, meaning '...??', well, I don't know what it mean but that' be my name now bwa. Salif. Oh sure, you saying – I know you. That ain't no Salify bwa. I went to school with that bwa. That bwa his name be Nigel. Nah, nah, nah, nah, see – my name ain't Nigel. My name Salif. (3)

The use of the mirror as a reflective surface of self-fashioning emphasises the performative aspect of becoming 'a self'. Nigel turns himself into a black Muslim subject by using what he perceives as an African Muslim name and speaking black vernacular – omitting the endings of verbs, using the uninflected *be*, substituting *brother* with 'bwa' (see also Berton 160). Reviewers perceived this mode of speaking, and more generally the acting style of Fraser Ayres in the original production, as echoing comedian Sacha Baron Cohen's white 'gangster' character Ali G, who similarly borrows from Jamaican patois and 'rude body' attitude (Loveridge, "*People*"). In contrast to Lacan's model, the mirror image does not assist in the constitution of Nigel's subjective position, but challenges it by acting out the interpellation of the state that would have people known by their given names. Despite the slang, the overall humorous tone of the speech, and the fact that Nigel's mental issues associated with an unspecified "borderline" condition (34) may be foreshadowed by this naive self-referential practice, the scene can still be read as a valid attempt to resist interpellation into the white identity connected to Nigel's British citizenship. This brief, blissfully ignorant moment – with regard to the subsequent symbolic entrance of post-9/11 discourse – is characterised by a playful relationship to ethnic and religious differ-

---

3 For better readability, I will provide the full source whenever I am first citing from a playtext; every subsequent quotation will be followed solely by page numbers in brackets (unless this could lead to ambiguity).

ence and an endorsement of the 'cool' black Muslim subject, or "Malcolm X Moslem", as Nigel later puts it (15).[4] The scene affirms the fluidity of cultural identities as a question of reflexive positioning.

With the symbolic onset of the post-9/11 world, Nigel's deliberate processes of subjectivation are replaced by subjection to disciplinary power. Phil forcefully enters Nigel's apartment and reiterates the hail that Nigel had previously only anticipated: "You're Nigel Brunswick, 34 C Warrender Gardens. I mean that is your name, isn't it?" (7). Although Nigel attempts to resist the policeman's call, "My name is Salif, see. You got the wrong guy" (7), it becomes clear that no such imaginative self-fashioning is permissible before the law. Going through the cards in Nigel's wallet, Phil drily observes: "Nigel Brunswick. Nigel Brunswick. Nigel Brunswick" (7). In the context of state interpellation, the playful friction between Nigel's (official) white British and (imagined) black Muslim subject positions is transposed into a more serious register. It is precisely this contradiction that makes him vulnerable to the – quite possibly unauthorised – policing effort single-handedly undertaken by Phil. On the one hand, the 'Hey, you there' of the hail addresses Nigel Brunswick, the "(white) originary citizen" that M. Jacqui Alexander identifies as eligible for the construction of the "new citizen patriot" (234–235).

On the other hand, Nigel's ambiguous ethnic position – in conjunction with his lower-class status – is exploited: in order to intimidate Nigel into cooperation, Phil avails himself of racialised and classified discourses of belonging. When Nigel insists on his rights to his "house" that he feels are being violated, Phil makes it clear that Nigel lives in a "housing association flat you cunt and don't you forget it. You don't own it. It doesn't belong to you. [...] They're letting you stay here" (7). Nigel's sense of entitlement to a home, his sense of being integrated into the community, is harshly rebuked by a reminder that his presence may be suffered but he 'doesn't belong'. Phil's speech evinces the way in which the traditional values associated with home ownership (and the seemingly timeless 'home sweet home' mentality) have become overlaid with patriotic claims to the nation home and the attendant rights and duties of defending it in the 'war on terror'. In addition, Phil invokes a climate of suspicion when he warns Nigel that his "neighbours might start asking questions", that, if police were to knock down Nigel's door, "your neighbours are going to be on the blower faster than a

---

4 As Aisha Phoenix observes, "'black' [...] in twenty-first-century Britain can be an indicator of cultural prestige and 'urban cool'" (326). Importantly in this context, Phoenix documents the ways in which practices of self-formation by young British Muslims are founded on a mix of 'casual' styles and dispositions that both draw on white British culture and emulate black identities (322, 328).

bunch of Albanians who got their Euro-tunnel timetables mixed up" (8). The racist joke draws on anxieties surrounding immigration and asylum seekers, implicitly establishing a connection between Albanians entering the UK through the Eurotunnel and Nigel's parasitic status on the housing estate. The patriotic speaking position explored here is structured around what Imogen Tyler has described as "anti-refugee publicity", which collapses the subjects of refugees, illegal immigrants, and terrorists "into one revolting parasitical figure" (91).[5] The framing of Nigel as suspicious anti-subject, pushed beyond the shifting frontier of the social, is emphasised at the close of the scene, in which Phil's threats are realised when "MRS MAC *keeps close watch from her door*" (12).

Significantly, the discursive construction of the white patriotic citizen "in sharp contradistinction to the (dark) naturalized citizen" (Alexander 235) is destabilised through the contradictory interpellation of Nigel. While his position as racialised 'other' can be exploited to render him suspicious under the changed historico-discursive circumstances, his subjection to law and citizenship as Nigel Brunswick makes him answerable to the discourse of community responsibility. Calling on Nigel to assist in the effort to find his half-brother, a suspected terrorist, Phil instructs him: "You'll ask questions. You'll go looking ... family, friends" (10). Although much of the play's comic energies derive from this contradictory positioning as both patriotic and suspect, it can yet be read as critically reflective of the ambivalent position of Muslims in British society after 9/11. This tension also generates the dramatic conflict, as Nigel is forced to participate in community policing against his own drive to position himself on the margins of society, as black outlier instead of white patriot. The external categorisation of himself as suspicious further clashes with Nigel's continuous attempts to reflexively position himself as an 'innocent' black subject: "I'm a young man who [...] gets picked on cause of the colour of his skin, who gets harassed by Babylon night and day for no fucking reason" (47). The fact that Nigel holds some cultural knowledge regarding institutional racism again makes for the comedy: he can read Phil as a representative of "Stephen Lawrence killing Babylon" (33), yet he never fully understands that he is not being targeted because he self-identifies as black but because he can be racially profiled as Asian. So Phil constantly has to remind him of the new grids of classification: "[t]his is not the time to have a brown skin and a wise-arse disposition" (29). The shades of skin colour assume a comically excessive importance in this context:

---

[5] For the "anti-asylum tabloid hysteria" and its normalisation within a nationalist rhetoric under New Labour, see also Burnett (11).

NIGEL. [...] I's fucking black, see. Black!
PHIL.   Brown.
NIGEL. Black! (33)

The differential subject positions Nigel is forced to inhabit are further linked to conflicting internal and external desires. To begin with, Nigel's self-relation is largely formed in the type of interobjective practices that could be deemed characteristic of the postmodern consumer subject. Listening to pop music, watching TV, playing video games, smoking marijuana, and dining on "*Campbell's Cream of Tomato soup*" (3) – that most iconic of mass-produced consumer goods – Nigel aspires to be the 'innocent' consumer of items of popular culture (and the occasional 'soft drugs') without being affected by the changed sociopolitical context. His infatuation with Ms Dynamite is a good example of that. In one scene, he sings along to the hip hop artist's music (19), and he playfully calls his half-sister "Miss Dynamitee-ee" (23). While audiences might be able to draw a connection to Ms Dynamite's prominent appearance in the protests against the Iraq war just months before the premiere, Nigel is completely oblivious to these new significations of (pop-)cultural trends. His own desire to continue his innocuous lifestyle jars with the two conflicting ways in which he is positioned: as terrorist suspect, his community wishes to fix their anxieties on him; as patriot, he is called upon to collaborate in the counter-terrorism effort and infiltrate the local mosque.

The play's critique of the climate of suspicion hinges on the personal and societal fissures emerging from these contradictions. Whereas Nigel's pre-9/11 subjectivation had enabled him to live in a relatively peaceful multicultural community with his old Scottish neighbour Mrs McCallum and young Afro-Caribbean Marco, the external construction of him inhibits intercultural cohabitation. The play illuminates this foreclosure by, first of all, rendering the process of suspectification absurd. This is achieved primarily through the figure of Mrs McCallum, who goes through different stages of suspicion concerning Nigel: she first accuses him of having smoked on the stairs (5), then suspects him of having become a victim of "usury" (18), and – only after her own encounter with the bearer of post-9/11 power/knowledge – begins to read Nigel in terms of her newly acquired knowledge about the enemy within (46). Her suspicion culminates in caricature as she goes off "looking for bombs" in Nigel's apartment, naively reiterating patriotic propaganda: "He said you were conspiring [...] with enemies of the state. Terrorists. He said to keep my eyes open for a Paki ... stani ... a Pakistani with a beard" (57). The comic conclusion of Mrs McCallum's search for bombs places the suspicion of the Muslim-as-terrorist on a par with neighbour disputes surrounding the more mundane matters of living together. Through the figure of the hypervigilant neighbour, the play satirises what Sara Ahmed calls the translation of post-9/11 citizenship "into a form of Neighbourhood Watch" (*Cultural Politics* 78). The absurdity of the idiom of suspicion is amplified by the characterisation of Nigel as naive, innocent misfit. For lack of 'real' terrorists on the housing estate, Nigel has to stand in for the enemy within, purely by virtue of his ambiguous racial appearance. He becomes the comic surrogate terrorist par excellence, epitomising W.J.T. Mitchell's notion of the terrorist clone as the "icon of our time" (167). Mitchell suggests that "the terrorist is often portrayed as a clone, a [...] suicidal life form comparable to a virus, a cancer, or a sleeper cell that 'incubates' inside the body of its host" (74). This idea is transposed into the workings of the farce, where the 'sleeper cell' is suspected to 'incubate' in the most unlikely body.

In this context, it is worth noting that the genre chimes particularly well with the discursive overdetermination of the terrorist subject position. As Issacharoff explains, substitution is "a basic semiotic ingredient of farce", mobilising "the device of quiproquo – something that stands for (that is mistaken for) something else" (107). The grotesque substitutions that operate in this farce, where a socially inept young man of the Ali G 'gangster' type is mistaken for a bomb-plotting terrorist, comically inflect the prescriptive positions of a discursive regime keen on identifying the 'next terrorist'. By representing the patriot as clown and the terrorist as clone, the play can be seen as providing comic relief in a strained situation as it renders persistent cultural anxieties laughable: as one reviewer remarked, "[i]t is so satisfying to reel with laughter at some of those things we fear most" (Fletcher). The suspicious mindset induced by low-intensity warfare on the home front is thereby ridiculed and invalidated. In the original production for the Traverse Theatre, the farcical take on suspicion and surveillance was encapsulated by Miriam Buether's set design – a frontal cross section of the two-storey council house, which offered both Nigel's and Mrs McCallum's flats to the spectators' and the characters' scrutiny. Not only does this set capture particularly well the cultural trend whereby the "injunction to suspicion [...] incited citizens to 'see' as/for the State" (Biesecker 162), but it is also reminiscent of the "vignettes" of a comic strip (Berton 167). It is this opening up of the set(ting) to the spectators' gaze that potentially implicates them in the plays' critique. If the spatial arrangement positions audiences as both the recipients of the comedy of neighbour terrorism and the watchful citizens that 'see' as/for the state (as, indeed, they may have been urged to do by public transport posters on their way to the theatre), then the implied spectator position activates the kind of "political humour" that "allows the audience to laugh at the joke while becoming aware of its own subjectivity and complicity" (Millie Taylor qtd. in Hutnyk 132).

Moreover, the play's farcical elements converge in a criticism of counter-terrorism policies as worse than ineffective. Ironically, it is through subjugation to the position of the patriot that Nigel comes closest to being the terrorist. By acting as an undercover agent in the local mosque, he drifts towards that other external construction of himself, as becomes evident in an encounter with Phil:

> I told them [...] [in the mosque] I'm a young man who [...] gets so het up by uncompromising white authority he wants to get a gun and start shooting and shooting and shooting! And man, that is the truth. I do want to shoot man. I want to shoot you. I want to shoot your wife. I want to blow up the whole fucking world man. (47–48)

This speech testifies to the way in which the patriot requires the terrorist but is also inseparable from him. Phil's investigations are, ultimately, designed to produce the terrorist, to render visible and punishable the amorphous enemy in the 'war on terror' whom he described in an earlier scene: "We're fighting a bunch of fucking ghosts. We don't know who they are or where they are or what they're planning" (29). Hence, the corporeal presence of the terrorist is essential for the patriot, who derives his subjective position from this antagonism. Conversely, the interpellation of Nigel into patriotic citizenship and the responsibilities that come with it has led to his increased identification with and desire for the actions of the terrorist, or assassin, instead of producing any kind of valuable evidence. This outcome can be seen as an ironic take on New Labour's continued emphasis on community responsibility.

The People Next Door also offers a satirical take on the script of arrests made under the Terrorism Act. Between 2001 and 2005, there was a significant surge in these arrests, for which a "template" developed, as Steve Hewitt recalls:

> Early morning raids [took place] and suspects would be taken away; a wave of publicity would follow, as the media vainly searched for ties to al-Qaeda [...]. Often with some of the spectacular arrests there would not be any charges, acquittals would occur, or the individuals would be found guilty on lesser charges [...]. Left in the aftermath would be damaged lives, poisoned community relations, and hysteria over the extent of terrorism in the United Kingdom. (41)

In a similar vein, John Hutnyk reads the emergence of "high profile security raids" as conducive to precisely the kind of neighbourly paranoia that Adam's play critiques: "Emblematic here would be the aftermath of a raid, with police cordoning off areas of quaking middle English suburbia; the nightly news interviewing people living on the same streets of suspects" (26). The fact that the constant appearances of the policeman at Nigel's flat never produce any evidence of value to the counter-terrorism effort highlights the performative quality of the raids as an empty show, "designed to demonstrate [...] that the government was doing something [...] consequential in terms of curtailing terrorism" (Hewitt

44). With its comic turn on the raid plot, Adam's play effectively reveals how (community) policing efforts feed cultural anxieties, rather than assuaging them.

On the whole, *The People Next Door* creates an ironic-critical distance to the normative subject positions of terrorist and patriot, shows their qualities as caricature, and exposes their mutuality in a way that resonates with Puar's point that the patriot and the terrorist are 'close cousins', rather than structural opposites. If its critically mimetic potential thus consists in mirroring the processes of patriotic and suspicious subject formation while refusing the (values attached to the) associated subject positions, the play is also responsive to the question of survivability reiterated by Jenny Hughes ('how can we live here?'). Its answer lies in affirming the feasibility of multicultural cohabitation – or, in Holger Südkamp's reading, intercultural convergence and "communal respect" (167). This becomes particularly evident in the final *"picture of domestic bliss"* (84), which has Mrs McCallum, Nigel, and Marco unite in front of the television after Phil has been killed. Thanks to the symbolic death of the power/knowledge complex, the characters can regress to their pre-9/11 blissful ignorance. When news about the impending Iraq war come on, Marco simply *"switches channels"* (85).

In a way, the play somewhat uncritically seeks refuge in this "wish-fulfilment ending" (Gardner, *"People"* 28), which – provided the scene is not read as ironic by audiences – celebrates the ideal of the multicultural community. The final stage picture poses an idealised, if transient, counter-image against social divisions in the aftermath of 9/11. I concur with Reid that "the contentment staged here is inherently problematic" as it relies "on ignoring events in the outside world" (193). Yet it is also important to acknowledge, as does Reid, that the play's ending affirms cultural identity as "hybrid, heteroglot, inclusive" and thus endorses the "flexible [...] Scottish citizenship model" promoted in the post-devolutionary context (193–194). This ties in with an emphatic rejection of New Labour's notion of 'cohesive' citizenship, which excludes anyone who refuses to conform to an inflexible set of values.[6] Ultimately, the ending thus posits a utopian image of the harmonious hybrid family against Labour's enlargement of the 'police family' and thus works towards undermining the "cultural homogenisation and forced assimilation" (Fekete 21) engendered by the securitisation of the home front.

---

[6] As Burnett's analysis of New Labour policies suggests, the notion of cohesive citizenship is intrinsically exclusive: "The debate over 'cohesive values' focuses upon those who are judged to be in diametric opposition to national identity" (11).

Who Gets the Part of the Terrorist? Dennis Kelly's *Osama the Hero*

Dennis Kelly's play *Osama the Hero*, first produced by Hampstead Theatre in London in 2005, similarly uncouples the antagonistic opposition of terrorist and patriot subject positions. Unlike the farcical subversion of these categories in *The People Next Door*, Kelly places greater emphasis on exploring the affective investments – or passionate attachments – of individuals who come to inhabit these positions. The play is equally set on a British housing estate that becomes deeply implicated in the larger sociopolitical context, as Gary explains to the audience in the first act: "Bins have been blowing up on our estate this summer and that's not me" (Kelly 57). This single line immediately conveys that the experience of terror is inseparable from the process of suspectification. The first act as a whole configures the subject positions of patriot and terrorist that become available in the face of the acts of terror on the estate, and it charts the characters' attempts to negotiate these categories. Gary's engagement with the audience via direct address reflects the dynamics of suspicion and repudiation; there is a meta-theatrical commentary about the parallels between seeing/being seen in society and in the theatre: "the entire estate, curtains twitching, every window, [...] and for a second I see the view from thirty or forty different perspectives, looking down at me" (57). The different perspectives of the estate-dwellers are refracted through the architecture of the theatre space. With the audience thus placed in the potent position of those who are watching (and judging), Gary insists that they should assume his innocence: "just so you know and are aware that that's not me" (57). It is, however, not the position of the innocent pre-9/11 subjectivity aspired to by Nigel in *The People Next Door* that is opted for here, as Gary does not refuse to engage with the new discursive grids of classification.

On the contrary, there is something in the subject position of the terrorist that he finds appealing: "I'm thinking of becoming a terrorist" (52). It becomes clear, however, that it is not the mindless vandalism of burning bins that he is interested in. Instead, Gary feels attracted to international terrorism because of his sense of not fitting in at home. Numerous reviewers have described the figure as a "naive misfit" (Croggon); one could even claim that the characterisation gestures towards a type of autistic disorder, as is hinted when Gary admits, "I never know when things are funny, so what I do is I wait until someone else starts laughing and then I join in" (59), and that he is constantly "trying to understand the complexities of the social structure and [his] place within it. No idea. No idea at all" (62). As Gary cannot accurately assess his place in social structures, bin Laden's unflinching dedication inspires him. Hence, becoming a terrorist seems a more straightforward career path to him than the many other professions he contemplates:

GARY. [...] I consider being a priest, a lighthouse keeper, a policeman, a taxidermist, a soldier, a tramp, an undertaker, a dancer in a gay bar, a footballer, a tube driver, a drug dealer, a surfer, an accountant [...], but I find myself wondering how much it costs to get to Afghanistan because maybe then
FRANCIS. This is our place.
GARY. maybe then
FRANCIS. We live here
GARY. maybe then
FRANCIS. We've always lived here
GARY. maybe then
FRANCIS. We always will live here. [...]
GARY. maybe then I'd have something to believe in. (70)

Gary's expression of desire and hope connected to the terrorist subject position interlaces with Francis's patriotic speech in significant ways. The intersecting lines present ostensibly antagonistic articulations of the terrorist's and the patriot's viewpoint; the former considers travelling to Afghanistan to find 'something to believe in', while the latter expresses strong sentiments about protecting 'our place'. Drawing on Chaudhuri's 'geoanalytical' terminology, one could say that the one derives his subjectivity almost entirely and in an unproblematic manner from place, whereas the other "experiences himself geopathically; when he is where he should feel at home, [...] where he supposedly belongs, then does he sense himself most deeply out of place" (65).

The structural terrorist-patriot opposition, however, is disrupted from within, for the rules of enunciation that prescribe ways of speaking about terrorism seem to be dispensed in the speaking position that Gary develops. Since he is unable to understand, or rather unwilling to accept – significantly, he speaks about his "non-acceptance of the world" (60) – preconceived notions about Islamic terrorism, he builds a self-relation based on an idiosyncratic conception of terrorism as one professional option among others. This enables him, albeit tentatively, to circumvent the regulation of positions from which one can make legitimate statements about terrorism and, instead, to develop a new set of enunciative modalities. When approached from Gary's perspective, bin Laden meets all the criteria stipulated by the instructions for his school presentation on a contemporary hero: he is "an inspiration to millions, a determined individual who'll sacrifice wealth, life and happiness for what they believe in" (66). The extent of the play's provocation to socially conditioned understandings of terrorism can be gleaned from two incidents that both hinge on the title *Osama the Hero*, one explicitly, the other implicitly: at the premiere in May 2005, police showed up at

Hampstead Theatre – a traditional new writing space that is not known for causing controversies – obviously alarmed by the sentiments a play thus entitled might stir (Kelly, personal communication); after the London bombings, which took place just two months after the premiere, a former school friend of Shezad Tanweer, one of the suspected bombers, declared: "Nobody can believe it. When he was at school his hero was Mike Tyson, not Osama Bin Laden" (qtd. in Seidler 87). It seems that the mere combination of the elements 'Osama bin Laden' and 'hero' makes for a statement that violates the "discursive 'policing' which one has to reactivate in each of one's discourses" (Foucault, "Order" 61).

In contrast to the insurrection of nonconceptual knowledges about terrorism in Gary's speech, Francis develops a speaking position that draws on discourses of nationalism, patriotism, and loyalty for its legitimation. Set against Gary's reflection on exiling himself to Afghanistan is a discourse of belonging, which links up with a sense of defending the home/land, metonymically represented by the estate. Echoing the 'Neighbourhood Watch' theme of *The People Next Door*, Francis positions himself as guardian of the community and begins to monitor the acts of vandalism: "sitting in here watching [...] curtain twitching" (58). Contrary to Gary's adoption of a minor viewpoint, Francis takes up cues from the popular media to diagnose the state of the nation: "worlds falling to pieces, terrorists and fucking perverts" (58). By showing how the patriotic subject position derives from populist discourse, the play illustrates what Allan Pred has referred to as the "production of widespread forms of anxiety-ridden 'situated ignorance' [...] that are infused with distortions, misrepresentations, and disinformation" (364). Whereas Francis articulates his subject position in dependence on the 'situated ignorance' of the 'war on terror' discourse, Gary inserts himself into a terrorist position that is almost entirely filled with subjective meanings.

The oppositional terrorist-patriot pairing is further disrupted by the trajectory of another subject position that is articulated towards the patriot, the figure of the sexual pervert. Since Francis, as community police agent, is at first unable to render the perpetrator of the garage and bin bombings accountable, he mobilises the position of the pervert as the anti-subject which patriotic subjectivation requires. Several reviewers have expressed their confusion concerning the "subplot about a 50-year-old man's creepy relationship with a celebrity-obsessed teenage girl" (Spencer, "Upsetting" 18). In my reading, the inclusion of the 'pervert' is central to the dynamics of positioning in the play. One could argue that, throughout the first act, the positions of terrorist and pervert overlap, for they are subject to an equivalential overdetermination. Both are given equal weight in Francis's construction of the enemy image, cultivated by the popular media ('terrorists and fucking perverts'). And, initially, Mark seems eligible as the suspect that occupies both positions. He is not only "an old man inviting a young girl into his garage" (57) but also becomes suspicious because he possesses the only garage left on the estate that has not been burnt out (59). The garage becomes an iconic space, signifying the breeding ground of the social evils of sexual deviancy and terrorism, an obscure niche in the terror city in which perverts and terrorists can stealthily seduce young girls and/or build bombs, unseen by the patriot whose 'curtain twitching' cannot penetrate its walls. Again, the technique of interlacing dialogues reinforces this point:

FRANCIS. [...] D'you know why he's put a door in the garage? [...] [H]e's put a little door in the big door so he doesn't have to open the big door and no-one can see inside.
MANDY. We like our privacy.
MARK. Yes, of course. (67)

The patriotic speaking position which Francis takes up articulates the anxieties linked to the new landscape of urban fear. His desire to probe into the garage becomes an ironic echo of the "security state's [...] insistence that 'they' may be anywhere and are everywhere, [...] hiding in the folds and interstices of 'our' freedom" (Katz 355). Francis answers the security state's call for mobilisation against those who are hiding out of plain sight: "you're just going to let a pervert walk around? [...] As if we have no morals? [...] If you think I'm going to let that happen you've got another think coming" (68–69).

The inclusion of the 'perverse' subject in the play serves to illuminate the dispersion of differential positions in the discursive regime, as lucidly described by Alexander:

> The meeting place that collapses the enemy, the terrorist, and the sexual pervert is the very one that secures the loyal heterosexual citizen patriot. Indeed, it is under his vigilant – one might even say vengeful – directives that the ostensible boundaries between the enemy and the patriot, the terrorist and the citizen, and the pervert and the morally abiding collide. (239)

Just as delineated by Alexander, Francis's vigilant and vengeful directives eventually lead to the blurring of the boundaries between the antagonistic subject positions of enemy/patriot, terrorist/citizen, pervert/the morally abiding in the second act. Essentially, the distances between subject positions collapse through the act of torture, which is set "*[i]nside the now burnt out and blown up garage*" (73). The brutal torture of Gary highlights that the would-be patriots, in seeking to punish the original crime, engage in acts of violence far worse than vandalism. Significantly, the second act is the only part of the play informed by realism, a linear structure, and symmetrical dialogue. As evident from reviews, the naturalistic acting style in the original production was reinforced by "horribly realistic sound effects" (Spencer, "Upsetting" 18). Through a representation of torture that agrees with realist conventions, the scene offers a sinister reflection of the "mimetic excesses of a system in crisis" (Hughes, *Performance* 18), that is, a democratic system which undermines itself in condoning acts of torture. The form and aesthetics at play here are also relevant for the positioning of the audience. Whereas Gary speaks *ad spectatores* in the first act, all characters recede behind the fourth wall in the second act. The way spectators are positioned towards this naturalistic display of aggression can be captured by drawing on Mary Karen Dahl's analysis of theatrical representations of state violence:

> Unless I refuse to watch, I become a guilty voyeur. My only exoneration must be by way of revulsion against the state that practices such violations. [...] By turns, I am one with the victims, victimised as a spectator, victimiser as long as I continue to watch. Sympathy, anger, and guilt combine to force a radical reassessment of values – and subsequently, of everyday actions. (118–119)

By way of caveat, some scepticism is warranted concerning spectators' projected 'reassessment of values'. Nevertheless, Dahl's argument is valuable for its suggestion that dramatic countermeasures to state violence can consist in the creation of an "audience-as-community in opposition to the false community of state terror" (116). This bears some relevance for the politics of positioning in Kelly's torture scene. As all the estate-dwellers join in a choreography of violence, consisting of graphic threats, repeatedly ripping the gaffer tape off Gary's mouth and putting it back on, and taking turns in hitting him in the face with a hammer, they emerge as a patriotic collective, offering equivalent articulations of the torturer's subject position. Regardless of their divergent personal motivations, the characters come to cohere in the 'false community of state terror'. Their synchronised collective act elucidates Puar's point that "the bonding ritual of the carnival of torture [...] is the ultimate performance of patriotism" (100).[7]

The fact that a 'false community' is being constructed in the 'carnival of torture' is highlighted by the integration of the formerly ousted 'perverse' subject in the bonding ritual. Here, it is worth recalling Puar's argument about the inclusion of queer citizens in the national project through a displacement of queerness onto the terrorist body. A similar mechanism is highlighted by Kelly's torture scene. A clear shift occurs from the ambivalent enemy image of act one to

---

[7] See also Allen Feldman's reading of the Abu Ghraib torture photographs as echoing the "celebratory and horrific carnivalesque atmosphere of the picture postcards that were sold as souvenirs of the lynching and mutilation of African-Americans in the 1920s" ("Actuarial Gaze" 218).

the punishment of Gary as terrorist enemy in act two. The swift cut from the arbitrary lashing out which concludes the first act, where Francis's final words are "I'm going / to fucking / kill someone" (72), to the gagged and shackled teenage body on stage resonates with the random arrest and incarceration of suspects, some of them underage, at both Guantánamo Bay detention camp and Abu Ghraib prison. The demarcation of the terrorist enemy is connected to a projection of the social evils previously identified by Francis onto this one body, which, in turn, allows for an integration of the 'perverse' patriot:

FRANCIS. Wife wasn't so lucky. [...] Looking for you [...] crying her eyes out looking for you and you with a girl [...]
MARK. Don't start with all the – [...] It's him we should be [...] He did it, he's the one who hurt me, [...] it's me that's hurt!
FRANCIS. Which is what we're saying to you Mark! [...] I thought you were sick of this shit.
MARK. I am sick of this shit. I am sick of this shit and I do want to do something, just don't bring that into this [...]
FRANCIS. Alright. (83–84)

The ambiguous coding of the signifiers *sick* and *shit* ceases to register with the characters on the level of the dialogue. Although they partly signify the sexual transgressions previously ascribed to the 'pervert', Francis and Mark come to interactively construct the speaking position of the patriot around a shared, unambiguous signified, the 'sick shit' of terrorism. With Francis's consent to Mark's plea to not 'bring that into this', the older man's relationship with the teenage girl can be naturalised for the sake of rallying around the patriotic position. These discursive manoeuvres articulate new chains of difference and equivalence between subject positions, thereby illustrating how the discourse of securitisation "enables the nation to be mobilized as coherent [...] through deployments against less coherent threats" (Katz 355). The characters of Francis and Mark exemplify those initially differential subject positions that come to cohere against the 'less coherent', yet markedly oppositional, threat of terrorism. The attendant displacement of queerness/perversion onto the terrorist body culminates in Mark's outburst: "Filthy little [...] pervert, [...] filthy pervert" (101). Mark's lashing out against Gary highlights the mechanism whereby the culturally acceptable construction of terrorists as "perverse figures" serves to rehabilitate subjects "*away from* these bodies, [...] signaling and enforcing the mandatory terms of patriotism" (Puar 38).

By scenically and verbally presenting these dynamics of subject positioning, the play makes transparent the effects of the epistemic regime of the 'war on terror'. Just as terms lose their ambiguity, as subject positions become sutured, the discursive formation provides speaking positions that iterate clear sides in the 'war on terror'. As briefly discussed in the theory chapter, Bush's paradigm, "Either you're with us or you're with the terrorists", exemplifies this combinatory logic. As Louise demands of Mark: "whose side are you on? [...] Because things have changed. [...] You have to pick a side" (81). Similarly, Bush's question, "Why do they hate us?", indirectly addressed to the 9/11 bombers, reappears in Mark's and Louise's questions for Gary: "Why did you blow up my garage?" (94); "Do you hate us?" (96). With the speaking position of the patriot being constructed around these Manichean binaries, Gary has no chance to assert any alternative form of subjectivity. He is invariably positioned as the terrorist enemy, and his remonstrations – "I didn't blow up your garage, honestly" (94); "No I am not a terrorist" (96) – go unnoticed. Gary's attempts at subjectivation are negated, as the only locus in the conversation offered to him is one that is defined in antagonism to the patriots. As Kelly suggests, "there is this thing that you can do when you declare yourself a patriot [...]. You declare yourself a patriot and you set the terms of debate. You set what it is to be a patriot" – and, conversely, what it is to be a terrorist (personal communication). The physical destruction of Gary's mouth in the torture scene epitomises the discursive policing of statements about terrorism. By contrasting the processes of subjectivation and insurrection of minor knowledges of the first act with the punitive subjugation to codes of populist discourse in the second act, the play highlights the fixation of subjectivities within the discursive formation of the 'war on terror'. The shift from modes of self-relation to techniques of subjection runs parallel to the displacement of Nigel's reflexive positioning by state interpellation in *The People Next Door*. One could infer from this the preliminary conclusion that theatre functions as a cultural space that permits reflection on the ways in which processes of active self-formation have become delegitimised in the 'war on terror'.

In addition, it becomes obvious that the terrorist position had never been eligible as that subjective position to which Gary aspired, as an empty subject form to be filled with subjectively selected content. As becomes starkly apparent in the torture scene, this circumvention of discursive policing cannot be durable. Particularly the external mechanisms of discursive control which Foucault specifies (prohibition, division, will to truth), as well as the systematic rarefaction of speaking subjects ("Order" 52–54, 61), apply here. Gary's construal of the 'professional terrorist' is not viable because it violates a taboo on the object of heroism, disrupts the division between 'good', hard-working citizens and those 'evil' terrorists who destroy the fruits of their labour, and cannot be established as a truthful statement in the historico-discursive regime. Moreover, it becomes evident that – although the first act had endowed Gary with a platform to be heard – the discursive framework does not provide a speaking position for the terrorist: "You don't need evidence for terrorists" (100), as Louise states. This is why the torture is not designed to obtain information, but to reinforce the validity of the patriotic positions the characters have already fully assumed. Kelly's torture scene is thus directly reflective of the functioning of torture in the 'war on terror', as thrown into relief by Anne McClintock's reading of the prisoner abuse at Abu Ghraib:

> torture is ultimately not the extraction of information from terrorists; it is [...] the determination to break down the tortured person's being and force them to 'confess': not to crimes they have committed, which mostly they have not, nor to provide actionable intelligence, which mostly they do not have, but rather to confess to [...] the godlike domination of the torturer. (72)

The 'godlike domination' that can be achieved over the torture victim becomes a strategy with which the estate-dwellers try to regain a sense of empowerment in a climate of urban vulnerability that leaves them largely impotent. Youngs has noted "the pervasive qualities of vagueness related to the war on terror", which she sees as distancing citizens from the "actions being taken on their behalf", resulting in a "perceived loss of agency" (932). This situation is aggravated in the social milieu of Kelly's housing estate, whose inhabitants additionally lack socioeconomic power. As a result, they turn to aggression in order to recover a share in a political configuration that does not actively involve them. The transposition of torture to the British housing estate blurs the real and imaginary geographical boundaries between 'home' and 'front', as it both traverses the spatial distance that supposedly separates 'us' from such violent acts and negates the division between 'barbarism' and 'civilisation'. The patriots' onslaught on the garage metonymically stands for the coalition's occupation of Iraq, "preaching liberation while practicing degradation" (Gregory, "Vanishing Points" 229). By illustrating how the terror brought to Iraq in order to 'punish' insurgents surpassed the crimes it had been designed to avenge, the torture scene divests received notions about the legitimacy of violence – "*endjustifiesthemeans*" is the mantra repeated throughout the third act (114–115) – of their self-evident nature.

To conclude, both *The People Next Door* and *Osama the Hero* engage with the new landscape of urban fear and the process of suspectification through various (recon)figurations of the terrorist-patriot binary. Both productions reflect how the ocular regime of the 'war on terror' establishes a pervasive system of surveillance on an urban and neighbourhood scale. In so doing, they illustrate the impact of the construction of a new suspect community on British society and culture. Interestingly, however, both plays refuse a mimetic engagement with the Muslim-as-terrorist. Although this may be to do with the date of the productions, which were both staged before the London bombings and the attendant discursive shift to the 'enemy within', the plays' refusal to engage with the overdetermined subject position of the male Muslim terrorist can, more importantly, be seen to heed Hughes's warning about theatre's role "in helping states invent images of phantom terrorists that are used to justify aggressive globalisation" ("Theatre" 163). While Adam shifts the position of suspect onto an ambiguously racialised yet blissfully ignorant young man, Kelly places a white teenage boy with unconventional notions about the 'war on terror' at the receiving end of suspicion. The embodied presence of the clumsy young men on stage does not sit comfortably with the discursive construction of the evil terrorist enemy around which those occupying the patriot subject position rally. Enunciated against these hapless and helpless bodies, the empty phrases and slogans reiterated by the patriots, though producing material results, ultimately fail to validate their truth claim, thus illustrating the shortcomings of the 'war on terror' as a literalised metaphor (see also Mitchell xvii–xviii).

Line of Flight I: Robin Soans's *Talking to Terrorists*

Even if Adam's and Kelly's plays are clearly issue-based, they cannot be seen in terms of the "empirical engagement" and "performance of the evidential" that has frequently been associated with post-9/11 theatre (Hughes, "Theatre" 152). Their staging of ersatz terrorist suspects is situated against the discursive construction of Islamic terrorists, rather than purporting to engage with the empirical validity of current conceptions of terrorism. It is on this basis that the plays can be contrasted with Robin Soans's verbatim piece *Talking to Terrorists*, which opened at the Royal Court Theatre in London after a national tour in 2005, only a few weeks after the premiere of *Osama the Hero*. Soans's documentary play, produced by Max Stafford-Clark's Out of Joint company, is largely based on interviews with ex-members of the UVF, the IRA, the PKK, the Palestinian al-Aqsa Brigade, and the National Resistance Army, Uganda. If the intertext for the fictional plays discussed in this section is the discourse on terrorists, *Talking to Terrorists* is framed as a 'direct' engagement with the 'real' people.[8] Verbatim theatre's claim to authentic re-presentation of original sources is precisely what makes the documentary engagement with the terrorist subject position problematic, in my view. Although it would be patronising to assume that spectators expect to meet, let alone talk to, 'real' terrorists in the theatre event (see also Heddon

---

[8] The blurb of the playscript, for instance, states that the company "interviewed people from around the world who have been involved in terrorism. They wanted to know what makes ordinary people do extreme things".

134), I would still argue that the performance at large operates on the untenable premise of achieving an authentic and balanced portrayal of terrorists, truthfully exploring their motivations, and accurately explaining their apparently inexplicable acts.

If the fictional responses to the terrorist-patriot binary engineer a critical awareness of the discursive operation of overdetermination that frames subjects for violent expulsion, *Talking to Terrorists* asserts an epistemological certainty about the causality of terrorism and an ontological certainty about the 'terrorist self'. Where the former plays stage failed replicas of the 'next terrorist', Soans and Stafford-Clark's project is based on a logic of equivalence that purports to throw into relief the commonalities that make for the "universal biography of a 'terrorist'" (Hughes, *Performance* 111).[9] This functions primarily through the provision of "a neat, monologic throughline […] in the form of an 'expert'", as Stephen Bottoms refers to the inclusion of Edward, the on-stage psychologist who comments on and explains the testimonies of the 'terrorists' (58). Within this "pathologising frame" (Hughes, *Performance* 111), the multiple positionalities of the 'terrorists', their differential locations in diverse (geo)political and social conflicts, their divergent gender and age, and their singular narratives of how they became involved in paramilitary forces are homogenised. Although, in the original production, the psychologist figure appeared somewhat endearingly ridiculous in the old-fashioned costume comprised of an out-of-style suit, a bow-tie, lapel handkerchief, and metal-rimmed spectacles, the actor's consistently stern yet sympathetic expression and use of typical lecturing gestures conveyed no sign that the psycho-pathological explanations were meant to be seen as ironic.[10] In the course of the play, the arc of becoming terrorist is traced from teenage peer pressure, through cultivating a conviction that another culture is "worth destroying", the experience of a personal crisis, the wish to become "extraordinary", to the development of "peak experience" (i.e. not thinking about the day after tomorrow) (Soans 30–43).

Admittedly, the portrayal of paramilitary fighters goes far beyond the vilification which follows from the labelling of terrorists in public discourse; the implied spectator position is linked to an empathetic understanding of the fighters, "whose humanity is presented as having been irrevocably damaged by their violent past" (Hughes, *Performance* 111–112). Nevertheless, the play affirms an op-

---

9 Similarly, Mary Luckhurst writes that "Soans offers an array of seemingly randomly selected 'terrorists' from different cultures caught up in different struggles, and appears to be engaging in making highly suspicious generalizations about them" ("Verbatim Theatre" 212–213).
10 All observations are based on the recording of the performance at the Royal Court Theatre on 29 July 2005 (National Video Archive of Performance).

position between these damaged individuals and, as Hughes puts it, the "affable, ethical and reasonable representatives of the values and anxieties of liberal democracy" (112). Though refuting the framing of terrorists as irredeemably evil, the production reinstates the terrorist-versus-patriot binary, at least to a considerable extent. Even if the representatives of liberal democracy that Hughes refers to must be seen as extremely moderate versions of the patriotic subject that labours in the defence of the 'homeland', the political, military, and humanitarian dignitaries represented in the play are still framed as highly responsible social agents who have made political and personal sacrifices to reduce the terrorist threat to the UK. Most notable in this context is the intersection of the testimonies of (the actors standing in for) former Member of Parliament Norman Tebbit and his wife Margaret Tebbit, who became permanently disabled in the Brighton hotel bombing in 1984 and appears on stage in a wheelchair, with that of former IRA member Patrick Magee, who was convicted of the bombing. Even though one could claim that the distance between the positions of terrorist and patriot is dissolved by the production's endorsement of dialogue and reconciliation as well as its repeated emphasis on the role of circumstance in the formation of terrorists,[11] I would argue that the terrorists represented in the play remain irrevocably 'other' – interviewed, pathologised, explained, yet clearly different from those who work to achieve and sustain peace.

Most significant in this context is the marketing of the production as a forum for 'talking to terrorists' past its capacity to create real dialogue. Not even on the level of dramatic discourse does dialogue take place, as Amelia Howe Kritzer points out: "the play alternates monologues to create a sense of communication where none actually exists" (205). The performers standing in for personae such as Mo Mowlan, who informs audiences in the opening scene that "[t]alking to terrorists is the only way to beat them" (25), never enter into any interaction with those speaking as/for the terrorists. In fact, the only figure who appears to listen to the terrorist testimonies in the mimetic space is that of the psychologist; his remediations of their narratives suggests that their pathological essence might otherwise get lost. If anything, then, spectators are "*Listening to Former Terrorists*" – which, as Joanna Rostek suggests, might have been a more appropriate title for the play (104) – and even the act of listening is interfered with by expert guidance. Moreover, the static staging, with the actors delivering "their heavily edited interview transcripts directly to the audience in much the same way that 'talking heads' might speak to a camera" (Bottoms 59), makes

---

11 As the British Army Colonel in the play says of his Northern Ireland tour: "I realised that if I had been born in Crossmaglen or South Armagh, I would have been a terrorist" (59).

for a problematic communicative situation. Listening to the effortless recitation of the terrorist testimonies in the theatre space cannot be conceived of as (a mediation of) "[t]rue dialogue", which, as sociologist Les Back writes in *The Art of Listening* (2007), "also means being open to the possibility that those involved will refuse to have dialogue" or may subvert the rules of conversation (19). Hence, I disagree with Christopher Innes's optimistic reading of the play as offering "a practical demonstration, onstage, of [...] how terrorism might be defused by talking and listening, how fundamentalism might be led into compromise by dialogue" (440). Although the production has to be credited for its endeavour to employ the stage as a platform where (former) terrorists are allowed to 'speak back' – or rather, where actors speak for them – the universalising frame as well as the swift succession of testimonies impose, on the micro-level of the show, various restrictions on the modalities of the terrorists' subjectivation.

In conclusion, at a historical juncture where the Islamic terrorist was produced as an object of knowledge in a way that allowed for the targeting, surveillance, and deportation of 'suspicious' populations, where the provision of a patriotic subject position enabled white citizens to mobilise exclusionary discourses of belonging and exert violence on a prerogative of defending the 'nation home', a more effective theatrical inflection of the discursive regime might be seen in evidence in plays that critically engage with the contingency and arbitrariness of terrorist/patriot subjectivities. *Osama the Hero* and *The People Next Door* variously trace and refract the mimetic excesses of democracy's crisis through the proliferation of global fault lines on the neighbourhood scale. It seems to be no coincidence that both plays are set on generic housing estates, a site that could be seen to exemplify both the heterogeneous structure of the urban and its particular density. In the context of their London productions, in particular, the plays may have spoken to contemporary anxieties surrounding vulnerability to terrorism. The fixation of urban fears onto the 'next terrorist' is exposed by the plays as a strategy that works to spoil community relations, rather than assuage panic. *Talking to Terrorists*, in contrast, defuses crisis by presenting "the world as ordered, liberal and reasonable over the chaos, incoherence and fantastic of war and terror" (Hughes, *Performance* 153). Where the former set of plays depicts subjectivities on the home front as coming under increasing pressure – and/or deriving their impunity – from a globally engineered conflict that they are in no position to fully understand, it is the play with the more ambiguous setting that maintains clearly demarcated boundaries between the home and the front, the local and the global. Even if place matters in the terrorist biography that *Talking to Terrorists* charts, the impact of the differential global distribution of hardship – and Britain's (neo)colonial role in sustaining it – is not scrutinised, and audiences are let off the hook with the mildly patriotic conviction that "liberal states have enough to make them worth defending" (94), with the assurance that their rational representatives will do the 'talking to terrorists' for them.

3.2 British Muslim Subjectivities

The fact that both *The People Next Door* and *Osama the Hero* engage with the formation of suspect communities through the staging of ersatz terrorists, albeit possibly related to their pre-7/7 production contexts, could also be seen as a strategic solution to problems surrounding the representation of British Muslims and a way out of the impasse of the good Muslim/bad Muslim binary. In a dispersion of subject positions that echoes the patriot/terrorist antagonism, the discursive regime of the 'war on terror' relies on maintaining a division between 'good' and 'bad' Muslims. Systematically repeated articulations of this dividing practice are absolutely vital to upholding the legitimacy of the 'war on terror' against the discourses of religious equality and tolerance that Western nations draw on for their collective imaginings. In other words, observing the distinction between the 'bad' minority of Islamic terrorists and the overwhelmingly 'good' majority of assimilated Muslim citizens is one of the crucial rules of discursive policing. The operation of this rule was in evidence, for example, in Blair's responses to 9/11, 7/7, and the invasions of Afghanistan and Iraq. After the 2001 attacks, Blair emphasised that "the acts of these people are wholly opposed to the teachings of the Koran" ("Statement" 219); after launching the Iraq invasion, he was careful to separate the "fanatical strain of religious extremism" from "the true and peaceful faith of Islam" ("Speech" 248); after the London bombings, he resorted to this dichotomy by promising to "promote the true face of Islam worldwide" ("Full Text").

Blair's enunciations illustrate the discursive dividing practices that Mahmood Mamdani has excavated in his work on the good/bad Muslim dichotomy. These practices consistently construe "a fault line [...] that separates moderate Islam, called 'genuine Islam', from extremist political Islam" (Mamdani, "Good Muslim" 767). Continuous efforts to distinguish between 'true' Islamic belief and its 'barbarous' perversion substantiate the notion that Islam is inherently problematic,[12] that 'good' Muslims are in constant danger of drifting towards

---

[12] Sara Ahmed persuasively argues that the coexistence of "[u]tterances like 'this is not a war against Islam' [...] with descriptions such as 'Islamic terrorists'" works "to restick the words together and constitute their coincidence as more than simply temporal" (*Cultural Politics* 76).

fundamentalism. Moreover, as Mamdani identifies "the central message of such discourse: unless proved to be 'good', every Muslim [is] presumed to be 'bad'" (*Good Muslim* 15). He criticises this dichotomous construction both for its reduction of Muslims to 'essential' cultural characteristics and for its veiling of the sociohistorical and political conditions behind the formation of "neofundamentalism", in whose creation Western powers have played a substantial role ("Good Muslim" 766, 772). That these discursive dividing practices served to justify the military invasions of Iraq and Afghanistan poses a challenge to cultural representations of Muslims in the post-9/11 context. Anis Shivani, for instance, reviews a whole list of British "good Muslim versus bad Muslim novel[s]" (41), which includes *Brick Lane* by Monica Ali (2003) and *White Teeth* by Zadie Smith (2000). Shivani criticises these novels for fostering a distinction between Islamic fundamentalism and the "labor-intensive processes of assimilation and meritocratic success" (47). The fundamentalism-versus-integration binary recurs across a number of filmic representations. For example, Kenny Glenaan and Simon Beaufoy's *Yasmin* (2004) as well as Peter Kosminsky's *Britz* (2007) use dichotomous modes of representation, the most obvious manifestation of which would be the choice of British Muslim siblings as protagonists, one of whom turns to terrorism whereas the other follows the path towards assimilation/success.

The challenge formulated here is not wholly unlike the question of the politics of representing black subjects raised in Stuart Hall's seminal essay "New Ethnicities" (1996). The development sketched by Hall's schema – "a change from the struggle over the relations of representation to a politics of representation itself" (442) – partly applies to the representation of (British) Muslims in the 'war on terror' context. The two, largely synchronous phases identified by Hall find their echo in a first wave of academic studies concerned with British Muslims' access to representation and the need to contest negative stereotypes (Richardson; Gottschalk and Greenberg) and, following on from these, a critical engagement with the politics of framing and representing Muslims (Morey and Yaqin; G. Nash). Despite a general proliferation of representations,[13] there is an ongoing need to resist uniform, negative imagery in the face of widespread Islamophobia. The application of Hall's framework essentially provides two research questions to approach theatrical representations of British Muslims in the post-9/11 context: first, to what extent do dramatic portrayals reach beyond the stereotypes and antagonisms that characterise this discursive field? Second,

---

[13] For a brief overview of the filmic/literary surge in representations of British Muslims, see R. Ahmed (286).

do they, to resume Hall's terminology, recognise "the extraordinary diversity of subjective positions, social experiences and cultural identities which compose the category [Muslim]" ("New Ethnicities" 443)? A progressive politics of representation would reject the discursive reduction of Islam "to one 'singular affiliation'" (P. Lewis 1), which obscures the multiple position-takings of British Muslims within and beyond religious communities. In short, the second issue pertains to the question whether or not, and to what extent, Muslim identities emerge as multidimensional and intersectional in British drama.

British theatre was, broadly speaking, somewhat slower than literature and film to respond to the steadily increasing interest in Islam after 9/11. The two dramatic responses discussed in this chapter were both first produced in 2009, after intensive efforts on the part of London theatres to instigate participation in the conversation about British Muslim identities: Alia Bano's *Shades* emerged from the Royal Court Theatre's "Unheard Voices" programme, initiated in 2008 with the aim of finding and promoting young Muslim playwrights; Atiha Sen Gupta's play *What Fatima Did...* was commissioned by Hampstead Theatre. Similarly product of a commission, in this case by the National Youth Theatre, was Tanika Gupta's play *White Boy* (2008). Gupta's portrayal of inner-city schoolchildren counters the essentialist reduction of Muslim identities by drawing on a hybrid mix of cultural and religious signifiers. Whereas her play endows its Muslim characters with the competence to navigate heterogeneous cultural scripts, David Edgar's *Testing the Echo* (2008), which offers a cynical look at the citizenship test introduced by New Labour,[14] frames its Muslim immigrant characters in relation to more static characteristics. Here, Islam figures as overdetermining subjectivities by prescribing set rules and rituals that do not easily translate into the British context: one of the central conflicts in the play revolves around an Egyptian woman's refusal to discuss images of sausages in the classroom because "[p]ig is unclean" and it "is *haram* to discuss unclean" (Edgar 75). The representation of Muslim figures on stage by *hijab*- and *niqab*-wearing actors speaking flawed English with a thick accent amounts to little more than caricature. A more optimistic, if overly romanticising, account of cultural translation was offered in *Mush and Me* (2014) by Karla Crome, which depicts the budding love relationship between two young Britons from Jewish and Muslim backgrounds. The two texts chosen for a detailed examination were selected because they place the conjunction of and contradictions between British and Muslim components of cultural identities at the heart of dramatic conflict.

---

14 Passing the "Life in the UK" test was introduced as a requirement "for those seeking citizenship in 2005 and permanent residence in 2007" (van Houdt et al. 417).

Shades of Muslim Cosmopolitanism: Alia Bano's *Shades*

Alia Bano's *Shades* was the most noted play to emerge from the Royal Court's "Unheard Voices" workshop and was almost universally lauded by critics when it premiered in 2009. Regarding the second question stipulated above, Bano seems tremendously successful in offering up an array of British Muslim experiences by acknowledging differential gendered, sexual, and religious positionalities. The romantic-comedy plot of *Shades* revolves around a moderately religious, independent Muslim woman, who shares a flat with her gay Muslim best friend and his white boyfriend, and who falls in love with a devout Muslim in the course of organising a fundraising fashion show for the West Bank. In one way or another, all characters in the play confound stereotypes, most visibly protagonist Sabrina, with her self-determined metropolitan lifestyle, and her best friend Zain, whose secularism, hedonism, and homosexuality stand in glamorous contrast to love interest Reza's traditional Islamic outlook, which, nevertheless, turns out to be more moderate than expected. In response, reviewers have praised the play as a "genuine eye-opener into the different attitudes of British Muslims" (Spencer, "It's Funny" 27).

With a view to the politics of resistance, it can easily be demonstrated that the play's figuration of British Muslim femininities resists prevalent cultural stereotypes. As Peter Gottschalk and Gabriel Greenberg's study of post-9/11 cartoons exemplarily demonstrates, "females [...] are almost always depicted as veiled and oppressed" (54). Against the backdrop of such popular visualisations, Sabrina is introduced as wearing "*a short-sleeved, quite low-cut top*" (Bano 3). That the first scene, set at a Muslim speed-dating event, challenges discursive correlations between gendered Muslim subject positions becomes apparent if one reads it against Sonya Fernandez's description of their presumed interdependence:

> Muslim women's identity is [...] never more than the experience of their oppression [...]. Within this prism, Muslim men are framed as forever denying Muslim women the freedom to explore and exercise their agency (read: sexuality) and, in so doing, are forever posited as the barbaric controlling Other. (275)

The construction of Muslim men as denying women the 'freedom to explore' is, in fact, mocked in the representation of Zain and Sabrina:

SAB. They keep looking me up and down.
ZAIN. You are dressed like the Whore of Babylon.
SAB. (*Looks down at her clothing.*) I'm not!
ZAIN. This is Muslim speed dating.
SAB. You said I should come as I normally dress. (3)

Presumed anxieties surrounding Muslim women's (in)appropriate behaviour are ridiculed in Zain's allusion to conservative perceptions of Sabrina. Instead of policing Sabrina's behaviour and delimiting her agency, Zain actively encourages her to "let loose" and have a "one-night stand" (9). His reproach about her dress is not connected to a discourse of correction but to an effort at helping Sabrina increase her chances at the speed-dating event – a format which is, effectively, designed around notions of choice and consent, rather than submission. Within this framework, Sabrina appears as the modern, worldly, independent woman who is free to choose or refuse partners that she deems (un)suitable. The emphasis on her style of dress both in the costume directions and on the level of stage discourse is important as it positions Sabrina within what Emma Tarlo insightfully describes as "new forms of Islamic cosmopolitanism in which fashion plays an important role" (145). Sabrina's choice of clothes signals a self-relation that draws on Islamic cosmopolitanism and female autonomy.

In addition, with the introduction of the character of Reza, *Shades* endeavours to debunk stereotypes surrounding orthodox Muslims, as it deliberately juxtaposes these with a more complex characterisation. The stereotyping impulse is represented within the dramatic cosmos by Zain, who caricatures "these fundos" as sexually and intellectually backwards: "If they weren't so busy denying their sexual frustration, they'd lose all that aggression and forget about *shariah*" (27). Reza explicitly rejects such popular misconceptions: "Not every brother wants to radicalise the world" (29). In fact, his enthusiasm for the debates ensuing from Islamic talks, which "allow people to interpret things in so many ways" (58), contradicts the notion that (all) Muslims promote one singular way of living according to the Quran, which the references to *shariah* connote. In contrast to fundamentalist interpretations of religious texts, Reza appears to be open to the idea of cultural translation and negotiation. Through this character, a moderate form of Islamism is explored, which is confined to a concern for "appropriate" behaviour (26), teetotalism (26, 31), regular prayers (28), rejection of premarital relationships (51), and endorsement of the *hijab* for Muslim women (68).

This largely positive version of orthodox subject positions is explicitly negotiated against the post-9/11 climate of suspicion. When Sabrina asks Reza whether he has ever thought of shaving his beard off, he replies:

> After the first attacks, having it made me feel like somehow I colluded with them. That people would think I believed what they did. I felt let down because I felt I was being asked to choose between Britishness and being a Muslim, and it's never been separate for me. (*Beat.*) I'm the kind of person – and it's a very British characteristic – I'll always side with the underdog. The underdog at the moment is a Muslim, and in an ironic way, by standing up for Muslims, I think I'm being very British. (30)

Reza's speech resonates with Bhikhu Parekh's thoughts on the different meanings of the term *British Muslim*, which can denote varying degrees of attachment to both Britain and Islam (179).[15] The subjective position adopted by Reza is self-reflexively articulated in relation to the discursive formation of the 'war on terror'. The 'first attacks' are used as the temporal marker of a discourse that provides new grids of classification according to which Reza is categorised as either British or Muslim. Yet Reza resists this subjection as the position he fashions for himself relies on a hybrid cultural identity that combines both Britishness and Islamic belonging. His positioning at the intersection of cultural scripts – epitomised by his translation of the British 'underdog' subject form to Muslim identity – does not sit comfortably with conceptions of Islamic fundamentalism. For instance, following 9/11 and the invasion of Iraq, the Islamist organisation Hizb ut-Tahrir hosted a conference entitled "Are You British or Are You Muslim?" (Akhtar 164), insinuating that such a choice had to be made. Societal pressures on British Muslims to 'come out' as 'good' Muslims and loyal Britons thus conflict with pressures from conservative Muslim groups, resulting in what Peter Morey and Amina Yaqin call "a double bind of performativity: called upon to demonstrate [...] their national identities, while at the same time performing [...] allegiance to the overarching Ummah" (40). Reza appears to creatively navigate a way out of this impasse without fully reneging on his allegiance to either British society or the Muslim *ummah*.

The representation of Muslim characters in the play also refutes the construction of Islam as a 'singular affiliation'. In the comic scheme that Bano opts for, this works via the pairing of seemingly opposing characters: Reza's orthodoxy and Zain's outright rejection of Islamic teachings sit at opposite ends of a religious spectrum; Sabrina's self-determined cosmopolitanism clashes with Nazia's uncritical endorsement of the *hijab* and arranged marriage; Zain's participation in gay subcultures runs counter to the other characters' embrace of heteronormative culture, encompassing Muslim speed-dating events and matchmaking websites such as "shaadi.com" (10).[16] This brief overview already indi-

---

15 Parekh elaborates: "the term 'British Muslims' [...] could mean *Muslims in Britain*, that is those Muslims who just happen to live in Britain or are its citizens but too alienated to have any commitment or attachment to it [...]. Second, the term could mean *Muslims of Britain*, that is those Muslims who see Britain as their home and feel loyalty and attachment to it [...]. Finally, the term could refer [...] to *Britishized Muslims*, that is those Muslims who not only feel loyal to Britain [...] but are shaped by the British way of life and thought, values, attitudes, etc." (179).

16 That the characters' participation in heteronormative dating culture fully integrates them into 'mainstream' society can be explained by drawing on Lauren Berlant and Michael Warner's

cates that the play may, paradoxically, reinstate the dichotomous structures of the discursive regime just as it appears to challenge one-sided portrayals of Muslims. While *Shades* resists the narrow characterisation of Muslims as overdetermined by their faith, it reproduces the dividing practices which appear to objectivise the subject according to binary pairs: fundamentalism versus secularism, self-determination versus oppression, homosexuality versus heterosexuality, etc. Most notably, the production at large can be seen to maintain the good-versus-bad-Muslim binary, as can be discerned in Reza's expressed worry that he 'colluded with them' and in the overall portrayal of eccentric or pious, yet peaceful and assimilated British Muslims against a constitutive outside where fundamentalism and terrorism reside. Implicitly, the play affirms the integration of 'good' Muslims against the foil of the 'bad' minority "who cannot assimilate" (Modood 17).

In addition, I would claim that *Shades* substitutes the discursive overdetermination of Muslims by their religious position with a narrow focus on their location within a heteronormative frame. What appears problematic about the production is that the different Muslim attitudes can presumably only be made palpable to the audience through the familiar narrative formula captured by the blurb of the playscript: "Sabrina, a single-girl-about-town, is seeking Mr Right in a world where traditional and liberal brothers sit side-by-side". In the speed-dating scene, Zain's first line already positions Sabrina within a popular script of heterosexual relationships: "I'm helping you with your Bridget Jones status" (3). While the need to reconcile a liberal lifestyle with the imperative to find a Muslim husband may be a largely unfamiliar challenge to British audiences, Sabrina's predicament can be made comprehensible through the *Bridget Jones* formula. In this manner, heteronormative assumptions about finding 'Mr Right' serve to contain the 'otherness' of Muslims in British society:

ZAIN. What exactly do you want, Sab?
SAB. [...] Just a normal guy.
ZAIN. There's plenty out there.
SAB. I just wish they were Muslim. (9–10)

The Muslim subject position is quantified as a formal requirement in the quest for a suitable marriage partner, an otherwise completely 'normal guy'. The plot thus becomes aligned with its predecessors of the *Bridget Jones* franchise

---

gloss of the "complex cluster of sexual practices [that] gets confused, in heterosexual culture, with the love plot of intimacy and familialism that signifies belonging to society in a deep and normal way" (169).

and their template, *Pride and Prejudice*. The commodification of Islam as a selection criterion in the match-making process is reinforced by the popular jargon that turns the search for a partner into a neoliberal project, as concepts such as "shelf life", "sell-by date", and "marriage rating" (10) recur across the dialogue.

I would argue that the uncritical subscription to the 'boy meets girl' narrative, whose validity and appeal is not once challenged in the play, contains its attempts at working against stereotypes. The protagonist may not be positioned under the thumb of an Islamic patriarch, but her subjection to discourses of procreation and heterosexual partnership is entirely normalised. In other words, the lack of emancipation ascribed to Muslim women in the 'outside' discursive framework, while ostensibly refuted on the level of dramatic discourse and in the visual codes of the performance, is unconsciously reproduced as an endorsed submission to the heterosexual matrix. Here, it should be noted that the inclusion of a gay couple in the play mainly serves to add colour to the cosmopolitan lifestyle of the protagonist, since both gay men not only turn out as generous aides to the love plot but also as bourgeois homosexuals, who themselves subscribe to a romantic notion of state-sanctioned marriage. In this manner, *Shades* replays what Sophie Gilliat-Ray's study of *Muslims in Britain* (2010) points out as "stereotypical concerns with marriage and the family" (206).

Within this frame, Reza's faith is naturalised as an inconvenient, yet not insurmountable, obstacle on London's cosmopolitan marriage market, not unlike the pride and prejudices of Mr Darcy. This can be clearly discerned in an exchange between Sabrina and her flatmate that draws on the conventional script and staple expressions of the popular heterosexual love story:

SAB.   Have you ever liked someone you never imagined liking? [...]
MARK. You like someone. (*Beat.*) Oh my fucking Lord! [...] You fancy him! [...] Son of a preacher man. [...] I knew it, I knew it. Sabrina has a crush, Sabrina has a crush. ZAIN, ZAIN, Sabrina –
SAB   *tries to stop* MARK *from calling out to* ZAIN. [...]
MARK. You can't help who you fancy. [...]
SAB.   He's funny, really respectful – always opening doors and checking if I got home OK [...].
MARK. The problem is?
SAB.   If anything was ever to happen, things would have to change. [...]
MARK. You always have to compromise in relationships. (35–36)

This sequence illustrates to what extent the play's interest in versions of Muslim identities remains limited to an attempt at recounting the *Bridget Jones* tale with a Muslim twist. Islamic difference is contained by the conventionalised narrative of falling in love with a potentially inappropriate partner, typified by the playground chant that taunts someone who 'has a crush' or the reference to Dusty Springfield's 1968 hit "Son of a Preacher Man". Thus, the orthodox Muslim position does not figure as a subjective mode worth exploring for its own sake.

To a certain extent, one could detect a progressive impetus behind the plot structure, if one reads the attempt to build a relationship between Sabrina, a Britishized Muslim, and Reza, a Muslim of Britain, to use Parekh's terms, as metonymically standing for a 'unification' of Britain's different ethnic/religious communities. In this sense, the love story explored in *Shades* could be understood as countering the injunction to choose one's loyalties. The play's positive outlook on multicultural conviviality is most evident in the overt ambiguity encoded in the image of the fashion show:

SAB. I was actually thinking we could do the ultimate in glamour and kitsch. Bring the two worlds together. [...] You know, the plastic flowers mums decorate the living rooms with. Eastern kitsch meets Western ironic cool. [...] So, people can come in a whole range of styles. [...]
REZA. I've made a start on the leaflets and posters. It'd be best for our budget if we went for black and white.
SAB. I'd rather we had colour. Different colours to attract the eye – [...] How about a few shades? Black and white is so severe. (23–24)

The fabrics, styles, and colours of the fashion show become obvious yet apt signifiers of cultural/religious difference insofar as "London [is] a city that, in spite of its multicultural pride and ethos, has surprisingly well-maintained ethnic and religious geographies of dress" (Tarlo 146). But the projected fusion of Eastern and Western styles is itself somewhat indebted to a 'kitsch' notion of liberal multiculturalism in the manner described by Slavoj Žižek, "as an experience of the Other deprived of its Otherness (the idealized Other who dances fascinating dances and has an ecologically sound holistic approach to reality, while practices like wife beating remain out of sight ...)" (11). With its forging of tropological links between 'mix and match' fashion and the fabric of multicultural London, the production works to promote what Helen Gilbert and Jacqueline Lo define as "'thin' cosmopolitanism, which lacks due consideration of either the hierarchies of power subtending cross-cultural engagement or the economic and material conditions that enable it" (9). In the representational economy of 'thin' cosmopolitanism, cities profit from the investments of ethnically diverse subjects, as they add variety to the urban landscape. The figuration of British Muslim subject positions in *Shades* functions within such a culture of fusion, a blend of traditional and 'exotic' lifestyle and consumer choices.

Despite responding to critics' call to work against the notion that Muslims form "homogeneous communities", *Shades* does not make their internal "tensions, histories and conflicts" (Seidler 14) matter beyond the trajectory of heterosexual love relationships. Ultimately, the play does not challenge audiences to see British Muslims otherwise but adapts Muslim subjectivities to narrative conventions that are already in place. The fact that Charles Spencer has hailed the production as "something both special and unexpected – Muslim *Bridget Jones's Diary*" ("It's Funny" 27) confirms that it is not the representation of Muslims that is 'special and unexpected' here, but the insight that Muslim experiences can be comfortably made accessible on 'our' terms, by being moulded according to the "essentialist truisms" that characterise the Bridget Jones "prototype" (Schlensag 145, 148). Bringing to mind Phelan's concern with the conversion of "the Other into the familiar grammar [...] of the Same" (6), the performance makes ethnic and religious minorities fit into the cultural mainstream, rather than modifying narrative frames in order to accommodate their subjectivities.

A crucial elision at the heart of the play's shading of differential Muslim subject positions comes into view here: the absence of class difference. This ties in with the perpetuation of "the myth of [...] a 'classless' society" in the *Bridget Jones* narrative, as uncovered by Stefan Schlensag; in similarly "representing the lifestyle of an urban and privileged class as normative" (146), *Shades* seems to speak primarily for and to middle-class subjects. Just as there is a somewhat uncritical endorsement of the prerogative of "romantic choice", which is often posited against unequal gender relations in Islamic cultures in order to mark the West's monopoly on women's rights (Bhattacharyya 135), the production displays no critical awareness of the classed nature of 'thin' cosmopolitanism. Evidently, 'mix and match'-types of self-formation are only available to subjects occupying a privileged socioeconomic position. With regard to the implied spectator position, the production caters Muslim experiences to the tastes of metropolitan, liberal audiences, whether through intertextual relationships with high-cultural items such as *Pride and Prejudice* or by echoing pop-cultural products that are already in high demand. Besides the *Bridget Jones* franchise, TV shows in the wake of the popular HBO series *Sex and the City* (1998–2004), such as Channel 4's *20 Things to Do Before You're 30* (2003) – in which Stephanie Street, the actor playing Sabrina, also had a part – are relevant intertexts with a similar focus on cosmopolitan women (and sometimes men) who are about to reach their 'sell-by date'.

In consequence, the particular conditions of the Royal Court's commission raise issues about the commercial value that is bound up with (theatrical) representations of British Muslims. In the context of the politics of resistance and Hall's concerns about coming into representation, it also has to be noted that all the actors who played the parts of the Muslim characters in the original production were already known for their appearances in TV series such as *Casualty*

(1986–), *Teachers* (2001–2004), *The Palace* (2008), or *Honest* (2008). In addition, while all these performers have mixed/Asian ethnic backgrounds, none of them is Muslim, which raises further questions about creating employment opportunities for as yet underrepresented actors. Undoubtedly, the play has to be credited for contributing to the scarce "positive, upbeat, or at least neutrally observant representations of the experience of what it is [...] like being a Muslim in the West [...] today" (G. Nash 118). Still, in light of its containment of 'otherness' within Western narrative formulas, the production remains vulnerable to the charge of commodification. As Braidotti cautions, there is, in late capitalism, always the danger of converting ethnic, cultural, or religious difference into the form of "marketable, consumable and tradable 'others'" ("Identity" 167). From this perspective, the cosmopolitan 'shades' of Muslim experience explored in the play reify a version of cultural identity that is "reshaped and reconfigured as ethnic stereotype in the form of the commodity's brand or its identified market niche" (Saha 737) – hence the novelty of 'Muslim *Bridget Jones's Diary*'. To the extent that pluralist differences are subsumed under the romantic-comedy plot, *Shades* evades what Hutnyk refers to as a "more difficult engagement" with multiculturalism, one that situates itself at the "sharp critical edge of postcolonial London" (25).

Unmarking the Veiled Woman: Atiha Sen Gupta's *What Fatima Did...*

Atiha Sen Gupta's *What Fatima Did...* is another mainstage production that engages with the mundane and metropolitan experiences of young British Muslims. The play centres on a multicultural group of teenage students who start fighting over classmate Fatima's decision to start wearing the *hijab*. As with *Shades*, the specific conditions of production – in this case, the circumstances of its commission by Hampstead Theatre – are noteworthy. Sen Gupta recalls how she "came for a meeting with the literary manager and the artistic director at the time, and [...] pitched three ideas, and they chose the *hijab* – I think because it was topical and it was very much of the zeitgeist" (personal communication). Again, it seems that British theatres were primarily interested in participating in a cultural conversation that was already ongoing, rather than inviting playwrights to explore as yet neglected aspects of British Muslim subjectivities. Like films such as *Yasmin* and *Britz*, Sen Gupta's play centres on a pair of British Muslim siblings, and, just as the twins in Richard Bean's farce *England People Very Nice*, which also premiered in 2009, Fatima and Mohammed are born on 11 September. This somewhat artificial (and, of course, ironic) construction highlights the characters' connection to 9/11, which serves as a temporal marker of changed social conditions for British Muslims. Towards the end of the play, Mohammed positions himself firmly within this context and, in so doing, differentiates his experience of Islamophobia explicitly from the racism his mother's generation of Pakistani immigrants had to endure:

> Times have changed! […] They don't even hate Asians anymore, they hate us … specifically us […]. Some days I can barely go out on the street, on the tube, to school […]. [T]he amount of fucking times I've got on the train and people have moved away from me […]. When you see a white person with a backpack on, everyone thinks backpacker. … But when you see an Asian with a backpack on, you're only left with terrorist. […] And you wanna know the worst thing? They give me that pathetic fucking I'm-ever-so-polite English half-smile like this (MOHAMMED *demonstrates this smile*) before they move away from me. (Sen Gupta 88–89)

Analogous to Reza's speech in *Shades*, Mohammed's subject position is explicitly articulated in relation to the 'war on terror'. Whereas Reza is responsive to societal pressures to disidentify with 'bad' Muslims, Mohammed's speech demonstrates that he is always already externally categorised as a terrorist. There are no techniques of self-formation available that would enable him to publicly position himself outside of this script. Instead, the label *terrorist* inevitably accrues to what one could call, pace Deleuze/Guattari, the assemblage of the racialised male body and the accessory of the rucksack on public transport (see de Waal, "'Do Not'" 2–7). Mohammed is subjected to the mechanism that Bharucha describes as the involuntary passing as Muslim/terrorist. Revising the conventional understanding of 'passing' in terms of intentionality, Bharucha declares that "the situation is different when *one is passed, irreversibly, against one's will*" (79). For him, the "logic of predetermined passing" entails that "one […] has no other option but to accept one's 'passed identity' as some kind of alter ego" (79).

Mohammed's cynical distinction between white travellers' passing as backpackers and those who are inevitably passed as terrorists not only highlights the racialised regime of visuality, but it also throws into sharp relief the collective panic surrounding what I would call the 'travelling terrorist'. That the racialised male carrying a rucksack on public transport has become an iconic figure of the new landscape of urban fear is evident, for instance, from the discourse surrounding the shooting of Jean Charles de Menezes, a Brazilian immigrant who was falsely identified (i.e. racially profiled) as a 'suicide bomber' and gunned down at Stockwell station in 2005. In the weeks after the incident, a photo of a service information board, supposedly taken at Notting Hill station, circulated widely on the internet. The depicted "notice to all passengers" reads: "Please do not run on the platforms or concourses. Especially if you are carrying a rucksack, wearing a big coat or look a bit foreign. This notice is for your own safety. Thank you" (qtd. in Pugliese 6). Although Pugliese fails to realise that the photograph was soon identified as a photoshopped spoof, he insightfully explains how it exposes the "governing racial schemas" that organise urban life "in marking the very spaces, sites and locations that a subject may traverse" (22). Mohammed's speech traces this spacing of race and the resulting unequal rights to mobility ('I can barely go out on the street, on the tube, to school'). The polite coding of the service information notice ('a bit foreign') also finds its analogy in Mohammed's outrage about the 'pathetic half-smile' of the white commuters. While Mohammed's mimicry of the 'polite' travellers shows his ability to imitate the white subject, his testimony to a sense of exclusion contrasts the gesture: he will never 'pass' as a 'backpacker', as he cannot shake off the terrorist 'alter ego' that sticks to his racialised appearance.

It would be premature to speak of a topos, let alone stock character, in post-9/11 drama, but the travelling terrorist figure recurs in a number of contemporary British plays. In Vinay Patel's monologue *True Brits*, first performed as part of the Edinburgh Fringe Festival in association with HighTide Festival in 2014, the speaker Rahul, a descendant of Indian immigrants to the UK, addresses a speech to the audience which notably resembles Mohammed's account. In a scene set in September 2005, he describes how "[t]he old lady on this train is looking at me, staring at me, she's been doing it since New Eltham, I can feel her eyes on the sweat of my neck. I turn to catch her out, and she flicks her head back [...] like she's subtle, but she ain't" (Patel 30). These performance segments resonate with Sara Ahmed's discussion of Audre Lorde's recollection of a childhood encounter with a white woman who shied away from her on the New York subway. As Ahmed elucidates, "bodies are disorganised and re-organised as they face others who are already recognised as 'the hated'. [...] How we feel about others is what aligns us with a collective" (*Cultural Politics* 54). In scenarios such as that considered by Ahmed or the ones dramatised in the two plays, it is important to note how "fear does something; it re-establishes distance between bodies whose difference is read off the surface" (63). It is the anxious orientation of the white commuters towards the 'othered' body that materialises the travelling terrorist assemblage.

This is precisely how audiences enter into the argument of the play(s): depending on their own position in the imagined racialised geography, they are enlisted on the home front as fearsome objects or fearful subjects. The mode of spectating that positions audiences towards the racialised bodies on stage, which are placed in a conflicting relationship with the 'outside' scripts of identifying the 'next terrorist', potentially undermines self-evident ways of looking at these bodies, of reading their difference 'off the surface'. If a particular subjectivity in performance is ultimately granted by the spectators' recognition, audiences are asked to resist the norms of intelligibility that make the travelling terrorist assemblage legible. Moreover, these characters' verbally presented testimonies of exclusion powerfully confound the script of the 'good' Muslim's confession. Spectators are not asked to corroborate their disassociation with terrorist subjectivity – throughout *True Brits*, Rahul notoriously evades even the question of whether or not he is a Muslim – but they are, at best, left with the task of reflecting on their own implication in maintaining these pernicious schemes of intelligibility. Ascriptions of guilt or innocence become obsolete for those individuals subjected to the punitive gaze of racial profiling, which does not discriminate between 'Asian with a backpack on' and 'suicide bomber'. This visual regime supersedes the "disciplinary apparatuses [that] hierarchized the 'good' and the 'bad' subjects in relation to one another" (Foucault, *Discipline* 181) by resituating the 'docile' bodies of all travellers in the "racial grafts and divisions" (Back 48) of the terror city.

Prior to this overt reflection on the coercive inscription of the (presumably) Muslim body with the overdetermined subject codes circulating after 9/11 and 7/7, the context of charged race relations is introduced in the very first scene of *What Fatima Did...*, in which black teenager Craig recounts his experience of attending a citizenship ceremony. The framing of his narration is significant, as the first words uttered on stage set the scene for this tense climate:

> And as we're getting on the bus to this place, I look out and I swear down I see this brood of youths. Bout four of them. All boys. Each wearing the England flag as a kind of home-made t-shirt. And they're sort of marching towards us like astronauts in a film or some shit. It was so weird. I thought, how fucking typical, get anywhere further than the Thames and you've got the BNP on your back. (9)

The most obvious thing to note here would be the extent to which the teenager maintains control over his narrative and refuses to insert himself into a victimised position. By ridiculing the BNP supporters as 'astronauts', Craig manages to salvage a sense of belonging in British society, despite the public presence of far-right groups. Recalling Mohammed's impression of having his access to urban infrastructures restricted, Craig traces a movement from the centre to the margins that leads him away from the areas he can safely navigate. His narrative charts what Back describes as the "tactically useful map" that London teenagers have been shown to develop of their neighbourhoods, comprising "a highly textured choreography of safety and danger" and a complex shading of 'racist' and 'multicultural' areas (62).[17] Craig's urban competency and resilience

---

[17] I am drawing on Back's gloss of his ethnographic "Finding a Way Home" research project

are echoed by the comments made by his classmates, who are "*sprawled lazily around*" him on stage (9), and whose benign banter accompanies Craig's speech.[18] The racist climate 'out there' does not intrude on the classroom atmosphere.

Nevertheless, the fact that the narrative of the citizenship ceremony is framed by an appearance of BNP supporters establishes an implicit association between extreme right-wing discourses and the new requirements for acquiring citizenship. The public ceremony where those wishing to become British citizens have to swear "some allegiance crap" (12), as Craig puts it, was introduced by New Labour in 2004. As a legislative move, the ceremony has to be seen both in the context of counter-terrorism measures – notably, it was included in Blair's twelve-point plan issued after the 2005 London bombings (Hewitt 51–52) – and in terms of the shift towards a notion of 'earned' citizenship. Implicitly, the play references the transformation of citizenship into "a process of manifesting that the potential citizen is worthy of the citizenship" (van Houdt et al. 419). In the context of the present study, the citizenship ceremony might well be read as a public performance in which those aspiring to the position of British citizen "declare aloud and intelligibly the truth about [themselves]" (Foucault, "About the Beginning" 201) – provided they have found themselves, and can be recognised by others, as 'worthy of the citizenship'. The public speech act of swearing the oath of allegiance is not unrelated to the mode of enunciation whereby speakers publicly confess to being 'good' Muslims, defending their entitlement to citizenship against the risk of (legal) exclusion. By opening with an account of such a ceremony, Sen Gupta situates her play in a cultural moment of increasing pressure on immigrants, especially those with a Muslim background.

It is against this backdrop that eponymous character Fatima apparently decides to don the *hijab*, the central action around which the play revolves, but which is never enacted on stage, just as Fatima never makes an appearance in the mimetic space. Her decision is first introduced by way of messenger report, and it is significant that the inarticulate character Stacey gets to fulfil this task: "I just saw Fatima guys! [...] She's Muslim. [...] No ... She's really *Muslim*. [...] I don't know how to call it ... [...] She's wearing that thing ... on her head" (18–19). Despite lacking the words to articulate what she has witnessed, and thus comically

---

(1996–1998), which examined the ways in which teenage students in the London boroughs of Deptford and the Isle of Dogs navigated the risk of racial abuse.

18 The playful, tongue-in-cheek tone of the dialogue and the camaraderie between the teenagers from diverse backgrounds recall the representation of multi-ethnic groups of friends in popular E4 teen drama series *Skins* (2007–2013), on whose writing team Sen Gupta had previously collaborated.

failing to report effectively, Stacey does grasp the import of the event. Her repeated attempts to verbalise her observation emphasise this significance, which is further reinforced by the dramatic suspense created at the close of the scene: "*The door opens slowly. The* CLASS *(apart from* MOHAMMED) *catch their first sight of* FATIMA *for six weeks. A collective intake of breath, audible. [...] Lights down*" (20). This ending, in combination with the play's title, substantiates the notion that the offstage act of putting on a *hijab* is a momentous decision.

The play as a whole, thus, centres on negotiating the subject position of the veiled Muslim woman. Evidently, the ascription of an often excessive significance to the piece of cloth with which Muslim women cover themselves has a long imperialist history. As Nachtigall observes, the veil holds a firm place in Western collective memory as a signifier of the patriarchal oppression of Muslim women, and fantasies of unveiling have long pervaded (neo)colonial strategies of domination (267, 381–384). These associations have carried over into current constructions of the *hijab* "as a symbol of [Muslim women's] stereotypical subjugation and also of the backwardness of the entire Muslim community" (Contractor 107). According to Fernandez, the veil has thus mutated "from a symbol of religious identity to a contentious marker of difference" (274). It could be argued that *What Fatima Did...* reinforces prevalent obsessions with the veil by having the dramatic conflict hinge on the act of putting on the *hijab*. Yet it is important to realise to what extent the *hijab*, as "an obvious visual shorthand for and stereotype of 'Muslim'" (Tarlo 155), functions as just that: a *visual* shorthand. Orientalist fantasies revolving around the exotic beauty hidden underneath the veil (Fanon 170), as well as associations with oppression, fundamentalism, and terrorism, are all founded on a visual imaginary. But the referent of the *hijab*-wearing female does not appear as an iconic sign in the production, even though it is all about the *hijab* as signifier. What this dramaturgical manoeuvre enables the performance to do is open up the room for a dialogic renegotiation of the subject position of the veiled woman while evading the risk of reinscribing the fetishisation of this figure or (re)submitting her to an objectifying or voyeuristic gaze.

Therefore, despite being the subject of much of the dramatic dialogue, the veiled woman remains crucially unmarked in the performance, in Phelan's sense. She is not made to appear within a visual regime in which the veil is always already overdetermined. As Phelan writes of the (im)possibility of staging the female body beyond scopic desire, "it can be effective politically and aesthetically to deny representing the female body (imagistically, psychically)" (164). While Fatima's presence in the diegetic space is often made felt, the mimetic space is palpably marked by her absence. The relegation of the character to the invisible offstage space – in spite of her inclusion in the dramatis personae –

resonates with Phelan's emphasis on the "immateriality" of the unmarked, which "shows itself through the negative and through disappearance. [...] I am speaking here of an *active* vanishing, a deliberate and conscious refusal to take the payoff of visibility" (19). This rejection of materiality somewhat falls short of Hughes's idea of critical mimesis. Concerning the figure of the veiled Muslim woman, Hughes finds Phelan's framework unsatisfactory. She proposes that only the staged embodiment of "our supposedly threatening and undecidable neighbours" can serve to counter constructions of veiled women as "frightening, demure and oppressed" (*Performance* 185). I would, however, argue that the play's refusal of visibility does 'pay off' insofar as the production manages to maintain a persistent tension between audiences' expectations of seeing the veiled woman and the continuous unmarking of this figure, its repeated and deliberate disappearance in the diegetic space just before crossing the threshold to visibility. The simultaneous mirroring and refusal of hegemonic values thus shifts from the realm of visuality to affect and desire. Continuously frustrated in their wish to see Fatima, the spectators' gaze is reflected back at them.

Moreover, the relegation of the referent to the diegetic space enables a profound engagement with the signifier. As no image of the woman in *hijab* is ever offered up to the spectators – apart from the cover of the playscript, which further sets expectations that are frustrated in the performance – there is no visual dimension that could contradict one of the views exposed or reinforce another. Chaudhuri's observation that "the figure of pedagogy" informs "the drama of multiculturalism" (216) certainly holds true with regard to the didactic impetus of the play. This becomes very apparent in the prolonged onstage classroom discussion where different perspectives on veiling are explored. These range from Craig's tolerant stance ("Obviously it's slightly different to what I'm used to. But I don't feel anything bad" [61]) to Aisha's rejection of "women covering up for men" (63). Although no definitive reason for Fatima's decision is given, the viewpoint that is most likely sanctioned by the play as a whole – for it receives the most extensive articulation – is also voiced through Aisha:

> It's political. [...] Fatima wants to show the world that she's proud of being a Muslim when it's so unfashionable to be one. The amount of women I have seen since 9/11 who have started wearing the hijab – they think they're starting a fucking revolution. (68)

The hunch that the climate of Islamophobia informed Fatima's choice is implicitly confirmed by Mohammed's subsequent speech, discussed above. Yet the idea that Fatima wants to visibly display her pride in her Muslim identity is somehow undercut by her marked absence, or unmarked presence. Following Rani Kawale's notion of 'coming out' as a South Asian, Ron Geaves has commented on how "British-born Muslims who have chosen to 'come out of the closet' of ethnic community politics [...] have also created a new space for the formation of Islam in Britain after the traumatic events of 9/11" (76). The idea that Muslim women 'come out' by wearing the *hijab*, though central to the play, is not given any visual substantiation. This does not entirely preclude such a reading, though. Ultimately, by leaving Fatima unmarked, the play posits her experience as generic. As there is no single explanation of her decision, it comes to stand more generally for young British Muslims' acts of publicly (re)claiming their religious identity without retrenching the range of motives underlying such a move. As Parveen Akhtar has observed, "what [...] is taken to be a return to religion is in fact a more complicated phenomenon: one that offers individuals [...] an alternative ideology, a sense of belonging, solidarity, and a means of political mobilisation" (165). In this regard, the play eschews reductive representations of British Muslims after 9/11 and one-sided interpretations of their religious and political choices.

Although the strain to create a balance between the different positions makes the dialogue somewhat heavy-handed, what the classroom scene does achieve is affirm the positive qualities of the *hijab* as a "dialogical tool which acts as a catalyst for initiating discussion" (Contractor 92). The play at large thus confirms the veil's significance as "one of the most [...] semiotically saturated contemporary symbols" (Tarlo 158), as a signifier that can be mobilised to forge a range of subjective positions. Yet, in contrast to its circulation in a discursive regime where it is always in danger of being sutured in a logic of difference, as a sign that is "made to stand for a range of problems" (Lentin and Titley 93), the strictly balanced treatment of the subject matter in *What Fatima Did...* unfixes the suggestive potential of the veil as a dialogical tool that can constructively contribute to debates in a multicultural and multi-faith society. Even if the play thus, to a certain extent, manages to inflect the visual regime of the 'war on terror', I would argue that the dramaturgical strategies employed to compensate for Fatima's absence in the mimetic space also obstruct this resistant potential. For the most part of the play, Mohammed functions as an intermediate figure, taking on the function of translating between the two spaces. This is realised in a most obvious manner in the climactic scene where Fatima's ex-boyfriend George appears dressed up as St George ("a proud national English hero") at a costume party (80). Literally standing on the threshold between the two spaces, on the doorstep, Mohammed informs Fatima about what is happening in the scenic space while reporting back about her response. The technical necessity of having Mohammed speak for his sister problematically reinforces the discursive correlations between gendered Muslim subject positions. By ordering Fatima to remain unseen ("Fatima go wait by the door" [83]) and denying her speaking subjectivity, Mohammed performs what is frequently understood as the compensatory "hyper-masculinity" of young British Muslims, which ostensibly seeks to make up "for its failure through the aggressive assertion of its (limited) power over the community's women" (R. Ahmed 287). The sequence alluded to here ultimately turns Fatima into a passive victim, whose brother manages her social interactions for her. Consequently, the liberating potential of the veil is at once facilitated and inhibited by the dramaturgical technique of keeping Fatima offstage.

To hark back to the questions formulated at the outset of this chapter, *What Fatima Did...*, just as *Shades*, resists negative stereotypes and makes the diversity of Muslim experiences accessible. Although the characters in both plays cohere around the shared experience of Islamophobia, Muslim subject positions interact with other gendered, sexual, and ethnic positions instead of forming a singular affiliation. Here, it should be noted that the absence of class difference and the concomitant normalisation of middle-class subjectivities points to a significant omission. With their heavily dialogic scenes set at speed-dating events, Islamic talks, or inside classrooms, both plays emphasise the need to reconcile intra- and inter-community tensions through discussion, debate, and compromise. With their stress on negotiation through dialogue, the plays promote Hall's notion that "cultural identities [...] are not fixed, but poised, *in transition*" ("Question" 310), thereby rejecting essentialist constructions. Against widespread perceptions of the incompatibility of Muslim and British values or identities, both plays promote versions of urban, cosmopolitan multiculturalism in which differences do not necessarily cause divisions, as long as diverging perspectives on cultural/religious symbols, rituals, and rules are consistently negotiated. Like the home-front plays that reconfigure the terrorist-patriot pairings, the plays concerned with the position of British Muslims after 9/11 reject the prevalent fixation on Islamic extremism. While the first set of plays engages with the terrorist subject position without reproducing its normalised conjunction with fundamentalism, the second group expounds varying degrees of Islamic religiosity without subsuming these subjects or their activities under the label of terrorism. Thus, the plays reviewed so far can be seen to critically inflect the combinatory logic and dispersion of positions in the discursive formation of the 'war on terror'.

3.3 Articulations of Citizenship

The ascription of the root causes of terrorism to Islam, or more precisely to the way in which 'bad' Muslims misappropriate the teachings of the Quran, largely precludes an inward gaze into 'our' positions and values. As Elizabeth Poole puts it, "the minority group's beliefs are problematised whilst dominant values remain unquestioned" (101). The extent to which the discursive regime of the 'war on terror' operates with a "civilizationist common sense" (Gilroy, "Multiculture" 433) that renders 'our' values beyond scrutiny is evident from the micro-level discursive actions surrounding various incidents since 9/11. In the aftermath of terror attacks striking the 'homeland', citizens are interpellated into subject positions that cohere around 'shared' values and civic identities, as discourse analyses of both 9/11 and 7/7 have demonstrated (Biesecker; Stephens; Bean et al.). Considering the displays of national pride in the US after 9/11, Žižek speaks of "an exemplary case of ideological interpellation, of fully assuming one's symbolic mandate [...] [by] taking refuge in the innocence of a firm ideological identification" (45). After the London bombings, the UK government was adamant that "defence of our common values" was the appropriate response (Blair, "Full Text"). Yet precisely what is meant by 'our' values is rarely submitted to interrogation. Even such seemingly universal values as freedom are historically, culturally, and (geo)politically specific, as Arun Kundnani emphasises:

> For some, freedom means freedom from the interference of the state, even at the expense of other values, such as fairness. For others, freedom is the absence of restraints imposed by poverty or by empire. [...] How values are expressed, how they are balanced with one another in a specific framework of social norms and how they are organised into a 'story' that gives them shape have always been mediated by a range of political, cultural and class differences. (38)

The 'regularity in dispersion' that is central to Foucault's definition of discursive formations functions such that a correlation, or set distance, is established between the elements of *dictatorship* and the collocation *freedom and democracy*. Situated within this logic of difference, *freedom and democracy* inevitably signifies the preferable option, as Rancière points out: "The difficulty", or the line of enquiry that is rarely realised as an enunciative option, "lies in knowing what this freedom consists in and to whom it falls to prefer it to servitude" (*Chronicles* 107). In making the choice of democracy over dictatorship seem self-evident,[19] the dispersion of elements naturalises the values offered up by Western neoliberal systems, which could be deemed the outcome of an "oxymoronic [...] conflation of freedom, democracy, free market, and free trade" (Alexander 245). The fix-

---

[19] As Blair has put it: "anywhere any time ordinary people are given the chance to choose, the choice is the same. Freedom, not tyranny. Democracy, not dictatorship" ("Speech" 249).

ation of 'our' values in opposition to a constitutive outside marked by extremism works to conceal the equivalential logic operating within the discursive field, which "collapses the liberal ideas of freedom and democracy into capitalist principles of the freedom to make money without state interference and the democratic right of everybody to [...] realize their own life projects inside a capitalist framework" (Featherstone et al. 170).

In this manner, the fixation of elements works to occlude the arbitrary and contingent nature of 'our' values in favour of representing them as self-explanatory, or even as universal, as Blair affirmed in a speech to the US Congress in 2003: "Ours are not Western values. They are the universal values of the human spirit" ("Speech" 249). Such micro-level discursive events as Blair's speeches substantially homogenise 'our' group, as captured by Gilroy's observation that, "if we Britons are to be united and robust in the face of terror, [...] we must become fundamentally and decisively the same" ("Multiculture" 435). The urge to create Western subject positions that cohere around a set of core values is both carried over from the Cold War project and an effect of the fluid enemy image in the 'war on terror'. Philip Hammond, for instance, surmises that it is the lack of a clearly definable enemy that necessitates "an almost incessant discussion of values [...] – although, amid all the values talk, one is hard pressed to find any very coherent or convincing account of what those values might be" (16).

In the context of the domestic 'war on terror' in the UK, 'all the values talk' has crucially affected, and in turn been shaped by, discourses of citizenship and their attendant legislation. British citizenship has effectively been redesigned around the notion of 'shared' values (Berg 42). Five particular trends are discernible in post-9/11 constructions of citizenship: shifts towards securitisation and privatisation and towards conceptions of citizenship as earned, contingent, and cohesive. First, the consolidation of the areas of border control, citizenship acquisition, and immigration with the 2009 Borders, Citizenship and Immigration Act encapsulates the "fact that citizenship [...] is something to be contained, controlled and secured" (van Houdt et al. 420). Second, citizenship has increasingly become equated with "integration into the market", reducing citizens to individualised consumers whose life projects are organised around personal accumulation, rather than civic duties (Haque 27). Third, with New Labour's introduction of new requirements for acquiring citizenship – language courses, passing the "Life in the UK" test, as well as participating in a public citizenship ceremony and taking the oath of allegiance – applicants are increasingly pressed to demonstrate that they have 'earned' the right to become UK citizens. Fourth, citizenship has been reframed as a tenuous status, due to the state's (increasing use of its) powers to strip it from individuals (Tyler 60). Fifth, and this aspect is connected as much to the 2001 riots in Northern England as to 9/11, citizenship has been redesigned as a resource of moral values and community responsibility: New Labour's ideal of "cohesive citizenship" promotes the notion that belonging to a citizenry motivates its members "to participate actively in creating their own solutions to community problems" (Burnett 1).

Theatre's interest in questions of citizenship evidently goes beyond the state or legislative level. The plays take their cue from the discursive strategy, commonly applied after potentially traumatising events, that mobilises citizenship as a collective identity in order to enforce solidarity and unity instead of division and unrest (see Bean et al. 445). They thus relate to citizenship as a crucial interpellative tool in governmental efforts to contain crisis. In post-9/11 drama, the site where all these aspects of citizenship converge, are embodied and enacted is the terror city, which is itself becoming a contested space. As Bülent Diken and Carsten Bagge Laustsen argue: "The contemporary city is no longer founded on the divide between its 'intramural' population and the outside"; rather, "the indistinct zones in-between" extend into and cut across the cityscape (298). Drawing on Agamben, Diken and Laustsen characterise the urban as a "zone of indistinction, in which the figure of the citizen meets the homo sacer in a struggle for survival" (303). The aspect of citizenship implicitly foregrounded here – which is central to post-9/11 drama – is the question of its articulation against disintegrating urban (infra)structures. As inhabitants of the contemporary terror city, citizens desperately hold on to their place in the polis and to a continuation of what Agamben theorises as *bios*, the collective and politically qualified life of citizens, or *eu zēn*, the "good life" (*Homo Sacer* 1–7). "If citizenship in the contemporary metropolis relates to the ways in which citizens imagine and negotiate their identities as city-dwellers", as Marissia Fragkou and Philip Hager fruitfully suggest, then "different dramaturgies of citizenship" can be seen to unfold in performances that engage with the terror city (541). It is on this basis that I approach the dramaturgies of post-9/11 and -7/7 citizenship in Mark Ravenhill's *Shoot/Get Treasure/Repeat* (2007) and Simon Stephens's *Pornography* (2007).

Privatised Citizenship: Mark Ravenhill's *Shoot/Get Treasure/Repeat*

Placing the iconic question, "why do you bomb us?", at its beginning, Mark Ravenhill's *Shoot/Get Treasure/Repeat: An Epic Cycle of Short Plays* departs precisely from the speaking position of an affectively united citizenry in the aftermath of a terrorist attack.[20] The cycle as a whole can be said to centre on the negotiation of Western sensibilities in the face of terror(ism) and war. The sixteen short plays (published alongside one epilogic scene in the playscript) were originally produced by Paines Plough Company as part of the *Ravenhill for Breakfast* reading series at the 2007 Edinburgh Festival and were first staged by a number of companies in various spaces in London in 2008. It is particularly the London run that is noteworthy in the context of urban battlegrounds for the way in which it combined the viewing of the plays with an experience of travelling across the city. For Hughes, the London production enabled audiences to "explore the reverberations of terror via a journey that engage[d] them in encountering the cityscape of London, which in turn gradually [became] inflected with a series of metaphors that evoke[d] a city utterly ruined by war" (*Performance* 120). The title of the cycle, which references the principle of video games, whose "increasingly narrow range of choices" seems to equally apply to citizens of the new global order (Spencer, "Terrorized" 66), here forms associations with the choices made by spectators who embark on their own "treasure hunt" across London, as reviewers have described it (Laera 6). I suggest that the doubling of the theatrical experience of volatile cities with the material experience of the London cityscape encourages spectators to associate the subjectivities negotiated in the play cycle with their own positions as inhabitants of the city and, by extension, citizens of the polity.

Of all the works discussed in this chapter, *Shoot/Get Treasure/Repeat* engages most thoroughly with the sense of a new urban vulnerability. Many of the playlets are set in generic Western (sub)urban environments that are constant targets of terrorist attacks. Although there are overt references to the bombed-out bus in Tavistock Square or a bomber carrying a backpack with explosives (Ravenhill 9, 11–14, 37), which clearly associate the staged incidents with the London bombings, the background and perpetrators of the attacks that strike in both the mimetic and the diegetic space remain largely obscure. This adds to a constant sense of threat, which feeds into "an ever-present, but undefined state of emergency that shapes and implicates [the characters'] behavior" (Spencer, "Terrorized" 65). Even though some of the plays are seemingly set in foreign war zones, these spaces also appear eerily familiar, since all the 'native' characters have English names, mainly speak perfect English, and engage in the same lifestyles and consumer patterns as Westerners. By refuting any strict sep-

---

20 Although Ravenhill informs those approaching the playtext that it is "up to [them] in which sequence [they] read or stage the plays", there is, as he admits, "a certain logic" to their order (Ravenhill [5]), which is why I consider the first playlet as the cycle's opening.

aration between 'here' and 'there', the plays dismantle the imaginative geographies that work in support of the 'war on terror' by designating "a familiar space which is 'ours' and an unfamiliar space beyond 'ours' which is 'theirs'" (Said 54). Ravenhill's "blurred geographies" (qtd. in Laera 6) allocate an equal share of violence, vulnerability, and anxiety to 'our' and 'their' spaces, which cannot be neatly differentiated anyway. Due to this spatial ambiguity, this chapter will discuss the playlets that negotiate citizenship in relation to the 'domestic' discourses of urban anxieties, securitisation, and Western consumer society, while the next chapter offers an analysis of those pieces that could be classified as front-line plays, whose characters or speaking figures are implicitly situated against the context of the Iraq invasion (see 4.3).

The setting evoked by the play cycle at large hovers between the two conceptions of the terror city that circulate in critical geographical analyses of the 'war on terror'. On the one hand, there are plays that reflect the imaginary geography of what Graham discusses as "dehumanized 'terror cities'", that is, dark, exotic 'target' cities that are delineated from the securitised, organised, high-tech environment of 'homeland' cities ("Cities" 256, 264). On the other hand, the urban territories of the Western home front have equally been redesigned as terror cities. According to Mitchell Gray and Elvin Wyly's "Terror City Hypothesis" (2007), this construct "redefines the urban by portraying all cities in terms of their *vulnerability to* terrorism or their *propensity to breed and harbor* terrorists" (331). Inhabitants of the Western terror city are characterised by an altered experience of and relationship to the urban, based on "[p]erceptions of fear, vulnerability, and exposure" (333). These affective scenarios find a material manifestation in – and are, in turn, fuelled by – the militarisation of urban space, the imposition of restrictions on urbanites' civil liberties and freedom of movement, and in the shape of "more divisions, separations, walls, and checkpoints" (339). Cindi Katz elaborates on the process which Peter Marcuse labels "urban citadelization":

> these spatial practices [...] involve the all too familiar forms of bunkering and fortressing of particular patches of real estate as well as the increased gating of communities; urban, suburban, and otherwise. Gating was an increasingly common practice globally prior to 9/11, but in the years since has been broadly expanded, democratized, and given the patina of a neat alibi. (353)

The subjectivity of the citizens that populate Ravenhill's play cycle is constructed in close conjunction with the spatial practices of urban citadelisation and militarisation. Two recurring motifs that epitomise these processes are gated communities (8, 47–48, 58, 111–112) and SUVs (7, 10, 60, 109). Sports utility vehicles are commonly read as recoding the urban as a battle zone; as Eduardo Mendieta notes, the SUV is "always advertised as a vehicle of war, a machine of escape and velocity in and through the urban jungle" (qtd. in Gray and Wyly 339). There is a curious parallel here between the characters' shared aspiration to own an SUV and the notion of "SUV citizenship" (Sparke 156), a term coined by Don Mitchell to describe those neoliberal processes that have turned the citizen into an isolated, individualised consumer, bent on personal accumulation and realising private life projects. Just as the SUV ostensibly provides armour to the civilian navigating the home front of the 'war on terror', the desire for gating is engendered by the experience of terrorism in the plays, as one character's outburst illustrates: "THE TERROR IS EATING US UP [...] WE NEED GATES. WE NEED TO, TO, TO ... DRAW UP THE DRAWBRIDGE AND CLOSE THE GATES AND SECURITY, SECURITY, SECURITY, SECURITY" (48). The compulsive repetition of terms like *security* – a stylistic feature which is employed throughout the cycle – stresses how citizens are continuously interpellated into, and activate their own subjectivation within, a community of anxiety.

Especially the choral scenes are of interest in this respect. The cycle contains five plays that are almost entirely spoken by "*A chorus*" (7, 119, 179) or "*A group of speakers*" (63) or "*A team*" (189).[21] Ravenhill's appropriation of choral aesthetics is noteworthy, for there is, supposedly, an intrinsic bond between spectators and the chorus. With regard to the classical conception of the chorus, Patrice Pavis explains that, "[i]n order for the real spectator to recognize himself in the 'ideal spectator' of the chorus, the values transmitted by the latter must be his own, and total identification must be possible" (55). This close correspondence still applies to contemporary choral formations, as Lehmann explains:

> the chorus (owing to its character as a crowd) is able to function scenically as a mirror and partner of the audience. A chorus is looking at a chorus [...]. It is obvious that it hardly takes any directorial effort to make the audiences associate choruses on stage with masses of people in reality (of classes, the people, the collective). (130)

In line with the thesis ventured above, that the doubling of the journey across London with the theatrical experience of the terror city encourages audiences to relate the dramatised subjectivities to their own position as citizens of the metropolis, spectators might be expected to perceive Ravenhill's choruses as a mass of people representative of themselves. A London audience, in particular, pre-

---

[21] Lehmann's definition would support considering these segments as choral scenes: "Whenever [...] drama mobilizes a multitude of figures for depicting a world, it tends towards the chorus, in so far as the individual voices add up to a general chant, even if there is technically no choral speaking" (129–130).

sumably finds an echo of their experience of 7/7 in the chorus of *Women of Troy*, reinforced by references to "the bus" and "the bombings" (9), the "MAN CARRYING A BACKPACK" (11), and the numerology of the "SEVEN PATIENTS AND STAFF" that die in the attack reported on stage (12).

However, in Ravenhill's adaptation of choral aesthetics, the audience are not placed into an affirmative relationship to the group of speakers, for the chorus strategically fails to fulfil its role as 'mirror and partner of the audience'. This is due to the fact that the choral speakers cohere around such an exaggerated identification with and propagation of the values around which 'we' are supposed to rally in times of crisis that these are rendered conspicuous, contingent, and ridiculous. The Manichean moral absolutes that pervade Bush's and Blair's discursive articulations are qualified by their recoding within a Western narrative in *Women of Troy*:

- We want to ask you this. I want to ask you: why do you bomb us? [...]
- You see. We are the good people. Just look at us. [...]
- Can I talk about me? I'd like to talk about me. Every morning [...] I make smoothies for my family. My good family. [...]
- And me. Every morning I sit down with my good mother, with Marion, and we eat bacon and eggs and pancakes. A good meal. [...]
- Me. Every morning I read the paper. I read about the ... There is suffering in the world. There is injustice. [...] I am moved about that. I care. As any good person would. [...]
- My husband likes to be out early washing the SUV [...], it's a good car. We live in a good place. It's a good community. All of our neighbours are good people. Here, behind the gates, we are good people. [...]
- I only eat good food. Ethical food. Because I believe that the good choices should be made when you're shopping. (7–8)

In a crudely ironic manner, Bush's choice of good versus evil is reframed as a question of making the right consumer decisions. The speakers' efforts to (re)think ethics in terms of consumption could also be seen as a cynical echo of Bush's notorious advice after 9/11 to "go shopping" (Mitchell 6). Similarly, Blair's warning that terrorists "detest [...] our way of life" ("Iraq Debate Speech" 241) resonates with the satirical collective introspection into what precisely is at stake when 'we' deem 'our' way of life threatened. The chorus inadvertently exposes the concerns covered by the "falsely naive question 'Why do they hate us?'", behind which, as Rancière argues, "lies a dismay that is more sincere: 'Why [...] don't things obey that simple reason according to which, when goods multiply, people live better and [...] become more peaceful?'" (*Chronicles* 76). A critical mimesis operates in the choral scenes through a comically amplified incantation of 'our' supposedly universal values: "Our way of life is the right, the good, it's the right life"; "It's the only way of life" (9). The arbitrary fixation of 'our' values and subjectivities in opposition to the irrational violence exerted by those who bomb 'us' is dislodged by means of exposing the equivalential articulation between 'good' and neoliberal values. The consumerist overdetermination of these subject positions denies validity to any claims to goodness that transcend the possession of 'goods'. The chorus of women, hence, falls dramatically short of enabling Pavis's 'total identification' but appears as a corrupted version of the powerful force that the chorus could potentially become (Lehmann 130).

By making explicit how the 'good' values around which citizen subjects are invited to cohere in the face of terror are structured by a neoliberal paradigm, the piece highlights the curtailing of the collective dimensions of citizenship. As Zillah Eisenstein's critique of global capitalism evinces, the privatisation of citizenship ties in with the erosion of public spaces: "As spaces for public life are downsized and emptied of their interactive and deliberative purposes, people [...] seek refuge in private schools, private housing enclaves, private gyms, private playgrounds, and private transportation" (2). Ravenhill's choruses conspicuously recruit speakers from such private enclaves. It is particularly telling that the one place which haunts the characters' geographical imaginary throughout the cycle is the commercial space of the "garden centre" (10, 75, 90–91, 108, 113–117). And even though the speakers appear as a choral collective, they do not manage to speak collectively. This failure becomes apparent in the very first line of *Women of Troy*: 'We want to ask you this. I want to ask you: why do you bomb us?'. The effort to build a unified choral voice fails immediately, as the subject of enunciation recoils into the singular subject of the statement. The speakers recede into their privatised narratives and consumer selves ('Can I talk about me?'; 'And me'; 'Me'). Although this type of "non-conflictuous, additive language" is typical of choral formations in postdramatic theatre (Lehmann 129), the deployment of a singular speaking position jars with Ulrike Haß's explication of the functioning of the modern chorus as an act of collective speaking that combines constituent voices in polyvocal, simultaneous speech, with no personalised voice standing out from this acoustic mass (78–79). The failure to articulate a collective/choral voice testifies to the neoliberalisation of citizenship, whereby

> citizens are being redefined as the customers of the state [...]. Such a notion is likely to encourage consumerist behaviour based on narrow self interest, and thus, may be detrimental to the formation of collective public interest [...] needed for effectuating citizens' power [...]. Fragmented individuals (as customers) without a collective identity are relatively powerless in relation to the state and the market forces. (Haque 24)

This development can be clearly discerned in the speakers' failure to relate to themselves and each other as sharing a collective identity or interest. This is not to suggest that these citizens have nothing 'in common', yet they cannot forge a subjectivity that rests on "a common", in David Harvey's sense of "a shared symbolic space that relates to the livelihood of the collective" (Fragkou and Hager 533). The commonalities of these neoliberal citizens appear to be delimited by the boundaries of an affective community of consumers, which only shares an orientation towards the same 'happy objects', as Sara Ahmed lucidly describes in *The Promise of Happiness* (2010): "such objects are passed around, accumulating positive affective value as social goods" (21). As SUVs, smoothies, and fair-trade products become the 'happy objects' in which Ravenhill's citizen consumers invest, it becomes clear that there is, in fact, no shared orientation towards their incessantly flaunted "core values: freedom and democracy" (125). Ultimately, consumption of the same 'happy objects' does not create durable links between citizens, nor provide the basis for any form of collective empowerment, nor map out 'a common', non-commodified symbolic space. Rather, shared consumer patterns prove to fragmentise citizens, as the retreat of the common into the singular voice suggests.

Rancière provides a productive framework through which to consider the disjunction between the formal propensities of the chorus and the singular positions of citizen consumers. Defining an aesthetic community as a "community of sense", Rancière explores the political potential of staging a conflict between sensory regimes, of creating "dissensus" (*Emancipated Spectator* 57–58). This is precisely what might be seen to be in operation in Ravenhill's choral scenes. To recall Lehmann's description of the chorus's 'character as a crowd', these scenes stage a dissensus between embodiment and voice, a conflict between the sensory impressions of the crowd on stage and the individualised, singular voices. Whereas, for Lehmann, the "chorus formally negates the conception of an individual entirely separated from the collective" (130), Ravenhill's speakers continuously retreat into singularity, both acoustically and ideologically. Consequently, the critically mimetic deployment of the chorus throws into sharp relief the disjunction between discursive articulations of 'cohesive' citizenship as built around 'shared' values and the isolated position of citizen subjects who can only assess their place in the polis as privatised consumers. The dissensus highlights the failure of 'war on terror' discourses to hail citizens into a powerful public collective.

My reading here has points of contact with Hughes's conclusion that "*Shoot/Get Treasure/Repeat* stage[s] critical, direct engagements with the failures of the voice as a political imperative" (*Performance* 121). These failures of the voice become apparent, beyond the collapse of a common voice, as the characters' incantatory repetition of their 'core values' turns these concepts into empty slogans of war propaganda. As Ravenhill asserts, "there's something special about the word *freedom*, and special about the word *democracy*. But if you just keep on saying them over and over again, you sort of cheapen them" (personal communication). Due to the emptiness of 'all the values talk' that citizens are supposed to derive their collective identity from, this mode of positioning ultimately leaves the speakers (and citizens) isolated, passive, powerless. The rallying cry of unity is exposed as disingenuous when, in *War of the Worlds*, one of the choral speakers suggests: "Can we all join hands please? Everyone join hands? The whole city? Queer banker trucker mum junkie immigrant second-generation lonely celebrity wheelchair bohemian?" (123–124). The random list of citizen subjects supposed to 'join hands' in a community of grief jars with the characters' perpetually expressed desire to keep the "scum" out of their gated communities (60), disclosing the exclusionary principle on which the "characteristic affirmation of a British community in unity" is predicated (Stephens 156).

Just as the speakers do not manage to build a shared voice, they do not develop any civic responsibility. Rather, the affective community of consumers recodes any emotion as a private gain ('I am moved about that. I care'), achieved by individual consumption of media narratives ('Every morning I read the paper'). As Julia Boll writes, "[t]here is an aspect of 'buying one's way out' of wider, more far-reaching ethical responsibilities" (97). The notion that even such supposedly shared affects as empathy can be counted as personal accomplishments that warrant instant gratification in the neoliberal system is taken up in various plays throughout the cycle; it is most directly parodied in *War of the Worlds*, where one speaker draws attention to their performance of grief: "Watch me as I do this. Watch me as I do this for you. Please see my grief. See it. Watch. Watch. See. (*Acts out this grief*)" (122). Drawing on Eva Illouz, one could explain this failure of the affective community of citizens to achieve empathy and responsibility by means of the translation of affects (i.e. shared orientation towards 'happy objects') into emotions, which she defines as "cultural meanings and social relationships" (11). The only emotions that Ravenhill's citizen subjects are able to build are thoroughly coded by what Illouz terms *emotional capitalism*; in other words, their emotional life "follows the logic of economic relations and exchange" (60). With respect to the replacement of 'a common' with the 'garden centre', *Shoot/Get Treasure/Repeat* critically reflects the building of neoliberal citizenship on the shared symbolic and economic place of the market.

In the cycle at large, anxiety proves to be another affect that isolates rather than unites citizens, as it provokes the same individuated consumer patterns emphasised by the choral scenes. The cycle variously exposes the process whereby "we seek *substitute* targets on which to unload the surplus existential fear" that is caused by the neoliberal mode of uncertainty which Zygmunt Bauman characterises as 'liquid' modernity (11). In *Fear and Misery*, Harry's constant displacement of fear, from house fire (41) via 'gypsies' (45) to terrorists (48), and the precautionary measures he undertakes in relation to all these threats would be a prime example of Bauman's "vicious circle of fear and fear-inspired actions", which has been displaced "from the area of security (that is, of self-confidence and self-assurance, or their absence) to that of safety (that is, of being sheltered from, or exposed to, threats to one's own person and its extensions)" (13). I find Bauman's distinction between *security* as a genuine feeling of being protected in and insured by the (social) state and the surrogate character of *safety*, related to the tenuous protection from potentially infinite threats, immensely useful for explaining why Ravenhill's characters, despite their obsessive investments in safety, fail to achieve any durable sense of security. The play cycle elucidates how terrorism can be made to function within the neoliberal system of what Bauman terms the "personal safety state", which replaces the "spectre of social degradation [...] by threats of a paedophile on the loose, of a serial killer, an obtrusive beggar, a mugger, stalker, poisoner, terrorist" (15). Just as the threat is conveniently shifted from the 'pervert' to the terrorist in Dennis Kelly's *Osama the Hero*, the privatised citizen's subjectivity in *Fear and Misery* feeds on the constant displacement of anxiety, which culminates in the fearful orientation towards the terrorist threat: "look around you, [...] they are selling heroin at the station, they are in gangs on buses, they have knives, they are fighting on the streets and now and now and now there are bombs" (48).

In conclusion, when terrorism becomes the ultimate object, or the master signifier, in the 'vicious circle of fear and fear-inspired actions', citizens are invited to fixate their anxious energies on the terrorist threat. This effectively forestalls any introspection into the underlying causes of their anxiety: the general sense of insecurity and precariousness in a neoliberal capitalist system. By opening up the route to that introspection, *Shoot/Get Treasure/Repeat* interrupts the "ideological short circuit that occurs in order to screen out neo-liberalism and provide a direct link between anxiety and terror" (Featherstone et al. 172). The play cycle illustrates how discursive constructions of the terrorist threat incite an individuated, privatised form of subjectivation instead of allowing for a political mobilisation or a collective response. In so doing, it offers a potent critical mimesis of the disempowerment of citizenship in the discursive regime of the 'war on terror'.

The City as Autoimmune Network: Simon Stephens's *Pornography*

International ethics scholar Dan Bulley has called for "a response to the London bombings [that] must contain a politicisation and displacement of the boundary between the 'domestic' and 'foreign', the national and the international, [...] the self and the other" (392). This politicisation and displacement is, as I will be arguing, dramatised in Simon Stephens's *Pornography*. The play was commissioned by Deutsches Schauspielhaus in Hamburg and premiered at Schauspielhannover in 2007, it had its UK premiere at the Traverse Theatre during the 2008 Edinburgh Festival, and transferred to the Tricycle Theatre in London in 2009. The reason for its delayed British and even later London premiere has been ascribed to the difficulties of formulating both a social/political and an artistic/theatrical response to 7/7 (Hughes, "Theatre" 159–160). Especially the fact that the London bombers were British citizens, not foreign radicals, rendered established discursive devices unfit to make statements about the bombings. In this context, Mark Featherstone, Elizabeth Poole, and Siobhan Holohan note the inexpediency of the "discursive construction of the terrorist as (foreign) ethnic other" (175). It seems that, by way of solving these difficulties, a discursive strategy was adopted that preserved the differential logic of 'war on terror' discourse by exteriorising the bombers. As Featherstone, Poole, and Holohan establish, this worked through emphasising the 'foreignness' of their ideology, their alleged links to international terror networks and the role of 'outside' influence, and by pathologising the perpetrators as 'deviants' (175–177). The distance between 'us' and 'them' was further reinstated by calls to defend the British way of life against 'foreign' incursion: the "resilient Londoners", in an echo of the Blitz narrative of the Second World War, were hailed as 'True Brits', "evoking unsullied and unified Britishness" (Morey and Yaqin 67). Curiously, media interviews on the day of the attack and subsequent talks with prominent figures of the British Muslim community were declared the responsibility of the foreign, not the home secretary (Bulley 381).

If the official response to 7/7 can thus be characterised by manoeuvres of exteriorisation, Stephens's play enacts a reverse movement: the character that carries analogies to the 7/7 bombers is not represented as foreign, Islamic, or extrinsic to the body politic. Instead, his narrative, which is put squarely at the centre of the monologues and duologues spoken by diverse Londoners, shares many of the same desires and concerns. While London's then mayor Ken Livingstone portrayed the terrorists as "fundamentally incapable of acquiring the values that Londoners represent", as Angharad Stephens summarises (168), *Pornography* structurally and thematically integrates the bomber into the community of Londoners, whom official commentators were at pains to distance from these 'outsiders'. By blurring the "boundary lines between terrorists and 'normal' characters" (Rostek 106), Stephens's piece dismantles the putative distance between 'us' and 'them'; rather than figuring the attack as coming from outside, it is firmly embedded in the social and political system indicted by it. The play can thus be seen as responsive to Bulley's injunction to 'redomesticate' the discourse surrounding the bombings.

Positioned in close proximity to the incident, Stephens's characters fail to achieve the "sense of collective purpose" that post-7/7 commentators were keen to invoke (Bean et al. 435). Just as Ravenhill's choruses do not manage to build a shared voice, these figures develop only individualised speaking positions in response to crisis. Most of the subjects in the play "speak themselves into existence" (Bolton lv) in the form of monologues, held entirely in the present tense. The immediacy of the enunciation works towards constructing a conversational location in the here and now, yet reinforces the impression of provisional, tentative subject formation. If 7/7 was officially mobilised as "a rallying cry for national unity" (Bean et al. 435), no comm/unity can be created among the singular positions constituted in an unfolding "cacophony of voices [...], none of which listen to each other" (Finburgh). Instead, the city-dwellers articulate thetic subject locations from the limited vista of their place in the polis (and the terror city), despite positioning themselves against events that concern the collective of citizens.

Regarding the integration of the bomber's narrative in this framework, the structural arrangement of the play is significant. As Stephens points out in the introduction to his collection *Plays: 2* (2009), each of the seven parts has been "inspired by one of the seven ages of man, that stoical medieval philosophy so forcefully articulated by Jacques in *As You Like It*" (xviii). Notably, the bomber's part has been inspired by the fourth 'age of man', the middle stage of maturity. The bomber is representative of Shakespeare's

> [...] soldier,
> Full of strange oaths and bearded like the pard,
> Jealous in honour, sudden, and quick in quarrel,
> Seeking the bubble 'reputation'
> Even in the cannon's mouth. (124)

It is only in the intertextual relationship between Jacques's speech and the recorded video message of suspected ringleader Mohammad Sidique Khan, part of which is quoted at the beginning of the play, that the figure of the Islamic suicide bomber emerges: in the video message broadcast on Al Jazeera in August 2005, Khan describes himself as a "soldier"; he utters 'strange oaths', promising to "the one true God" to avenge his "Muslim brothers and sisters"; he appears to be 'bearded', as is sometimes considered obligatory for devout Muslims; in a sense, he seeks 'reputation' through his sacrifice for what he considers a "war" (BBC News, "London Bomber").

Beyond these intertextual elements, scene four does not make any reference to an ideological or religious motivation for the attack insinuated here. There are, however, various allusions to the London bombings: there are four "of our number" (41), who travel on the same tube lines from King's Cross as the London bombers did, and the "train pulls out of Liverpool Street and moves towards Aldgate" (41) as the scene cuts off, which is precisely where one of the bombs exploded. Yet the journey to London, which the character narrates for the most part of the scene, does not correspond to the route taken by the bombers, and the trip is initially framed as an ordinary commute. The comments made during the journey contain numerous "echoes and resonances of observations expressed previously by other characters", as Jacqueline Bolton notes (lix). Most significantly, Bolton astutely observes how "the bomber's own psychic territory [is] crisscrossed by needs, wants and desires to be fulfilled through the consumption of Western products" (xlix). The bomber's speech is replete with references to consumer items and 'happy objects', towards which the bomber ostensibly shares an orientation with the affective community of citizens: he wants "the morning *Metro*" with his "horoscopes" (36), "coffee from Upper Crust", an "almond croissant" (38), etc. The repeated references to objects of consumer desire intersect with his diatribes against the commuters he observes. The bomber charts the imprint of commodity culture on the (subjective) territories of citizens, who are characterised as the "[w]eary-eyed and bloated. Breakfasting on McDonald's or Breakfast Bars or Honey and Granola. Lugging their laptops. Clicking their heels. Pulling their shirt cuffs. Pressing their phones" (37). On the one hand, his own subjection to consumerism fails to register with him in a way that undermines his criticism.

On the other hand, the singularity of the unrepeatable journey the character narrates introduces a rupture into the almost mechanical functioning of the neoliberal citizen subject. The anonymity of the mass of commuters stands in stark contrast to the silent trust that connects the bombers: "We don't need to check that each other is here. We trust one another. We're here" (37). The bombers' mute alliance counters the technocratic rhythms of metropolitan existence ('Clicking their heels. Pulling their shirt cuffs. Pressing their phones'). In a body politic where each member is isolated, citizens – albeit contributing to the functioning of the whole, i.e. its orientation towards profit – are unable to develop any sense of collectivity, for there is no shared 'common' social imaginary where they could come together. The dislocation between the constituent parts becomes evident in the bomber's observations about repeatedly not being recognised: the bus driver "doesn't say anything" (36) when the bomber thanks him; the man "sat across the table [...] furrows his brows at an early-morning anagram" (38); the "teenage girls in the counter of Boots didn't even check the signature on [his] card" (40); "the man who holds the gate to the platform open [...] doesn't smile back. He doesn't check [his] ticket. He doesn't even look at [him]" (41). The multiple instances of not being looked or smiled at, not being noticed or spoken to, and, indeed, of not being prevented from carrying out an atrocity become legible as symptoms of a larger sociopolitical failure to create an inclusive sense of citizenship. The bomber's speech traces the contours of "a certain sensory fabric, a certain distribution of the sensible", which, following Rancière, "defines [people's] way of being together" (*Emancipated Spectator* 56). In the distribution of the 'sensory fabric' of the polis that the bomber delineates, he does not have a part; he is not visible, audible, perceptible. My reading here resonates with Alan Read's commentary on the London bombings: "It is the *failure* of their representation in post-(Iraq) war British politics, in Rancière's terms, a *miscount* has serially occurred concerning these four young men that has forced them into the open" (182). Due to the 'miscount' that denies the bombers a "part in the perceptual coordinates of the community" (181), they are driven to carry out an act so momentous that it cannot fail to register as a spectacular 'sensation', forcing the community to sense, perceive, to 'count on' them.

If this insistence on understanding the bombing as an act that 'we' must account for, rather than exteriorise, constitutes the play's critique, its ending somehow works against this impetus. In the final list of the 52 victims of the London bombings (with one left blank), the perpetrators are omitted. In this manner, the play reiterates the (body) miscount that it appears to critique and perpetuates the omission of the bombers' deaths from "the inventory of multiculture" (Back 134). The fragmentary obituaries of which the scene is made up have quite obviously been copied and pasted from the BBC website which listed the "Victims of the Bombings" (see also Bolton xxxvii). The slightly haphazard mode in which these obituary snippets have been stitched together may introduce a self-reflexive and ironic note to the theatrical tribute. Whether or not the ending positions spectators as a community of grief that collectively remembers the 52 victims, thereby resuscitating the us/them mentality ostensibly refuted by the play at large, decisively depends on the staging. In the Tricycle production, for instance, the list was projected after the curtain call as audience members began to walk out.

In contrast, the bomber's narrative is given considerably greater emphasis. The character comes closest to articulating a purpose for the projected attack in one of his diatribes, triggered by watching the industrial landscape:

> Here there are food-makers and the food they make is chemical. It fattens the teenage and soaks up the pre-teen. Nine-year-old children all dazzled up in boob tubes and mini-skirts and spangly eyeliner as fat as little pigs stare out of the windows of family estate cars. In the sunshine of mid-morning in the suburbs of the South Midlands heroin has never tasted so good. Internet sex contact pages have never seemed more alluring. Nine hundred television channels have never seemed more urgent. And everybody needs an iPod. Any nobody can ever get a *Metro* any more.
>
> If I had the power I would take a bomb to all of this. (39)

Contrary to the notion of 'outside' influence, the speaker's hatred is provoked fully within British society, substantiated by observations made during a regional journey, with clear geographical references to the South Midlands. It is his smug 'diagnosis' of the moral debasement and late-capitalist obsession with ownership and surplus production that triggers his rage. Again, however, the speaker's own affective investments in consumer culture undermine his critique. For example, he tells us how he "pick[ed] up a copy of the morning *Metro*" (36) shortly before he denounces commuters' infatuation with media and technology that allow for a forged isolation. These contradictions recall the CCTV footage of the 7/7 bombers, widely circulated after the incident, which supposedly shows them doing a 'test run' on the London transport network, wearing T-shirts and baseball caps with oddly discernible Western brand logos standing out against the otherwise grainy images.

To some extent, then, it is the bomber's hypocrisy which goes to show that the attack is looming inside, not outside of the sociopolitical system. The generic features of the bomber, who – like all but one of the other characters – remains nameless, whose narrative assumes a central position, and who is fully immersed in Western lifestyles, disable any discursive efforts to exteriorise the attack(ers). Yet these generic features are, at the same time, a potentially problematic point, for they render the act of terrorism somewhat indiscriminate. With its adaptation of the 'seven ages of man' framework, the play seems to make suspicious generalisations about the human subject by sketching a universal, timeless, essentialising code according to which 'man' appears to be modelled, regardless of the sociohistorical conditions in which subject formation takes place. Despite these reservations, I take issue with Charles Spencer's criticism of Stephens's construction of the bomber as a "cop-out", as ignoring the fact "that there are disaffected British Muslims among us who want to destroy our way of life and cause whatever carnage they can" ("Lives" 24). In my view, Spencer's uncritical reiteration of the explanatory categories offered up by official discourse is more disconcerting than Stephens's generalisations. Although it is certainly true that some responses to 7/7, particularly on the left, have tended to unduly deny the role played by the "rhetorics of political Islam" (Back 139), I would contend that Stephens offers a politically progressive analysis of the attack precisely by firmly locating it among 'us'. As suggested by the play, the root causes of the attack may not primarily lie with 'disaffected British Muslims', but with disaffected citizens.

As Jonathan Burnett and Dave Whyte have demonstrated, the formative conditions of terrorism, particularly its roots in socioeconomic and political issues, are largely ignored in the influential model of "new terrorism", which considers terrorists as ideologically rather than politically motivated: 'new terrorists' are supposedly acting because of a fundamentalist or extremist mindset, instead of being driven to violent resistance by political, historical, regional, and socioeconomic factors (4–14). The 'new terrorism' framework construes terrorists as "incorrigible" (i.e. "beyond the boundaries of negotiation or reasoning") and thus rejects engagement with the motives underlying their violent acts (5). This refusal is nowhere as evident as in the public dismissal of the "explicit and planned message bequeathed to us by [...] Khan in his justificatory videos", as Hutnyk writes of the apparent impossibility "to hear the call and recognise the [...] sense of responsibility articulated in [the] video message" (5, 57). Against the urge to condemn this message as 'beyond reasoning', Pugliese insists that one has to 'listen to terrorists' in order to make them "the subjects, and not the objects, of their own histories" (34). Admittedly, the 'seven ages of man' framework of *Pornography* might be seen to dehistoricise terrorist atrocities by turning the bomber into the universal 'soldier', yet it clearly turns terrorists into the subjects 'of their own histories'. By providing a subjective and a speaking position to the perpetrator – regardless of whether or not spectators give credence to his narrative or read the figure in analogy to the London bombers – Stephens could be seen to allow for the articulation of at least some of the gaps and silences that emerge between the discursive grids of the 'war on terror'.

The play's effort to re-stitch the bomber (and his narrative) into the fabric of civil society – while concomitantly tracing the loosening of the strings that bind citizens together – ties in with an evocation of the autoimmunity of British society. In his interview on 9/11 with Giovanna Borradori, Jacques Derrida interpreted the attacks in terms of "an autoimmunitary process", which refers to "that strange behavior where a living being, in quasi-suicidal fashion, 'itself' works to destroy its own protection" (qtd. in Borradori 94). Derrida 'diagnoses' as the "first symptom of suicidal autoimmunity" the fact that the 9/11 hijackers obtained the technological know-how, the training, and the weapons in the very nation-state against which they directed the aggression (95).²² Bulley has transferred Derrida's idea that democratic states incubate the seeds of their own destruction to the London bombings. He reads the discursive exteriorisation of 7/7 as "an attempt to make 'Britain' appear less autoimmune (as the attack came from the *other* not the *self*)" (391). I would propose that the resistant potential of *Pornography* could be traced to a critical mimesis of autoimmunity. The play evokes the image of an autoimmune society by embedding the bombing as an 'antibody' attack on the social body's own 'tissue'.

The central image in this regard is the network. The idea of the network as infrastructure, as technology, and as social (auto)immune system informs the play as a whole and functions as the central vehicle for its critique. The contemporary terror city is characterised both by its reliance on high-tech networks and the attendant risk of disruption. As Graham outlines,

> the potential for catastrophic violence against cities and urban life has changed in parallel with the shift of urban life towards ever greater reliance on modern infrastructures. [...] In a 24/7, always-on, and intensively networked society, urbanites [...] become so reliant on infrastructural and computerized systems that they creep ever closer to the point where, as Bill Joy puts it, 'turning off becomes suicide'. ("Demodernizing" 309)

The terror city is an inherently autoimmune system in that it constantly expands the very (infra)structures that make it vulnerable to ('suicidal') attack. Although the network connects citizens in the different parts of the city/polis, its intrinsic flaws hinder attempts at forging connections. The city-dwellers in Stephens's play all rely heavily on public transport: they "get the bus from Holborn" (4), take the tube to work (5, 33), "need to get to Edgware Road" (54), or "take the bus to the entrance of the faculty" (55). Yet these links systematically fail to create human connections. The widow in scene two, for instance, dreads the coexistence with other people on public transport because she has "absolutely no interest in speaking to anybody" (54). Notably, it is only when the transport system breaks down that she develops the desire to 'reach out'. The reason for this is that the existing urban infrastructure is not built and used in such a way as to facilitate contact. The only 'common' environment these citizens share is mediated. The events of the Live 8 concert (which took place at Hyde Park on 2 July 2005) and the announcement of the successful London Olympics bid in Singa-

---

22 To some extent, Hélène Cixous's and Jean Baudrillard's analyses of 9/11 serve as precursors to Derrida's thought. Cixous argued that "the pain that the United States is experiencing was suicidally concocted in America's chemical and political laboratories" (432); Baudrillard similarly expounded that "[i]t was the system itself which created the objective conditions for this brutal retaliation" (9).

pore a day before the bombings are followed by all the characters via the media. No immediate, communal, local experience of these events is accessible. Notably, the only character that reports a sense of shared joy at the Olympics announcement is alone in his car at that moment: "I honked my horn in celebration. Other people did too. It was like having a big party on the road, in our cars. Everybody was grinning at each other" (48). It is only possible for these citizens to express and share in their sense of elation from within the protective borders of their own vehicles, while remaining confined to the "privatized bubble spaces of an atomised 'SUV citizenship'" (Sparke 156).

The affective qualities of the Live 8 concert and the Olympics announcement to connect and unite Londoners are thus rendered questionable. The heavily mediatised and commercialised events enter into the same nexus of production and consumption that ultimately leaves citizens isolated, serving as mere background noise for the everyday routines of consumer society: "in the shops everybody's got the concert on" (3). This substantiates both Mark Fisher's reading of Live 8 as a "hyper-corporate event" that nourishes the "fantasy [...] that western consumerism, far from being intrinsically implicated in systemic global inequalities, could itself solve them" (14–15) and Michael Silk's discussion of "the Olympic Games [as] a correlative to a consumer society that requires [...] the appropriation of spectacle" (735). Just like the infrastructural links of the city, these supposedly shared events do nothing to effectively connect the city-dwellers in a 'common' space: the schoolboy walks out as his sister watches Live 8 on TV (13), and the widow scornfully watches the televised images of the drivers who "toot their horns at one another with idiot inane grins on their faces" (57). The characters' sarcastic reactions to Live 8 and the Olympics bid expose the self-congratulatory sentiments that underlie the notion that poverty can be abolished if we "buy the right products" (M. Fisher 15), as well as the Olympic branding of London "as a city of multiple communities" (Stephens 164). Since the only common signifiers that emerge from the citizens' speeches are consumer products, brand names, and these highly commoditised events, the play, like Ravenhill's cycle, powerfully demonstrates "the collapsing of consumerism into citizenship" (Mohanty 15).

To sum up, the figuration of citizens' subjectivity in *Pornography* takes place within the dislocated, privatised 'bubbles' that are tenuously woven into a disintegrating social tissue. In the territory of the autoimmune urban network, citizens' subjectivation is realised within the defective infrastructures that fail to provide connection or create 'a common'. The imaginary geography operative in the discursive formation of the 'war on terror' – i.e. the "inside/outside spatial imaginary of the domestic and foreign" (Bulley 380) – is disrupted by the play's effort to direct critical scrutiny both inwards and underground. These two movements of the gaze have been refused by official representations and visualisations of the bombings. The ubiquitous images of the wrecked red bus, for instance, functioned as "a specifically London manifestation of the brute force which, in three other locations, remained subterranean and ill-illuminated" (Read 73). The underground-overground dualism of official discourse, according to which, "above-ground, the capital was still basking in the glory of having won the bid [...] [while] underground a horrific narrative was beginning to unfold" (Seidler 46), is dismantled by a critique that implicates the 'subterranean' causes of the terrorist attacks and the 'overground' spectacles of the Olympics and Live 8 in the same neoliberal, autoimmune system.

If citizenship is "a contract between citizen and state" (Burnett 13), then *Pornography* and *Shoot/Get Treasure/Repeat* track citizens' attempts at navigating the demands imposed on them by a 'war on terror' regime that rewrites this contract with a view to private responsibilities, whereas, off stage, their "elected representatives make wise decisions" (Ravenhill 125). The contractual obligations felt by Ravenhill's citizens are restricted to a neoliberal agenda of self-optimisation on their side and an effective performance of managerialism by the state. The official representatives of this state are conspicuously absent. "Sovereignty", in these plays, "works through an act of *abandoning* subjects" (Diken and Laustsen 292); citizens are left to fend for themselves and pursue their own private initiatives. The resulting impression is of a society that has been, in Stephens's words, "massively orphaned" (personal communication). Far from a vision of anarchy, however, the terror city envisaged in these plays is emblematic of Deleuze's notion of the societies of control, in which power takes shape in "obscene, off scene" forms: "physical geography is cancelled by networks, the political is foreclosed in transpolitics, and the real implodes into simulation" (Diken and Laustsen 300). The 'obscene, off scene' type of power is conveyed in both plays: one of Ravenhill's groups of speakers informs audiences that "[t]here are CCTV cameras watching you at the moment" (76) and that the disciplinary apparatus consists of "government-recognised but privately owned centre[s]" (80); the city-dwellers in *Pornography* are bombarded by rolling news and service information updates, yet never is there any pronouncement made by politicians. The political, in these plays, appears to have recoiled not so much into 'transpolitics', but into a neoliberal consensus. The state-citizen contract, in the critique of these plays, has arguably succumbed to the imperatives of the market.

Line of Flight II: David Hare's *Stuff Happens*

David Hare's *Stuff Happens*, which premiered at the National Theatre in London in 2004, contrasts with the two fictional responses to post-9/11 citizenship on precisely this account. The semi-documentary "public evidence play" (Colleran 144)[23] about the run-up to the Iraq war stages a version of politics where "history is shaped in the hands of the powerful" (Soto-Morettini 313). Power, in the framework of the drama, accrues to concrete historical agents – mainly white, male politicians and diplomats – who may not always 'make wise decisions', but who essentially act in good faith and have considerable scope to shape the destiny of the nation. In the top-down model of sovereignty that informs the play, there is no 'obscene, off scene' of power. The thesis I would like to put forward in this analytical interlude is that Hare reinstates a straightforward state-citizen contract, on whose terms there is principal agreement; while this contract may be strained by the mendacity of politicians, it is in no way constrained by the market.

Although, as was indicated in the introduction, these 'line of flight' sections are designed to break up the supposedly neat contours of 'home' and 'front' territories, it becomes at once apparent that Hare's play – despite having a setting that cannot easily be mapped in terms of either category – is the one with the most well-defined geopolitical boundaries. Against Ravenhill's 'blurred geographies' and Stephens's autoimmune network, Hare posits surprisingly stark separations between nationally specific spaces.[24] Admittedly, many of the places evoked in *Stuff Happens* are locally situated but globally relevant sites such as the United Nations Security Council. Also, the play contains numerous scenes where locally articulated statements are simultaneously broadcast globally, as the audience will be aware from recalling familiar media sound bites like Donald Rumsfeld's infamous 'stuff happens' comment. Nevertheless, scenographic elements such as national coats of arms, the information supplied by the narrator figures, or the stage configuration of personae (e. g. Blair's office or Bush's entourage) always clearly demarcate the staged world in national terms. Globalisation, here, has neither eroded the sovereignty of the nation-state nor shifted citizenship towards membership in a global public (see Bhattacharyya 2). The

---

23 As Bottoms has polemically yet not inaccurately argued, "upwards of 80 percent of *Stuff Happens* takes place 'behind closed doors' – that is, on the stage of Hare's mind" (60). The play was, however, "essentially criticized as a verbatim piece", as Brady points out (27).
24 The only exceptions are the interspersed "Viewpoints", where different perspectives are offered by single figures addressing the audience, who are not located in a geographically demarcated space.

explanatory framework offered to make sense of the developments building up to the Iraq invasion – i. e. Bush and Blair led their nations into war on false evidence – seems to miss out on a crucial point, raised in Baudrillard's analysis of 9/11:

> Even in their failure, the terrorists succeeded beyond their wildest hopes: in bungling their attack on the White House [...], they demonstrated unintentionally that that was not the essential target, that political power no longer means much, and real power lies elsewhere. (50)[25]

With one exception, *Stuff Happens* does not raise any critical awareness of the 'real power' that might eclipse the level of conventional politics. There is one remarkable moment in the performance where a group of journalists who are applauding Rumsfeld's report on the Afghanistan mission at a press conference almost seamlessly merge into a crowd of "defence contractors" (Hare 27), who continue to cheer enthusiastically as Rumsfeld carries on in an ever more aggressive tone.[26] In this brief performance segment, one might obtain a glimpse of the intricate interrelations between politics, the media, neoliberal economy, and the military. Problematically, however, this moment is immediately succeeded by a switch to "Europe, [where] the British Foreign Secretary, Jack Straw, is regularly put forward to control the impact of statements from Rumsfeld and the Pentagon" (28), as An Actor explains. The critical moment is thus contained by "expelling the disorder and chaos of the war on terror to the other side of the Atlantic" (Hughes, *Performance* 115). If there is any enquiry into the profit to be made from invading Iraq, this is limited to administration officials' personal ties to the industry; there are, for example, repeated comments on Dick Cheney's links to Halliburton (57, 116–117). Hence, the interest is more in pinpointing personal gain than in exposing the structural economic foundations of a war system that works irrespectively of the individual politicians operating the machine. The possibility that British citizens – or Western consumers more generally – might be implicated in the forceful 'integration' of Iraq into a globalised free market is nowhere considered.

With its line of critique directed entirely at "the irresponsible, self-serving, and irrational qualities of current political leaders" (Kritzer 82), the play might somehow miss its target. If political leaders are shown to have failed their elec-

---

[25] Other sources claim that the plane which crashed in a field in Pennsylvania had aimed for the US Capitol, rather than the White House – Baudrillard's argument holds in both cases.
[26] All observations are based on the recording of Nicholas Hytner's original production held by the National Theatre Archive (undated recording; viewed on 2 December 2014).

torate by acting on flawed proof concerning the necessity of invading Iraq, this argument leaves both the basic configuration of the democratic system of representation and the state-citizen contract intact and exempts the citizenry from accountability. In showing how politicians fall short of the expectations of responsible leadership, the play nevertheless instates these qualities in the form of an obverse ideal. This contrasts with the way in which the 'off scene' location of conventional politics explored in *Shoot/Get Treasure/Repeat* and *Pornography* appears to reveal what Žižek phrases emphatically in one of his trademark rhetorical questions: "are not 'international terrorist organizations' the obscene double of the big multinational corporations – the ultimate rhizomatic machine, omnipresent, albeit with no clear territorial base?" (38). In *Stuff Happens*, the Iraq invasion is not brought about by a remorselessly grinding, 'rhizomatic' war machine, but by a linear succession of decisions, diplomatic negotiations, and public speech acts made by individually accountable, spatiotemporally situated agents. This ties in with the conventions of tragedy, which the play observes to a certain degree. If "[t]ragedy examines an individual at a particular moment of crisis making a terrible decision", as Elizabeth Kuti states (469), then *Stuff Happens* casts Colin Powell and/or Tony Blair as tragic hero.[27]

Concerning the emphasis placed on agentic individuals, the question of the play's adherence to tragic conventions ties in with its status as a history play. Donna Soto-Morettini insightfully reads *Stuff Happens* as indebted to "Formist" conceptions, which foreground the uniqueness of historical agents, rather than the context of their actions (315). Glossing the play as "a series of meetings, involving [...] very powerful men having discussions", Soto-Morettini remarks that "the field against which these discussions take place is never the focus of attention" (315). These observations chime with the tragic turning point that one could identify in the play, the moment where Powell finally gives in to Bush's insistence on war, "I don't disagree" (91) – an exemplary case of an individual 'making a terrible decision'. Tragedy, importantly, "also shows how close [the hero] came to making the opposite decision" (Kuti 469). Even if *Stuff Happens* engages in a "lampooning of administration officials" (Westgate 409), it conveys the clear sense that history would have taken an alternative course if the players had decided differently or if only more responsible and honest politicians would have been in charge. Although it is doubtlessly highly critical of the Bush administration and – albeit to a lesser extent – of the Blair government, Hare's play is not

---

27 Kuti reads Powell as engaging in a tragic "hero-quest" (467), and Colleran charts the "arc of Powell's downfall" as "tragic or romantic hero" (152), whereas Hughes sees Blair as most eligible for the position of "fatally flawed tragic hero" (*Performance* 115).

critically mimetic of the larger configuration of power relations. In this regard, Lehmann's pessimistic verdict about the critical potential of the "representational form 'drama'" appears to hold true, for "the real issues are only decided in power blocs, not by protagonists who in reality are interchangeable" (182).

With its "series of conventionally realistic scenes depicting reimagined meetings" (Bottoms 60), the staging replicates the visual economies of the 'war on terror'. As is evident from the abundant printouts of photographs depicting the senior politicians featured in the play at the Security Council or at press conferences, which were collected by Hytner's team and stored in the National Theatre archive of production materials, the performance aimed at a faithful imitation of the iconography of the 'war on terror'. As critical mimesis gives way to mimetic copy, the play "reassure[s] audiences that there is a mirror of their own sense of ethical probity in global space" (Hughes, "Theatre" 153). Again, the fact that the politicians represented in the play fall short of fulfilling their mandate of 'ethical probity' does nothing to question the validity of the state-citizen contract. The corrupted representatives merely need to be expelled and replaced: at the end of the play, the protagonists "momentarily take centre stage, confess their mistakes, and then vanish", leaving audiences "rather complacent, even satisfied with themselves" (Westgate 410). The stability of a democratic order is thus reinstated by the dramaturgical frame. If these protagonists are shown to have violated the terms of the state-citizen contract, the spectator-citizens are implicitly positioned as its guardians ("the guardians of an ideal, the guardians of a conscience", as the French prime minister puts it in the play [107]); they are the ones who call politicians to account by attending the performance. Even the play that most explicitly suggested it would do just that, *Called to Account* (edited) by Richard Norton-Taylor, which premiered at the Tricycle Theatre in 2007, ended its over two-hour long, naturalistic hearing of evidence for indicting Blair for the crime of aggression against Iraq on a more sinister note: as is typical of the Tricycle's tribunal plays, there was no curtain call, but a photograph of the grinning prime minister came up on the screens, calling the earnest theatrical endeavour retrospectively into question.[28]

The reading offered here challenges Colleran's argument that *Stuff Happens* constructs a "complex spectatorial position" (140). Rather, the implied position seems to be one from which spectators affirm the play's "underlying truth" (Weidle 70), namely, that the pro-invasion argument is untenable. Chris Westgate provides an excellent analysis of the way in which the 2007 Seattle production of

---

[28] I am drawing on a recording of the matinee performance of *Called to Account* at the Tricycle Theatre on 9 June 2007 (National Video Archive of Performance).

Stuff Happens eschewed controversy just as it overtly promoted it, since it did "nothing to challenge how liberal audiences know the Iraq War" and encouraged them "to defer accountability" (409–410). I would hold that Westgate's argument is more applicable to the original London production than he assumes. While he suggests that the political climate at the time of the Seattle production had markedly evolved from the London debut (411), the same tendencies to induce complacency in audiences can be detected in the original production. Indicative of this is a segment in the performance where Blair tells the head of MI6, "If these weapons inspectors go back in, and – God forbid – any of these weapons are found not to exist, then my life as Prime Minister will become very difficult" (63). In the recorded performance that I viewed, this statement was greeted with derisive laughter from the audience. With Hare's consistent use of the type of dramatic irony that comes with dramatising 'true stories', audiences are continuously positioned towards the staged representation with the benefit of hindsight.

Accordingly, rather than seeing the play's function as "helping people analyse the debate over weapons of mass destruction", as Reinelt optimistically suggests ("Selective Affinities" 312), I would hold that its discourse mainly taps into what they already know. In the straightforward state-citizen relationship proposed here, it is enough for these politicians to take the blame and disappear from the stage. There is not the slightest (pre)figuration of the more complex and ambivalent relationship that led to Blair being re-elected in 2005, despite widespread public dissatisfaction with the Iraq invasion. In my view, the reason why *Stuff Happens* does not reconfigure the symbolic social order, or the distribution of the sensible, is that it locates conflict on the level of (lacking) consensus concerning the Iraq invasion. This line of critique does not go to the "core of the consensual times" chronicled by Rancière (*Chronicles* viii) – or by Ravenhill and Stephens, for that matter. Whereas the fragmented, privatised, singular citizen voices in the fictional plays dismantle the ideal of a united citizenry invoked after 9/11 and 7/7 by highlighting the processes whereby a neoliberal consensus has always already eroded the 'common', Hare's dramatic universe sustains the notion that politicians are accountable to and act on behalf of a community of concerned citizens. Thus, the piece can be shown to invest in the "continued hegemonic belief that if only We, 'the people', could elect", as Nandita Sharma writes more generally, "the 'proper representatives', we would finally realize liberty" – a view that "has led to the denial of the deep ties between [...] capital, state and national identity" (138). Underneath the veneer of the obvious disagreement around which dramatic conflict revolves in *Stuff Happens* thus lies a much more tacit agreement, the uncovering of which might do more to explain the failure of the protests against the Iraq war and the re-election of the Blair government than a topical engagement with post-9/11 diplomacy.

3.4 (Un)Grieving Femininities

Just as Ravenhill's blurred geographies and Stephens's autoimmune network refute neat separations between 'home' and 'front', these boundaries are traversed by "exchanged narratives of grief" and the formation of "communities of bereaved", as Carol Acton's study *Grief in Wartime* (2007) has demonstrated (13). British wartime subjects both at home and on the front participate in the formation of these communities by exchanging information on soldiers' deaths and offering each other condolences and strategies for coping with the loss. Yet the iconic representation of grief that has probably been most central to the visual economies of the British 'war on terror' originates from a ritual invented 'at home': the Wootton Bassett repatriations.[29] The small Wiltshire town served as the locus of collective mourning rituals, as the hearses carrying dead soldiers passed through its high street on their way from RAF Lyneham to hospital in Oxford between 2007 and 2011, and it gained widespread public attention for the increasingly huge turnout of mourners that gathered at the roadside paying tribute as the corteges passed.[30] Wootton Bassett may well be considered one of the primary sites of the British home front, as is illustrated by Gillian Youngs's consideration of the tributes as expanding "the significance of notions of the home front" (931). Notably, the collective performance of mourning and its widespread visual documentation in the national media is specific to the British 'war on terror' context because, in the US, coffins were paraded through the deceased soldiers' hometowns (Drake 127), and visual representations of flag-draped coffins could not be shown in the US media until a ban on them was lifted in December 2009 (Taylor 1892).

As a brief survey of photographs and news reports circulating in relation to the commemoration ritual indicates, the cultural performance of mourning at Wootton Bassett has predominantly been framed in terms of what Puar and Rai aptly call "heterosexual family narratives of trauma and grief" (125).

---

[29] Michael Drake discusses the Wootton Bassett commemorations as an invented tradition (127).
[30] In 2011 repatriations switched back to RAF Brize Norton, and the commemoration ceremony was taken over to the Oxfordshire town of Carterton. Yet the ritual performed there never attained the same status in the national imaginary, which is why Wootton Bassett is my key referent here.

Media coverage has persistently constructed a grieving feminine subject in relation to the (predominantly) male dead bodies contained by the coffins. This reinforces the stereotype of the tearful, bereaved female, as can be gleaned from tabloid descriptions of a "weeping daughter [...] [who] was comforted by friends and family as her father's repatriated body was paraded" or references to a widow who "watched tearfully as shots were fired over the coffin, kissing her husband's wedding ring several times" (Taylor and O'Shea 4–5). Here, grieving femininity is proffered as the subject position through which to focalise the ritual of mourning. It seems that the 'Blitz spirit' ideals of resilience and stoicism associated with British unity after 7/7 were salvaged in the staunch postures of male veterans. This points to the mutual constitution of gendered war identities: the valour of the dead soldier induces the female tears that, in turn, reinforce – eroticise, even – heroic masculinity (Schott 25). It is this correlation of female grief and martial masculinity that representations of Wotton Bassett exemplify so well, which is why I consider the tributes an ideal site against which to trace the mapping of femininities in home-front drama.

In respect of this dualism, the commemoration ritual can be seen as participating in what Graham Dawson, in *Soldier Heroes* (1994), describes as a

> nationalist discourse, [in which] martial masculinity [is] complemented by a vision of domestic femininity [...]. The 'feminine' narrative stance concentrate[s] on the tearful goodbyes of girlfriends, wives and mothers; on their hopes, anxieties and grief; on their sense of the terrible vulnerability of those they waited for, and pride in their suffering of loss. (2)

A cultural imagination that assigns the role of mourning primarily to women reaches back to the 19th-century interpretation of grief as "a properly feminine condition" (Walter 178). The association of mourning with femininity applies particularly to wartime constructions of gender, as feminist scholarship since the 1980s has consistently pointed out. This is encapsulated by Jean Bethke Elshtain's well-known description of women as "designated weepers over war's inevitable tragedies" (4).[31] Although the construction of grieving femininity is hence by no means a post-9/11 phenomenon, it gains particular salience through its intimate links with questions of legitimacy, national identity, and subjectivity.

First, although rituals of mourning are common to every war, they are differently performed and interpreted depending on public attitudes to the conflict in question. Expressions and representations of grief sit in a spectrum that, broad-

---

[31] Elshtain's formula is corroborated by Acton, who claims that, in the context of the war in Iraq, "binaries wherein women portray themselves and are portrayed as the primary mourners" have persisted (177).

ly, reaches from affirmation to subversion of the 'war story'.[32] Because the dead bodies of soldiers are empty signs that become imbued with meaning only through the ritual of memorialisation (Drake 126–127), mourning can work to either support or destabilise official strategies. One would expect that the latter is more likely to be the case with contentious wars. Indeed, as research on the Vietnam war has shown, the divisive political climate effectively led to a silencing of grief, which suggests that the legitimacy of mourning is bound up with public support for the military campaign (Walter 45–46). There is, however, an interesting disjunction between the perceived (il)legality of the Iraq and Afghan wars and the public displays of mourning, whose intensity harked back to cultural responses to the First World War (Acton 6). The fact that viable subject positions could be constructed around grief and mourning in a rather unproblematic fashion, whereas the legitimacy of the war(s) at large has remained questionable, points to a discursive dispersion of contradictory elements that is worth deeper examination.

Second, the collective performance of mourning at Wootton Bassett, though resuscitating traditional wartime constructions of gender, can be read as a manifestation of contemporary versions of national identity. The public ritual is an exemplary act whereby the nation collectively imagines itself. This is evident from newspaper reports that deem the ceremony "a very British way of mourning" and mark Wootton Bassett as a "town [that] came to represent us all" (Jardine and Savill 15). In this regard, Drake notes a striking persistence of the national imaginary at the site of Wootton Bassett (126). For Benedict Anderson, the soldierly sacrifice is key to imagining the nation "as a *community*, because [...] the nation is always conceived as a deep, horizontal comradeship. Ultimately it is this fraternity that makes it possible [...] not so much to kill, as willingly to die for such limited imaginings" (7). The death of a soldier, inscribed as "the ultimate sacrifice" into the national military-civilian contract known as the military covenant (Forster 1044), necessitates both personal and national strategies of mourning. Wootton Bassett is a place where private and public modes of grief collide: not only are the grieving relatives joined by a collective of mourners at the roadside, but their personal reactions also stand in for the response of the wider public that consumes these images via the national media. The mourners at Wootton Bassett and the media audience form "a nationwide bereaved community", which, according to Edward Linenthal, "is one of

---

[32] Krista Hunt and Kim Rygiel define the *war story*, based on Miriam Cooke's work, as "the official, state authorized story about why we go to war and how wars are won" (4).

the only ways Americans [and Britons, one might add] can imagine themselves as one" (111).

Third, with its potential for either undermining or supporting the war agenda, the subject position of (un)grieving femininity becomes an apt lens through which to consider the resistant potential of subject formation. Even though the "grieving wartime subject" (Acton 6) is a construct that recurs in virtually every conflict, this subject form is shaped by the historically malleable cultural narratives forming around each war. This is reflected by the varied approaches to grieving (or griefless) females in contemporary British home-front drama. A recurring subject position in post-9/11 plays is that of the returning male soldier's girlfriend or wife; the contradictions between the perceived illegality of the war(s) and the injunctions stipulated by the cultural script of domestic femininity are often at the heart of dramatic conflict. The traditional gender constellation of fighting men and weeping women is disrupted in two plays by Simon Stephens, *Motortown* (2006) and *Canopy of Stars* (2009). Both refract the compensatory masculinity behind the prisoner abuse in Iraq and the soldiers' sense of impotence in the Afghan campaign, respectively, through disintegrating relationships with their cynical, emotionally detached female (ex-)partners. Cat Jones's *Glory Dazed* (2012) is another play that deliberately juxtaposes the heteronormative ideals evinced by conventional images of "passin' out parades" or narratives about Falklands veterans who "got old dears' kisses and young girls' knickers" with the appearance of a disillusioned and disappointed wife, who refuses to be stylised as the domestic 'angel' that helped the soldier 'get through' the Afghan war (Jones 35, 37–38).

This chapter looks in detail at two plays whose production history coincides with the beginnings of the Wootton Bassett repatriations, based on the assumption that the larger cultural discourse on grief and mourning surrounding the ritual informs, and may in turn be informed by, theatrical negotiations of grieving femininity. Steve Gilroy's *Motherland* (2007) and Roy Williams's *Days of Significance* (2007) both locate female grief, or the absence thereof, at the centre of their interest. In light of the theorisation above, my analysis of these productions will seek to excavate the resistant or conservative potential of the subject position of grieving/griefless femininity with regard to the wider discursive formation of the 'war on terror'. One initial thing to note in this chapter is that the dramatic mapping of this subject position 'takes place' in locations that are at a remove from the dense housing estates of the first subchapter, the cosmopolitan metropolis of the second, or the infrastructures of the terror city illuminated in the third section. The more marginal places conceptualised in the plays discussed here aptly reflect the sense of dislocation felt by the returning soldier protagonists and echo the locale of the Wootton Bassett repatriations more than an urban setting might do.

Domestic Versions of Female Grief: Steve Gilroy's *Motherland*

Steve Gilroy's *Motherland*, directed by the writer himself, premiered at Live Theatre in Newcastle upon Tyne in 2007, was invited to the 2008 Edinburgh Festival, and toured the UK in 2009. Beyond what is already a fairly substantial production history for a new play, *Motherland* has continued to receive stagings up to the time of writing – most recently, for instance, at the Assembly Rooms Theatre in Durham in 2014. Extracts from the piece further circulate outside the frame of the playtext, as its monologues are popular with drama school auditions and competitions; in this way, the text or parts of it are constantly extended to new audiences.[33] In addition to its premiere following just months after the first Wootton Bassett tributes, the 2009 UK tour of the play is notable for its coincidence with abundant news items on British soldiers' deaths in Afghanistan, as "2009 was the bloodiest year for British forces" (Edwards 87). The thematic concerns of the play thus enter into a close relationship with its performance history, and performances have variously participated in the wider discourse on troop deaths. For example, one reviewer noted the "particular resonance" of the play's 2008 Edinburgh run, as the verbatim testimony of a mother who lost her daughter in the Iraq war reflected contemporary reports on the death of the first British servicewoman to be killed in Afghanistan (Laing). Viewed against the media representation of troop deaths, the play appears to give a voice to those subjects who also take centre stage at the Wootton Bassett repatriations: Gilroy interviewed "over twenty women from the North East of England", including "mothers, stepmothers, sisters, wives and girlfriends of service men and women who had served or were currently serving in Iraq and Afghanistan" (Gilroy [3]).

Motherland is part of the verbatim tradition that gained enormous popularity in the UK after 9/11. The fact that it engages with original primary sources is central to the way the play has been advertised. This is evident from the blurb's announcement of a "powerful and moving drama that shares the true stories of women whose everyday lives have been touched by the recent conflicts". The use of original sources is further highlighted by the staging. At all points in

---

[33] Two monologues from *Motherland* are contained in the second volume of the *Oberon Book of Modern Monologues for Women* (2013), edited by Catherine Weate.

the performance, it is made palpably clear that the four actors re-present the voices of 'real' subjects who exist outside the theatrical frame. This functions, for instance, through projections of the names of the interviewees onto a screen as the actors start their speeches and through precise imitation of their speech patterns, including hesitations, interruptions, and repetitions. The faithful reproduction of "local idiom, tics of speech and linguistic markers" is a typical feature of verbatim theatre (Luckhurst, "Verbatim Theatre" 203). In highlighting its documentary status, the play makes a claim to presenting the 'authentic' voices and experiences of the women it portrays.

Verbatim theatre's strategies of authentication have increasingly garnered criticism. In his much discussed article "Putting the Document into Documentary" (2006), Bottoms criticises the British variety of documentary theatre for its truth claim (57–58). *Motherland* is, in part, premised on the illusionism that he takes issue with: "it is as if, in the theatre, we can be given unmediated access to the words of the originary speaker" (59). The production purports to provide this kind of access by reproducing the communicative situation of the interview in the theatrical frame, with most speakers addressing the audience as interviewers. A mimetic style of acting is designed to further reinforce the impression of an absence of mediation, as is evident from reviewers' comments on the "tremendous skill on the actresses' part. With little outward show [...] they have to portray a wide range of characters [...], relying purely on voice and body language" (Lathan). Yet a distance between actor and role may emerge precisely where the technique of impersonation fails, as one review inadvertently reveals: "The four actresses [...] struggle when playing outside of their age range – twenty-odds offering testimonials from mothers of twenty-odds is a serious challenge and one that *Motherland* doesn't quite pull off" (Hickson). Despite its aspirations to faithfully re-present the 'original' word, then, the fact that the 'real' subjects remain at a remove can be glimpsed in the gaps emerging from the failure of mimesis.

The play partly answers Bottoms's call for theatrical self-reflexivity insofar as it includes various segments that implicitly point to Gilroy's role in editing and arranging the playtext. There is also an emphasis on the technical modalities of the interviews in performance, as a dictaphone is used to replay parts of the original testimonies, for example. These strategies expose the play's processes of representation. Nevertheless, I would argue that its elements of self-referentiality, paradoxically, also serve to enhance its claim to authenticity. Reviewers' impressions of the play appear to confirm this, as they have described the interviews as "faithfully transcribed" and the "real speech" as "reproduced [...] in such an accurate fashion" (Chadderton). The production is, on the whole, highly likely to be received as a truthful portrayal of the interviewed women.

Its claim to veracity seems to bring the production into even closer proximity to media representations of grief and mourning. Colleran claims that "documentary art reframes, recontextualizes, and thereby reopens the already seen and heard media event for a second look, a different interpretation" (139). The question whether or not the play offers a 'second look' at grieving femininity warrants closer scrutiny. To that end, I will read the play against what Acton identifies as prevalent discursive attempts at "[p]rescribing and controlling grief through consolatory rhetoric that emphasises the meaning of the death in the service of the state", which assist in "the overall 'manufacture of consent' through which the state persuades its citizens to participate in war" (3).

To a certain extent, the speakers in *Motherland* employ the discursive strategies of a 'consolatory rhetoric', in particular by mobilising the script of the eulogy. Conventionally, obituaries shed an entirely positive light on deceased soldiers; among their "easily recognizable and celebratory tropes" (Saal 358) are an emphasis on the soldiers' heroic qualities, their contribution to a successful mission, and the fact that they died doing a job they loved.[34] John Kelly has criticised the British media for acting as the "primary messenger of the nation" in the event of a soldier's death, publishing "tributes to bravery, selflessness, courage and heroism [...] in order to assuage the nation's grief" (733). Indeed, most of the speaking figures in *Motherland* declare their pride in 'their' soldier (37, 48, 68) and emphasise how much that person loved (working in) the army and/or never considered another profession (20, 25, 41, 61). Yet the play goes beyond what is 'sayable' in the official script of the soldier's obituary insofar as it provides these women with a speaking position that draws on discourses of both mourning and protest. From within this position, it becomes possible to grieve for the loss and, at the same time, question the legitimacy of the campaign – which is a combination of discursive elements that is never encountered, for instance, in the eulogies reprinted in newspapers after a soldier's death.

The narrative development of Pat's subjective position as a grieving mother illustrates this. Pat begins her speech by commemorating her son's blissful childhood, including his eternal fascination with soldiers and cannons (66–67, 71), declares her pride in him (68), attests to the intensity of her grief ("not just he died that day. Part of me died" [69]), goes on to challenge the army's official account of and response to her son's death (69–70), and ends with voicing resistance to the Iraq war: "I don't think it should have been started anyway" (72). The anger expressed by Pat is echoed in the testimonies of several other women, who

---

[34] Concerning the latter aspect, Acton explains that "families less ambiguously console themselves with the idea that their son, brother or husband died in his chosen occupation" (93).

denounce the lack of a justifiable rationale for the Iraq/Afghan war (21, 72), the notion of humanitarian interventionism (32–33, 73), systematic failures of the military relating both to equipment shortages (34, 74) and their policies of information disclosure in the case of troop deaths (59, 62–63, 72). These anti-war arguments, as such, by no means transgress the boundaries of the 'sayable', as they are well-rehearsed by activists and protesters. Equally, the mobilisation of grieving femininity in modes of resistance is not unusual if one considers Acton's point that, in the context of the Iraq war, "images of [...] the grieving mother have [...] come to dominate the anti-war movements in both Britain and the United States" (176). Nevertheless, I would argue that it is the combination of the scripts of protest and the obituary within one dramaturgical frame that unsettles the dispersion of elements in the discursive formation, which does not provide for such a correlation. That is to say, while the grieving mother might be welcome to mobilise her speaking position at an anti-war rally, protest statements cannot be seen to emerge in the discursive field of commemoration, whether in the frame of the eulogy or at Wootton Bassett.

This becomes particularly apparent if we read the order of elements in Pat's speech against the media representation of "the woman who has best articulated the loss suffered by wives and lovers since the fighting in Afghanistan began" (Grice, "'In'" 23). *Telegraph* journalist Elizabeth Grice first wrote about war widow Christina Schmid in the 'bloodiest' year for British troops. In an article about Schmid's response to her husband's death in Afghanistan, Grice described Schmid's public appearance as follows: "In front of thousands of people, she applauded as the hearse carrying Staff Sgt Schmid's coffin passed the war memorial at Wootton Bassett; declared her pride in him as a soldier, husband and father and reassured him of her love" ("'We'" 31). The journalist also gave Schmid room to publicly voice her support for the troops: "I believe that they are there to protect our homeland – that's why they go to war – and they should feel loved and appreciated". In the media frame constructed around the soldier's death through the lens of grieving femininity, dissent cannot be articulated; in Butler's terms, resistance is "suspended or shut out by [this] frame" (*Frames* xvii). Significantly, it is only when Grice revisited Schmid's story in an article published in 2014, the year of troop withdrawal, that Schmid could (be allowed to) articulate a moderate version of resistance to the war story: "As Task Force Helmand comes to an end, it is very, very hard to see a genuinely positive impact. In my darkest moments, I do question the wisdom of what we did" (qtd. in Grice, "'In'" 23). Read against the five-year lapse between public endorsement of the Afghan campaign and its questioning, Gilroy's play appears to undermine consolatory rhetoric by forging a speaking position that combines grief and resistance within a single act of enunciation.

Beyond this resistant potential, however, there are various ways in which *Motherland* fails to offer a 'second look' at grieving femininity. If we hark back to Dawson's outline of a nationalist discourse that conjoins martial masculinity with domestic femininity, it becomes apparent that the piece largely stays within traditional gendered wartime scripts. All the ingredients of what Dawson describes as the feminine narrative stance of the war story – 'the tearful goodbyes of girlfriends, wives and mothers'; 'their hopes, anxieties and grief'; 'their sense of the terrible vulnerability of those they waited for' – are endorsed in *Motherland*. In spite of its inclusion of two testimonies about female soldiers, the play largely reinscribes the archaic subject codes of fighting men and weeping women through its singular focus on female dependants. In this sense, the grid of classification that, as Cynthia Enloe elucidates, "categorise[s] women as peripheral, as serving safely at the 'rear' on the 'home front'" (*Does* 15), remains firmly in place. The delimitation of the experience of grief on the 'home front' to the female point of view is remarkable insofar as "bereavement is particularly well placed to contest conventional wartime binaries", as Acton has shown (13).

Indeed, the set design of the original production initially seems to transcend spatial and gendered dichotomies: the actors are "[s]at on or walking amongst neat little piles of ammunition boxes around the stage, which have the appearance of tiny suitcases in the half-light as the audience enters", as one reviewer details (Chadderton). The ambivalent signification of the scenographic elements is echoed on the level of auditory signs with a cross-fade from the "*sound of a military helicopter encircling*" to the "*stirring of 100 cups of tea*" (17), which establishes a link between the (masculine) battle zone and the (feminine) domestic space. Similarly, the iconic sign of the ammunition boxes oscillates between its indexical quality, which locates the performers and the viewers on the front line, and its symbolic connotation as 'tiny suitcases', which situates them in transit, somewhere between the 'home' and the 'front'. The boxes signal the entry of war into the peaceful setting inhabited by the women, who nevertheless continue to perform an unperturbed version of domestic femininity: in the opening scene, they "*sit facing the audience holding cups and saucers; stirring*" (17). The ambivalence of the setting seems to dissolve further in the first speech, rendered by an apron-wearing performer:

> She is a formidable lady. She always has been. (*Pause.*) Erm. A lady that was in charge of the household. She worked hard, in the house, being a mother. And a wife of course, because me dad worked at the mine [...], and she still believes every woman should sort of, look after their husband and look after their family, you know? (17)

The editing work undertaken by Gilroy is of particular relevance here. Although the meticulous reproduction of the interviewee's speech pattern, including her hesitations and local idiom, points to the fact that an original account over which the writer has had limited influence is re-presented, it is striking that Gilroy chose to open the play with a testimony to the 'formidable' working-class mother, rather than soldier. In conjunction with the title, *Motherland*, a version of essential motherhood is offered already in these early moments of the play, which naturalises women's role as primary caregivers. Here, one has to take into account the script's ties to the northeast of England with its history of (de)industrialisation. The absent father who descends into the mine becomes, for lack of employment opportunities after the pit closures, the prototype for the male soldier who departs for the foreign war zone. Both versions of male work leave women to look after the household and await the men's return, resulting in an iconography of "women as caretakers and mourners" (Cohler 246). This binary frame extends all the way to the ending of the play, which closes with "*a view through a net curtained window of a tree*" (76), in other words, with the anxious yet hopeful perspective of domestic femininity looking out for the man's return.

It hardly makes sense to criticise the experiences of the female interviewees for an adherence to traditional gender binaries, and it is essential to bear in mind the socioeconomic factors that might have restricted their life choices. Instead, a critical analysis of the piece must excavate those aspects of the editing process that remain concealed in the script. Apart from framing the play with images of formidable motherhood, the questions the playwright asked in the interviews but that are omitted in the playtext point to specific interventions in what would appear as the original account of these women. This is especially noticeable in the scene in which "*four women enter slowly and self consciously, gradually plucking up the courage to turn and face the audience*" (46). They begin to address the spectators, presumably in response to an unheard interview question:

SARAH. I'm married to John.
JANE.   I'm married to Phil.
GEMMA. I'm married to James, I've been with him for eight years we've been married for seven [...] with two children. [...]
CAROL. I'm married to Richard, we got together about eleven years ago and we've been married eight years. (46–47)

Since the spectators are positioned as the mute interlocutors, they are inserted into an as-if communicative situation in which their own enunciations are always already predetermined. The neat parallelism of the lines works to elide alternative options of 'where to begin'. The request with which the playwright presumably approached the interviewees is thereby occluded. In this manner, the structuring of a female speaking position around heterosexual marriage and maternalism is naturalised. One could even claim that these speakers acquire no subjectivity outside these scripts, as they can posit a thetic 'I' only in relation to their husbands. Like Christina Schmid in the *Telegraph* interviews, the women appear very aware of the public speaking position made available to them: "People don't realise outside what a difficult life we actually do lead" (49). Their self-formation within the verbatim playtext does not, however, work in terms of a theatrical technology of the self, such that they could use their 'appearance' therein to publicly proclaim the truth about themselves, for all their articulations are carefully framed, selected, and (re)arranged. As an outcome of the editing procedure – or possibly as an effect of the interviewees' (subconscious) response to the audience's expectations – all of their statements are designed to reinforce the ideal of domestic femininity set out at the beginning, if sometimes in a tongue-in-cheek manner: "Not only are we wives and mothers, we're also the comforting voice [...] for the parents as well. God we're fantastic aren't we?!" (50).

Accordingly, the dramaturgical arrangement inserts speakers and spectators into complementary positions within official scripts of commemoration. In *Precarious Life*, Butler writes about the "hierarchy of grief" that is perpetuated in the soldier's obituary, which distributes grievability unevenly:

> [I]n the genre of the obituary [...] lives are quickly tidied up and summarized, humanized, usually married, or on the way to be, heterosexual, happy, monogamous. But this is just a sign of another differential relation to life, since we seldom, if ever, hear the names of the thousands of Palestinians who have died by the Israeli military [...] or any number of Afghan people, children and adults. Do they have names and faces, personal histories, family, favourite hobbies, slogans by which they live? (32)

The functions of 'tidying up' and 'summarising' the soldier's life can also be discerned in the discourse of the play. With the exception of one lesbian servicewoman, all soldiers are positioned as 'heterosexual, happy, monogamous'. This is illustrated perfectly by Elizabeth's act of showing photos to the audience: "he's err, a very handsome man. six ft three. And that's his wife god bless her and she, she's gorgeous as well. That's the two girls" (37). Significantly, "*[a]ll the photos are blank*" (37), which might be seen to undercut the ideal image but also gives her description of the good-looking couple and nuclear family a generic quality. The performance thus largely validates the heteronormative frames that make the soldiers' lives appear real, worthy of support, and grievable.

Most significant is Butler's claim that the narrative ordering of the dead soldier's biography establishes a 'differential relation to life'. The humanising function of the obituary works against the obscene underside of the life that cannot be mourned: the 'ungrievable' life that is not intelligible within the established ontology of the human, which cannot be mourned because it was never apprehended as 'living' (Butler, *Precarious Life* 32–33). The life of the 'other' vanishes into the blind spots of all the testimonies in *Motherland*. This is problematic, to say the least, insofar as "discourse itself effects violence through omission" (34). What is more, the play's duplication of the Wootton Bassett ritual's heterosexual narratives of grief actively works in the service of derealising 'their' lives. As Gargi Bhattacharyya discusses the "recurring narrative of mothering" (51) in the 'war on terror':

> The implication is that 'we', participants in humane and western-inspired values, have learned the importance of affective family relations in the creation of balanced citizens, unlike these others who neglect their children and their parental duty and sacrifice their offspring to faceless causes. (53)

In mobilising the 'affective family relations' of absent or dead British soldiers in order to build empathy, the play implicitly affirms the differential distribution of grievability; as participants in the theatrical community of mourners, 'we' need not grieve for those who have no such familial ties, 'favourite hobbies, slogans by which they live'. 'Their' losses are, at best, implicitly recognised in the speeches:

JANE.   I remember when I first knew my husband, one of my friends said to me: 'Has he killed anyone yet then?' And I was just absolutely stopped in my tracks [...].
GEMMA. It's not even a question I'd ask.
JANE.   I never asked it, because if I get down that road [...] where do you go from there?
GEMMA. I would think it would open a massive door then wouldn't it? (47)

The question of the soldiers' culpability and their use of violence is consciously pushed beyond the boundaries of the 'sayable': a soldier's wife should not be expected to 'get down that road'. This statement is significant in two respects. First, it points to women's complicity in the war system.[35] There are, for instance, various passages where the mothers remember their sons' early fascination with (playing) soldiers, which they evidently never discouraged. Again, Elizabeth's speech is exemplary, for she remembers hoping "he'll grow out of it" when

---

[35] Joshua Goldstein has usefully defined the *war system* as "the interrelated ways that societies organize themselves to participate in potential and actual wars" (3).

her son engaged in non-conforming gender performances (i.e. wearing high heels, necklaces, and carrying handbags) but happily "talked about the RAF" with him (24–25). While the play endows the women with speaking positions from which to denounce the 'war on terror', their agency as mothers in processes of socialisation that train and enable men to fight this very war is not explicitly addressed (see Goldstein 252). In order to keep intact the basic premise of the piece – that these women's testimonies to bereavement are worth listening to and empathising with – the play does not openly problematise the way in which, as outlined by Lindsey Feitz and Joane Nagel, "femininities can give aid and succor to militarized masculinities" (202). Second, just as the interviewer obviously left the speakers' staking of the discursive territory of the 'sayable' uncontested, there were evidently no questions designed to 'open the door' to a conversation about the loss of Iraqi and Afghan lives. While these mothers and partners are prepared to receive their returning children, siblings, or spouses, whether alive or in coffins, and dutifully take on the ensuing tasks of nursing the injured or mourning the dead, there is no hint at 'our' ethical responsibility for those who may be at the receiving end of violence abroad. Where 'their' fate in the war zone is concerned, the home/front boundaries remain impermeable. In tactfully glossing over these gaps in the discourse of mourning, the performance exempts spectators from scrutinising the norms governing grievability or reflecting on the lives that are shut out by the frames of war.

On the whole, then, there is not only an undercurrent of conservatism beneath the surface of the play with regard to its reinstatement of traditional gender binaries, but the production also enacts a conservative closure of thought when it comes to the ethical framing of war. Although the play's trajectory can be seen as reaching from the reactive to the resistant, I would conclude that the performance at large cannot be seen to critically inflect the discursive regime of the 'war on terror', despite its voicing of protest. In this I concur with Acton, who argues that "the focus on 'our' grief to the exclusion of the grief of the 'other' [...] limits the extent to which [...] protest narratives actually do interrogate the binaries that make war possible" (197). Even though the subject position of grieving femininity becomes a vehicle for protest, its disruptive potential is contained by the reinscription of the gendered and spatial binaries that sustain war. This bears important implications for the issues surrounding subjectivity and national identity formulated at the outset of this chapter. If the obituary is "an act of nation-building", then the documentation and re-enactment of grief in *Motherland* reproduces the grievable life of the soldier as "an icon for national self-recognition" (Butler, *Precarious Life* 34). As the title signals in an obvious manner, the production seeks to acknowledge the contribution of mothers to the collective imagination of the nation. But instead of excavating any female roles that have been obscured by the grand narratives of nation-building, the play only brings the traditional subject positions of 'formidable' mothers into view. Standing metonymically for the nation, the 'motherland' constructed in the cosmos of the play positions spectators in the feminised domain of the home front by inviting them into the dramatic company of "[t]hese women, who live in our street and drink in our local" (blurb). To the extent that the derealisation of 'other' lives serves to legitimise military violence, spectators become enlisted in the war effort insofar as they accept the interpellative invitation to mourn 'our' losses against the omission of 'theirs'.

Tearless Girlfriends, Failing Men? Roy Williams's *Days of Significance*

Roy Williams's Iraq war drama *Days of Significance* was commissioned by the Royal Shakespeare Company and written as a response to *Much Ado about Nothing*. It premiered in the same year as *Motherland*, at the Swan Theatre in Stratford-upon-Avon in 2007, a rewritten version of the piece was shown at the Tricycle Theatre in 2008, and, just as Gilroy's play, the piece toured the UK in 2009.[36] With the production history spanning these three years, performances contributed to various contemporary conversations surrounding British involvement in Iraq. The premiere in January 2007 coincided with a court martial hearing into British soldiers' alleged abuse of Iraqi prisoners, a context in which the plotline about a returning British soldier facing trial for mistreatment of detainees had particular resonance. During the play's Tricycle run in March 2008, the Ministry of Defence admitted to breaching the human rights of Iraqi detainees, which resulted in payment of damages later on that year. The UK tour in late 2009, again, resonated with various news items on British soldiers' deaths in Afghanistan, so the play's events surrounding a soldier's death on the front line and his friends' attempts at coming to terms with the loss had "real currency", as one reviewer remarked (Vale).

Although performances of *Days of Significance* thus spoke to the same cultural moment as *Motherland*, Williams's play is a markedly different response to that context, the most obvious difference being one in form. *Days of Significance* is a piece of original new writing, developed from the RSC's commission to craft a response to one of Shakespeare's plays. The intertextual relationship with *Much Ado about Nothing* is most evident in the first part of the three-act

---

36 In the following, all quotations are based on the first version of Williams's playscript. All cited passages were only subject to slight alterations in the second version.

play, where Williams turns Shakespeare's young lovers into snappy, drunk, and brawling working-class youngsters, roaming about "*the middle of a city centre somewhere in the southeast of England*" (Williams 5).[37] The sociogeographical setting established in this first act frames the play as a whole: there is a striking continuity between the young men's sexist, racist, and belligerent conduct in the British town centre and on the front line, which transpires in the second act set in Basra: "The violence that British soldiers engage in [...] appears as an intensification of the everyday violence that simmers in England, evident in the drink culture and abrasiveness of the first act" (Gupta 101). Despite alternating home and front settings, then, the primary interest of the piece lies with the effects of the war in Iraq on British society in general and white working-class communities in particular (see also Reinelt, "Selective Affinities" 317). Williams's extended front-line scene, which traces the impact of social and ethnic tensions in the UK on the behaviour of troops abroad, will be discussed in the next chapter (see 4.1).

The tense atmosphere evinced in the home-front scenes is a far cry from the homely feminine sphere constructed in *Motherland*. If the groups of men and women are kept apart for some time during the first act – Maria Aberg's production at the Tricycle Theatre had them enter the stage separately via a catwalk extending into the audience – it is only to establish equivalences between the habitus and manner of speaking cultivated in each of the homosocial environments.[38] The play opens with a fight between Dan and Jamie, with the latter accusing the former: "Spilt my beer. [...] I'll split you in your head" (5). This conflict is echoed in the women's group where "DONNA *accidentally spills her drink over* HANNAH's *top*", with the latter retorting: "Do you wanna get hit? [...] I'll cut yer face" (16–17). The men's response to the appearance of a policewoman, whom they objectify throughout the scene by making sexually explicit comments and touching her bottom (5–8), is mirrored by the women's encounter with a "*dishevelled-looking* DRUNKEN MAN *[who] comes running out after the girls [...] holding his penis in his hands*" (10), and to whom they react with equally explicit talk, taking photos of his penis, licking their lips, and cheering him on (10–12). Both the men and the women seem driven by the same habitual dispositions and heated emotions. What is noteworthy about the aesthetics of the first act is that, despite the heightened theatricality of the use of an exaggerated and grotesque physicality – e.g. prolonged stage fights, excessive vomiting on stage,

---

[37] Questions of adaptation are beyond the scope of this study; for a brief discussion of the relation between the two texts, see Ledent (297–298).
[38] All observations are based on the recording of the performance at the Tricycle Theatre on 28 March 2008, held by the National Video Archive of Performance.

the men's incessant touching of their crotches, use of hip-hop hand gestures – the setting appeals to audiences as instantly recognisable. One of the lines that attracted the most laughter in the recorded performance of the Tricycle production that I viewed was the policeman's dry comment, upon Steve's showing his bottom to the policewoman: "I hate weekends" (41). The spectators' acknowledgement of how that line resonated with them signalled a willingness to read "those yobbish displays of vileness and vulgarity" (Cavendish) as a realistic representation of the street scenes taking place outside the theatre.

The way audiences are positioned on the home front, accordingly, diverges considerably from the mise-en-scène of *Motherland*: they are not invited into a protective environment that sends soldiers away and welcomes them back. In *Days of Significance*, the binaries of safe/dangerous and feminine/masculine spaces are undercut by the evocation of continuities between fighting and violence as well as feminine and masculine behaviour both at home and on the front. Although, to some extent, the persistent aggression in Williams's play appears related to the working-class position of its characters, this is not an inevitable connection; after all, many of the women represented in *Motherland* hail from a less privileged class background and similarly live in regions where young, uneducated men have few professional options. Whereas Gilroy taps into the 'respectable working class' topos by evoking a harmonious environment that is conducive to healing and recovery, Williams seems more interested in illuminating the extent of young working-class men's 'home-grown' despair and sense of impotence when they are sent into the war zone.

The atmosphere of 'vileness and vulgarity' sets the scene for Williams's version of the 'tearful goodbyes' inscribed into the war narrative. As soon as they engage in their first romantic encounter, Hannah and Jamie have to take leave due to Jamie's imminent departure to Iraq:

HANNAH. Right. You're not scared. [...] Despite what they all say?
JAMIE. Who?
HANNAH. Geezers on the telly. The papers. Another soldier getting killed.
JAMIE. Was it a bomb?
HANNAH. Think so. I just hope it's not Basra you're going to. Nuri al-Maliki has declared a state of emergency now.
JAMIE. Nuri who?
HANNAH. Iraqi Prime Minister.
JAMIE. What have you been reading?
HANNAH. Just telling you what I see, what I hear. I'm going to college.
JAMIE. [...] Look, I have to go. I don't have a choice. (22–23)

Hannah's understanding of the campaign does not induce her to lament Jamie's vulnerability but, instead, to nonchalantly display her superior knowledge. What is more, her declaration that she is 'going to college' suggests that she will not be waiting at home, perturbed by grief or anxiety, while Jamie is stationed in Iraq. With Jamie's disappointed realisation that Hannah is "like the rest of them. [...] Don't give a toss about what we're doing" (22), it becomes clear that the women in *Days of Significance* largely refuse to occupy a position that supports and gives succour to military masculinity, which in turn impacts on the men's ability to fight. In spite of its similar emphasis on the economic necessity that forces young working-class men to deploy to unpopular wars, the play – unlike *Motherland* – does not reproduce the complementary subject position of the anxious female waiting for the man's return. The lovers' farewell, essentially, remains tearless.

Hannah's refusal to be confined to a domestic position of anxiety corresponds to the disruption of Ben and Trish's relationship in the second act. The structural framing of that act with video messages sent from the front line positions spectators alongside the tearless girlfriends on the home front who are receiving these videos. The play highlights the role of the media in present war contexts, in particular "their influence on bringing 'fronts' into closer connection with home" (Youngs 928). Despite the use of "sophisticated technology", however, Reinelt calls attention to the fact that "Ben's crude attempt to communicate and be remembered is uncomfortably close to the kind of theatricality of the Abu Ghraib photographs. These constructions of identity [...] are utterly reduced by clichés and machismo" ("Selective Affinities" 318). There is a significant discrepancy in tone and mood between the first and the second video broadcast. In the first, Ben seems to succeed in addressing Trish as a soldier's sweetheart awaiting his return:

> Got yer photo. [...] You are a dirty bitch, you know that. Who took this picture? Better not be Dan, or Steve, it better be one of them timer things [...]. Anyhows, I'm putting it to good use, every night, toilets, you know what I'm saying? Course you do. (*Blows kiss, laughs again.*) Dirty bitch. (49)

This scene highlights the interdependence of wartime gender roles in various ways. It points to the salience of heterosexual eroticism in military culture, which evidently has a long history, dating back to the publishing of 'pin-ups' in newspapers for servicemen in the Second World War, for example (Goldstein 334). The exchange of titillating photos enables Ben to position himself as a heteromasculine hero: when there is the "*[s]ound of a distant explosion*", Ben relishes the fact that "we're gonna be seeing some action already. Oh, yes! [...] Love yer, don't worry, my luck's in. (*Waves photo.*) Got you, dirty bitch!" (52). This ending signals the relevance of the feminine object position as sexually available for maintaining men's willingness to fight. It also demonstrates soldiers' reliance on imagining "a place to return to, or at least die trying to protect – a place called home or normal or peacetime" (Goldstein 301). Yet Ben's attempt to position Trish as the sweetheart watching over his home instantly appears fraught with problems. The construction of a normalised, feminised peacetime environment can only fail, for the home has already been exposed to be as violent as the war zone, and the feminine sphere of experience as aggressive as the men's. This is indicated by the latent anxieties surrounding infidelity, which resurface in the second video. Sitting with his legs spread open towards the camera, Jamie Davis in the original production emphasised the intense desperation linked to the threat of emasculation:

> So how you doing, baby girl, my Trish? Thought you were gonna send me new pictures, it's bin three months now, you letting me down. Or are you too busy, going out every weekend, getting some new dick, eh? [...] Wanna show you summin. (*Holds up a pair of bolt-cutters.*) I got bolt-cutters ... (*Shows a dagger.*) Knife ... (*Flashes a torch.*) Torch ... Word is we're going on a raid later, bust down the doors of a couple of houses. (68)

Trish's presumed lack of faithfulness unsettles Ben's martial masculinity. In response, he has to restore his virility by displaying a range of phallic tools and weapons to his girlfriend (and the audience). Equipped with these ersatz penises, he pictures penetrating the foreign environment. Significantly, the necessity to thus retrieve his heteromasculinity originates from Trish's refusal to perform her femininity as the chaste, anxious girlfriend at home.[39] The scene thus reveals once again the "intimate connection linking gender, sexuality, and war", on which Feitz and Nagel elaborate:

> There [...] are the sexualized depictions of both sides in armed conflicts: from 'our' men who are honorable and virile, to 'their' men who are perverted and/or impotent; from 'our women' who are virtuous and vulnerable, to 'their' women who are promiscuous and treacherous [...]; and there is the phallic discourse of 'war talk': from weaponry – guns, bullets, missiles, and bombs, to military campaigns – assaults, penetration, conquest, and surrender. (201)

---

39 Male soldiers' preoccupation with the fidelity of wives and girlfriends at home is a recurring topos in war narratives. There is, e. g., a passage in Anthony Swofford's Gulf War memoir *Jarhead* (2003) that describes the soldiers' creation of a "Wall of Shame, a post covered in pictures of and comments on women who are cheating or are assumed to be cheating" (Peebles 1666), which is echoed in Williams's front-line scene, where an ex-girlfriend is denounced as the "queen of whores" (60).

Both the 'phallic discourse' of war, including displays of weaponry and penetration imagery, and the construction of 'our women' as virtuous are illustrated by the video messages. Yet, again, it becomes apparent that the girlfriends' refusal to perform according to gendered expectations disturbs the war system: Ben's positioning in relation to martial masculinity fails because Trish cannot be constructed in a complementary manner, as 'virtuous and vulnerable', but takes on the 'promiscuous and treacherous' characteristics of 'their' women. *Days of Significance* thus inflects the mutual constitution of gendered and sexual positions. This critically mimetic strategy exposes the centrality of dualistic gender constructions to the war effort. This is reinforced by the fact that, in response to Trish's implied performance of griefless femininity, Ben fails to perform professionally as a soldier, which leads to him and his sergeant getting killed in the second act.

The third act continues to uncouple the conjunctions of grieving femininity and martial masculinity. In the original production, the opening of the final act conveyed the further merging of home and front territories: as soon as the second video message had faded out, flickering flashlights came on in the British town-centre setting, and metallic sounds suggested that the raid announced by Ben was carried out 'at home'. The constellation of the third act, where every scene revolves around Hannah, reinforces the impression that the fighting continues, with Hannah becoming embattled in "verbal duels" from all sides (Wierzoch 117). The different parties in this confrontation each represent specific expectations surrounding women's wartime roles, some of which Hannah is unable or unwilling to meet. With her boyfriend having returned as an alleged war criminal and his best friend coming back in a coffin, Hannah is supposed to support Jamie and mourn for Ben, whereas the discussions she is having at college induce her to politically denounce the incidents in which she finds herself increasingly embroiled. The conventional expectation that Hannah will stand by her soldier boyfriend, regardless of his culpability, is represented by her stepfather, who keeps asking her if she will accompany Jamie to court, generalising this expectation into a bland truism: "Life only throws at you what it thinks you can handle" (88). The position of supportive girlfriend, however, conflicts with Hannah's academic socialisation, which requires her to denounce the atrocities committed by British soldiers: "You should hear them at college, [...] with all their PC shit, those poor Arabs, blah blah blah" (88). The pressure on Hannah to assume a firm anti-war stance is represented by Dan, another student, who challenges the script of supportive femininity: "Go to that courtroom with Jamie. Hold his hand, like some sad divvy cow" (81). The option of taking the moral high ground by opposing the war is, in turn, problematised by Trish, who expects Hannah to adopt the position of soldier's sweetheart: "I wanna talk about the war. [...] How often did Jamie write to you? Was that place getting to him?" (84). What becomes starkly apparent from these interlocking dialogic sequences is that there is not one (gendered) way of talking 'about the war'. As soldier's (ex-)girlfriend or as college student with a growing political and moral consciousness, Hannah has to navigate incompatible subject positions that are tied to the discordant impulses to either distance herself from or acknowledge her personal connection to the atrocities committed in Iraq.

With this configuration, the act as a whole exemplifies the location of the subject in the discursive field of the 'war on terror': Hannah occupies a series of contradictory subject positions at the intersection of the conflicting discourses and concomitant subject codes of grief, support, protest, dissent, and disengagement. Other characters make these positions available to her in the form of loci in (dramatised) conversations, yet she retains some leverage to choose between or reflexively negotiate her own positions. Hence, what also becomes evident from this dramatic constellation is the way in which subjects can exploit the potential for resistance within the boundaries of a discursive field, in the interstices emerging from their conflicting positions. Interesting in this respect is also the "graphic staging" of the original Swan Theatre production, in which "a chalked square marked the confining space into which characters stepped to confront Hannah, while also suggesting that the dialogues take place in her mind" (Reinelt, "Selective Affinities" 319). With this delineation of the interactive and internal battle zone of subjectivity, the staging could be seen as realising an iconography of subject positioning. In contrast to the way in which *Motherland* offers a singular subject position to its speakers, which they willingly come to occupy, subjection does not function as smoothly in *Days of Significance*, where Hannah continues to resist interpellation.

The final act of *Days of Significance* throws into sharp relief the fact that traditional wartime gender roles, despite retaining an extraordinary appeal in present conflicts, may not be suited to straddle conflicting loyalties in the controversial campaigns of the 'war on terror'. "Wartime's Beautiful Soul", in Elshtain's framework, "can respond simultaneously to [...] the 'family claim' and the 'social claim', for, she is told, without her unselfish devotion to country and family each would be lost" (9). In contrast, with the character of Hannah, Williams explores how civic responsibilities and personal commitments might be at odds with each other in present war contexts. *Motherland*'s enunciation of protest from within a position of grief and loyalty to the fighting (wo)men is problematised in the figure of Hannah, who realises that she either has to distance herself from Jamie or from the 'PC shit' discussed at college, as any articulation of an anti-war stance from the position of supporting soldier's girlfriend would appear disingenuous, whereas talking like her "fucking college mates" alienates her from Jamie (92).

The only discursive option that is not available to Hannah, it seems, is that of disengagement, for she is invariably "called up to take a position" (Wierzoch 117). Despite retaining some agency with regard to the way in which she performs her positions, subject formation inadvertently takes place in the discursive field, or the 'chalked square', circumscribed by the 'war on terror'. Even if Hannah exclaims, "I don't want that war to matter to me. I wanna go out, I wanna dance, I wanna get so fucking drunk" (87), the final act makes it very apparent that this war matters to all characters – and, by implication, to all spectators – to varying degrees. The play neither allows for an allocation of blame to working-class soldiers nor for exempting civilians from shared responsibility for the war. As a response to contemporary debates surrounding allegations of war crimes, *Days of Significance* complicates versions of female grief that heroise the deceased while eliding issues of culpability.

In conclusion, there are ways in which both productions discussed in this subchapter offer a 'second look' at the grieving femininity exhibited at Wootton Bassett. *Motherland*, to some extent, rejects the co-optation of this figure into efforts at legitimising the military strategy. *Days of Significance* illuminates the dispersion of complementary and contradictory gendered elements in 'war on terror' discourses and disrupts the stable correlation between versions of grieving femininity and martial masculinity. If Hunt and Rygiel are right in claiming that, in order for it to work, "the War Story depends on traditional gendered tropes" (4), *Days of Significance* has to be seen as the more critical response. Despite its subversive combination of grief and protest in one mode of enunciation, Gilroy's verbatim piece largely recounts the familiar war story focalised through the feminine narrative stance of the Mater Dolorosa. It leaves the spatial and gendered polarisation of war intact by positioning women mainly at the safe and peaceful 'rear' on the home front. Williams's piece, in contrast, refuses to impose order on the confusing and chaotic experiences of the Iraq war by positioning (un)grieving women in-between the home and the front, embattled by conflicting gendered, civic, and social expectations.

3.5 Traumatised Masculinities

To mark the ten-year anniversary of the London bombings, the *Huffington Post* published an article with the headline: "7/7 Bombings: How London Bravely Carried On after a Harrowing Day of Trauma" (Hopkins). Spanning the poles of bravery and trauma, this single line encapsulates the discursive balancing act that has been performed in official statements about the bombings. Initial responses can be primarily characterised by a recurrence to the Blitz narrative and the associated values of stoicism and resilience. The *Huffington Post* article, for instance, cites Prince Charles's admiration of "the incredible resilience of the British people who have set us all a fantastic example of how to react to these tragedies", next to Blair's praise for "the stoicism and resilience of the people of London" (qtd. in Hopkins). It seems that early cultural coping strategies were mainly designed around the discursive provision of courageous and undaunted positionalities for the collective of citizens, whereas anxious and traumatic responses were foreclosed (Bean et al. 445). The wide appeal of articulations of stoicism and resilience is evident from numerous (eyewitness) accounts (see Seidler 34); one could, via Butler, almost speak of a collective passionate attachment to these modes. The Blitz discourse was, however, soon complemented (and partly superseded) by discussions of the traumatic impact of the bombings, as psychologists drew attention to Londoners' experience of "'substantial stress' relating to the attacks" (Rubin et al. 350, 353). The subject position of the 7/7 survivor, accordingly, sits at the intersection of therapeutic discourses on post-traumatic stress and cultural expectations surrounding the ability to bounce back from national catastrophes.

The rise of the trauma paradigm has been attributed to advances in medical and psychological research, specifically the inclusion of post-traumatic stress disorder (PTSD) in the *Diagnostic and Statistical Manual of Mental Disorders* in 1980 (Luckhurst, *Trauma Question* 1). Even before the current terminology was coined, the phenomenon of a compulsive return to the 'scene' of traumatisation had been diagnosed in relation to train accidents from the late 19th century onwards, and the well-known antecedent *shell shock* gained currency in the context of the First World War (Chamberlin 361). Nevertheless, the particular forms of knowledge and the attendant subject positions emerging with the PTSD discourse can be connected to more recent sociocultural changes. These have been described in terms of the "'rise of the trauma culture' in Britain" and an increased social acceptance of traumatised subjects, especially war veterans (McCartney 46). Roger Luckhurst goes so far as to claim that the "trauma paradigm [...] has come to pervade the understanding of subjectivity and experience in the advanced industrial world"; he identifies "post-traumatic subjectivity" as a new mode of self-formation (*Trauma Question* 1, 15). In her work on *Trauma Culture* (2005), E. Ann Kaplan corroborates the notion that traumatic events "produce new subjectivities through the shocks, disruptions and confusions that accompany them" (20).

How are such (post-)traumatic subjectivities socially constructed and culturally mediated? A genre that is particularly embroiled in the rise of the trauma paradigm is the autobiography, or more precisely the memoir. In this context, Illouz points out the significance of "confessional autobiographies" of the type of the 'illness' or 'misery' memoir that gained widespread popularity in the 1990s (182), and Luckhurst suggests that "the success of the memoir genre was a result of its re-organisation around trauma" ("Traumaculture" 36). Memoirs about traumatic incidents have to adapt the conventional autobiographical organisation of experience to narrative attempts that "centre precisely on that moment which escapes self-apprehension", as Luckhurst notes (*Trauma Question* 118). Although the appeal of the 'trauma memoir' is not immediately connected to the post-9/11 moment, the reorganisation of narrative and cultural constructions of the self around incomprehensibility appears particularly suited to address the anxieties pervading the 'war on terror' decade. In fact, Luckhurst links the resurgence of traumatic narratives to the "psychic costs" of late modernity (*Trauma Question* 214), which – as the previous discussion of 'liquid modernity' has shown – are a central concern in plays produced after 9/11. As these deliberations indicate, "trauma's centrality to contemporary self-representation" (Gilmore 129) persists in significant ways in the context of the 'war on terror'.

If it is true that, in contemporary trauma culture, "extremity and survival are privileged markers of identity" (Luckhurst, *Trauma Question* 2), then prominent subject forms that exhibit those markers are not only those of the 7/7 survivors but include returning Iraq and Afghan war veterans. Indeed, the subject positions made available to returning soldiers in public, media, and clinical discourses are almost invariably organised around a trauma frame. Yet post-traumatic subjectivities are not limited to those directly involved in violent and catastrophic incidents. Kaplan calls attention to "a series of positions" that subjects with varying proximity to the traumatic event come to occupy, from "the direct trauma victim" to "a person geographically far away" (2). To her list of different degrees of trauma, Kaplan adds the relatives of victims, who may be affected by "'family' or 'quiet trauma'", and the vast number of people who come in contact with "mediatized trauma" and might, in extreme cases, be "'vicariously' traumatized" (1–2, 87). The implied position for readers/viewers of eyewitness accounts of the London bombings or first-person testimonies of soldiers involved in the Iraq and Afghan campaigns, for instance, may be structured around a shared sense of 'extremity and survival'. Similarly, the public who participates in the commemoration ceremony at Wootton Bassett may experience the "collective sense of survival" that is typically exuded by 'dark sites', and which potentially triggers the feeling that "we are all victims now" (Walklate et al. 159–160). In this manner, the wider public might obtain access to articulations of traumatised subjectivity.

This is not to suggest that those consuming news items or paying tribute at Wootton Bassett are traumatised patients in a pathological sense. Rather, what comes to bear on these collective subjectivities is what Kirby Farrell, in *Post-Trau-*

matic Culture (1998), defines as a post-traumatic mood: "It reflects a disturbance in the ground of collective experience: a shock to people's values, trust, and sense of purpose; an obsessive awareness that nations, leaders, even we ourselves can die" (3). In his analysis of trauma as a cultural trope, Farrell offers "four characteristics of post-traumatic stress that make the concept useful for thinking about culture" (11), one of which appears particularly relevant in this regard, namely, the contagiousness of post-traumatic stress. Farrell proposes that, as members of a society are susceptible to each others' fears and panics, post-traumatic stress connects the individual with a group or culture (11–12). At issue here is what Luckhurst terms the "affective transmissibility of trauma" (*Trauma Question* 119). I find it necessary to caution, via Sara Ahmed, that the social contagion model of emotions is flawed for its reliance on the integrity and stability of affects, for ignoring the "contingency of how we are affected" (*Promise* 39). It would be fallacious to infer that post-traumatic stress could simply be passed around in society. Nevertheless, Farrell's argument holds with regard to the general pervasiveness of a post-traumatic 'mood'. Beyond clinical categories, contemporary culture can be seen to rely on trauma for "a strategic fiction [...] to account for a world that seems threateningly out of control" (Farrell 2). In other words, PTSD is not merely "a narrow medicalizing label", or an individual psychological problem; rather, it has become recognised as "a socio-political category that has routed a significant strand of identity politics into the language of survivorship" (Luckhurst, *Trauma Question* 62).

In drama, the traumatising impact of war is most often encoded in the figure of the returning soldier, who has been physically and/or psychologically wounded and struggles or fails to readjust to civilian life. The body of the injured soldier transports the horrors of war and destruction into the civic everyday life of the home front. This is why the returning soldier is a generic border-crossing or "liminal figure", as Matt Jones suggests (26). His claim that "Canadian theatre's engagement with the war in Afghanistan has centred almost entirely on the figure of the traumatized soldier" (29) can be partly corroborated from a British perspective. Next to plays that centre on traumatised Iraq war veterans, such as Jonathan Lichtenstein's *The Pull of Negative Gravity* (2004) and Simon Stephens's *Motortown* (2006), the damaged warrior returning from Afghanistan is at the centre of Morgan Lloyd Malcolm's *Belongings* (2011) – which will be discussed in detail in chapter four – and Cat Jones's *Glory Dazed* (2012). Evidently, these plays employ a literary trope with a long tradition (see B. Martin 78). But they also raise questions about the contemporary cultural and therapeutic frames that help to understand, and possibly heal, trauma in the context of controversial wars. This chapter charts the dramatic negotiation of post-traumatic subjectivities against the critical issues of legitimacy and culpability in regard to the 'war on terror', which have been touched upon in many of the preceding analyses. Broadly speaking, it contrasts a production that affirms the validity of the trauma paradigm with a play that, though reflecting a pervasive post-traumatic mood, rejects the position of the victim. While Owen Sheers's *The Two Worlds of Charlie F.* (2012) is about trauma in the most visual and visceral sense in that it stages the real bodies of injured war veterans, Chris Goode's *Men in the Cities* (2014) offers a more oblique engagement with extremity and survival in the 'war on terror'.

Recuperating Trauma Victims: Owen Sheers's *The Two Worlds of Charlie F.*

The Two Worlds of Charlie F. was originally developed by the newly founded Bravo 22 Company at the Theatre Royal Haymarket in London's West End in 2012, where it premiered in a fundraising gala performance in support of the Royal British Legion. It went on its first UK tour and to the Edinburgh Fringe Festival in the same year and toured the UK and Canada in 2014. A live recording was released on DVD in 2012, and a making-of documentary (*Theatre of War*, dir. Chris Terrill) aired on BBC One in the same year. In *The Two Worlds of Charlie F.*, the real bodies of psychologically and physically wounded service personnel irrupt into the theatrical frame of an otherwise fictionalised play about their front-line experiences and return to British society. Lehmann discusses the "irruption of the real" in the context of postdramatic theatre, which is seen to have turned "the level of the real explicitly into a 'co-player'" (100). This production, however, cannot be neatly situated in a postdramatic paradigm: while Lehmann postulates that "the main point is not the assertion of the real as such [...] but the unsettling that occurs through the indecidability whether one is dealing with reality or fiction" (101), it is precisely the reality of the injured bodies that becomes the 'main point', or at least the unique selling point, of the show. An analysis of the play, beyond exploring its figuration of traumatised subjectivity, thus also has to take into account the affects and effects related to the staging of real injured bodies (see de Waal, "Staging").

In the production, real veterans appear alongside a small number of professional actors who take on subsidiary roles. "Drawn from the personal experiences of the wounded, injured and sick Service personnel involved", as the blurb states, the playwright created a frame that spans the soldiers' recruitment and departure for the front line in Afghanistan, the traumatic moment of their injury, their ongoing struggle with the symptoms of post-traumatic stress disorder – nightmares, flashbacks, relationship problems – to their recovery in physio- and psychotherapy. The play, which combines dialogue with song, dance, movement, and verbal narration accompanied by physical acting, largely situates itself within a post-traumatic frame. Audiences are confronted with subjects after the traumatic incident has taken place; they are invited to witness their post-traumatic development and growth. This dramaturgical arrangement resonates with Christina Wald's definition of "Trauma Drama", which "approaches trauma from an almost invariably *post*-traumatic perspective" (156). The piece does hence not so much illuminate the formation of subjectivity through traumatisation as dramatise a subject position that has already been scarred by trauma. In this regard, it is perhaps not surprising that Cassidy Little, who plays the semi-fictional protagonist Charlie, addresses the audience in the opening scene with the stump of his amputated leg resting on a crutch. Whereas Charlie "*wears his prosthetic leg*" in other scenes (Sheers 24), the play begins with a set-up that accentuates the visible injury. The opening scene stages the mutilated male body, quite literally, as a body of evidence, as a visual signifier of trauma in a way that resonates with Cathy Caruth's famous description of trauma as "the wound that cries out" (*Unclaimed Experience* 4). Caruth explores the communicative encounter at the site of trauma as "an address that remains enigmatic yet demands a listening and a response" (9). To a certain extent, the production forges such an encounter between the dramatised subjects as the speakers and the audience as the hearers of trauma.

Although potentially intimate, this encounter can never be fully immediate. First of all, a certain distance is already built into the structure of trauma, as the subject cannot consciously access the traumatic event or possess the traumatic memory. Rather, the event returns repeatedly and uncontrollably in the form of nightmares and flashbacks. In addition, it is questionable to what extent spectators can be made to listen to, acknowledge, and comprehend the 'enigmatic' address of trauma. What is at stake here is the question of intelligibility raised by trauma theory. Caruth's highly influential, if controversial, work on trauma posits that there is always a degree of incomprehensibility about trauma, which makes it difficult to process both for the victim and the listener (*Unclaimed Experience* 6). The performers' (self-)narratives often work to occlude the incommunicability of the traumatic memory in favour of a linear, coherent representation. Such representational engagements with trauma rarely grasp, as Amanda Stuart Fisher argues, the "traumatic truth that fail[s] to be disclosed by a literal and factual account of 'what happened'" (112–113). A tendency to privilege a version of trauma that verges on the comprehensible can be detected in a scene where a psychologist enquires, "Do you want to talk about your 'when', Charlie?", upon which all performers begin positioning themselves within a linear narrative:

CHARLIE.	Sure. I was taking part in an op ... [...]
DANIEL.	I was commanding a company ...
RICHARD.	I was on top cover ...
FRANK.	I was against a wall ...
ROGER.	I was in a Snatch ... [...]
ALL.	When / When / When / When ...

> *A sudden simultaneous moment of contact. The sound of explosions and gunfire. In slow motion* FRANK *is hit by an RPG.* RICHARD *is blown from his vehicle.* ROGER's *Snatch turns over.* CHRIS, DANIEL, CHARLIE *and* LEROY *are hit by IEDs. [...] As the medics work the wounded* SOLDIERS *sit up to speak.*

DANIEL.	I was blown twenty metres ...
FRANK.	I heard the rocket coming in ...
RICHARD.	I was blown sixty feet ...
CHRIS.	I caught the backlash ...
ROGER.	The Snatch went over and I hit the roof ... [...]. (47–49)

The structural parallelism between the lines conveys the sense that 'what happened' is relatable in a clear narrative formula triggered by the 'when' question. Fisher's criticism of factual accounts for failing to grasp traumatic truth is relevant here. It is questionable whether the distance inherent in the structure of trauma is sufficiently acknowledged in the performance. The speaker who tells us, 'I was blown twenty metres ...', or 'I caught the backlash ...', insinuates some kind of conscious access to and narrative authority over the event. Although these formulations seem to resonate with the testimonial mode, they fall short of the dramaturgy of testimonial theatre, which – according to Fisher – allows for "unknowingness and the fragmentary way the testimonial subject encounters an event" (119).

Yet the fact that these accounts are not re-presented by intermediaries, but by the traumatised subjects themselves, also calls for a slightly different critical perspective. Griselda Pollock argues that the conversion of trauma from incomprehensibility to narrativity and linear temporality "encases but also mutes trauma's perpetually haunting force by means of a structuration" (40). The combination of parallel narratives and simultaneous body movement in the moment of the onstage explosions constitutes just such a structuration. Drawing on Freudian psychoanalysis, Wald explains the difference between acting out and working through trauma: "The process of working through trauma [...] paradoxically allows for a gradual liberation from the repetition compulsion through the very mechanism of repeating, albeit repeating in a slightly different form" (106). With regard to the production, Leigh Gilmore's point that "[t]elling the story of one's life suggests a conversion of trauma's morbid contents into speech, and thereby, the prospect of working through trauma's hold on the subject" (129) has particular pertinence. The stylised and schematic re-enactment of the original traumatic incidents, repeated throughout rehearsals and performances, could be seen as an artistic mode designed to counteract trauma's grip on the affected soldiers. Although Caruth problematises "the transformation of the trauma into a narrative memory that allows the story to be verbalized and communicated", she concedes that it may work to "tell a 'slightly different story' to different people" ("Recapturing" 153) – which is precisely what the performers do. Instead of speaking as the 'experts' of their own biographies, like the non-actors in Rimini Protokoll's 'theatre of experts', for instance, they are offered an alterego character and a script that is not identical to their original testimonies. The presentation of the traumatic material within a fictive text-cosmos could be seen to protect the participants from retraumatisation, providing a safe mode for retelling and re-enacting their traumatic experiences with a difference.

I would, however, argue that the narratives are still highly likely to be (mis)read as authentic testimonies due to the apparent fit between representational and material orders. Even though the performance doubtlessly highlights the materiality of the injured bodies appearing on stage in wheelchairs, on crutches, with prosthetic legs, or moving on their stumps, these bodies are never merely self-referential. Unlike the grotesque bodies that inhabit the stage world created by Socìetas Raffaello Sanzio, for example, the soldiers' bodies continuously bear a distinct relationship to the dramatic characters they represent. Drawing on Fischer-Lichte's terminology, one could state that the materiality of the phenomenal bodies never fully overrides the semiotic attributes, as the injuries always 'make sense' as part of the semiotic bodies of the characters (*Transformative Power* 76). Since the phenomenal bodies function as real referents of injury and damage, they seem to validate and authenticate the characters' re-enactments in ways that at times obscure their representational status. This is problematic insofar as the semblance of proximity to the 'wound that cries out' may undermine the audience's ability to keep a reflective and emotional distance. The focus of the play ultimately remains on the figuration of the soldiers' suffering, thereby constructing them as victims within the trauma paradigm and absolving them of complicity in acts of violence.

Ostensibly, the emphasis on injuries points to a thorough engagement with the costs of war, as evident from Sheers's expressed hope that the play is about saying "this is what those three letters mean, this is what war is" (Terrill 46:37–46:40) or from the protagonist's invitation, "Let's go on a tour" (12), extended to the audience in the first scene. At the heart of this engagement, however, is a crucial elision, for the injuries and deaths inflicted on the 'other' are rendered invisible, insignificant. Arguably, there is one scene that alludes to Afghan casualties, yet the fact that it is entitled "Flashback" already indicates that its concern is primarily with the impact of war on the British soldiers, rather than the Afghan population. Positioned as the second scene of act two, which is initially set in a physiotherapy room with the soldiers doing exercises, it begins with a *"massive blast"*, upon which *"the patients and physios collapse to the floor"* (55). Their motionless bodies are meant to signify as Afghan civilians who were accidentally killed by the soldiers. However, since these same bodies almost instantly begin to *"shift and turn [...], repeating a sequence of movements of discomfort"* (56–57) and rise in the next scene to sing a song about nightmares and insomnia, the scene is clearly framed as an obstacle in the soldiers' recovery process, rather than in terms of an ethical sensibility. Throughout, the audience's empathy rests with the British soldiers. In this manner, the performance perpetuates the differential grievability of lives. There is a concern, then, with how the sense of immediacy conveyed in the staging of real injuries builds on a series of blind spots, occluding not only the inaccessibility of trauma but also the wounds inflicted on distant 'others'.

In my view, the suffering of the 'other' cannot be made to matter within the frame of the play due to its singular focus on the traumatised 'self'. The performance avails itself of the trauma paradigm so as to avoid raising questions about the soldiers' culpability, for "trauma proposes a passive, 'acted-on' victim or culture" (Radstone 457). Trauma is almost invariably connected to victimhood, as Farrell implies: "The idea of trauma may help put a problematic victim safely beyond blame" (14). Cultural ambivalence towards victims certainly pertains to the status of British soldiers in a controversial war. Helen McCartney's study of the public image of the British soldier in the 21st century has demonstrated how the discourse of victimisation provides soldiers with a preferable (self-)narrative (43). McCartney discusses the revision the traditional image of the heroic soldier has undergone in the context of the Afghan campaign in favour of constructing the soldier as the victim of an unwinnable war, of Improvised Explosive Devices (IEDs), and equipment shortages (44–46). The undeniable material impact of the war, evident in the visible injuries paraded on stage, reinforces the legitimacy and ease with which these performers can position themselves and be recognised by spectators as victims. As suggested in the scene cited above, many of them were injured due to IEDs – popularly seen as "a cowardly weapon", as McCartney points out (45).[40] Significantly, an IED explosion takes place at a spa-

---

[40] A number of filmic and televisual representations of the Iraq and Afghan wars have prominently focused on the use of these bombs against coalition forces; notable examples include Kathryn Bigelow's Oscar-winning *Hurt Locker* (2008) and the BBC series *Bluestone 42* (2013–2015), which centre on American and British bomb-disposal teams operating in Iraq and Afghanistan, respectively.

tiotemporal remove from the enemy. Although Taliban fighters, for example, can ultimately be made accountable for them, there is technically no enemy contact. A body damaged by an IED is hence a body damaged by war, but not by battle.

The implied spectatorial position is thus one that affirms the soldiers' status as victims and puts them 'safely beyond blame'. This is the basic premise of the performative contract for the more important interpellative invitation to be realised, namely, an apprehension of the soldier-performers' recovery process. This operates, first of all, on the level of visual signs. The exhibition of disabled bodies on stage inevitably recalls the visual regime of the freak show. The frequent dance routines and sequences of physical movement in the production (choreography: Lily Phillips) indeed have the quality of spectacle. Yet what appears spectacular is not the deviance of the injured and amputated bodies thus exposed, but their dynamic and vigorous movement alongside the able-bodied performers. In all cases, the audience's gaze is directed towards the ways in which these bodies can perform in line with the norm, rather than fall outside of it. This is where the "therapeutic ethos" (Illouz 156) underlying the aestheticisation of the disabled bodies becomes apparent. It not only codes the performers' narratives but also their physicality in terms of recovery and recuperation. A scene that offers a variation on the *pas de deux* is paradigmatic in this respect: three of the male performers who have lost limbs enter the stage in wheelchairs and engage in dance duets with the professional actresses, who take on the roles of their mothers or partners within the diegesis. The disabled performers appear dignified and strong, fully capable of holding and steadying their dance partners. The aesthetic representation does not capitalise on the extreme qualities of the unusual bodies but foregrounds what they are still able to do, such as performing a strong and supportive heteromasculinity. Instead of the objectifying stare of the freak show, the spectators' gaze becomes a therapeutically inflected look of recognition that validates the recovery process of the injured bodies.

As the *pas de deux* exemplifies, the play's project of recuperation is chained to a restoration of martial masculinity. The play is entirely affirmative of military values, as evidenced by its framing: the performance begins with Charlie's invitation to 'go on a tour' and ends with his speech on the "regiment of the wounded":

> we're leaving the services, but we're also joining the oldest regiment there is. The regiment of the wounded. It's a regiment with an illustrious history [...]. You might not be familiar with all its victories, but believe me it has thousands to its name. [...] And it's deploying too. Every day. Not to a battlefield, or to a base. But to you. [...] Because we don't live in two worlds, do we? (85)

In performance, the sentimental tone of the speech was underscored by an acoustic version of Snow Patrol's popular ballad "Chasing Cars" (2006). As the song increased in volume, the stage filled with wounded soldiers, who froze at the edge of the stage, looking into the auditorium. This confrontation turns the spectatorial act of looking into a reciprocal gaze, one that seeks to forge an emotional bond, reinforced by the inclusive metaphor of the 'regiment of the wounded'. The theatrical event is designed to create a community that transcends the us/them binary between the 'two worlds' of soldiers and civilians. When I saw the performance at Richmond Theatre in 2014, I felt gently coerced by this final scene into an emotional identification with a "preemptory 'we'" (Diamond 404), bound to the soldiers on the terms of an emotional contract I had neither been able to negotiate nor dissociate myself from. What appears problematic about the production then and now, upon reflection, is the way in which inclusion in the affective community of the theatre event entails an unquestioned acceptance of military codes and values. The solution the play offers at the end is enmeshed in military paradigms, as the healing process culminates in the subjects' reintegration into a 'regiment'. The visceral engagement with injury and disability does not lead to a critical engagement with violence.

Similarly, the play aims at reconciling traumatised subjectivities with versions of martial masculinity. Generally speaking, traumatic symptoms could be regarded as incompatible with the type of dominant, hegemonic masculinity that is promoted in military culture (Chamberlin 359). Self-control and self-reliance, (physical) strength, power over women, and sexual performance are among the features of hegemonic masculinity identified by R.W. Connell (see Tosh 47–51). All these characteristics are at stake when the impact of trauma sets in. Many of the injured bodies staged in *The Two Worlds of Charlie F.* cannot maintain the physique associated with soldierly masculinity, and the performers' narratives address concerns with loss of control, virility, and continence. For instance, in an interview contained in the BBC documentary, Stephen Shaw admits,

> I don't really have a social life anymore ... Because basically ... the risk of falling over, because occasionally I've actually pissed myself – with the pain, when you go down, your bladder just lets go ... There's always that ... worry that you'll be out, having a good time, something will happen, you'll be on the floor in a puddle of piss, basically. [...] And everybody just looks at you like you're a freak. (Terrill 45:30–45:57)

The hesitant articulation of a voice that speaks from a place of damage and embarrassment is converted into a more stabilised speaking position in the play: Shaw's character, Roger, tells a businessman who incredulously asks him, "what's wrong with you?" (since he has no visible impairments), that "I broke my back in two places, [...] I'm addicted to meds and sometimes the pain is so bad I collapse and piss myself in public. What's wrong with you?" (81). While Shaw understandably has difficulties articulating his concerns about public exposure to the camera, the staged character is snappy, aggressive, and pushes the intrusive civilian brusquely away. The vulnerable masculinity to which the documentary testifies is transformed into a resilient one that is more in line with the idealised warrior image. This might be seen as another case of the theatrical frame providing protection, for Shaw does not risk the dreaded exposure as a 'freak' on stage, where he appears self-possessed and in control. In this manner, though, the performance misses the opportunity to make spectators bear witness to the anxieties that characterise traumatised masculinities or motivate a reconsideration of military masculinities in the face of trauma.

It might have to be clarified why the piece's central concern can be seen in the reconstruction of military masculinity despite its inclusion of two female soldier-performers in the cast. This is the case because the subject positions of the female soldiers are continuously marginalised on the level of acoustic and visual codes. Regarding their voices on stage, the women's experience is systematically split off from the men's by means of the conventional division of songs into male and female parts. In a particularly iconic scene revolving around the generic soldierly experience of receiving 'blueys' on the front line (i.e. air mail sent to service personnel via the British Forces Post Office), the female narrative stance focuses on the letter writing, while the male perspective is that of the recipient. The women soldiers sing along with the professional actresses, designated as Letter Writers in the script: "Hope you get this, hope you're safe, hope everything's alright. Miss you. [...] Look after yourself, my love, and come home soon" (35). The female voice enunciates a position of dependence and anxiety, recalling the way in which the women at the 'rear' on the home front await the soldiers' return in *Motherland*. In contrast, the male voice has recourse to a discourse of homosocial bonding, which explicitly excludes the female soldiers present on stage: "Please don't worry, I'm with a good bunch of lads. And, you know, we look out for each other" (36). Overall, the configuration of the scene resonates with gendered narratives of war that construct "letter writers as participating in a heterosexual romance between a man in the theatre of war and a woman waiting at home" (Acton 10) – there is hence no room to address the female soldiers' experiences of the theatre of war.

Their experience cannot easily be integrated in the dramaturgical structure of the play due to the overall coding of femininity as complementary to military masculinity. The play reinscribes archaic wartime constructions of gender, fashioning male and female subjectivities in terms of "the personas of Just Warriors and Beautiful Souls", as Elshtain has famously described them: "Man construed as violent, whether eagerly and inevitably or reluctantly and tragically; women as nonviolent, offering succor and compassion" (4). The women on stage are positioned within a heterosexual frame, which recalls the gender binaries explored in the discussion of (un)grieving femininities. In articulating traumatised masculinity in correlation with the supportive femininity offered up by the soldiers' sweethearts, the play harks back to the "dominant cultural idea that psychological recovery [takes] place in the privacy of a serene domesticity facilitated by the love of a sympathetic woman" (Acton 127–128), a notion whose origins Acton traces back to such films as Samuel Goldwyn's *The Best Years of Our Lives* (1946). Regardless of the empirical validity of the potential of heterosexual love relationships to provide comfort to male PTSD patients (Goldstein 309), the play's negotiation of trauma within these heteronormative binaries appears problematic insofar as it occludes articulations of subjectivity beyond these dichotomies – most palpably that of the female veterans present on stage.

The crisis at the heart of the play, if seen through its protagonist, is linked to a failure to perform a soldierly, heterosexual masculinity due to the trauma accrued in Afghanistan. This is manifest in his inability to connect to his fiancée, Lauren. Again, military discourse is appropriated to speak about this crisis: "I know she's my solution. But I'm fucking it up. [...] It's a whole second tour [...]. I mean, I'll storm a fucking compound tomorrow. Even with one fucking leg. But *this* tour. I'm outnumbered" (74). The analogy goes as far as designating the soldiers' sweethearts the "casualties" of this second tour (74). At the end of the play, the process of healing charted throughout culminates in the appearance of a dancer in a lap-dancing club in nurse costume – an unlikely reincarnation of Florence Nightingale – who has designed a tattoo with his fiancée's name for Charlie, thus literally inviting him to reinscribe his heterosexuality onto his damaged body (83–84). In Charlie's final speech on the 'regiment of the wounded', he takes up the offer to refashion himself in terms of a military masculinity despite the injury. Accordingly, the crisis of masculinity engendered by trauma is warded off by an endorsement of the very ideals that brought these soldiers to the front line in the first place: strength, stoicism, resilience, solidarity, fighting for the male comrades.

With its potential for reshaping "the relationship of the self to culturally situated others", emotion, as Illouz declares, has the capacity to move to action (11). As I left the performance at Richmond Theatre, collection buckets for the Royal British Legion gave audience members an opportunity to donate money in support of (former) members of the armed forces. If the show works as emotionally effective theatre, spectators are likely to translate the affects experienced in the confrontation with the injured soldiers into culturally meaningful emotions and, ultimately, into charitable activity. The show's affirmation of the legitimacy of PTSD narratives also has significant economic implications, if one recalls that the diagnostic category emerged primarily in response to questions surrounding financial compensation. But the production does not primarily locate the responsibility for that compensation with the state; it is the audience to whom the 'regiment of the wounded' deploys. What appears problematic about the way in which the show emotionally enlists spectators is the fact that it draws them into identification with subjects who are already awarded a considerable degree of recognition. Without unduly diminishing the plight of wounded, injured, and sick service personnel, it has to be noted that wounded veterans have a noticeable (media) presence in the UK, with such highly public figures as Prince Harry – who, in 2014, launched the Paralympic-style Invictus Games for injured soldiers – championing their cause. While the participation of real soldiers in the production affectively enhances the engagement with trauma, pain, and suffering, the show does not realise its resistant potential by challenging audiences to see injured soldiers otherwise or think through their presence to the wounds they potentially inflicted on others. Ultimately, the play's effort at recuperation is not linked to a reconciliation between 'us' and 'them' in a global framework, but between soldiers and civilians on the home front.

Flailing, Falling, Fallen Men: Chris Goode's *Men in the Cities*

The articulation of traumatised subjectivity in *The Two Worlds of Charlie F.* can be contrasted with a performance that works within the trauma paradigm but problematises positions of victimhood and hegemonic masculinity. Whereas Bravo 22 Company's production purports to reflect women's experiences of war while subsuming them under heteromasculine viewpoints, Chris Goode's monodrama *Men in the Cities* presents a narrative from which women have been, deliberately and artificially, rendered absent.[41] *Men in the Cities* was originally produced for the Royal Court in 2014 and transferred to the Traverse Theatre during the Edinburgh Festival in the same year; it returned to the Royal Court for a second run in 2015, which is when I saw it performed. The solo performance cites the mode of stand-up comedy, with the writer-performer standing in a circle of lit white flooring and speaking into a microphone throughout. It is framed self-reflexively: "Hey. How's

---

41 As Goode reflects on this dramaturgical move, "as a speculative experiment, I wanted to lift almost all of the women out of the play. So it's a play in which all of the women are disappeared somehow. They're dead or they're divorced or they've left or they were never there" (personal communication).

everyone doing? This is a story called *Men in the Cities*. It starts in the middle of the night, with the sound of screaming" (Goode 17). The performance persona that Goode creates can perhaps best be described as a 'narrating subject', in keeping with Heddon's terminology of the "performing subject" of auto/biography (4). This narrating subject does not 'story' its own life, however, as is the case in most of the examples Heddon analyses.

Instead, one by one, Goode (henceforth used in reference to the narrating subject) lets more than a dozen male characters wake up in cities throughout the UK and provides glimpses and snapshots of their (sub)urban existence. What links these loosely connected stories is, first, that they are all set immediately after the 2013 Woolwich murder and, second, against this moment of collective shock, all the men either go through a traumatic event, recover a traumatic memory, or undergo a personal crisis. To a certain extent, this recalls the series of transgressions in Stephens's *Pornography*. Indeed, *Men in the Cities* similarly sheds light on the abandoned citizens of an 'orphaned' culture; this is encapsulated by a newspaper item that circulates 'in the cities': "David Cameron has gone on holiday" (43). In terms of its form, however, the monodrama differs markedly from Stephens's play, for there are no definable characters that are impersonated by actors, or one actor even. The metatheatrical framing as 'a story called *Men in the Cities*' aligns the piece with postdramatic techniques, as "the theatre becomes the site of a narrative act" (Lehmann 109). The production parts with postdramatic aesthetics, though, insofar as the playtext is still the primary offer of meaning and theatrical element. Although they are absolutely central to the dramaturgy, the technologies of storytelling are posited as faulty, unreliable, and potentially misleading. Narrative, in this production, does not function as a therapeutic response to counter trauma's hold on the subject, nor is it affirmed as a technique that works to transmit trauma to an empathetic listener. The traumatised subjects the audience encounter via Goode's mediation of their experiences remain twice removed: first, they are inserted into a narrative frame behind which the writer's voice, his textual choices and manipulations never disappear; second, they are distanced by their own inability to access their traumatic experiences.

This can be illustrated exemplarily by examining in more detail the storyline revolving around Jeff, an elderly widower who notices an urgent need to go and fetch something from the attic in his house. The significance of the object hidden in the attic – an overt symbol of a repressed memory lodged in the unconscious – is intricately connected to Jeff's response to the murder of British soldier Lee Rigby. It is after listening motionlessly to the radio news on the Woolwich attack for one hour that "Jeff takes a pink felt tip [...] and on his hand he writes the word: 'ATTIC'" (30). The visible and easily discernible signifier of his repressed memory immediately embarrasses Jeff, however: "And then he crosses it out because he doesn't want anyone to see that he's written it" (30). In performance, this passage was underscored as Goode – though generally using few gestures – indicated the act of writing on the back of his hand and erasing it. The pink "blotch" (30) that results from the blurring of the signifier gains an indexical quality as it aligns Jeff with the "theatrical red of those blooded hands" (40) of Michael Adebolajo, one of the murderers, as seen by Jeff on *Newsnight*. The fact that the media images of Adebolajo's hands lead to his "feel[ing] sick, deep down" (40) suggests that the blotch on Jeff's hand, similarly, points to an episode that is unpleasant and possibly violent. Upon finally visiting the attic, Jeff uncovers his wife's old doll and takes her into the woods, which is revealed as the site of the memory:

> That's where we did it, says Jeff, pointing at a tree on the other side of the clearing. [...] She kept saying we mustn't, we shouldn't, says Jeff, we shouldn't, I can't remember, we mustn't, something like that. [...] I regret it in a way, says Jeff. I don't think she really wanted to. [...] But then I think if she'd actually, you know, whatever the word ... consented, I think I would have ... I wouldn't have seen it through. (49–50)

The communicative transmission of trauma heralded by trauma theory and therapeutic approaches is twice deferred in this scenario. First, the subject addresses an inanimate object instead of an empathetic listener; the ensuing communicative situation is hence closer to apostrophe than to address. Lauren Berlant's gloss of Barbara Johnson's work on apostrophe offers further insight here. Berlant explains how the animation of a silent interlocutor speaks to a "desire to make something happen *now* that realizes something *in the speaker*" (25). This desire to realise something in the speaker, to resolve the repressed conflict, is – and this constitutes the second deferral – further mediated by Goode, who variously intervenes in the narrative over which he conspicuously retains control, evidenced by the frequent insertions. The audience are not invited to apprehend or empathise with the traumatisation of a speaking subjectivity. Instead, their access to the site of trauma is further barred by the fact that the subject himself fails to remember the event accurately. That Jeff cannot recall the precise words used by his wife is immensely significant; after all, language is decisive when it comes to sexual consent. Failing to remember what was said and struggling to find the adequate words, Jeff is not accorded a stable enunciatory position that would allow him to take control of a linear narrative (within the narrative).

The traumatic event that can be glimpsed through these distancing mechanisms is one of sexual coercion. The subject through whom the trauma is focalised is, however, not the traumatised victim but the perpetrator. The image of the 'blooded hands' that provides the link between Jeff's story and the Woolwich incident can now be decoded as a symbol of culpability in patriarchal modes of violence. This becomes more explicit as Jeff begins to reconsider the murder in light of his unravelling of the repressed memory:

> I'm looking at these Muslim lads, I'm reading this speech in the paper [...], these bits of this speech about we're the extremists and they're just fighting the war we started and I look at it all and I think, well, yeah. [...] I can't disagree.
>
> I think those boys out marching don't speak for me.
>
> That bastard with the blood on his hands. He speaks for me. (53–54)

It is his recollection of his own violent act that enables Jeff to discover a subject position from which the Woolwich murder begins to make sense to him. Linked by the 'blood' on their hands, Jeff gradually comes to recognise his own position as a perpetrator. The pink blotch that Jeff had been unable to erase restitutes the missing link of complicity, which had been repressed in the formation of the anti-war speaking position. Hutnyk captures the hypocrisy of the protest slogan when he writes, rather provocatively: "Blood on our hands but not even an attempt to wash it off; after its initial articulations, the slogan 'Not in My Name' was barely legible in the diminishing anti-war movement, itself indicative of responsibilities shirked, disavowed and ignored" (138). It seems that, in acknowledging the blotch that connects 'us' and 'them', Jeff disidentifies with the subject position expounded by both the political centre in the anti-war protests and the far-right English Defence League rallies in response to the Woolwich murder ('those boys out marching'). Instead, he identifies with the 'extremists', with those who own up to the violence exerted in 'our' name. This discursive move enables Jeff to synchronise his personal history with the narratives being created around recent events.

The moment where the personal collides with collective crisis is echoed in the other storylines. Soon after Jeff's discovery, Rufus, a ten-year-old schoolboy, undergoes a similar epiphany. Rufus runs away from school, presumably after – this is only hinted at – sexually abusing one of his classmates. What precisely happened is, again, obscured by an inability to remember that sets in almost immediately: "There was just the roar of his absolute unconditional love for Arthur. And then there was blood on the wall of the cubicle" (46). Escaping to the city that seemingly promises fulfilment of his explosive libidinal desires – "he's going to London where everyone has sex constantly" (47) – Rufus visits an exhibition where he contemplates the eponymous *Men in the Cities* drawings by Robert Longo:

3.5 Traumatised Masculinities — 155

> Large and isolated on a grey wall, three panels, on each of which is a figure. [...] And each man is drawn contorted in a different way, in his own way, flailing. As though falling, or fallen, or twisted somehow or bent. Rufus looks at the first contorted man. And at the second. And the third. [...] Looking at them in the way that he only ever looks at the very most fucked-up desperate porn. [...]
>
> He steps back. Looks again from a few feet away, at the three contorted men. [...]
>
> The capacity for love. The need for injury. (54–55)

The installation provides a quiet space for the kind of "solitary contemplation and meditation" that "committed art" facilitates, according to Rancière (*Emancipated Spectator* 53). The reception of art from this position differs from Rufus's hasty consumption of online porn, which is always geared to the purpose of sexual satisfaction. The suspended men elude the expedient gaze of the porn viewer; their movements are frozen in time. The men's expression is captured in a moment somewhere between agony and aggression,[42] and it is in this suggestive tension that Rufus discovers the inextricable link between the 'capacity for love' and the 'need for injury', which allows him to work through his own violent desires. The contorted men in the cities become the symbol of the masculinities that the play dissects; they are refracted through the various narrative snapshots which eventually converge in a "wide-ranging and depressing portrait of male lives in crisis" (Gardner, "Powerful Vision" 5). Just as Rufus contemplates the drawings, spectators are invited to look at this portrait from different perspectives; however, like Rufus's, their lines of sight are dependent on the writer-narrator's manipulations. In this manner, Goode weaves his own "complicity from the position of someone who is a cultural maker" (personal communication) into the play's framework of violence.

Rufus's description of the figures as 'falling, or fallen' could also be read as an allusion to Richard Drew's iconic photograph of the "Falling Man", which came to epitomise the innocence of those attacked in the twin towers. The predominant lens through which these victims were culturally represented is captured by Ilka Saal's reading of the much-discussed "Portraits of Grief" series published in daily instalments in the *New York Times* in 2001 in order to pay tribute to the lives lost on 11 September. According to Saal, these anecdotes relied on "the melodramatic logic that stipulates that undeserved suffering is always the telltale sign of an essential [...] innocence" (359–360). Although Berlant suggests

---

[42] I am drawing on the images and descriptions provided on the website of Adamson Gallery (Washington, DC), which holds a number of prints of the photographs that became the basis for Longo's drawings.

that the falling man is "an enigma", a "noted but de-eventilized affect site" (85), I would argue that the figure, though eternally suspended and potentially open to interpretation, has mainly circulated in the affective spectrum of grief. A 'melodramatic logic' sticks to this figure such that it is coded in terms of undeserved victimhood and essential innocence. At this point, it is useful to recall Colleran's point that, as a result of constant media coverage, "few spectators enter a playhouse without bringing some media-produced image of the drama's subject along with them" (20). It is safe to assume that audiences are able to recall the images of Adebolajo facing the camera with his blood-stained hands and the man falling from the twin towers, which are conjured up in the performance. As Colleran further elaborates, "Whatever political effect a drama may hope to create, it must first dislodge the images or assumptions the media has already manufactured" (20). It is my view that *Men in the Cities* does just that by offering up an alternative subject position from which to read these images. The preferred spectatorial position is one that avows complicity and disavows victimhood. Most of the characters do not recognise their experience of the 'war on terror' in the fated falling man, but in those flailing men that are agonised yet aggressive; if the former "falls without landing" (Berlant 86), they have always already 'fallen' into their position at the intersection of personal and collective histories of violence.

The production thus inflects the trauma paradigm so as to render it congruent with modes of complicity. If Luckhurst identifies new narrative forms that engage with the disruptions of trauma as "the places where we try out the re-significations of self that trauma has wrought on contemporary subjectivity" (*Trauma Question* 85–86), then *Men in the Cities* can be seen to explore these resignifications with a shift in perspective from victimised to violent subjectivities. In a way, the piece tells 'the other side of the story' in responding to the trauma discourse from the perspective of those normally granted an object rather than a subject position in it. The trauma narrative has been shaped essentially – and, of course, justifiably so – by those suffering from post-traumatic stress: "Vietnam veteran groups coincided in the mid-1970s with feminist activists who were determined to voice the hidden secret of patriarchy – that its power was [...] maintained by the actuality or threat of rape", as Luckhurst summarises ("Traumaculture" 30). With its plethora of male characters, Goode's monodrama provides glimpses of moments of epiphany in which traumatised subjectivity is forged precisely through discovering and voicing 'the hidden secret of patriarchy' – albeit from the perspective of those who derive their power from (the threat of) violence and abuse.

This focalisation of trauma through the perpetrator's perspective also pertains to storylines revolving around events that are conventionally understood as traumatising, such as Ben's suicide. The divergent reactions of his father Brian and his partner Matthew highlight the simple fact that traumatic reactions to distressing incidents are neither universal nor inevitable. Although being the one who more ostensibly displays his distress, Matthew can overcome his grief with a resilient response: again, it is the move to London that contains a promise, in this case of processing the painful memory. Brian, in contrast, descends into crisis when Matthew rejects his strategy of making sense of Ben's death – "there aren't [...] reasons" (63) – by calmly declaring: "It was your fault. Everything about him was damaged, says Matthew. You know that. You know that. You know it. Where do you think that came from? It was absolutely your fault" (64). The structure of trauma becomes apparent here: there is a tragic incident, a loss, and some kind of repressed memory or knowledge the subject would not avow, as Matthew's reiteration of 'You know that' emphasises. But this precise knowledge comes to possess the subject. In the subsequent sequence, a drunk and disorientated Brian is wandering the streets of London, losing control of language but gaining partial insight into what has been repudiated. Brian hallucinates the apparition of a "Gay Twink Angel", which is the name of the porn website that he consulted when trying to come to grips with his son's homosexuality. The communicative situation that ensues partly corresponds to the twice deferred frame of Jeff's apostrophic confession as Brian "raises his voice above the crowd to tell the angel everything" (65). But there is also a marked difference, for Goode here cedes control of the narrative and – for the only time in the performance – leaves the microphone as he begins to act out Brian's wanderings:

> HEY FRIEND hey pal hey supernatural radiant bender! [...] I need to try and speak all the language out of my mouth! – you toxic shining boy, you hanging-over-me threat of disappearance, dissolution, of splitting up like a failed marriage, my atoms are so stuck in this stupid configuration. // *And my father and his father and his father.* // Won't you read me? Won't you drag me by the tongue into whatever oblivion will have me now? I must get this poison out of my life, decommission this horrible apparatus. I have to re-hurt the wound that sprung me. I have to beg for the forgiveness of my son, that happy skeleton. (65–66)

The bereaved father's outburst illustrates what Gilmore calls the "consensus position [...] that language not only fails in the face of trauma, but is mocked by it and confronted with its own insufficiency" (132). The failure of language is underscored by the act of stepping away from the microphone as the locus from which speech is authorised and by Brian's attempt to mobilise all available linguistic resources. Language 'fails in the face of trauma' insofar as he cannot articulate clearly what is lodged in his unconscious, what it is that drives him to beg for his son's forgiveness. Language is also 'mocked', its insufficiency exposed, as, during the course of the monologue, Brian comes to manically repeat the same lines and phrases over and over again, as if they engendered no effect or advance in understanding.

Nevertheless, this moment of crisis is not without insights into the traumatic formation of subjectivity. The overarching theme of the monologue is captured by the phrase 'my atoms are so stuck in this stupid configuration'. The personal and sociopolitical 'apparatus' pointed to here is connected to the notion of structural trauma. As Pollock explicates, there is

> a necessary, if actually unsustainable, distinction between *structural* trauma and *historical* trauma. Structural trauma refers to what is theorized by psychoanalytical tradition as [...] the series of losses which mark and by which subjectivity is formed: birth, loss of the breast, castration and loss of the loved object as well as the primal scene, and/or seduction. (43)

The apparition of the Gay Twink Angel triggers Brian's introspection into his traumatisation since it functions as an icon of the 'threat of disappearance, dissolution, of splitting up', in short, as symbolic of the series of losses of which Ben's death is only one manifestation. Brian's homoerotic fascination with the Angel constantly gives way to homophobic repulsion, for the lean male body of the 'toxic shining boy' evokes the spectre of HIV/AIDS. Brian's insistence to 're-hurt the wound that sprung me' could be read as a reference to the structural trauma of birth, which Brian needs to work through in order to address 'the loss of the loved object'. In reflecting on the series of structural trauma events that constitute subject formation, the monologue could also be read as a statement on the transmissibility of trauma, as the recurring sentence '*And my father and his father and his father*' indicates. This explains the use of biblical register in this context; the phallocentric Christian image of God and his son provides the archaic foil against which the contemporary male subject situates his own position in a vicious circle of desire, violence, and loss. It is, again, not as victim that Brian positions himself within this system; rather, his asking for forgiveness indicates that he begins to own up to his complicity in Ben's suicide.

By evoking the insufficiency of language in the face of (structural) trauma, Brian's speech demonstrates that it is precisely the inability to 'speak all the language' that is being passed on from father to son (and his son and his son). What this performance segment conveys, and what is reflected on a meta-theatrical level by Goode's surrender of control over the speech are the systemic shortcomings of socially acceptable forms of language in articulating masculine affects, traumata, and crises. There is no language available for Ben to articulate his despair, which is why, although Matthew and Brian intuit that he was unhappy, "[t]hey just don't know how they know" (40). In parallel, Jeff realises that the

Woolwich murderer's crude reversal of subject positions cannot easily be dismissed, because it seeks to express something that 'we' know about (but just don't know how we know): namely, 'our' complicity in acts of violence, war, and terror(ism). In the videotape submitted to Al Jazeera, which is also cited in *Pornography*, suspected 7/7 ringleader Khan articulates this 'unspeakability': "our words have no impact upon you, therefore I'm going to talk to you in a language that you understand" (qtd. in BBC News, "London Bomber"). The lack of 'sayable' statements to address acts of patriarchal, structural, and state violence pushes men to 'act out' in the form of suicide, abuse, or terrorism, as *Men in the Cities* suggests. In this manner, the piece evinces the pernicious effects of the discursive policing and regulatory effects operative in the enunciative field of the 'war on terror'.

With its figuration of traumatised masculinities, *Men in the Cities* eschews the entrapments of "an addiction to 'wounded attachments'" (Kaplan 22). While Goode's flailing men are clearly entangled or stuck, they do not become caught in a reiteration of their own hurt or victimhood, but rather in what Berlant astutely characterises as the "impasse shaped by crisis" (8). Pace Berlant, one could argue that the play shifts the focus from notions of trauma culture, or wound culture, to "a notion of systemic crisis or 'crisis ordinariness'" (10). Berlant criticises trauma theory for failing to account for the pervasive and oddly permanent sense of precariousness in the present, since trauma always figures as that exceptional disruption of an otherwise solid, uneventful, ordinary life. What Goode's play illuminates, instead, is that – underneath the veneer of grief and outrage performed in response to the ostensibly exceptional events of 9/11 or the Woolwich murder – there are, as Berlant puts it, "always screaming men and falling men: one does not much witness them, they live offscreen" (93). The prolonged moments of 'crisis ordinariness' refracted through the experiences of the 'men in the cities' powerfully link the personal with the historical, the private with the political. This is where, in my view, Lyn Gardner's criticism that the piece "never quite ties the threads of its stories together to bring the personal and the political into focus" does not hold ("Powerful Vision" 5). It is precisely through forging these interconnections that the play mobilises trauma so as to enquire "how we in this era can have access to our own historical experience, to a history that is in its immediacy a crisis" (Caruth, "Recapturing" 6). Notably, the first performance took place around a year after the Woolwich murder, at a time when legal proceedings surrounding Adebolajo's appeal against his whole-life order and Michael Adebowale's plea for a reduction in his sentence were ongoing and when both the incident and the juridical response were still being discussed controversially in the media.⁴³ By participating in the formation of narratives surrounding these recent violent events, the play substantiates Catherine Silverstone's point that "performance can be read as offering a traumatic response to events, belatedly 'working through' that which is not yet fully known or accounted for" (16).

If we see the performances of *Men in the Cities* and *The Two Worlds of Charlie F.* as attempts at 'working through' the traumatic moments of the 'war on terror', they provide two opposite models for that process. The latter invites audiences to identify with injured and damaged British subjects, with the position of victims. The former invites them to consider issues of culpability and complicity. While both performances construct their subjects inside the trauma paradigm, *The Two Worlds of Charlie F.* seems more interested in overcoming the trauma, in tracking the post-traumatic growth of subjects worth reintegrating into the 'healthy' fabric of British society. *Men in the Cities*, in contrast, locates the moment of dramatic interest precisely in the subject's realisation of its traumatisation, or the trauma it has inflicted on others. There is no therapeutic arch here, no way of mending the agonies of 'crisis ordinariness'. One could thus also conclude that Sheers's play, through its emphasis on healing and recuperation, endorses the fantasy of the whole subject, or at least a subject that could become unified again if it were to gain control over its narrative(s). Goode's play, instead, illuminates the post-traumatic subjectivity of the "gapped subject" that "cannot remember itself to itself" (Luckhurst, "Traumaculture" 28). Finally, while *The Two Worlds of Charlie F.* seeks to restore the soldiers' heroic masculinity, *Men in the Cities* works to create critical reflexivity about the traumatising effects of hegemonic masculinity, both for those inhabiting this subject position and the social and (sub)urban fabric in which it is implicated.

---

43 Both convicts lost their legal cases in December 2014. The juridical response is explicitly mentioned in the play: "Talking heads on the subject of whole-life sentences" (69).

4 Front-Line Plays: Positioning 'Self', 'Other', and Other Selves in Iraq and Afghanistan

By transferring acts of torture to British housing estates, screening video messages from military camps in Iraq, accentuating the visible wounds of war, and consistently blurring the boundaries between spaces of security and threat, the home-front plays discussed in the previous chapter variously engage with the wars in Iraq and Afghanistan. Though primarily focused on the impact of the 'war on terror' on British society and subjects, they mediate experiences of the distant theatres of war by creating proximity with staged acts of violence, 'real' voices of grief, and the 'authentic' bodies of the injured. In this sense, most plays can be seen as interested in both 'here' and 'there', as tracing the diverse interconnections between the front line and the home front. But there is also a substantial number of post-9/11 plays that distinctly venture into the battle zone. Aleks Sierz, somewhat jocularly yet not inaccurately, subsumes these plays under the theme: "Britons go abroad but they fail to make the world a better place" (*Rewriting* 83). Suman Gupta approximates a genre definition by specifying "the theatrical conventions of frontline drama" as "focalizing the frontline and the participants of invasion there", often through "contemplating 'soldiers at war'" (101–102). There is a case to be made for a discussion of front-line drama as a category in its own right, without losing sight of how these representations oscillate between the 'home' and the 'front'. The label *front-line drama* can serve as a valuable shorthand for highlighting the plays' engagement with the themes, spaces, and participants of military, humanitarian, or economic intervention, even if it remains terminologically imprecise insofar as a clearly delineated front line was lacking both in Iraq, where "urban warfare and guerrilla tactics def[ied] conventional notions of battle zones" (Feitz and Nagel 203), and in Afghanistan, where British forces were routinely involved in firefights and counter-attacks occurring around dispersed forward operating bases (King 313).

An enquiry into the dramatic negotiation of subject positions along and across the blurry lines of the front has its merit in facilitating a continued interrogation of the spatial construction of subjectivity. Theatrical productions that create as-if scenarios of the Iraq and Afghan wars situate the British subject within foreign, distant, and potentially hostile environments. In drama in general, and war plays in particular, "space is an instrument which defines identity and determines the location of difference of self and other" (Starck 63). At issue, then, is the question of how British post-9/11 drama relates to the hegemonic geographies of the 'war on terror'. To what extent, for instance, do the plays contest, reinforce, or rechart the neo-imperial mapping of 'their' spaces as uncivilised, wild, chaotic, dangerous, threatening? Based on the work of Edward W. Said, human geographer Derek Gregory identifies three imaginative geographies, or performances of space, that have been at work since 9/11 in the construction of Iraq and Afghanistan: the first, "Locating", reduces and abstracts the spaces inhabited by the 'other' to the grids of maps and visual displays; the second, "Opposing", constructs an antagonism in terms of the 'clash of civilisations' discourse; the third, "Casting out", turns the 'other' into a political and legal outcast and legitimises taking 'their' lives ("Defiled Cities" 311). The digitised visualisation of the enemy positions as abstract impact points and the televised transmission of intensive bombing are developments carried over from the First Gulf War, which James Der Derian has famously discussed as inaugurating an era of "virtuous war [that] has taken on the properties of a game" (41). Stephen Graham expands on the imaginary geographies of foreign territories, and especially of Arab cities, that are constructed through the representational strategies of the immensely popular urban warfare games:

> Within such games, as with the satellite images and maps [...], it is striking that Arab cities are represented merely as 'collections of objects [...]'. When people *are* represented, almost without exception, they are rendered as the shadowy, subhuman, racialized Arab figure of some absolutely external 'terrorist' [...]. Here, then, once again, the only discursive space for the everyday sites and spaces of Arab cities is as environments for military engagement. ("Cities" 265–266)

This chapter will consider theatrical representations of the wars against the dominant configuration of 'their' spaces as abstract targets for military intervention, as invariably oppositional to Western spaces, and as lacking in ordinary everyday activities and inhabitants. The central question addresses how far the plays can be seen to construct differently situated subjectivities or whether they take over and sustain the geographical imagination, and attendant subject locations, that circulate in the visual and discursive fields of war.

In order to further trace the diverse interconnections between 'here' and 'there', this chapter maps each front-line section onto the trajectory of the previous chapter, creating a corresponding enquiry to the discussion of home-front plays. Since imaginative geographies rest on arbitrary lines of demarcation between "a familiar space which is 'ours' and an unfamiliar space beyond 'ours' which is 'theirs'" (Said 54), a recurrent focus of this chapter will be on the plays' iteration of 'our' and 'their' subject positions and the ways in which theatrical productions navigate the spatial, semantic, and ideological them/us binary. This concern will be especially salient in the first part of this chapter, which interrogates constructions of the enemy in the Iraq and Afghan campaigns, echoing the previous analysis of the positioning of terrorist suspects on the British housing estate. One of the most prominent object positions, which has repeatedly been sutured at the intersection of discourses of 'freedom and democracy' and the civilising mission, is that of the Afghan woman in need of liberation. The second subchapter considers dramatic negotiations of this position against the (neo)colonial trope, "White men are saving brown women from brown men" (Spivak, "Can" 92), corresponding to the previous chapter's emphasis on Muslim femininities. The third section focuses on the neoliberal brand of imperialism at work in the Iraq invasion, revisiting the construction of neoliberal subjectivities, with a shift from civilian citizens to citizen-warriors and from privatised consumers to the mercenaries fighting a privatised war in Iraq. Articulations of mourning on the home front serve as the backdrop for the fourth part, which examines the framing and reporting of grievability in the Iraq war. The final section picks up on the concerns surrounding the masculine subjectivities constructed within the trauma paradigm by analysing performances of military masculinity in front-line plays.

4.1 Determining the Enemy Positions

Attempts at delineating the enemy image in the 'war on terror' revolve around articulations of lack and absence: the post-9/11 enemy is "'shadowy', 'invisible', and 'unseen'" (McClintock 57), "unlocatable" (Mitchell xiii), "faceless" (Jackson 49), "amorphous" (Hunt and Rygiel 17), and "elusive" (Feldman, "Actuarial Gaze" 210). At the heart of the inability to describe, visualise, and locate the enemy sits the paradox of a war declared on an abstract noun, rather than an identifiable adversary. "The concept of a war on terror", as W.J.T. Mitchell declares, "has brought something radically new into the world, perhaps at last forcing a confrontation with the question of *what* – not 'who' – is the enemy" (1). That the enemy cannot be easily captured, neither semantically nor militarily, is problematic insofar as the discursive construction of an enemy 'other' is essential for defining and differentiating the 'self'. As philosopher Carlo Galli posits, "if, to produce a fully formed Us, we need an enemy to exclude, this means that we cannot do without the enemy, that the enemy is somehow constitutive of our own identity" (195).

In the following, I will sketch three ways of theorising the lack of a clearly definable enemy in the 'war on terror', which variously resonate with the representation of the enemy in front-line drama. The first is a historical approach, as proposed, for instance, by media scholar Philip Hammond. He reads the end of the Cold War in 1989 and the 11 September attacks as the pivotal events which have shaped contemporary Western understandings and depictions of the enemy. With the end of the Cold War came what he refers to as "enemy deprivation syndrome", which the declaration of a 'war on terror' promised to resolve: "Radical Islamists and Arabs, it was suggested, might be able to fill the enemy-shaped hole left by the Russians, perhaps in the form of a 'clash of civilisations'" (14). Chantal Mouffe had already anticipated in the early 1990s that, due to the West's dependence on the "existence of the Communist 'other' that constituted its negation", the identity of Western democracy depended on "the creation of a new frontier" (*Return* 3–4). However, due to the "diffuse and elusive character" of terrorist networks like al-Qaeda, where precisely the new frontier was to be located "has not always been as straightforward as some had feared and others had hoped" (Hammond 14). The dominant reading of the 'war on terror' as the successor to the Cold War is evident from discursive articulations well into the last phase of British military involvement. Speaking on the occasion of troop withdrawal from Afghanistan in late 2014, David Cameron offered a brief historical sketch leading up to the present conflict:

> If our great grandfathers were fighting against the Prussian domination of Europe, if our grandfathers were fighting fascism, if our fathers were fighting the cold war against communism, then I am afraid to say – and let us be frank about this struggle against Islamic extremism and terrorism – this is the struggle of our generation. (Qtd. in Wintour)

In Cameron's statement, 'Islamic extremism' becomes a totalitarian worldview comparable to communism during the Cold War. What is also evident from the phrase 'the struggle of our generation' is the hegemonic notion "that terrorism is now considered the greatest danger to western security since the threat of superpower confrontation" (Jackson 92). This perception is manifest in concrete political developments such as the two-and-a-half-fold growth of the UK's Special Branch as compared to the Cold War and the Troubles in Northern Ireland (Fekete 7).

The proposal of a linear succession that leads from the Cold War to the current 'war on terror' conceals the close contiguity between the two conflicts and the concomitant enemy narratives. In fact, constructions of the enemy as "a 'threat to our way of life'" echo back with "well-worn cold war expression[s]" (Jackson 99). As Derrida has pointed out, "'September 11' is [...] a distant effect of the Cold War itself, [...] from the time when the United States provided training and weapons, and not only in Afghanistan, to the enemies of the Soviet Union" (qtd. in Borradori 92). Mahmood Mamdani's work on the 'good Muslim, bad Muslim' narrative, discussed in the previous chapter, provides a coherent account of the Cold War roots of a terrorist movement based on political Islam (*Good Muslim* 11–14). Yet the function of such historical sketches as Cameron's is to present the Cold War and the 'war on terror' as discrete temporal units that follow upon each other but do not overlap. This enables the discursive construction of the 'war on terror' as "unfolding [...] across some kind of geopolitical *tabula rasa*", instead of "landscapes that bear the marks of pre-existing and multiple struggles over enduring colonial, Cold War and other geopolitical orders" (Ingram and Dodds 7). In conjunction with an obliteration of all traces of Cold War connections between Western governments and the mujahideen in Afghanistan or Saddam Hussein's regime in Iraq in policy discourses and documents, this erasure of Cold War and colonial geographies enabled the construction of Iraq and Afghanistan as distinct enemies of the West, legitimising military intervention in their territories (Jeffrey 47–48).

The arbitrary fixing of an amorphous threat onto discrete nation-states ties in with a second reading of the enemy deprivation syndrome. Anne McClintock writes that, as a consequence of the crisis of the visible inaugurated with 11 September 2001, the US government was "faced with an immediate dilemma: how to *embody* the invisible enemy and be visibly seen to punish it?" (57). McClintock suggests that three strategies have worked together to produce the enemy: first, the threat was individualised, given a body and a face in the shape of Osama bin Laden and Saddam Hussein; second, the danger posed by terrorist networks such as al-Qaeda was territorialised within the boundaries of the 'rogue' states Iraq and Afghanistan; third, the enemy was, literally, embodied through practices of incarceration and torture (57–58). The three moves of individualisation, territorialisation, and embodiment can be seen as the most salient attempts to reify the anonymous, unlocatable, and invisible post-9/11 enemy. And yet the enemy continuously resists containment: for instance, until his capture in 2011, bin Laden remained notoriously mutable and elusive, appearing to a global media public only in grainy videos filmed at unknown times and in unspecified locations (Colleran 18).[1] The multiple deflections and disappearances of the enemy are intensely problematic for a war system predicated on a fixed antagonism, as Jonathan Burnett and Dave Whyte point out: "If wars on terrorism are to be successfully represented [...], the terrorist must be ideologically represented as knowable, actionable and controllable in a particular form" (2). Although the elusiveness of the enemy thus poses problems for discursive attempts at warmongering, it also facilitates a constant readjustment and continuation of the war strategy, as Judith Butler argues: "The infinite paranoia that imagines the

---

[1] There is a distinction to be made here between the two prime enemy figures. For Mitchell, bin Laden "seemed less than satisfactory as an iconic figure of the enemy" and it "proved easier to focus attention on Saddam Hussein, a more visible and locatable target" (3).

war against terrorism as a war without end [...] justifies itself endlessly in relation to the spectral infinity of its enemy" (*Precarious Life* 34).

A third and final reading of the invisibility of the enemy is offered by Derrida's identification of the moment "[w]here the principal enemy, the 'structuring' enemy, seems nowhere to be found, where it ceases to be identifiable and thus reliable" (qtd. in Feldman, "Structuring Enemy" 1704). Allen Feldman proceeds from the loss of the structuring enemy to discuss the emerging incommensurability of an unending 'war on terror'. He aptly describes the representational strategies employed to compensate for this loss:

> The principal enemy is replaced by *figures* of the enemy, metaphors, doubles, typifications, traces, apparitions, place holders, envoys and specters that operate as mnemotechniques for political identity threatened by the loss of the enemy as a political archive and exteriorized support. (1705)

The theatrical undertones of this passage are unmistakable. The infinitely mutable enemy makes multiple entries on the 'war on terror' stage in the form of doubles, traces, and apparitions. There is something in Feldman's description that resonates with John Orr and Dragan Klaić's remark, in the introduction to *Terrorism and Modern Drama* (1990), that terrorists "must remain inaccessible and their methods unpredictable. No one must know where they will strike next. They lurk in the wings, hoping their timing and precision will land them in centre stage" (2). Here, the architecture of the theatre, with its division of diegetic and mimetic space, and its differential onstage positions, serves as a metaphor for terrorist (in)visibility. Yet, if "the chief characteristic of terrorism *tout court* is the invisibility of its instruments and agents" (Mitchell 84), this raises questions surrounding the representability of the enemy in contemporary war drama. What is at stake here is a negotiation of the slippery divide between knowability and containment. How best to contest a discursive system that exploits the enemy's elusiveness for an infinite extension of warfare and at the same time strives to render the enemy visible, controllable, locatable? The oscillation between the seen and the unseen, "the *fort/da*, the show, the stage and offstage", which is "the very definition of the theatrical experience" (Colleran 14), provides the point of departure for this enquiry into the representation of the enemy in post-9/11 drama. It seems adequate, then, that this section should start with a discussion of a play in which the enemy is never seen, but merely heard, sensed, and intuited. I will begin by resuming the analysis of Roy Williams's *Days of Significance* (2007), whose home-front scenes were discussed in the previous chapter, followed by a discussion of an Afghan war drama which scenically enacts yet variously problematises the capture of the embodied enemy, DC Moore's *The Empire* (2009).

Spectral Enemies: Roy Williams's *Days of Significance*

In the second act of *Days of Significance*, we follow Williams's working-class protagonists to Basra. Throughout the extended front-line scene – which is structurally bookended by the video messages that were previously discussed – the British soldiers are seeking shelter behind a wall in an alleyway while they are being pursued by a crowd of Iraqis after Ben opened fire on a group of unarmed children. When it comes to theatrical conventions, the scene quite literally yields a teichoscopic perspective on the battle – with a slight variation, as the characters do not primarily report the action but are caught in the middle of it – and thereby evades the difficulty of staging it. This strategy resonates with Karen Malpede's observation that "the formal messenger speech from classic tragedy becomes in contemporary plays of war and witness the memory speech" (xxvi). Rather than seeing acts of violence performed on stage or having them reported in a coherent, chronological manner, audiences are confronted with characters who have just become embroiled in these acts and have not sufficiently processed them yet.

In the original production, the two-part concrete wall, which enclosed performers from behind and from stage right, and the floor in front of it where the soldiers were crouching were positioned further upstage than the scenographic elements of the home-front setting, with the effect that the action taking place in Basra appeared more removed and inscrutable. This impression was reinforced by the use of sidelights, which dimly lit the camouflage patterns of the costumes and partly sculpted the soldiers' bodies and their shadows against the wall.[2] Another effect of this spatial configuration was that the soldiers were orientated towards the offstage space behind the wall, rather than towards the audience as in the acts set in the UK. A ray of light falling on the back wall from behind animated the diegetic space, in which the unseen Iraqi pursuers appear. Lighting and stage design here contribute to a mise-en-scène that resembles the photographic representation of British soldiers in the print media in the context of the Iraq and Afghan wars. Rachel Woodward, Trish Winter, and K. Neil Jenk-

---

[2] Set and costumes were designed by Lizzie Clachan; lighting was by David Holmes. All observations are based on the recording of the performance at the Tricycle Theatre on 28 March 2008, held by the National Video Archive of Performance.

ings discuss a generic photograph (credited to Rob Knight/PA) that accompanied different news stories about the Afghan war in 2006, the year before the premiere of Williams's play. The image shows a group of armed British soldiers positioned around the edges of a doorway set into the wall of a compound. Its composition closely resembles the arrangement in *Days of Significance*, and the scholars' description is therefore worth quoting at some length:

> Bright sunlight streams in through the doorway. Three armed soldiers are intent on what is going on outside the doorway and seem poised [...]. [S]heltering behind the wall and around the perimeter of the door, they are portrayed as vulnerable within potentially hostile territory [...]. The idea of the vulnerability of the soldiers [is] evident [...] by the suggestion of an unseen enemy in the glaring white sunlight seen through the door. (216–217)

Evidently, then, the second act of Williams's play draws on iconic war photography and one of its most common tropes, British soldiers' vulnerability 'within potentially hostile territory'. To hark back to the question of theatre's engagement with the images circulating in the 'war on terror', the production cannot be seen to offer a different visualisation of British involvement in the Iraq war. As the comparison between the conventionalised photographic motif and the image created on stage further suggests, *Days of Significance* does not seem to map out an alternative imaginative geography of Iraq. Just as outlined by Graham's analysis of representations of Arab cities as abstract targets, Iraqi space in the play appears solely as an environment for military engagement, whereas the population inhabiting it is reduced to 'shadowy' figures behind the wall.

The fact that the Iraqi pursuers are relegated to the diegetic space is highly relevant for the play's politics of representing the enemy. This technique can be read against Slavoj Žižek's analysis of a structurally similar sequence from a 1996 film about the Bosnian war, Srdjan Dragojević's *Pretty Village, Pretty Flame*, as a prefiguration of the shift from the reliable to the spectral enemy. Žižek discusses an extended scene where a group of Serb soldiers is trapped inside a railway tunnel by Bosnian fighters:

> The key feature of the narrative [...] is that this stand-off between the two sides [...] is presented entirely from the perspective of those inside the tunnel, the Serb fighters; until the very final dénouement, the 'Muslim side' is presented only as an assemblage of what Michel Chion called 'acousmatic voices' [...] which [...] acquire an all-powerful spectral dimension. [...] The narrative device [...] compels us, the spectators, to identify with the besieged Serb group [...]. In contrast to the Muslims – an unidentified spectral Entity of insults, threats and wild shouts – the Serbs are [...] fully individualized, basically characterized as a bunch of 'crazy but sympathetic' antiheroes. (38–39)

Similar to the film sequence described by Žižek, the Iraqi presence in *Days of Significance* remains completely 'acousmatic', an 'unidentified spectral Entity', audible only through "*[s]ounds of massive gunfire*", "*Arab voices in the distance*", and "*approaching footsteps*" (Williams 52, 65, 67). In a sense, then, the audience are – just as in the dynamics outlined by Žižek – compelled to identify with the trapped British soldiers. Although it is revealed that it was Ben who initiated the action, shooting at a group of children because they presumably gave a "sign to open fire" (58), the three British soldiers are offered as the only point of identification. They are fully individualised too: the audience learn about the football clubs they support (56), their home towns (57) and girlfriends (60 – 63), and they witness Brookes dying from an injury accrued in the initial shoot-out, a process which he eventually speeds up by stabbing himself (67). To a certain extent, then, the spectators are encouraged to identify with the soldiers as 'crazy but sympathetic' antiheroes and share their anxiety about the approaching sounds, voices, and footsteps. There is something in this set-up that conveys the conditions under which the British army operated in Iraq, as captured in innumerable news reports at the time of the performance; for instance, Graeme Lamb, commander of UK ground forces in south-eastern Iraq in 2003, detailed how "[t]he troops worked in dreadful physical conditions, never knowing when, in a moment, an apparently benign situation would turn into a lethal attack" (qtd. in Kerr 408). The suspense generated due to the opacity of the situation (did the soldiers shoot at innocent children, or were these used as decoy for a group of insurgents?) further encourages audiences to side with the British soldiers on the visible side of the wall.

In this regard, the wall could be seen to function as the dividing line between 'self' and 'other'. In contradistinction to the invisible enemies that remain as indistinct as the diegetic space beyond it, the British soldiers are invariably encoded as the 'self'.[3] The spatial configuration enables the soldiers to self-reflexively position themselves against the unseen enemy beyond the wall by employing what Richard Jackson defines as the "derogatory terms [...] by which fellow human beings [...] are discursively transformed into a hateful and loathsome 'other' who can be killed" (60). For example, Sean calls the unseen Iraqis "fucking sand-niggers" (57) or a "fucking tribe" (59), and Ben justifies opening fire

---

3 My reading here is inspired by Merle Tönnies's pointed analysis of the positioning of the Western characters who are kept hostage in a Lebanese prison in Frank McGuinness's *Someone Who'll Watch Over Me* (1992) as the 'self'. Resonating with Žižek's argument cited above, Tönnies observes that "the audience clearly identifies with [the visible Westerners] rather than with the unseen Arabs, who in their turn strengthen the Western group by being encoded as its 'Other'" (78).

with reference to the subhuman status of Iraqis: "Those kids, they're nothing but maggots. [...] They are not people, they aren't human, they are the enemy, alright?" (58). In particular the tag question at the end of Ben's speech invites his fellow soldiers to cohere around a patriotic subject position forged in wartime propaganda, one that constructs the British soldier in opposition to the inhuman enemy 'other'. Yet it is precisely the soldiers' attempt at positioning themselves as righteous warriors that alienates spectators from the characters. Especially the fact that these discursive strategies are mobilised against (quite possibly innocent) children underlines the cruelty of such appellations. Uttered against an invisible enemy, the derogatory terms employed by 'our' soldiers turn against themselves: it is the speaker, not the object designated by the racist insults, who appears morally debased. The fact that the front-line act is entitled "On the Side of the Angels" adds another ironic note to the soldiers' attempts at stylising themselves as 'a force for good'.

Moreover, the idea of a clearly circumscribed 'self' that can be neatly delineated from the 'other' beyond the dividing line is variously undercut on the level of dramatic discourse. An essential aspect in this is Brookes's ethnic identity. As Bénédicte Ledent argues, "'race' is not wholly irrelevant to *Days of Significance*" (301), in spite of its emphasis on white working-class characters and uneasy categorisation as black British drama. Ledent foregrounds the role of Brookes as an ethnic minority soldier in the British army, holding that, "if race sets Brookes apart, so does his moral sense" (301). The presence of the black soldier makes the othering process at work in Ben's and Sean's speeches untenable. Brookes condemns Sean's use of the epithet *sand-niggers* by pointing out his own status on the margins of white British society: "A white boy don't say the N-word in front of a brudda from Harlesden" (57). The fact that the only black soldier is seen to die on stage, whereas the white soldiers die *entr'acte*, is quite significant. For Ledent, Brookes becomes "fully part of England through his war sacrifice" (303), which confirms British national identity as a multicultural one. Yet there is something deeply disturbing about watching the scenic presentation of the black soldier's death. Mary Louise Pratt's note on "war as a mechanism whereby human collectivities renew and revitalize themselves by sacrificing a select number of their own members" (1521) offers further insight here: rather than reading the sacrifice as an inclusive ritual that makes Brookes 'fully part of England', it could also be seen as a purifying one. The inclusion of ethnic minorities within the British subject position is, accordingly, tenuous and conditional, which does not allow for a stable manifestation of a homogeneous British 'self' on the visible side of the wall. The putative separation between 'us' and 'them' is thus redrawn in a way that imagines "the nation split within itself", as Homi K. Bhabha writes of the "liminal signifying space" of the Western nation (148).

Divisions within the signifying space of the nation are further highlighted by the use of the metaphor of football rivalries, a theme that Williams had explored at length in *Sing Yer Heart Out for the Lads* (2002). Before Ben joins them behind the wall, Brookes and Sean speak about the child at whom he shot:

BROOKES. How old you reckon the kid was? Ten?
SEAN. Twelve.
BROOKES. How can you be so sure?
SEAN. He was the same height as my brother. Looked like him as well – he was always running around with a bloody football in his hands, wearing that stupid Arsenal top.
BROOKES. Eh, you have a problem with Arsenal now?
SEAN. I do, as it goes.
BROOKES. Oh Jesus, you are, innit, a Spurs man [...].
SEAN. Eat shit and die. (56)

Significantly, the Iraqi child becomes intelligible to the soldiers not in terms of the enemy image but for the similarities they share. The supposed enemy is legible precisely because he appears in the same shape and garments (Sean's reference to 'that stupid Arsenal top' is ambiguous; is he referring to his brother only or the fact that his brother wears the same shirt as the Iraqi boy?). The Iraqi children are killed for engaging in the same practices as Westerners, in a game whose codes the invaders understand, or think they understand: Ben is sure that, "when he dropped that ball, that was their sign to open fire" (58).

What the scene clearly demonstrates is the paranoid perspective that makes 'us' misread the 'other' as the enemy. Ben's alleged spotting of a 'sign to open fire' recalls the way in which military strategies in the Iraq war have been heavily based on structures of gaming. A notorious example would be the deck of playing cards issued by the US military to help soldiers identify personae such as Saddam Hussein (the ace of spades); this practice came to popular attention through films like Kathryn Bigelow's *Hurt Locker* (2008) or Paul Greengrass's *Green Zone* (2010). Writing on the pervasive culture of video war games, Sara Brady notes that "we all play the 'good guys' – US soldiers. There is no option to play the 'enemy'" (88). The workings of a virtualised first-person perspective geared towards detecting and eliminating the enemy are put into sharpest focus in this scene from *Days of Significance*. Due to the modes of seeing and judging inculcated by these popular practices, Williams's soldiers cannot apprehend the Iraqi child as the same, but misrecognise him as an uncanny double: if the 'other' appears familiar, it must be a deliberate deception to unleash violence on 'us'. The tragic moment of anagnorisis is not dissimilar to the realisation of

William S. Wallace, commander of US ground forces during the 2003 invasion, who "complained to the *Washington Post* that '[t]he enemy we're fighting is different from the one we'd war-gamed against'" (Mirzoeff 1740).

Implicitly, the scene criticises the discursive enlistment of children in the 'war on terror' effort as a justification of the military intervention. As Catherine Scott has observed, "Kids in Afghanistan, Iraq and the US are depicted as having their childhood innocence stolen or interrupted by the Taliban, the dictator Saddam Hussein, and the September 11 terror attacks" (101). Scott discusses a notable discursive strategy that consists in juxtaposing the plight of Iraqi children under the dictatorship or of Afghan children under the Taliban – interestingly, one of the most frequently cited facts was that they were not allowed to play football – with images celebrating "the 'return' of their childhood thanks to the [...] rescue operations" (102). By throwing into relief the violence endured by children in the war zone, which is occluded by the rescue narrative, the scene does more than just replicate the imaginative geographies of 'their' spaces as prototypically dangerous. It rather reveals how the lack of a more complex geographical imagination leads to the violent disruption of 'their' everyday lives, sites, and activities – for there is no way to mark these mundane spaces in the digitised maps informing the invasion.

To go back to Brookes and Sean's exchange, a further analogy between 'them' and 'us' is established with their discovery that they support the long-standing rivals Arsenal and Tottenham Hotspur Football Club respectively. Considering Kritzer's comment regarding the "racial and regional loyalties" expressed through football enmities in Williams's work (160), one can read this exchange as a metaphorical rearticulation of the confrontations that have dominated perceptions of the Iraq conflict, most prominently the Sunni-Shia divide, in 'our' terms. The excessive importance placed on football loyalties in a situation of acute emergency exposes the British subject position as split rather than unified, and it could be read as an allusion to British complicity in fuelling sectarian tensions in Iraq, "as part of their policy of 'Divide and Rule'" (Chalabi). By retracing these divisions on 'this' side of the wall, the play shifts the focus from the them/us dichotomy to the fault lines within each culture, suggesting that "what we are witnessing today are, rather, clashes *within* each civilization" (Žižek 41). In other words, the refusal to embody the 'other' and concomitant emphasis on the 'self' conveys the sense that, as Paul Gilroy puts it, "the fissures, folds and leaks within civilizations deserve more attention than the much-vaunted clashes between them" ("Multiculture" 439).

In conclusion, there are essentially two, fairly irreconcilable, ways of thinking through the implications of withholding the enemy's body from the mimetic space of the stage. As was outlined at the outset, the discursive regime works to both exploit and contain the invisibility of the enemy, on the one hand justifying itself 'in relation to the spectral infinity of its enemy', as Butler submits, on the other hand carving out discursive attempts to individualise, territorialise, and embody the enemy, as McClintock demonstrates. Certainly, *Days of Significance* challenges hegemonic attempts at suturing the position of the enemy. Since the spectral entities refuse to become visible on stage, the discursive construct of the 'other' never obtains a material substantiation. Furthermore, if the enemy is constitutive of 'our' own identity, the refusal to give a voice, face, and body to the enemy also calls into doubt the homogeneous collectivity that makes up 'our' group. One might, however, also detect reactionary tendencies in this dramaturgy of absence. As with the shadowy figure appearing in the doorway of the routine war photograph, the sense of the British soldiers' vulnerability conveyed in the scene is heightened through the purely acousmatic appearance of the pursuers. Mitchell expounds that invisibility is "a crucial property of terrorism as such. The idea is to turn the imagination against itself by provoking a psychotic state" (84). It follows from this that the spectral enemy device could serve to reinforce paranoid perceptions of the enemy's multiple, undetected (re)appearances in the form of traces, doubles, and apparitions. If the spectral enemy does not appear on stage, he or she may still be lurking in the wings, as Orr and Klaić might put it. I would nevertheless contend that the dramatic strategy of withholding the 'other' from view can be seen to exhibit, rather than reinforce, the workings of this paranoid perspective. Žižek concludes his reading of *Pretty Village, Pretty Flame* with the question: "if the Enemy is purely [...] spectral, what if it is just a paranoiac projection of the Serbs themselves [...]?" (39). Ultimately, if 'our' subject position depends on 'their' inhumanity and barbarity but these features do not manifest themselves on stage, 'our' position is fundamentally destabilised. And if the spectral enemy persistently refuses to become visible, locatable, embodied, the enemy figure may be exposed as a (paranoid) projection of 'our' own attributes.

Embodying the Enemy, Encountering the 'Self': DC Moore's *The Empire*

The paranoid scheme at work in constructions of the enemy 'other' is further elucidated in a play that centres upon the difficulty of encountering and embodying the enemy. DC Moore's *The Empire*, which premiered at the Royal Court Theatre Upstairs in 2010, revolves around the capture of a supposed Taliban fighter who turns out to be a British citizen. The dramatic style of *The Empire* could be characterised as *Pinteresque:* like Harold Pinter's room plays, the piece is set in an enclosed space, "*[a]n empty room, part of an abandoned compound in a remote region of the Helmand Province*" (Moore 3). Moreover, there is a constant atmosphere of menace, an individual's power struggle with authority, and the rhythmic back-and-forth of *Pinteresque* exchange (see Shaw 211–214). Having said that, the sense of menace is clearly a less abstract one in Moore's play, which locates itself, literally and figuratively, in the heat of the Afghan war. As indicated in the script, it is set in "*Summer 2006*" (3), right after the start of Operation Herrick 4, which saw "a major escalation of British involvement in Afghanistan, involving the assumption of responsibility for Helmand" (King 314). The set and lighting design of the original production,[4] aptly described by one critic in terms of a "hazily filtered glare" (P. Taylor 15), made the stifling heat of Afghanistan in the summer, and more generally the heat of battle, viscerally palpable. Similar to the enemy's silhouette appearing in the doorway of generic war photographs or the sounds of gunfire and shouts beyond the wall in *Days of Significance*, the performance maintained a constant sense that the situation might escalate, or that the fighting might erupt into the wrecked room that made for the scenic space, full of bullet holes and filled with rubble.

The play begins with the very act of producing the enemy's body: British soldier Gary and Afghan soldier Hafizullah, who has gone AWOL from the Afghan National Army (ANA), "*carry a dirtied and bloodied body*" that "*is dressed in local traditional dress (shalwar kameez, etc.)*" (3) into the derelict room. Even before the dialogue provides clues as to how to interpret this body, the visual codes enable spectators to read it according to the knowledge distributed about the Afghan conflict. The apparent capture of a Talib in an isolated makeshift compound appears like an exemplary incident in the British forces' Helmand campaign, which was "defined by the dispersion of forces into isolated forward operating bases (FOBs) and recurrent but indecisive offensive operations against the [Taliban]" (King 313). The dialogue begins with a reading of the man's physiognomy:

HAFIZULLAH. Punjabi.
GARY. Punwhat?
HAFIZULLAH. Punjabi. From Pakistan.
GARY. Is he? [...] How can ya like, tell?
HAFIZULLAH. His face.
GARY. OK, yeah, suppose he does look a bit more.
He gestures vaguely to his own face. A pause as they both look down and consider the body.
GARY. Whatever he is, he's a bit fat, inny? [...] [F]or a Terry. [...]
HAFIZULLAH *shrugs*. (4)

---

4 Set design: Bob Bailey; lighting design: Jason Taylor.

The brief exchange testifies to the divergent scripts from which the characters derive their knowledge about the conflict. Being a 'native' of Afghanistan, Hafizullah can seemingly effortlessly distinguish between people's ethnic origins. Gary, in contrast, lacks awareness of these ethnic categories, let alone their application. There is only one reading of the foreign body available to him: anyone captured in traditional dress on a battlefield must be a Talib ('Terry').[5] While Gary's assumption is preconditioned by the scripts of war, Hafizullah is reluctant to combine the signs exhibited by the captive body to the labels circulating in British army talk.

Gary's assessment is confounded, however, as soon as the captive regains consciousness. It is then that the play turns into what Peter Buse has elsewhere called a "drama of contested interpellation" (100; see chapter two). Buse's application of Althusser's theory to Trevor Griffiths's play *Comedians* bears relevance to the opening of *The Empire*. "If the instant of ideology is the act of recognition – the answer 'Yes, it's me' to the policeman's 'Hey, you!'", as Buse writes, "it is significant that *Comedians* starts with a hesitation over recognition" (99). For him, the play thus stages "a refusal to be positioned as a subject, or interpellated" (100). A similar mechanism can be discerned in *The Empire* once the captive begins to speak. Groaning with pain, the first lines spoken by Zia, with a British accent, are "Oh my days" and "Oh my gosh" (21), which position the speaker in the same linguistic register as Gary and immediately disrupt the previous reading of the body as Taliban fighter. The resulting confusion is evident from their first exchange:

A moment as they all consider each other.
ZIA. (*To both of them.*) Who ... who are you?
GARY. No.
ZIA. And what you ... what you doing?
GARY. No. [...] Let's. Let's. OK. Let's. Start. With the start.
ZIA. (*Gesturing to his plasticuffs.*) And wha's this about?
GARY. That's to stop you ... fucking ... No, no – actually, right? – [...] you're not *asking* questions here, mate. That's not ... that's not how it's gonna fucking work, OK? Let's establish that now. (22 – 23)

Where, before, the British and Afghan soldiers claimed the prerogative of interpretation, Zia now seeks to establish his own subjectivity on stage. He will not be reduced to the object position of enemy 'other', but is determined to shape his relationship with his captors by turning around the mode of enquiry. Yet Gary

---

[5] "Terry Taliban" is a typical name given to presumed Taliban fighters by British soldiers on the ground in Afghanistan; Gary uses this phrase at a later point in the dialogue (31).

refuses to participate in an interlocution in which speakers interactively position each other. Since answering Zia's questions would make him accountable to the prisoner, he declines to respond and, instead, tries to gain authorship over the conversation. Gary's attempt at achieving dominance reflects his own subordination in the army ranks. By seeking to establish a hierarchical relationship in which he is the one in command, Gary attempts to place Zia into the same subjugated position in which he normally finds himself, one of unquestioningly following orders. His status in the army, manifest in the continuous refusals by the corporal, Simon, to explain operating procedures to Gary ("You don't need to understand. Though it is pretty simple" [19]), is transferred into subjugation of the enemy 'other'.

Rather than taking up the location offered to him in the conversation instigated by the captive, Gary tries to assert a position from which he hails the 'other' by starting an impromptu interrogation: "Proper, first off. [...] What's your name?" (24). As in the scene discussed by Buse, there is a noticeable hesitation over recognition, a refusal to be interpellated. It is only after Gary reiterates the question several times that Zia responds: "OK. (*Pause.*) Zia" (25). Just as in rhythmic *Pinteresque* dialogue, the pause here is significant, for it indicates some awareness of and struggle against subjection. Moreover, this illuminates what Butler, glossing Emmanuel Levinas, describes as the subject's situation in discourse: "there is a certain violence already in being addressed, given a name, [...] compelled to respond to an exacting alterity" (*Precarious Life* 139). The power relations of captivity and the structure of interrogation in *The Empire* heighten the subject's vulnerability to the violence at stake in providing 'an exacting alterity' with one's name. "To be addressed", as Butler continues, "is to be [...] deprived of will, and to have that deprivation exist as the basis of one's situation in discourse" (139). This is precisely the discursive dynamic that is established as soon as Zia tells Gary his name.

This explains why it is possible for Gary to keep positioning Zia as a terrorist enemy, in spite of the latter's continuous demands to be recognised as an innocent British subject. Zia makes one attempt after another to reflexively position himself: "I wanna let you know I'm not ... [...] I'm not ..." (27). Notably, he cannot even bring himself to use the appellation *terrorist*, as if the mere utterance would invariably associate him with the attendant subject form. Zia does manage to get across parts of his narrative in an attempt at subjectivation:

> I'm on holiday [...] – I don't drink or do none of that, yeah? Though, though I used to, back in the days, I was a bit of a boy, yeah? But, but not now though, [...] cut it all out [...]. So yeah, it was just meant to be like a quiet family holiday thing this time. Went to Pakistan first and I just came over with some, some business. (29)

4.1 Determining the Enemy Positions — 177

Zia's speech could be read in terms of the Foucauldian technique of the confession, as "self-examination, explanation of oneself, revelation of what one is" ("About the Concept" 2). Zia's endeavour to reveal himself as a reformed 'rude boy' ultimately fails, however, since Gary refuses to recognise Zia as the subject he projects himself to be. Gary constantly interrupts the narrative by recurrence to signifiers of Islamic terrorism: "What, like jihad business?" (29). Zia's attempts at positioning himself as a disoriented traveller ("I was with my uncle in Lahore, [...] and I was a bit ..." [32]) are all channelled into this direction as Gary finishes his sentences for him ("Of a terrorist" [33]). Although these lines are intended for comic effect – when I saw the original production in 2010, the audience laughed a great deal at these repartees – Zia's increasing despair conveys what is at stake for him in having his 'true' identity established. The speaker may employ confessional markers of speech, but the confession has ceased to work as a technology of the self. The formula 'I am', supposedly one of the most straightforward methods of identifying oneself, entirely loses its validity here. The only type of confession available to the speaker is the one established in the penal system, whereby "the accused accept[s] the charge and recognize[s] its truth" (Foucault, *Discipline* 38). The fact that Zia can only confess to a predetermined truth that confirms the "founding interpellation" (Butler, *Bodies* 8) as terrorist is underscored when he eventually makes the statement expected of him: "I can't lie to you no more. [...] All started. This day. I was. I was walking round Whitechapel – [...] and Osama Bin Laden [...] comes up to me" (79). Zia's parodic enunciation of the terrorist confession not only exposes the sheer absurdity of the scripts of war but it also points to the subject's access to strategies of subversion despite being caught in the asymmetrical power relations of captivity (see Foucault, "Will to Knowledge" 292), as he effectively sabotages the interrogation.

Zia's inability to attain a subject position other than that of terrorist/Talib, assigned to him before he could even come into enunciation, highlights the arbitrary ascription of such labels. As is the case with Gary in Dennis Kelly's *Osama the Hero*, Zia's attempts at subjectivation are negated. Just as the only subject position offered to Kelly's character in the torture scene is defined in antagonism to the patriots, the British soldier in *The Empire* cannot allow for a self-determined positioning of the captive. The discourse on the Afghan campaign regulates the identity of the players in a way that does not allow for much ambiguity. Gary's stubborn persistence emphasises the paranoid structure that underlies what Talal Asad terms a "hermeneutics" which "always presupposes that what appears on the surface is not the truth and seeks to control what lies beneath" (31). Asad's description of the hermeneutics of suspicion resonates with the shift, in *The Empire*, from the reading of the body to contested interpellation in speech:

> One begins with a human body having an appropriate appearance and origin: racial, sexual, and religious categories are what give the interrogator his starting signs. But he has to go beyond the words spoken by the subject to other signs – mode of speech, gesture, posture, etc. – that indicate hidden meanings. (32)

The more Zia tries to establish a subjective position for himself, the more firmly Gary objectifies him as a terrorist. Ironically, Gary increasingly has to draw on knowledge not about the Afghan conflict but about British society in order to be able to interpret the 'hidden meanings' underneath the traveller's feeble alibi. Zia strives to create a bond with Gary by positioning himself in terms of a shared cultural identity: "I just. Missed it. [...] England. Home. [...] Everything bruv. [...] Decent cars. Decent TV. Decent. Women" (33). But Gary only concedes a racially marked, 'improper' Britishness to Zia. He maintains the separation from Zia as 'other' by mobilising what Bhabha deems the liminal signifying space of the 'nation home': "in my class at school, there was only three white kids, including me. So all I heard, all day long, was exactly this kinda gangsta singsong" (36). It is precisely his knowledge, or rather "situated ignorance" (Pred 365), about ethnic 'otherness' in British society that supposedly enables Gary to detect lies in Zia's speech: "And you get used to 'em – [...] denying *everything* under the fucking sun" (37). As Ellen Redling has accurately pointed out in her brief commentary on the play, *The Empire* thus links the Afghan conflict to cultural anxieties and class issues on the home front by posing "the civic question of who fights England's wars and why" (164).

The perceived unreliability of Zia as speaker of his self-narrative exemplifies the departure of the structuring enemy. The techniques of capture and interrogation, designed to produce the body of the enemy and render him/her accountable, turn out to be inapplicable to the convoluted Afghan conflict, where the subject positions of 'self' and 'other' variously intersect. It is extremely relevant for the politics of the play that Zia's innocence cannot be safely established by the other characters, nor by the audience. His narrative about having gone on a family holiday to Pakistan, then travelled to Afghanistan, where he was kidnapped and abandoned on the battlefield, is strongly reminiscent of the tale(s) of the 'Tipton Three', the young British Muslims who travelled from Pakistan to Afghanistan, where they were captured by Northern Alliance soldiers, sent to Sheberghan prison, and eventually deported to Guantánamo Bay detention camp. Their ordeal has become widely known in the UK and internationally through Michael Winterbottom and Mat Whitecross's docudrama *The Road to Guantánamo*

(2006), which interleaves interview segments with dramatised sequences about the men's (forced) travels and imprisonment. Notably, the film fully assumes the perspective of those affected, offering "a limited focalisation through the eyes of its protagonists, whose account is taken for granted and never juxtaposed with another point of view" (Haschemi Yekani 71–72). In marked contrast, Zia's account is continuously interrupted by Gary's interjections. Whereas *The Road to Guantánamo* implicitly affirms the men's claim to innocence, spectators of Moore's play are likely to be equally repelled by Gary's racist rejections of Zia's speech as by the latter's increasingly unnerving pleas and his self-indulgent, digressive narrative.

Although Zia's account is not altogether implausible, there are a few hints that he is not entirely trustworthy. First of all, due to the excessive emphasis on the spelling of Zia's name ("*Zia*. Z-I-A. Rhymes with, Leah, yeah, but with a Z" [25]), spectators might wonder if the name was chosen to associate the character with Ziad Jarrah, one of the suspected hijacker pilots in the 9/11 attacks.[6] Second, Zia's attempt at bribing Hafizullah when they are alone, telling the young Afghan that his "father is. Quite rich. [...] GP. Could set you up. For life" (49), raises questions as to his avowed innocence. Third, after Gary's and Simon's persistent refusals to give credence to his narrative, the captive eventually loses his poise:

> *Shut*. I've had enough *white boys* talking today. They can listen now. [...] I come to Lahore, just to get away from the, the *noise of you* [...], making all your *shit*, buying all the, all this *shit* you buy, watching all the *shit* you people, [...] while other people, my people, real people are ... And then you get all like, all this like: 'Why are all these people so angry? Why are all these people so *fucking angry all the fucking time?*' [...] How could I not be angry? (81)

The inarticulate, repetitive, and incoherent manner in which Zia voices his anger betrays the genuineness of the sentiment. Zia's outburst bears resemblance to the articulation of despair by that other terrorist suspect on the home front, Nigel in Henry Adam's *The People Next Door*. It is expressive of an antagonism that belies his previous attempt at bonding with Gary over a shared cultural identity. Consequently, as much as Zia's anger could indicate his culpability in committing acts of violence against British soldiers and thereby confirm the charge against him, his speech is also a powerful demonstration of how the vio-

---

6 Ziad Jarrah's prominent role as the pilot of the notorious United Airlines Flight 93 and his centrality to various films and docudramas on the topic (especially Greengrass's critically acclaimed *United 93* [2006]) might trigger such speculations.

lence perpetrated by state armies abroad produces the very terrorists they seek to track down and punish.

The confrontations between 'us' and 'them' on the front line bear striking similarities to the dynamics of positioning in home-front plays. The subject position of the citizen patriot at home is transferred to the citizen-warrior sent out to fight against the enemy 'other' in the war zone. The lack of visible enemies in the mimetic space of Williams's *Days of Significance* throws into relief the processes whereby racialised subjects come to stand in for the enemy, as surrogate terrorists. Mitchell's notion of the terrorist as clone, "or a sleeper cell that 'incubates' inside the body of its host" (74), underlies not only the attribution of terrorist credentials to an unlikely 'host' in plays such as *The People Next Door*, but it is also reflected by Williams's soldiers' suspicion of and attack on Iraqi children. In the case of Adam's play, it is the quirky innocence of the terrorist suspect and, in *Days of Significance*, the enemy's marked absence in the realm of vision that critically inflects the operations of a discursive formation that categorises subjects according to particular forms of knowledge. Within this visual and discursive field, subjects that fall into categories liable to suspicion are denied access to the active process of assuming subjectivity that is associated with subjectivation. This is exemplified by the torture scene in *Osama the Hero*, which oscillates between the culture of suspicion generated at home and the production of the enemy's body in interrogation centres and prisons abroad, and by the struggle over recognition in *The Empire*. Similar to Gary's failed attempts at subjectivation in Kelly's play, Zia stands in for those racialised subjects who cannot assert their subjectivity outside the strictures of a discourse that overdetermines their position as 'other'. The inherent multiplicity of subject positions ceases to provide the agency that comes with the subject's negotiation of (contradictory) positions when agents of state power regulate processes of interpellation. Overall, with the divisions emerging between subjects on 'our' side of the wall and the capture of a British subject instead of Taliban fighter, both front-line plays revolve around scenarios in which, instead of seizing on the enemy 'other', British subjects are invariably confronted with the 'self'. Consequently, the resistant potential of staging spectral or unreliable enemies may be seen to lie in exposing "the delusion of a visible confrontation" in the 'war on terror' by showing that, instead, the "fundamental antagonism [...] points [...] to *triumphant globalization battling against itself*" (Baudrillard 11).

The lack of 'a visible confrontation' in these front-line plays is critically reflective of the disjunction between the conventional military 'boots on the ground' offensive and the deterritorialised nature of terrorist organisations. While international terrorism and insurgency-related violence defy the traditional notion of the battlefield, these plays somewhat stubbornly stick to the theatrical conventions of front-line plays. Their contemplation of "'soldiers at war' – especially 'our soldiers'" (Gupta 102) can, in the context of its apparent incongruity with asymmetrical warfare, be read in terms of a critical mimesis. The 'dissensus' between the staging of the traditional figures of war drama and the acousmatic, spectral, or unreliable presence/absence of the enemy interrupts "the atrophic, petrified projections of self and other mobilised by the mimetic excesses of a system in crisis" (Hughes, *Performance* 18). These front-line plays set a distinct spatial imaginary against the iconic places that mark earlier wars, such as the trench warfare of the First World War, as dramatised, for instance, in R.C. Sheriff's *Journey's End* (1928). Although Sheriff's play similarly conveys the "claustrophobia and terror of an enemy invisible yet horrifyingly close" (Luckhurst, "Wounded Stage" 307), Williams and Moore base their dramaturgies on the hazy contours not only of the front line but also of the enemy profile. It seems to be no coincidence that both chose makeshift structures as their setting, derelict spaces into which dispersed firefights might erupt at any time. There are no trenches that would enable 'us' to determine the enemy positions. If state surveillance and violence aim to "visualize, expose, display and to affix the identity and location of hidden terrorist agency" (Feldman, "Actuarial Gaze" 208), the plays reviewed here deliberately refuse to contribute to that endeavour.

Line of Flight III: Victoria Brittain and Gillian Slovo's *Guantanamo*

While *Days of Significance* employs the invisibility paradigm and *The Empire* reflects the hermeneutics of suspicion in order to critically inflect readings of the enemy image in the 'war on terror', Victoria Brittain and Gillian Slovo's much-discussed verbatim piece *Guantanamo: 'Honor Bound to Defend Freedom'* contests the juridical frames whereby the 'other' is reduced to subhuman status. The spoken evidence play was commissioned by Nicolas Kent and premiered at the Tricycle Theatre in 2004. As one of the earliest theatrical responses discussed in this study, it made for an urgent intervention at the time of its original production: it was staged just months after five of the British detainees had been released from Guantánamo Bay detention camp and at a time when two of the UK residents/citizens on whose testimony the play relies were still held at the facility. Performances thus called considerable attention to the incarceration of British suspects at Guantánamo at a time before Moazzam Begg (one of the characters) became a highly mediatised figure (see Colleran 183) or films such as *The Road to Guantánamo* made the case of the 'Tipton Three' widely known.

The play explicitly juxtaposes a humanising representation of the detainees with the "anonymity, voicelessness and disempowerment" (Rubik 55) effectuated by the widely disseminated photographs of shackled men wearing surgical masks, blackened goggles, and industrial earmuffs. Whereas "the men behind the hoods were not identifiable as individuals", the piece "restored individual voices and fates to some of the (British) detainees [...], so that they regained their subjectivity", as Margarete Rubik argues (55). The fact that the detainees are given a speaking position in the performance is relevant. Following Emily Mann's definition of testimonial theatre, Wendy Hesford writes that the re-presentation of testimonial letters in the piece not only individualises and humanises the detainees but also positions spectators as empathetic listeners (36). Consequently, the representational strategies of *Guantanamo* could be seen to successfully counter the photographs that render the enemy "faceless and abject" (Butler, *Precarious Life* 73). How does this restitution of subjectivity work against the topographical conditions under which subject positions emerge in the field of the 'war on terror'? *Guantanamo* is, perhaps, the play that reaches most severely beyond the ostensible division between 'home' and 'front' territories. Its deterritorialising impetus is already implicit in the title. The toponym *Guantanamo* appears noteworthy for the spatial and legal ambiguity it evokes. While it is, as Ursula Canton suggests, arguably "a clear reference to a place in the world outside the theatre" (88), Guantánamo, at the same time, eludes the certainties of place identity and territorial sovereignty. This is where Giorgio Agamben's point about the camp as the fundamental biopolitical paradigm comes back into view: Guantánamo Bay is an exemplary site of the "zone of undecidability with respect to the state of exception" (Agamben, *State* 2). Its geopolitical and legal indeterminacy is manifest in the fact that the detention camp is placed outside the juridical order. Within this zone of indistinction and the permanent state of emergency established therein, detainees "undergo a suspension of their ontological status as subjects" (Butler, *Precarious Life* 67). For Agamben, those who enter the camp become *homines sacri*, "situated in a limit zone between life and death [...], in which they [are] no longer anything but bare life" (*Homo Sacer* 159). In McClintock's reading, this effacement of the detainees' subjecthood jars with the concomitant need to produce the enemy through incarceration and surveillance; Guantánamo is, accordingly, simultaneously a site where certain subjects "are made juridically spectral, conjured into legal ghosts" and spectacularly displayed as enemy bodies, "in however phantasmagoric a form" (67).

Even though the play indisputably contests – and possibly provokes outrage at – the legal manoeuvrings that have led to the men's detention, it bears scrutiny to what extent the spectatorial act of "collective rhetorical witnessing" (Hesford 35) remains confined within precisely those geopolitical boundaries that the space of exception exceeds. Clearly, the testimonies re-presented in the play achieve a high level of reflexivity about the suspension of law and the implications this entails for the prisoners' (lack of) status. There are a number of passages where the detainees reflect on the arbitrary interrogation script, the kind of "fanatical questions" they were asked, or the euphemistic labels applied to that process, such as "reservation" or "exhibition" (Brittain and Slovo 17, 39). The additional contextual information provided by the figures of lawyers elucidates how the detainees had to be redefined as "unlawful combatants" in order to circumvent the Geneva Conventions (32). Over the course of the testimonies, the play traces the elimination of the men's legal and political subject status, their reduction to what Agamben calls *bare life*. There are a number of passages which provide poignant glimpses of the process whereby "the human body is separated from its normal political status and abandoned, in a state of exception, to the most extreme misfortunes", as Agamben writes of the camp (*Homo Sacer* 159). These include references to the detainees' exposure to scorpions, mice, and spiders whose bite "causes flesh to decay" (37) and a detailed description of the modification of the human body and posture through the different chains placed on the men (37–38). A stark illustration of the way in which the prisoners have, in visual representations, been "likened to caged and restrained animals" (Butler, *Precarious Life* 73) was also provided by the staging, "with detainees wearing orange jumpsuits in mesh prison cages or on narrow cots" (Hesford 35).

The fact that audiences are brought into close proximity with performers standing in for these *homines sacri*, positioned as listeners to their painful testimonies, could point to the formation of a kind of border-crossing alliance. Gargi Bhattacharyya surmises that "[i]t is impossible for the consumer of [...] global media to be unaware that horrors are being carried out 'in our name'", and she sees the formation of a "global audience and consciousness" as one of the central features of the 'war on terror' (1–2). Indeed, the performance might be seen to build an empathy that reaches beyond the "lush atmosphere of a West End theatre" into "the wire cages modelled on those of Camp Delta" (Canton 87).[7] Yet the kind of solidarity that the play seems to foster is not unconditional, neither is it genuinely global. The indistinct juridico-political status of both the prisoners and the space of the camp is 'domesticated' by means of an exclusive focus on British detainees. Although the play ends on the reference, spoken by a

---

7 Canton is here referring to the Ambassadors Theatre in the West End, where the play transferred in the 2004 season.

voice-over, that most of the detainees still held in Guantánamo at the time of performance "are from countries with even less power than Britain to influence events" (62), the play's singular interest is in the fate of the British captives. The outrage at the erasure of the men's subjectivity thus becomes inseparable from the consternation that UK residents or citizens could be treated in such inhumane ways.

Significantly, the play begins with relatives recounting the life stories of the detainees as prototypical British biographies, of hard-working students acquiring their GCSEs and A-levels (6–7), participating in extra-curricular sports activities (8), or being popular and helpful with the neighbours (19). As Rubik summarises, "their memories of normal British life serve to transpose them U.K.-wards as one of 'us'" (57). In the testimonial letters, the detainees display the sense of irony and sarcasm that is often associated with 'British humour'; some question how they could have been deprived of their human rights, given that they are British citizens ("I'm from Manchester, what am I doing here?" [41]). The testimonies of the relatives and lawyers invariably position the men as British and as 'good' Muslims, as comments such as "Bisher [...] was reasonably devout but he's the sort of guy that can sleep for England – he used to sleep through morning prayers" (19) establish. The humanising function of the testimonies doubtlessly works to resist the reductive enemy image operating in detention discourses and practices, but this seems to be facilitated through a replication of the good-versus-bad-Muslim binary and a focus on the men's Britishness. Overall, the testimonial letters and narratives serve to construct a "victim identity" (Hesford 37), which ties the audience's empathy to the men's presumed innocence. This brings to mind Gregory's cautionary remark that "our horror ought not to be measured by the innocence or guilt of the prisoners [...] but by the calculated withdrawal of subjecthood from all of them" ("Vanishing Points" 215).

Ultimately, then, what audiences are witnessing is not so much the violent reduction of subjectivity but the restoration of life, or more accurately, the "politically qualified life" (Agamben, *Homo Sacer* 2) of British citizens. This raises questions about the limits of the play's potential in resisting the frames that enable indefinite detention. The play's overall gesture "toward a juridical resolution" (Hesford 36) possibly exempts the audience from responsibility. Although scholars have argued that "what emerges [...] from the accounts of why these men were arrested and sent to Guantanamo is the pervasive climate of suspicion under which Muslims lived" (Colleran 180), British audiences barely enter into the critique of the play. Whereas, in *The Empire*, spectators are positioned towards the body of the supposed enemy in terms of a hermeneutics of suspicion, the juridical framework heralded in *Guantanamo* absolves 'lay' audiences from involvement, unless one gives credit to the view that the play "urges each individual in the audience to [...] exert political pressure towards restoring human rights to the imprisoned" (Kritzer 199). Butler makes a striking point about the contiguity between the legal practice of detention without trial and 'our' own participation in a public culture of "indefinite containment", as the body of the 'other' "becomes visually rounded up, stared down, watched, hounded and monitored by a group of citizens who understand themselves as foot soldiers in the war against terrorism" (*Precarious Life* 77). There is, in my view, no association drawn in the play between the unlawful seizing and deportation of suspected combatants on or near battlefields abroad and 'our' participation in racialised schemes of visuality and surveillance on the home front. In contrast to Williams's and Moore's front-line scenes, then, *Guantanamo* does not move the 'fissures, folds and leaks within civilizations' (to recall Gilroy) into view. Although it clearly contests the hegemonic enemy image, it suggests that those who have become unjustifiably subsumed under that label can be reintegrated into the social fabric of multicultural Britain.

While clearly offering a potent critique of the biopolitical reduction of the detainees to bare life, Brittain and Slovo's play seeks closure in the restitution of (British) subjecthood. Despite ending on the pessimistic note, provided by the voice-over, that over 650 prisoners "are being held indefinitely" at Guantánamo Bay (62), something of a rite of passage is performed in the testimonial narration, which includes, towards the end of the play, an unnecessarily lengthy description of the procedure whereby the returning detainees leave their fingerprints at Paddington Green Police Station (48–49).[8] What this emphasis on the re-identification as British citizens shrouds is the fact that the release of a handful of British detainees does nothing to contest the persistence and – more importantly – the stability of the globalised system of detention in the 'war on terror'. As Agamben has shown, the camp exists as a "stable spatial arrangement inhabited by the bare life that [...] can no longer be inscribed in [the juridico-political] order" (*Homo Sacer* 175). At issue here is the stabilising function of an enemy image that – even if openly contested – functions to sustain practices and discourses of securitisation 'at home': "as a profiled bearer of risk, the sleeper body is the enabling currency of the public safety apparatus", as Feldman so astutely argues ("Actuarial Gaze" 209). The Western citizen situated in the 'safe' space of the democratic order is thus bound to the detainee at

---

8 *The Road to Guantánamo* closes with a strikingly similar sequence; as Elahe Haschemi Yekani outlines, it contrasts a voice-over referring to the remaining detainees with the "cathartic moment" of the returning British citizens' "social rebirth" into the "welcoming home" of British society (75).

Guantánamo Bay in infinitely more complex ways than expressions of outrage or consternation could serve to avow. This is why, for Agamben, the camp exists as "the hidden matrix of the politics in which we are still living" (*Homo Sacer* 175). This structural relationship between the polis and the camp is not easily grasped, and it makes for a troubling conjunction that theatre productions like *Guantanamo* do not, or perhaps cannot, work to elucidate.

4.2 Appropriating Afghan Femininities

Many of the narratives that legitimised intervention in Iraq and Afghanistan were discredited almost as soon as they had begun to circulate. The most notorious piece of misinformation doubtlessly springs from the Iraq war dossier and the infamous claim that Saddam Hussein's regime could launch weapons of mass destruction within 45 minutes of an order to do so. The Iraq war was, from the beginning, far less popular in the UK than the Afghan campaign and sparked a much bigger protest movement. Even though public distaste for the Afghan campaign grew as the war went on, it seems that, at least in its earlier stages, the promotion of intervention on humanitarian grounds proved to be the "arguably more successful [...] war story" (Hunt and Rygiel 7).[9] One of the most tenacious lines of this war story was the notion of freeing Afghan women from Taliban oppression: "Protecting the rights of women became the most politically powerful rationale for invading Afghanistan", as Christina Ho suggests (433). Since the beginnings of the invasion, (feminist) researchers have continuously striven to point out that "the rhetoric of women's liberation was a lie as monumental as the claims about WMD" (Stabile and Kumar 779). Due to largely favourable attitudes to the doctrine of humanitarian interventionism, however, this myth has appeared harder to debunk. Indicative of this is the tenacity of the image of the burqa-wearing Afghan woman as the signifier of Taliban repression; examples of the circulation of such images can be drawn from media discourses up to the very last phase of the war.[10]

---

[9] Officially, "humanitarian justifications were not part of the original authorization"; the Security Council approved military action in Afghanistan based on self-defence (Weiss 125–126). Still, humanitarian arguments loomed large. Tony Blair sought to persuade the British public that "[w]e have to act for humanitarian reasons to alleviate the appalling suffering of the Afghan people" ("Statement" 218).

[10] See, for instance, the photograph accompanying a news report on the German news website *Spiegel Online* on 20 June 2013 ("Die Kapitulation des Westens in Afghanistan"), where an image of burqa-wearing Afghan women is used to illustrate the West's surrender in the country.

"White men are saving brown women from brown men", Gayatri Chakravorty Spivak's well-known formula about British colonial endeavours to abolish widow sacrifice, or sati/suttee, in India ("Can" 92), has often been revisited in this context. In opposing self-immolation, British colonisers fashioned themselves as the liberators of subaltern women, whose own voices about the practice could not be heard; what was successfully abolished in this campaign, then, was the free will and testimony of the 'Third World' woman. The trope of protecting 'brown women from brown men' reappears in the discourse on freeing Afghan women. As Miriam Cooke elaborates,

> The burka recalls suttee and the four-stage gendered logic of empire: (1) women have inalienable rights within universal civilization, (2) civilized men recognize and respect these rights, (3) uncivilized men systematically abrogate these rights, and (4) such men (the Taliban) thus belong to an alien (Islamic) system. (469)

Although the Taliban's mistreatment of women should by no means be denied, researchers have pointed out the various blind spots in the liberation narrative, which work to camouflage neo-imperial interests, inconsistencies, and desires for domination. In particular, three broad concerns with this war story can be discerned.

First, scholars have pointed to the dehistoricisation at work in Western policymakers' sudden focus on the plight of Afghan women, where before they had turned a blind eye. The "protection scenario", as Carol Stabile and Deepa Kumar demonstrate, relies on an "Orientalist version of Afghan history, suggesting that women's oppression began with the Taliban" (772). This decontextualising representation serves to both justify the West's previous non-involvement and press the case for intervention. Moreover, the Orientalist version of history overlooks the various ways in which Afghan women had been empowered and had empowered themselves before the Taliban regime. Stabile and Kumar restore a much-needed historical perspective to the discussion of women's rights in Afghanistan:

> Even in the early 1990s, large numbers of Afghan women in urban centers participated in the workforce and in public life. Afghanistan's Constitution, written in 1964, ensured basic rights for women such as universal suffrage and equal pay. Since the 1950s, girls in Kabul and other cities attended schools. Half of university students were women, and women made up 40 percent of Afghanistan's doctors, 70 percent of its teachers and 30 percent of its civil servants. [...] The ascendance of the mujahideen government in 1992, who would later form the Northern Alliance, meant that women's rights were severely curtailed.

What rights remained would be summarily denied when the Taliban came to power in 1996. (768)[11]

The ahistorical perspective applied in the discursive field of the 'war on terror' insinuates that Western intervention would bring unprecedented liberties to Afghan women. Jasmin Zine, for instance, quotes a 2002 White House report claiming that "Afghan women are experiencing freedom for the first time" (34). Images of the oppressed Afghan woman rely on an essentialising conception of an immovable Muslim culture and an erasure of imperial cartographies. Ultimately, a historical view of women's rights in Afghanistan would also have to acknowledge that the situation has not substantially improved with Western intervention.[12]

A second broad concern with the protection scenario is with its reinstatement of an Orientalist opposition between 'First World' and 'Third World' femininities. As Rosi Braidotti elaborates,

> The dominant discourse nowadays is that 'our women' (Western, Christian, white, or 'whitened' [...]) are already liberated and thus do not need any more social incentives or emancipatory policies. 'Their women', however [...], are still backwards and need to be targeted for special emancipatory social actions or even more belligerent forms of enforced 'liberation'. This simplistic position reinstates a world-view based on colonial lines of demarcation. (*Transpositions* 46)

The neocolonial lines of demarcation that separate 'our' from 'their' women occlude the ongoing (need for) feminist struggles in the West. This is another blind spot with a long history: "The Victorian male establishment", as Katharine Viner reminds us, "fought bitterly against women's increasingly vocal feminist demands and occasional successes [...]; but at the same time, across the globe, they used the language of feminism to acquire the booty of the colonies" (26). In this context, Viner refers to the British colonial governor of Egypt, Lord Cromer, who condemned the degradation of Muslim women but founded the Men's League for Opposing Women's Suffrage upon his return to the UK. One of the

---

[11] Mary Anne Franks looks even further back in her short overview of women's rights in Afghanistan, referring to the reign of King Amanullah (1919–1929), who banned child marriage and polygamy, and to the reforms of Prime Minister Muhammad Daoud Khan from 1953 onwards, which included various initiatives to improve women's situation (138–139).
[12] Stabile and Kumar concede that, "[w]hile some things have changed since the collapse of the Taliban for women, much remains the same. [...] [T]hey still do not enjoy basic human rights" (775). Ho, writing in 2010, is more pessimistic: "violence against women and women's self-harm in many areas of Afghanistan is more prevalent now than it was under the Taliban" (436).

most drastic points in this regard has been made by legal scholar Mary Anne Franks, who argues that "an implicit ideological affinity exists between the oppression of women in Afghanistan and Western 'liberal' gender equality" (142). Franks may be stretching her argument quite far by resituating the Taliban as "America's own specter, its obscene underside" (150), but the value of her analysis certainly lies in its stark illustration of the fallacies of the "'things might be bad here, but they're better than over there' attitude", which "posits real horror as being eternally 'over there'" and makes "intervention from 'here' [seem] the only possibility" (146).

A third element of the liberation discourse that has attracted criticism is the notion that Afghan women cannot speak for themselves and that their concerns must therefore be voiced by their benevolent Western 'sisters'. One of the most frequently cited aspects of Spivak's analysis comes into view here: "The subaltern as female cannot be heard or read [...]. The subaltern cannot speak" ("Can" 104). In this context, much attention has been paid to the radio addresses of First Lady Laura Bush, who was "speaking on behalf of and instead of Afghan women" (von der Lippe and Väyrynen 23). In fact, a similar phenomenon could be observed in the UK, where the prime minister's wife and human rights lawyer Cherie Blair simultaneously launched a campaign to 'liberate' Afghan women. "Goggling through her fingers, to illustrate the view from inside a burqa", as Catherine Bennett recalls, Blair declared that 'we' needed to help Afghan women in order to "free [their] spirit and give them their voice back" (20). The demand to give back a voice to Afghan women implies not only that they had been entirely mute under the Taliban but also that only Western powers can enable them to speak. This assumption evidences the workings of a "feminist Orientalism", which is "blind to the ways in which women in the East resist and empower themselves" (Bahramitash 222). What these speeches ignore is the existence of an Afghan feminist movement, with the most prominent organisation, the Revolutionary Association of the Women of Afghanistan (RAWA), having been founded as early as 1977.[13] Again, this blind spot bears the imprint of colonial histories, as Lila Abu-Lughod's discussion of a Christian missionary document from the early 20th century shows, which was tellingly entitled *Our Moslem Sisters: A Cry of Need from the Lands of Darkness Interpreted by Those Who Heard It*. Importantly, Abu-Lughod highlights how the assumption that Afghan women cannot speak for themselves creates "an imaginative geography

---

[13] While I find it important to draw attention to the ways in which Afghan women have engaged – and are still engaging – in their own struggles, it is also imperative to acknowledge that RAWA is a middle-class organisation, which might do little to "represent the subaltern", as Spivak has pointed out ("Terror" 84–85).

of […] cultures in which First Ladies give speeches versus others where women shuffle around silently in burqas" (789).

This pointed sketch of the spatial imagination underpinning the liberation discourse can be taken as a starting point for an interrogation of theatrical representations of the 'humanitarian' intervention in Afghanistan, and in particular the negotiation of Afghan femininities in war drama. In line with the scholarly concerns identified above, three broad areas of enquiry can be specified. First, there is the question of the (a)historical perspective applied in drama. Plays should be considered against the dehistoricising function of a discourse that decontextualises Taliban oppression and Western intervention. A second concern is with drama's relationship to the Orientalist opposition between 'our' and 'their' women. Do the plays challenge this binary worldview by offering an alternative vision, for instance, by outlining the "continuity between our grievances and those of the women of Afghanistan" (Michaele Ferguson qtd. in Ho 435)?[14] Finally, questions have to be raised about who represents and speaks for whom, and on whose behalf. Are victimised Afghan women the "silent props, present to vivify the barbarism of dark men cast as threatening other" (Haaken 457), or does theatre open up a space where their voices can be heard without the need for Western amplification?

This chapter zooms in on one of the most profound theatrical engagements with the war in Afghanistan. *The Great Game: Afghanistan* play cycle, which premiered at the Tricycle Theatre in London in 2009, was one of the first British theatre events to address the Afghan war explicitly and exclusively. Artistic director Nicolas Kent devised the cycle, as he writes in the introduction to the published script, in response to a perceived lack of public debate on and artistic responses to this war (7). The three-part cycle consists of twelve short plays, which were originally staged alongside verbatim pieces about the political situation at the time of the production and monologues/duologues about episodes in Afghan history as well as films, talks, and ceramic displays. The *Great Game* festival has been labelled "the biggest teach-in on the country ever conducted in Britain" (Whitaker) and been described as "part collective ritual […] and part crash-course in the complexities of a land whose past has been little known by those eager to shape its future" (Cull, "Staging" 125). Its didactic impetus is also evident from the British Council's 'export' of the cycle to the US, and from special performances for expert audiences such as the British armed forces. Contrary to the fixation on the Taliban regime in public discourse, the structure

---

14 Approaches to a global feminist solidarity might, however, as Rustom Bharucha cautions, come at the risk of eliding differences or turning into patronisation (47).

of the cycle seems to allow for a more balanced engagement with Afghanistan's complex history. Each of the parts deals with a distinct period: part one starts with the defeat of the British at Jalalabad at the end of the first Anglo-Afghan war and is entitled "Invasions and Independence: 1842–1930"; the second part on "Communism, the Mujahideen and the Taliban" focuses on the period from 1979 to 1996; the final part derives its title, "Enduring Freedom: 1996–2009", from the latest Afghan campaign. With its hint at "the strategic rivalry and conflict between the British Empire and the Russian Empire for supremacy in Central Asia" (Kent 9), the title of the cycle points to a thematic focus on (neo-)imperial involvements in Afghanistan and the responsibility of British, Soviet, and US players for the current geopolitical configuration of the country, whose very borders were drawn by outside forces (see Žižek 55).

The Subaltern Can Speak: Abi Morgan's *The Night Is Darkest Before the Dawn*

Seen against this broad historical canvas, the title of Abi Morgan's contribution to the cycle, *The Night Is Darkest Before the Dawn*, seems to tap into the (a)historical imagination established in the discursive field. With its focus on women's rights and education under the Taliban and post-invasion humanitarian efforts to reopen a school for girls, the play's proverbial title seems to suggest that the 'darkest' phase of Afghan history, the Taliban regime, is about to give way to the 'dawn' of a new era, brought about by Western forces. This resonates with the overly optimistic outlook that gained traction soon after the invasion, as captured by Jason Burke: "With the Taliban apparently defeated and dispersed, a bright new era for Afghanistan seemed to be dawning" (xvii). In fact, this notion frames the play as a whole. Its opening is stipulated in the stage directions: "*Dusk – A bombed out building –* Minoo *(early 50s) sits making bread by a fire. She is dressed in the familiar blue burkah of the Taliban era*" (Morgan 193). The play closes with lights fading on Berukh, whom local teacher Huma has just recruited for the girls' school, relearning, with Huma's help, how to sharpen a pencil. Its arc hence leads from the 'darkest' hour in the history of women's rights in Afghanistan, epitomised by the image of the 'familiar' blue burqa with which the play opens, to the hopeful 'dawn' of sending girls back to school after the defeat of the Taliban. In consequence, the framing of the play affirms an Orientalist version of Afghan history and reinstates the correlation between the burqa and women's plight under the Taliban. The use of the burqa as theatrical costume does nothing to reframe its emblematic signification as the epitome of oppression or contextualise the practice of veiling.[15]

Yet, although the silent stage presence of burqa-clad Minoo, who never speaks and only carries out household chores, testifies to the apparent need for liberating 'brown women', the rescue effort is unlikely to be performed by 'white men'. American NGO worker Alex is represented as utterly incompetent and inadequate in the face of the inscrutable Afghan tribal relations and customs; "the modern-day aid worker [...] is little more than an uncomprehending spectator", as one reviewer comments (Whitaker). He cannot muster up enough patience to wait for the tribal chief (193–194), is unable to communicate with him without Huma's translation (194–195), fails to establish any authority with the Afghans, who merely sneer and laugh at him (195–201), and lets himself be enticed to smoke an opium pipe with the tribesmen (207), until he eventually admits: "I'm not built for this country" (208). Even if Morgan's play does not endorse the positioning of Western powers as liberators, the restoration of women's rights to education in the play is at least facilitated by Western intervention. As Huma explains to Berukh and her father, Omaid: "[Alex] works for an international charity. [...] They want to put funding into our school. [...] I have nine girls already who have agreed to return" (195). The emphasis throughout is on a 'return' to the state of affairs before the Taliban's arrival, which partly debunks the myth of women's freedom starting with Western intervention. Nevertheless, the framing of the Taliban's seizure of power as a caesura which marks the beginning of repression is affirmed by the play: "'94 the Taliban arrived. Ara cried all night", is how Omaid begins his narrative about his daughter having to leave school, his sons being sent to a *madrasa* (i.e. a religious school instilling militant versions of Islam into young boys), and the Taliban's torture of his brother (201–203).

Despite the *Great Game*'s overall endeavour to cover more than the past 150 years of Afghan history, the trope of the 'darkest' hour of the Taliban's arrival also inaugurates the cycle as a whole. In the original production at least, the cycle opened with a short monologue written by novelist and political activist Siba Shakib, which is not included in the published playtext.[16] The monologue

---

15 As Abu-Lughod points out, "it should be recalled that the Taliban did not invent the burqa. It was the local form of covering that Pashtun women in one region wore [...] as a convention for symbolizing women's modesty or respectability. [...] What had happened [...] under the Taliban is that one regional style of covering [...] was imposed on everyone as 'religiously' appropriate" (785).
16 All observations are based on the performance recorded at the Tricycle Theatre on 17 May 2009 (National Video Archive of Performance). The playscript, for reasons that are not specified,

is spoken by a painter finishing a mural (designed by Pamela Howard) as the Taliban seize Herat in 1996. Immediately upon entering the stage, a group of men wearing the traditional Pashtun dress associated with the Taliban switch off the small boom box from which music had been playing and prevent the artist from completing the mural by arresting him. The painting of Afghan history he had been working on serves as the backdrop for the ensuing plays. The unfinished mural depicts, amongst other things, the statues of the Buddhas of Bamiyan, which the Taliban notoriously destroyed in 2001. In conjunction with their interruption of the other artistic practices on stage, the Taliban are positioned as the supreme enemies of art. With this opening, the cycle self-reflexively situates itself as a liberal artistic response against the threat posed by the Taliban. *The Night Is Darkest Before the Dawn* affirms this framing of the Taliban as the ultimate evil; as one review states, the play "is as oppressive as the regime and shows the terrible position of women under the Taliban" (Loveridge, "*CurtainUp* London Review").

Certainly, condemnation of the Taliban's reign of terror is by no means misplaced. Yet, when it comes to the dramatic figuration of subject positions associated with the 'other', a number of political and ethical concerns have to be raised. As was discussed in chapter two, it is disputable whether and under which conditions the practice of 'speaking for others', as Linda Martín Alcoff puts it, can ever evade the risk of misrepresentation and appropriation. In particular, her concern with authoritative 'First World' subjects who speak for groups in the 'Third World' is relevant here ("Problem" 26). That the play subscribes to the narrative of Taliban repression is problematic insofar as it reinstates Orientalist oppositions between 'First World' and 'Third World' femininities and reinforces the imaginative geographies that situate the 'real horror' irrevocably 'over there'. This reproduction of spatial and gendered binaries is evident from an article that Morgan published in the *Guardian* in 2009, where she explains how news stories about acid attacks on Afghan schoolgirls in 2002 inspired her play:

> Supporters of the Taliban have attacked schoolgirls in the street, angered that they should now demand an education after years of being denied this basic freedom. [...] The urge to write kicked in. Here was a chance to illuminate a world where school is a luxury, and where the decision to become a teacher in Afghanistan – particularly a female teacher – could mean courting death. (24)

---

only contains the short pieces of new writing commissioned from (mainly) British playwrights, not Shakib's contributions.

From her comfortable position among "first-world viewers who seek to understand 'what happened over there'" (Butler, *Frames* 78), Morgan seeks to 'illuminate' a 'dark' world. She describes being haunted by a "grainy image [she] saw on the web, filmed on a mobile phone, of a burka-clad woman being flogged in Pakistan's Swat valley", adding accounts of how "a 75-year-old widow in Saudi Arabia was sentenced to 40 lashes" and how "14 women, all students and teachers in Kandahar, had been attacked with acid. It happened as I was taking my daughter to school" (24). Morgan's list establishes an equivalence between atrocities against women in diverse Islamic societies, regardless of their particularities. Although there is doubtlessly a historical connection between Saudi involvement in Afghanistan and the formation of "the Taliban's brand of extreme Islam" (Stabile and Kumar 769), the way in which such pointed sketches homogenise instances of violence against women in one single narrative remains problematic. Without wishing to condone any of these brutal acts, there is a difference to be made between the inhumane legal punishments officially sanctioned by the Saudi state and the Taliban's terrorising of the population after they had seized Swat. The universalising account of structural violence offered here points to the workings of an "Orientalist feminism", based on the assumption that "women's ill-treatment is first and foremost grounded in an essentialised, monolithic Islamic culture" (Ho 435).

Morgan's speaking position firmly situates her in a secure 'First World', where her daughter can safely attend school and where violence against women is only encountered in images from the 'Third World', without scrutinising the limitations this vantage point might bring with it in order to understand and legitimately speak about 'what happened over there'. The spatial/gendered dichotomy of civilised versus barbaric spaces and subjectivities partly structures *The Night Is Darkest Before the Dawn* as a whole. After having witnessed Omaid's narrative about Taliban atrocities and having experienced the difficulties in convincing Afghan tribesmen of reopening the girls' school, Alex's final speech testifies to 'First World' privilege:

> What am I doing here? I take my kids to school every day. I don't even think about it. My eldest. She wants to be famous. I'm ashamed of that. I say 'You can be anything you want to be. A doctor? A lawyer? [...] Don't you know how lucky you are? You have the world [...]'. (209)

Alex's inadequacy in handling the negotiations gives way to a more profound insight into the benefits of living in that part of the globe where people 'have the world'. Crucially, his speech is articulated for the benefit of the audience, as the only onstage listeners are presumably – within the internal system of communication established in the play – unable to understand English. The preferred position offered to audiences is, therefore, one that corresponds to the dominant viewing position provided in media discourse. Narratives and images of burqa-clad women or of teenage girls who are unable to sharpen a pencil position Western audiences as 'First World' viewers attempting to understand the plight of these women. The conclusion that empathising viewers of these images on the news – or in the theatre – are likely to draw is that Western intervention in Afghanistan is necessary, and it must be long-term intervention at that. After all, the "oppressive regime [...] might return at any time", as Morgan says in her article (24); or, as Omaid puts it in the play, "They are only a few kilometres away. Hiding across a border or in the mountains" (202). Critics have hence read the play as the one that strikes "the only positive note" regarding Western intervention within the largely anti-interventionist cycle (Whitaker).

Accordingly, the play can be shown to both affirm an Orientalist version of Afghan history and endorse a type of Orientalist feminism that contrasts 'our' privileges with 'their' suffering. When it comes to the third question about representing Afghan women stipulated above, the playwright's detection of 'a chance to illuminate a world' indeed points to the notion that Western women should give a voice to their suffering. Afghan girls and women, however, are not entirely 'silent props' in Morgan's play. Although Minoo initially appears mute and ignorant, she performs a meaningful stage action during Alex's final speech, challenging his account of 'First World' safety. Alex "*is wearing a flak jacket*", the stage directions specify upon the opening of the play (193). The emphasis placed on this iconic sign reveals its significance; it marks Alex's life as one that needs to be protected in a dangerous place. The onstage characters notice the loaded signifier too; pointing to Alex's chest, Omaid says: "We don't have flak jackets [...] to protect us" (198). Ironically, it is the only person who profits from the unequal geopolitical distribution of precariousness, living in "America's safest town" (200), whose life is thus safeguarded when he confronts a group of vulnerable rural Afghans, who have all lost large parts of their families in US air raids or Taliban assassinations.

In a meaningful transfer, however, when Alex regains full consciousness as the opium wears off, he "*realizes he's not wearing his flak jacket. He looks around, searching, stopping on seeing* Minoo *wearing it. He hesitates, shrugs, resigned*" (209). When Alex delivers his narrative about 'First World' safety, Minoo crosses the stage wearing the vest. By transferring the signifier of a grievable life to an Afghan woman, the play renders her life valuable. With the empowering act of putting on the protective garment, Minoo claims her vulnerability and performs a stage act that undercuts Alex's First-versus-Third-World dichotomy. Like Bhuvaneswari Bhaduri, of whom Spivak writes in "Can the Subaltern Speak?",

Minoo is "a woman who use[s] her gendered body to inscribe an unheard message" ("Terror" 97). She may not be speaking, but, as Spivak reminds postcolonial scholars, they need to be "*measuring* silences, if necessary" ("Can" 92). The transfer of the flak jacket could be 'measured' in terms of a performative extension of the norms that stipulate whose life is worthy of protection. It becomes an act that destabilises the official war story, since to "call into question [the] frame by which injurability is falsely and unequally distributed is precisely to call into question one of the dominant frames sustaining the [...] wars in Iraq and Afghanistan" (Butler, *Frames* 182).

Just as Minoo uses a powerful symbol to publicly claim grievability, Berukh eventually emerges from her father's shadow. Responding to his challenge, "[Huma] says you are a storyteller?", Berukh begins to tell the "story of the farmer and the silver" (210), all the while moving slowly from the margin of the stage, where Berukh and Minoo are positioned for most of the piece, nearer the downstage centre position. It is her competent storytelling that persuades her father to give his consent to her school attendance, albeit tentatively: "We will see" (211). As with Minoo's act of putting on the flak jacket, Berukh transforms her own status, for "if the subaltern can speak [...], the subaltern is not subaltern any more" (Spivak qtd. in Cohler 248–249). That Berukh can become a speaking subject only through an act of storytelling is somewhat troubling, given its recourse to the trope of the "Oriental storyteller", or "native narrator", in colonial writing (Behdad 85). The notion that the subaltern woman can only speak in stylised language is reinforced by another short piece written by Shakib, staged in the first part of the play cycle. In the duologue, a female performer appears as the 19th-century folk heroine "Malalai the brave" (Malalai of Maiwand), also featured in the scenographic mural of Afghanistan, who urges Afghan men to fight against the British invaders in a highly poeticised speech that is abundant with pathos. The fact that some of the female Afghan voices in the *Great Game* cycle can only gain audibility through the formalised scripts of folk-cultural sources obscures the many ways in which Afghan women voice their resistance to violence on a daily basis in such outlets as blogs, websites, or weekly newspapers (see Kumar), using excellent English and 'ordinary' speech registers. Yet Berukh's act of storytelling is more than a rhetorical device designed to add "an exotic flavor" to a colonialist narrative (Behdad 85); it functions as an empowering speech act that transforms her subaltern status. Within the cosmos of the play, then, the voice of the Afghan woman can eventually be heard without Western amplification. In spite of its heavily stylised approach to the subaltern woman's speech, attention arguably shifts from 'our' humanitarian efforts to 'their' own struggles. In consequence, although the play clearly subscribes to the notion that 'brown women' need to be saved, it subtly indicates their own power to do so.

Selling Brown Women: Richard Bean's *On the Side of the Angels*

The implicit pro-invasion argument of *The Night Is Darkest Before the Dawn* is somewhat weakened by its position in the play cycle. The subsequent play, *On the Side of the Angels* by Richard Bean, offers a cynical view of humanitarian intervention and liberation. Morgan's pro-interventionist stance is hence, as one critic holds, "immediately contradicted" (Whitaker). The British NGO workers in Bean's play try to solve a land dispute between rivalling Afghan tribes; after learning that the eventual deal brokered by an Afghan colleague includes the exchange of a 'bride price' of three teenage girls,[17] two of them die en route to Herat in the attempt to rescue them. In contrast to the optimistic message encapsulated in Morgan's play, Bean's piece contains an ironic, self-reflexive comment on its title in the final scene, when aid worker Jonathan reassures his disillusioned colleague Fiona that "we're on the side of the fucking angels" (Bean 226). This notion is continuously problematised in the short play, which centrally deals with finding the right balance between "impos[ing] our values" and "some kind of moral vacuum", as protagonist Jackie puts it (225), in dealing with another culture.

In the opening scene, set in the "*Head Office of Direct Action World Poverty in Croydon*" (215), Bean's aid workers explicitly position themselves in opposition to the war story on liberating 'brown women'. In performance, before the scene started, a series of short video clips was projected against a screen at the back of the stage; these intercut news about the Afghan conflict with the familiar opening credits of popular soap opera *Eastenders* (1985–) and extracts from a chat show with an all-female panel. The use of video projections, repeated at each change of scene, positions audiences as televisual spectators; the scenically negotiated attempts to promote understanding of human rights issues in Afghanistan compete with the lure of soap-opera and chat-show formats in the Western mediasphere. The difficulties of 'selling' humanitarian concerns are reflected on the level of dramatic discourse, as Jackie, Fiona, and Jonathan discuss appropriate aid projects for the Afghan region. Fiona reads out titles from a list of proposals that would appeal to the narrative of improving Afghan women's situation – "Awareness Raising of Post Natal Health issues for Women", "Conference and Event production skills training for … women" (215) – but Jackie

---

17 Exchanging Afghan girls for marriage is part of "an old tradition called 'Baad' aimed at settling disputes between the parties in conflict"; the persistence of this type of forced marriage was recently reported on the news website run by RAWA (Musavi).

rejects each proposal before Fiona has even finished reading out the titles. Upon Jonathan's reminder, "You know how this business works", she bursts out:

> Yes. Out of work actors hang around tube stations mugging career women for direct debits so that I can be sent off to fight a war against the Taliban on the ideological battleground of women's rights. I'm not a soldier. I don't want anything to do with Women's Rights, human rights, children's rights; rights are individualistic concepts and the one thing that Afghanistan doesn't have, and has never had, is any individuals. [...] All Afghans belong to a family, then a tribe, and then Islam. It's not my job to change that. (215–216)

Jackie is aware that "show[ing] a photo of a young Afghan girl on her first day of school looking 'happily bewildered'" (216) would be an effective strategy to raise money for NGO efforts – an essential argument for humanitarian work that depends on the laws of the free-market economy – but rejects involvement on that 'ideological battleground'. The sarcastic undercurrent of her speech emphasises the utilitarian considerations underpinning the humanitarian discourse and points to the monetary dimension of 'all the values talk' (see chapter three): 'we' only choose to defend those values in Afghanistan that can be converted into actual cash value.

Implicit in Jackie's speech is what Ho calls "a rejection of the role of Western 'liberator'" (438). Ho proposes a critical feminist project that, instead of "a preoccupation with Islam as the greatest threat to women's rights", shifts the focus to "the requirements for human security, which women and men share across the globe" (438). Jackie positions herself in explicit opposition to the liberating discourse by proposing to refocus attention from an obsession with women's rights in particular, and human rights more generally, to "reduce poverty and improve their diet" (216). Her rejection of rights as 'individualistic concepts' echoes Butler's criticism of imposing "a language of politics developed within First World contexts on women who are facing the threat of imperialist economic exploitation and cultural obliteration" (*Precarious Life* 49). In part, the opening scene also dispenses with an Orientalist version of Afghan history that frames the Taliban's arrival as the 'darkest' hour. Upon Fiona's remonstrations about Jackie's ongoing support for a school in Taliban-controlled Kandahar, Jackie drily remarks: "The Taliban kill women in football stadiums, hey nobody's perfect" (216). Contrary to the accepted wisdom that the Taliban represent the ultimate evil, her account foregrounds the detrimental effects of policies based on an absolute opposition to them: "If you close that school the boys will be sent to a madrassa in Pakistan" (216).

The pragmatic approach represented by Jackie thus runs counter to the overall gesture of the play cycle. Not only does *The Great Game*, as has been outlined, start with a short scene about the crushing impact of the Taliban's arrival, but in a verbatim piece (edited) by Richard Norton-Taylor, which was staged immediately after Bean's play in the Tricycle performance, a Taliban commander is introduced as persona non grata. Resonating with the chat-show format briefly referenced at the outset of Bean's play, the short verbatim piece places five speakers into static positions, most of them seated, speaking towards the audience. The actor reciting the interview statements made by Taliban member Mullah Abdullah Ghazni is positioned on stage in a way that suggests he does not fully belong to the panel of experts: he is standing behind the four speakers with his arms crossed in front of his chest throughout the scene, and he is the only speaker that the others do not listen or respond to (and vice versa), which indicates that no insights can be gained from his testimony. His speech and appearance amount to little more than a caricature of the evil enemy 'other': pointing at the audience, he speaks in a sombre voice about "these infidels that occupied and invaded our country" and promises a return to *shariah* law in a threatening tone.[18] Whereas the cycle as a whole thus positions the Taliban as a group that 'we' should neither speak nor listen to, let alone negotiate with,[19] Jackie's speech highlights how experiences on the ground in Afghanistan diverge from this dominant point of view.

Her more pragmatic take on political options in Afghanistan ties in with Rashid's assessment of "Prospects for Peace in Afghanistan" (2010). The Pakistani journalist, who, incidentally, also features as one of the expert-speakers in another verbatim piece in the cycle, explains that:

> Afghanistan is a tribal community, a clan community. Many in the West may view this as a negative, but [...] [a]s a tribal society, Afghanistan has an enormous absorptive capacity for forgiveness. The example of the Afghan government shows that, if done in the right way and in accordance with Afghan custom, the enemy can be brought into the peace process. (366)

A similar take on the peace process informs the NGO effort depicted in *On the Side of the Angels*: the team of aid workers get "both parties to [...] stand on the disputed land" in order to disempower the "aggressor [...] by a sense of negative honour" (218). The chief aggressor, Dawood, is played by the same actor as

---

[18] All quotations are transcribed from the performance recorded at the Tricycle Theatre on 17 May 2009 (National Video Archive of Performance).

[19] What seems like a foregone conclusion in the play cycle in fact runs counter to policy developments at the time of its staging, at least in the context of the festival's 2010 run: as Ahmed Rashid sums up, one of the conclusions of the international Afghanistan conference held in London in early 2010 "was that all the countries agreed that they would start talking to the Taliban" (355).

Omaid in Morgan's play; in consequence, a stock figure of the Afghan tribal chief emerges, who essentially remains a flat character. Dawood's appearance chimes with the critical impetus of the play, however, insofar as he (mis)appropriates the statements circulating in the discursive regime of the 'war on terror': "*Yes, I am free, it is good, I am enduring freedom*" (221). The pun on the official designation of the Afghan campaign brings out the contradictions in the liberation discourse. The mission has brought libidinous liberties to the tribal chief. Jackie's pragmatic approach to humanitarian work does nothing to challenge this. Since her relativism induces her to accept "[a]nything so we have a deal" (222), the agreement brokered by her team entails the loss of freedom for the three underage girls who are promised to Dawood's clan.

The notion that Operation Enduring Freedom is more connected to 'selling' than to 'freeing' Afghan women is reinforced in the final scene, which reveals the eventual convergence of the official liberating mission and the pragmatic outlook explored in the play. Even before the characters begin to speak, the consolidation of Jackie's and Jonathan's seemingly antagonistic positions becomes apparent through an iconic sign: the scene opens with Jonathan using the exercise bike that was sent back to the Croydon office, just as the previous scene had begun with "JACKIE *on the exercise bike*" in Kabul (226). This establishes a correspondence between 'here' and 'there', the liberation discourse forged 'at home' and the mission on the ground in Afghanistan. The play ends with Jonathan preparing to pitch the photograph of a 'happily bewildered' Afghan schoolgirl – precisely what Jackie had refused to do – to the NGO's trustees: "What a photo, eh? It's the bandage isn't it. Brilliant. Almost fetishistic" (227). This final reversal of Jackie's position on humanitarian work also inverts the very position of the rescuer: it is the Afghan girl who "saved us. Rescued us. Credit crunch? Qu'est-ce que c'est?" (227). This inversion unsettles the regular dispersion of subject positions in the discursive formation, which "not only constructs the 'victimized women to be rescued', but also their 'hyper-masculine rescuers'" (Hunt and Rygiel 9). Bean's play, in contrast, demonstrates to what extent the subject position of rescuer depends on the object position of the Afghan woman, and not the other way around, in order to 'sell' the war. This ultimately undermines the hegemonic representation of 'brown women' in need of saving by divulging the constructedness of this image: the photograph has been "photoshopped" (227).

This point is underscored by the absence of Afghan female characters from the dramatis personae. Just as some of the female Muslim subjects in home-front plays remain 'unmarked', Afghan femininities in *On the Side of the Angels* are wholly situated off stage. In spite of their centrality to dramatic discourse, they remain markedly invisible – even the photoshopped image is handled such that the audience never see it. In Bean's play, then, Afghan women have no face and no voice. This dramatic strategy, however, does not work to reinforce the dominant assumption that Western subjects need to speak and act on their behalf, but it unveils some of the inconsistencies, contradictions, and detrimental effects of the liberation discourse. As Stabile and Kumar point out: "As long as women are not permitted to speak for themselves, they provide the perfect grounds for an elaborate ventriloquist act, in which they serve as the passive vehicle for the representation of [Western] interests" (778). The commodification of the image of Afghan schoolgirls in the final scene illustrates this appropriation of their muted voices. Rather than seeing it as further disempowering Afghan women by denying them a voice of their own, I would argue that the resistant potential of the play lies in exposing the discursive mechanisms whereby Afghan women are bereft of speech, agency, and subjectivity in the first place. The persistent negotiation and, in particular, the final fetishisation of Afghan femininities forcefully demonstrate the reduction of multiple subjectivities to a sutured object position.

In addition, Bean's play accentuates some of the continuities between 'our' and 'their' struggles and thereby works to undercut Orientalist oppositions. In the initial debate on appropriate aid projects for Afghanistan, Jackie has to assert her opinion against her male colleague. After interjecting her proposals with slightly aggressive interruptions, forcing her to protest, "I'm not stupid" (216), Jonathan angrily concedes that he needs to hear his female colleague out: "Pitch" (217). Jackie comments on his hyper-masculine habitus when she proposes: "Land rights brokering. Ah! I said the word 'rights' and he got a hard on!" (217). To some extent, the scene points to Western women's need to defend their expertise in professional contexts. Moreover, in contrast to British colonialist contradictions between strengthening 'their' and opposing 'our' women's rights, there is an allusion to the legacy and necessity of feminist struggles in the UK when aid worker Graham reminisces how "mum bought me my first keffiyeh, when I was five, to go to Greenham Common" (219). The reference to the anti-nuclear protests is significant, for the site "became an exemplar of women's peace organizing", as Joshua Goldstein explains: "The Greenham Common women created feminist symbolism designed to contrast with the masculinist war-culture of the air base" (328). On the one hand, one could argue that the reference to feminist protest movements of the 1980s dates this form of activism firmly in the past; on the other hand, the allusion to feminist mobilisation against a 'masculinist war culture' points to the endurance of gender binaries in the current 'war on terror'.

By way of conclusion, Christiane Schlote's verdict on representations of humanitarian aid in contemporary British drama has particular resonance:

> the absence of well-rounded non-Western characters is clearly noticeable and partly troubling in all plays. In this respect, we may even ask whether the gradual shift from a focus on refugee figures to the character of the aid worker may be read as indicative of a return to First World and middle-class concerns and a desire for the 'humanitarian hero'. (130)

I certainly share Schlote's concern about the representation of non-Western characters in the *Great Game* cycle in general, and these two plays in particular. Emphasised by the technique of multiple casting, certain stock characters emerge over the course of the performance: Daniel Betts, playing Morgan's aid worker Alex, reappears as Jonathan in Bean's play; Ramon Tikaram has the parts of Omaid and Dawood; Sagar Arya and Danny Rahim are cast as Afghan tribesmen in both plays. The naturalistic approach to casting in the cycle neatly divides the roles of Afghan and Western characters, respectively, among white British actors and those with a minority ethnic background. Casting non-white actors (irrespective of their ethnicity) for the parts of Afghan characters, rather than for any of the British/American/Soviet roles, reinforces ethnic stereotypes. The casting strategy's claim to verisimilitude is doubtful, moreover, given that Pashtuns (who feature in Morgan's and Bean's plays) would in fact have to be seen as white – if one were to accept these registers of skin colour at all.

An intensely problematic point of the production is the fact that – although the as-if communicative frame of the plays induces audiences to believe that, even though they speak English on stage, Afghan characters communicate with each other in local languages such as Pashto – the English that the non-Western characters speak is tinged with a fake foreign accent and frequent grammatical mistakes. The overall effect is one that creates all Afghan characters as foreign and linguistically/culturally 'other', as incapable of speaking 'our' language properly and, by extension, of adequately understanding 'our' benevolent efforts in Afghanistan. In this sense, the plays reinstate a colonialist framework that denies to the 'other(ed)' characters what Nicholas Ridout has called "the Full English capacity", that is, the ability to engage and participate in cultural, communicative, and economic activities in a globalised community of English speakers (Ridout). With the pseudo-naturalistic staging of performers wearing traditional costumes and speaking with a foreign accent, the cycle as a whole disturbingly recalls the "[p]ictorialist stage orientalism" developed in the colonial era; Gilbert and Lo have described this representational style as a "fetish" that "betrayed a deep Western fascination with Otherness" (30). What seems to be missing from the staging, then, is any "gesture towards [the] instable, performative subject positions" that make up ethnic and cultural identities, which Eckart Voigts has identified as the "essential point" (12) raised by *England People Very Nice*, Bean's immensely successful and controversial play that premiered in the same year as *The Great Game*. This line of critique can only somewhat be mitigated by the fact that – contrary to Schlote's assumption about the return of the 'humanitarian hero' – Western characters rarely escape an equally scathing criticism as those of Afghan drug lords or tribal chiefs.

All in all, various interconnections between the dramatic negotiation of Muslim femininities on the home front and the front line emerge. The plays display a heightened awareness of the reductive media images and representations that posit female Muslim subjectivities as submissive, oppressed, backwards, dependent. As a response to the object position of Muslim women in the image war, Bano's *Shades* employs a politics of resistance to counter negative representations. While *Shades* revolves around a cosmopolitan sense of Islamic identity and places an excessive significance on different middle-class (life)styles and choices, *The Night Is Darkest Before the Dawn* implies the replacement of the oppressive fabric of the burqa with the emancipated appearance of young female storytellers. Female Muslim characters in both plays have to resist, to varying degrees, reduction to stereotypes both within the internal communication system and the external one, in asserting unexpected aspects of Muslim subjectivities in their interaction with more traditionally minded characters and the audience. A different strategy is employed in Sen Gupta's and Bean's plays, for both *What Fatima Did...* and *On the Side of the Angels* seek to counter the voyeuristic gaze at and objectification of the Muslim woman with absence. On the whole, a distinctive advantage of this dramatic technique emerges, insofar as it does not reify the visual regimes that fuel the war story. Whereas a mimetic representation of veiled Muslim femininities risks refracting the objectifying gaze within the theatre space, indulging the audience's desire to look at 'Oriental' females, the relegation of unmarked Muslim femininities to the diegetic space can be seen as a vital dramatic resource for opening up a space for a critical reflection on these desires, as well as a critique of the appropriation of women's voices and subjectivities.

4.3 Neoliberal War Agents

If the gendered protection scenario was specific to the Afghan campaign – even if it finds its echoes in the way Western forces stylised themselves as rescuing Iraqis from a brutal dictator – one of the defining aspects of the Iraq invasion was its 'shock and awe' tactics.[20] In terms of military doctrine, 'shock and

---

[20] For a reading of the liberation narrative in the context of the Iraq war, see Brittain (73–81).

awe' may be more directly associated with the US forces than with British involvement in the conflict (Carpenter 145); yet both the leader of the 'coalition of the willing' and its closest ally employed and profited from the strategy:

> 'Shock and awe' was about fighting a war on terror through terror itself. The massive bombardments of Baghdad were designed not only to dishearten the Republican Guard and [...] the rest of the Iraqi army; they were also intended to strike fear in the hearts of the Iraqi people at large – the very people that Bush and Blair constantly announced they had no quarrel with. (Gregory, "Who's Responsible?")

Gregory's description reveals two of the central paradoxes at the heart of the Iraq campaign. First, the 'war on terror' was fought 'through terror itself', although terrorising a foreign population by military means was accepted as a legitimate response to avenge the terror unleashed on US territory. Second, 'shock and awe' tactics deliberately targeted civilian populations, despite Blair's assertions, pre-invasion: "I hope the Iraqi people hear this message. [...] Our enemy is not you, but your barbarous rulers" ("'Britain'").

The doctrine of 'shock and awe' is bound up with the imaginative geographies underpinning the invasions of both Iraq and Afghanistan. In *The Shock Doctrine* (2007), Naomi Klein coins the label "disaster capitalism" for the conversion of devastated public spheres in the aftermath of natural or human-made catastrophes into neoliberal free-market societies according to the Chicago School prototype (6). The idea that Iraqis could be 'shocked and awed' into submission to the invading forces betrays the fundamental geopolitical misconception of post-invasion Iraq as a "blank slate" (48). The geographical abstraction of Iraq as "an empty space on a map" facilitates the operation of what Klein identifies as the neoliberal 'shock treatment': "the use of ultimate shock to forcibly wipe out and erase all obstacles to the construction of model corporatist states free from all interference" (330–331).[21] In the context of reducing Iraq to a 'blank slate', Klein discusses the looting of key cultural institutions in the aftermath of the US-/UK-led invasion, such as the stealing of artefacts from the National Museum of Iraq, as a calculated side effect of the military intervention (336–337). Another example in this respect is the US forces' seizure of archaeological ruins and cultural heritage sites in Iraq (Feldman, "Actuarial Gaze" 220). British complicity in – or at least indifference towards – the erasure of Iraqi culture was

---

[21] Klein traces the shock treatment back to the CIA-funded MKUltra mind control programme, and in particular the psychiatric 'shock shop' experiments conducted by Ewen Cameron, which laid the foundation for the infamous manual *Kubark Counterintelligence Interrogation* (1963), "based on [Cameron's] idea that shocking his patients into a chaotic regressed state would create the preconditions for him to 'rebirth' healthy model citizens" (47).

addressed, for instance, in a symbolic yet overt manner in Mike Bartlett's play *Artefacts*, first staged at the Bush Theatre in London in 2008, which hinges on a British schoolgirl's impulsive act of smashing an ancient Mesopotamian vase salvaged by her truant Iraqi father from the National Museum.

In a similar vein, Nicholas Mirzoeff traces how the coalition's counterinsurgency strategy sought "both to produce an acquiescent national culture and to eliminate insurgency [...] under the imperative 'culture must be defended'" (1738). The 'shock and awe' treatment is accompanied by the application of techniques whereby the invading force creates "a culture in its own image" (1739). Post-invasion (re/de)construction of Iraq is hence intricately connected to the 'values talk' examined in the previous chapter. The notion of bringing (neo)liberal values to Iraq is, in turn, linked to a geographical imagination that conceives of 'universal' values as spreading with the 'reach' of globalisation, which has "in reality been about westernization – the export of western commodities, values, priorities, ways of life" (Kevin Robins qtd. in Hall, "Question" 305). "Arab cities", writes Graham, "have long been represented by Western powers as dark, exotic, labyrinthine and structureless places that need to be 'unveiled' for the production of 'order' through the ostensibly superior [...] technologies of the occupying West" ("Cities" 256–257). This geographical imaginary finds expression in Blair's public pronouncements on the West's task to bring "order" to that other "part of the globe, [where] there is shadow and darkness, where not all the world is free" ("Speech" 248, 250). This move was in line with his earlier foreign-policy stance on crises such as the civil war in Sierra Leone in 2000, where he instigated a unilateral intervention without UN approval, acting "upon the premise that [...] 'global interdependence requires global values commonly or evenly applied'" (Jamison 371). This normative understanding is intricately connected to "the imposition of globalization on those who are not integrated", as Simon Dalby suggests (298).

With regard to the dramatisation of the neoliberal venture into Iraq, a pivotal question revolves around the agents of the 'imposition' of globalisation. Chandra Talpade Mohanty sketches a list of "imperial actors – the salesmen and planters, the brains and technicians, and the executives and military/security personnel" (8). These neoliberal war agents "tell very particular stories – not just of political economy and territorial control but also of [...] racialized patriarchies and heteronormative sexualities of empire" (8). Beyond their investment in gendered/racial power structures, a further connection can be drawn between the imperial actors deployed to foreign territories and the societies from which they hail. In practical terms, British companies and institutions have been heavily involved in the project of privatising the Iraqi economy. For instance, UK firm De La Rue printed the bills for the new currency in Iraq (at a time when people were lacking electricity and drinking water), and "Britain's Adam Smith Institute was contracted to help privatize Iraq's companies" (Klein 346–348). As Tariq Ali delineates, senior executives met at conferences in London, hosted by US reconstruction company Bechtel, soon after the beginning of the invasion in 2003: "It was agreed that a tiny proportion of the loot could be shared" (165). And in 2011, after the last British troops had withdrawn from Iraq, it transpired that energy giant BP profited from operating Iraq's largest oilfield in Rumaila to a previously inconceivable extent, fuelling the controversial notion of a 'war for oil' (Macalister 10). With the entanglements of transnational capital flows and company structures, the specific British role in disaster capitalism is not always easy to discern; yet the plays that accompany neoliberal war agents to the front line variously trace the impact of UK institutions, socioeconomic structures, and histories on the 'shock therapy' project in Iraq. In order to chart these interrelations, this chapter will continue the investigation into Mark Ravenhill's imbricated subjectivities, situated in-between 'here' and 'there', in *Shoot/Get Treasure/Repeat*. The discussion of Ravenhill's front-line playlets will be preceded by an analysis of Adam Brace's *Stovepipe* (2008), which similarly inserts audiences into a dense field of associations between the neoliberal capitalist system at home and the one being designed in Iraq.

"From Blank Slate to Scorched Earth":[22] Adam Brace's *Stovepipe*

One of the surest indicators of the privatisation of war is often taken to be the exponential rise in the deployment of private security/military contractors,[23] who are among the most prominent, if not infamous, neoliberal war agents. "And when there is killing to be done", Jonathan Rutherford writes of the foreign policy of post-industrial nation-states, "a denationalized imperialist war will find its proxies, mercenaries and the growing number of private military firms to undertake the dirty work" (639). Private security contractors, often inaccurately called *mercenaries* in public discourse,[24] figure as the protagonists of Adam

---

[22] "From Blank Slate to Scorched Earth" is the subtitle of Klein's concluding chapter on the Iraq war in *The Shock Doctrine*, which heavily influenced the reading offered here.

[23] In 2007, a year before *Stovepipe*'s premiere, more than 160,000 people in the UK were employed in the private security industry, which almost equalled the number of UK service personnel at the time (around 190,000), and the total number of private military forces in Iraq had surpassed that of UK troops (Zabci 3–4).

[24] What differentiates private contractors from mercenaries is the broad range of services they provide (e. g. logistics, consulting, hostage negotiation, guarding of sites) and the fact that pri-

Brace's *Stovepipe*. The promenade production premiered at the HighTide Festival in Halesworth, Suffolk, in 2008 and transferred to West 12 Centre in London in 2009 (in collaboration with the National and the Bush Theatre). As explained in the playscript, a "'stovepipe' is a common firearm malfunction. It occurs when shooting a firearm with a limp wrist" (Brace 12). The title could, on the one hand, be read as an overt comment on the errors and miscalculations of the Iraq invasion; on the other hand, it foreshadows the many glitches that occur during the contractors' rotation in the play, involving equipment and human failures ("People malfunction. In this industry" [69]).

The play offers, as Brace has put it in an interview with Sierz, an "episodic look through Alan's [its protagonist's] memory" revolving around his deployment to Iraq as a contractor (qtd. in Sierz, "Playwright"). The non-chronological structure corresponds to a high-paced promenade performance with frequent changes of rooms, situations, and temporalities. It is in particular the London production that is noteworthy in the context of the neoliberal elements of the Iraq invasion, for the play was staged in the basement of a shopping centre in Shepherd's Bush, a designated place for Western-style consumerism. This is how one critic described the promenade framing:

> The audience assemble in an abandoned shop [...] and is then led [...] down steep steps to the huge concrete basement. At first, we are treated as delegates at a Project Rebuild Iraq Conference, where military equipment and glossy posters promising a vibrant commercial future are on show, and the key speaker advises us of the importance of private security companies once the troops have moved out. And then sirens blare, the speaker is knocked to the ground and we are ushered to safety. (Spencer, "Most Thrilling Drama" 25)

Site-specific performance has risen in prominence and garnered much critical attention over recent years. "The increased visibility of site-specific practices points", as Fiona Wilkie assumes, "to a wider need to reconsider our relationships to the spaces we inhabit" (89). Wilkie argues for two shifts in emphasis in site-specific performances, which have particular resonance for an analysis of *Stovepipe*: first, she notes a turn "from performance that *inhabits* a space to performance that *moves through* spaces"; second, she identifies a shift "from a concern with the political and cultural meanings of particular locations to a focus on broader questions of what *site* as a category might mean" (90). Clearly, the promenade style of *Stovepipe* is indicative of the first phenomenon. When it comes to the second change, the way the performance has been conceived (and

---

vate military companies have a legal structure and corporate identity (Zabcı 4; Higate, "Drinking" 451).

received) would testify to a more general interest in 'site' too. In the above-cited interview, for example, Brace and Sierz discuss the "atmosphere" of the venue at length: Sierz recalls his sensations as an audience member in "all these gloomy corridors; [...] it all feels very abandoned and very unpleasant, it makes your skin crawl a bit", and Brace confirms that, for the production team, "the atmosphere of the place [...] was a real concern" ([qtd. in] Sierz, "Playwright"). In contrast, there is nowhere any consideration of the multiple associations between the space created in performance and the political and cultural meanings of the location.

This lack of an explicit enquiry notwithstanding, there are various connections to be drawn between the vacated shop used as a starting point for the promenade and the staged "Rebuild Iraq" conference. As this site signals, a previous system – embedded in existing economies – is replaced with new structures. The invitation extended to audience members as conference delegates positions them as possible investors and profiteers: "If you want lasting peace in Iraq, you won't do it without *international* investment" (13). I would argue that the identity of the place of performance, the shopping-centre basement in an "upwardly mobile" area of West London (Fisher, "*Stovepipe*"), productively interacts with the place produced in performance, the safe zone of air-conditioned conference centres in Amman, where the fate of neighbouring war-torn Iraq is settled. The spatial imaginary resulting from this convergence of real and staged place at once recalls Ali's description of the conferences held in London, where the imperial 'loot' was divided between Western investors. Klein relates a similar anecdote which has pertinence here: she writes about attending the "Rebuilding Iraq 2" conference in Washington, DC, where she was advised that "[t]he best time to invest is when there is still blood on the ground" (326).

Stovepipe positions spectators as consumers in three ways: first, on a pragmatic level, via entering the place of performance through a shopping centre; second, by an appeal to their investing power within the script's diegesis; third, as participants in a monopolistic performance, in the sense suggested by Michael McKinnie: as "spectators [who] are invited to 'purchase', through the performance, temporary 'ownership' over a distinct and non-replicable time, place, and experience" (29). The sense of an exclusive ownership is unmistakeably heightened in site-specific performances that make disused spaces available for temporary 'acquisition'. It is extremely fitting, then, that one reviewer has referred to the production as the "Iraq Experience" (Fisher, "*Stovepipe*"). As is the case with such tourist attractions, theatregoers book a virtual tour of Iraq with the aim of being entertained and potentially also enlightened. Their role as consumers of the theatrical experience interacts with their position as conference delegates within the dramatic frame, which prompts them to consider their indebtedness to the activities of contractors in Iraq: "electricity [...] government [...] investment. [...] [T]hese things are impossible. Impossible. Without private security companies" (13). In this manner, the framing device also paves the way for approaching the 'Iraq Experience' through the eyes of the contractors.

This takes shape as Carolyn, the "business brain" (14) of the company that recruits protagonist Alan, reads out the employment contract, which stipulates a long list of "dangers and voluntarily assume[d] risks" (16). The functional language of the document, which reduces the potentially ethical issue of "responsibility" to a mere technicality ("to obtain personal insurance" [17]), underlines the extent to which the privatised approach to war formalises the relationship between participants. The contractual relations established in the private sector stand in sharp contrast to the "unspoken contracts of brotherhood and camaraderie" that are commonly seen to characterise the "combat family" (Peebles 1667), as well as the collective rituals of military parades and "deference and demeanour ceremonies" (J. Kelly 729), where a bond is created not on economic terms, but on the basis of a moral duty towards one's monarch (and nation). Although the scene thus illustrates the discrepancy between modes of work for a private company and a state institution such as the military, Alan's intimate banter with the men who will be on his team undercuts Carolyn's technocratic speech. Notably, Alan already has a connection with Eddy and Grif from the "Paras"; they "were the ones who got [him] involved" (15). Not only can the men rely on the group solidarities forged in the army, but Alan also recurs to statements of purpose more familiar from a military context: "I like to think that in some small way, by going out there and doing this work, with the people of Iraq, that I can really. Help" (17). Even though the men discuss their salary in detail, "[s]ix hundred dollars a day. Twenty-four hours seven days a week job [...]. Twenty-five dollars. Fifteen pound an hour, that is" (17), the suggestion is that they are not purely driven by the prospect of personal gain, but that there are traces of the moral duty and "desire to act" that is associated with "the ethos of the British military" (King 322). Importantly, the dialogue closes with "ALAN *sign[ing] on* EDDY*'s back*" and the men "*clasp[ing] hands*" (17–18), which connotes that the 'real' contract will be between the men in the field.

In a broader sense, the shift from military to corporate roles, and the men's transition from soldiers in the Parachute regiment to employees of a British security company, is indicative of what Rutherford describes as the new "imperialism of the nation state", whose "neo-liberal marketized variant will draw upon its historic personality structures, update its militarism and liberalize its economics" (639). Accompanying this transition is the 'outsourcing' of the legitimate right to violence, dissolving the state's monopoly on the use of force. Significantly, until 2009, private companies operating in Iraq were not accountable to Iraqi law and could therefore act with relative impunity, as is reflected later on in the play (45–46). In a broader sense, the choice of private security contractors as the protagonists of front-line drama corresponds to their unprecedented centrality to the Iraq war. As Klein explains:

> The 'Baghdad boom', as it was called in the financial press, took what was a frowned-upon, shadowy sector and fully incorporated it into the U.S. and U.K. war-fighting machines. [...] The longer the war wore on, the more it became a privatized war, and soon enough, this was simply the new way of war. (378–380)

Filiz Zabcı corroborates the view that, as a result of the Iraq invasion, "a war or conflict without any interference of private military industry is considered to be out of question" (4). In light of these developments, there are remarkably few cultural responses to the phenomenon of private militarised companies. *Stovepipe* seems to have been the first British play about Iraq that stages contractors rather than soldiers,[25] which makes the conventions of front-line drama as focalising 'our soldiers' appear almost old-fashioned. British film has been even slower to pick up on the issue; after a short appearance of contractors in the Hollywood-produced Iraq war films *The Hurt Locker* (2008) and *Green Zone* (2010), where they are portrayed as stereotypical 'bounty hunters', British director Ken Loach turned a PSC employee into the protagonist of *Route Irish* (2011). Akin to Brace's play, Loach's film offers a fairly sympathetic representation of the men who decide to join the industry for financial gain but nevertheless retain an acute (if somewhat twisted) sense of moral principle.

In *Stovepipe*, the creation of an empathetic relationship to security contractors functions primarily by stressing the men's multiple position-takings, which reach beyond the economic-legal discourse that regulates their deployment. For the most part, Alan seems to believe that they are acting as a 'force for good' in Iraq, as evident, for instance, from his astonishment about an angry crowd of Iraqis appearing at a building site the contractors are guarding: "Don't they want the police station finished?" (56). Despite his contractual obligations, the language Alan uses to speak about his professional activities persistently highlights a sense of solidarity: he assures Eddy that he will not "walk out" on the team (27) after Grif's death, and he tells Carolyn that he "wouldn't want to let you guys down" (73). These assertions emphasise that, despite acting with relative impunity in Iraq, the contractors nevertheless feel accountable, if only to each other and to their employer. The play thus negotiates a subjectivity for

---

[25] To my knowledge, the only other example is the as yet unpublished *Dagestan* by SJ Fowler, which previewed as a scratch performance at Rich Mix in London in 2015.

the men that exceeds prevailing views of contractors as "vectors of [...] (controversial) forms of privatised power played-out on the ground, often for reasons of self and company gain", as Paul Higate's research on the public profile of the contracting workforce has shown (*Critical Impact Report* 40). Debate on the conduct of contractors in Iraq has often converged around scandals, such as the shooting of Iraqi civilians in Nisour Square in Baghdad in 2007 by employees of the US firm which was then known as Blackwater. As a consequence, Higate emphasises that negative perceptions of "trigger happy mercenaries" and "cowboys" have become quite firmly rooted in the popular imagination, whereas there are few constructions of "complexity in contractor [...] subjectivities that point to the flourishing of a professional conscience" (3, 40).

The most emphatic rebuttal of the mercenary stereotype and the associated traits of self-interest and recklessness comes at the plot level. That ethical and personal bonds take precedence over economic motivations becomes starkly apparent as both Grif's and Eddy's disappearances drive the entire plot. The flashback scene in which Grif is killed as their convoy is escorting a truck from Baghdad airport is staged twice, in an almost identical manner, and the performance ends with a memorial service. Eddy's disappearance, in turn, provides the central plot device, as Alan embarks on a search for him. Notably, this brings Alan into conflict with the terms of his contract; he goes AWOL not only at the cost of forfeiting his profit but also at the risk of legal consequences, as the company threatens to "begin proceedings" against him (47). While one may sense traces of the cowboy or frontier identity in Alan's single-handed search operation and Eddy's private vendetta against the company CEO, which both highlight the "legal/lethal impunity" of contractors "working to their own rules of engagement" (Higate, "Drinking" 454), the drastic means to which the characters resort appear morally motivated and Alan, especially, retains audience sympathy throughout. Although the play's idealisation of homosocial camaraderie, whose values are nowhere called into question, makes for a problematic affirmation of the type of militarised masculinity that is conducive to warfare – an issue that will be explored in detail in the final subchapter – it has to be noted that it here serves to challenge simplistic popular imaginations of security contractors. In other words, the 'stories' these imperial war agents 'tell' are of more complex loyalties than the stereotypes of privately hired killers driven purely by personal gain would suggest.

The 'blank slate' of Iraq is, in fact, only a minor location in the performance. Similar to the negotiations of Afghan femininities that are situated off stage in plays about the 'humanitarian' intervention, Iraq features primarily as a bartered good. The fact that the neoliberal war agents engage as "salesm[e]n" marketing a particular version of Iraq is reflected on a meta-level by Carolyn's comment about the conference: "expect not to recognise the Iraq they talk about" (65). In the flashback scenes that are set in the war zone, the country is represented as a chaotic, volatile place, much in line with popular imaginative geographies. Similarly, the search for Eddy unfolding across Amman, which takes audiences swiftly "around the dungeons" beneath the shopping centre (Fisher, "*Stovepipe*"), draws on "popular geopolitical representations of [...] intrinsically devious [...] Orientalized streets" (Graham, "Cities" 264). Centrally, the two nigh-on identical scenes which restage the airport run during which Grif dies feature heated, hectic exchanges between the men in an increasingly opaque situation. Audiences are very much 'thrown' into these scenes the same way the contractors are, and the spectators' sense of confusion about what is happening might make them more prone to affectively register the anxiety and disorientation of the men. Again, in these front-line scenes, Iraq is conjured up as a 'wild' place, lacking 'ordinary' inhabitants or everyday life; it is primarily the locus of ubiquitous, unspecified threats.

Yet the way in which the British characters are positioned against this spatial backdrop is critically reflective of the role 'our' imaginings have played in the construction of Iraq. The dialogue is interspersed with references to the invaders' remapping of pre-existing cartographies. Most prominently, the "airport road's called Route Irish", as Alan tells the audience (18). The name Route Irish is a fair indicator of the neo-imperial geopolitics at the core of the Iraq invasion: as Brace explains, US forces named the routes in Iraq after college sports teams; Route Irish goes back to the Notre Dame University teams, which are known as the "Fighting Irish" (qtd. in Sierz, "Playwright"). Alan signposts other elements of these neocolonial topographies for the audience, who come to imagine Iraq on the invaders' terms: he explains that "[t]he first bridge [is] called J for Jihad" (19), or he describes how "we enter the Kill Zone" (20). What becomes clear from this collectively imagined tour of the airport road is that the occupying forces have labelled the existing infrastructure according to their own uses and perceptions of the foreign place. This is, moreover, reflected by the vocabulary Alan employs when invoking images of Iraq: "There's a shit loada charred date trees lining Irish. [...] The ground's all scorched" (19). Possibly, the choice of the descriptor *scorched* is not incidental, but a reference to the 'shock and awe' tactics of the occupying forces, which have produced a 'scorched' ground. The semantics of Iraqi place in the play are thus critically mimetic of the geographical (mis)imaginings of Iraq as a 'blank slate', waiting to be remapped, renamed, and restructured. "This is what happens with projects to build model societies in other people's countries", as Klein declares: "when the people who live on the land refuse to abandon their past [...] the dream of the clean slate morphs into its doppelgänger, the scorched earth" (374). The fierce reaction the contractors encounter on Route Irish, then, becomes legible as a response to neo-imperial efforts at remodelling a foreign society. It is, again, perhaps no coincidence in this regard that the contractors mistake a "Big Mac wrapper" for an IED (22). The post-invasion optimism, epitomised by "talk of a McDonald's opening in downtown Baghdad – the ultimate symbol of Iraq joining the global economy" (Klein 346), here gives way to despair as the very symbols of 'benign' globalisation turn against the invading forces.

A critical potential to expose the structure of the neoliberal 'shock treatment', which may or may not be realised in performance, inheres in the frequent references to such brands and icons. As can be seen from photographs, the original production (designer: takis) deliberately used props with highly visible brand names, such as Evian water bottles or ASUS notebooks. The critical reflection on the nexus of consumer capitalism, globalisation, and imperialism by reference to (the export of) Western commodities is most evident in another flashback scene set in Iraq. After their increasingly forceful attempts at dispersing the aforementioned angry crowd who appear at the building site the contractors are guarding,

> *they don't notice a figure breaking from the darkness.* ALAN *does. In the torchlight an* ARAB MAN *can be seen running. His jacket looks stuffed with something.* [The contractors attempt to stop the man and give the obligatory three warnings.] *The* ARAB MAN *ignores them, tries to scurry away. A hail of gunfire brings him down.* [...] ALAN *approaches with* EDDY, *who shines the torch while* ALAN *delicately undoes the jacket. Cans of Coke and Pepsi fall out.* (56–57)

While Alan displays a sense of consternation, Grif surmises that the man "heard us alright. Must be stolen" (57), and Eddy shrugs the man's death off as a "[s]hitty state of affairs dying for blackmarket soft drinks" (58). At the site of the corpse, Eddy and Grif, clearly bemused, engage in a "taste test" with the pierced cans, and they finally "*swiftly drag the body away*" (58).

The fact that reviewers have commented on this brief scene as "rais[ing] awareness of the futility of an occupation that can leave a boy dead having committed no greater crime than pilfering four cans of cola" (Fisher, "*Stovepipe*") strikes me as indicative of its centrality. In my reading, the scene reveals the detrimental effects of the imposition of globalisation. Seen against Blair's statement on the values at stake in the Iraq war – "they detest the freedom, democracy and tolerance that are the hallmarks of our way of life" ("Iraq Debate Speech" 241) – it appears that the Iraqi is killed precisely not for hating 'our' values, but for trying to emulate them. The free market, or rather its shadow, the black market, fatally entices the man into the freedom to consume. He dies not because he lacks but strives for the Western values signified by American brands. The scene can be understood as an ironic echo of the mujahideen's credo that was circulated after 9/11: "The Americans love Pepsi-Cola. We love death!" (qtd. in Reuter 139) – it is because he, too, loves 'Pepsi-Cola' that the man meets his death at the hands of the Western forces. Similar to the shooting of the football-playing children in *Days of Significance*, resemblance is here decoded as the enemy's uncanny deception. The scene thus makes a crucial point about the continuities between 'our' and 'their' consumer desires. It is not incidental that the Coca Cola brand was relaunched in Baghdad in 2005 thanks to the economic conditions established by Western forces (Carroll 14). In alluding to the geography of commodity chains, the scene exemplifies how the (re)opening of the market to the influx of Western consumer goods and investors proved lethal for Iraqi civilians. On the whole, the flashback scenes set in Iraq span a certain trajectory, reaching from the 'scorched' ground to the death of the Iraqi man, if read against Klein's cynical summary of the "game plan for Iraq: shock and terrorize the entire country, deliberately ruin its infrastructure [...], then make it all okay with an unlimited supply of cheap household appliances and imported junk food" (339). *Stovepipe* thus throws into sharp relief the operation of the neoliberal 'shock treatment'.

"There's No Food in Zone Eight": Mark Ravenhill's *Shoot/Get Treasure/Repeat*

If the link between Western routines of consumption and the neoliberal Iraq war venture is implicitly established through site-specificity and negotiated through commentary on the privatised market of warfare in *Stovepipe*, Mark Ravenhill's *Shoot/Get Treasure/Repeat* cycle explicitly and repeatedly evokes connections between economic-ideological systems 'here' and 'there'. As has been outlined in the analysis of the home-front playlets that form part of the cycle, most of the pieces are marked by blurred geographies that variously transgress the boundaries between the 'safe' spaces of Western consumerism and the 'dangerous' territories that are yet to be 'integrated' into a globalised free market. The cycle as a whole highlights, as John Hutnyk writes in another context, "the imbrication of here and there as co-constituted operative centres of a never-ending battle" (159). Therefore, even when shifting the focus to the front line, the multiple links created between neoliberal subjectivities at home and abroad deserve tacit attention. Indicative of their convergence is the fact that, in the London production, four of the five pieces that could be classified as front-line plays were staged as double or triple bills alongside plays with more clearly recognisable home-front settings. In this way, the stereotyped Western worlds of middle-class citizen consumers depicted in *Women of Troy* or *War of the Worlds*, as analysed in the previous chapter, come to intersect and interact with "a middle-class household in an occupied country" in *Love (But I Won't Do That)* or an interrogation centre in a "country [that] has been invaded" in *Twilight of the Gods* (front matter).

Specific associations between modes of subject formation at home and on the front emerge from this particular combination of plays. There is, for instance, the concern with medication for stomach pain by the speaker of the monologue *Intolerance*, which was staged alongside the front-line play *Crime and Punishment* at the National Theatre in the London run. Helen's pain is clearly a symptom of the larger social malaise of a thoroughly neoliberalised world, where relationships are forged through ticking boxes on a form (19) and family life consists in "snuggling up together in front of a DVD" (23). Helen's suppression of a profound sense of discontent is echoed in the soldier's description of the Western world in *Crime and Punishment*: "My country is safe. It's a safe, numb place. The people are happy people. Underneath I ache but still I ... I can go to the supermarket" (90). In line with this characterisation, Helen is convinced that the right diet, the intake of "zinc and calcium and iron" (27), works towards healing her condition – that is, suppressing the 'ache'. What is more, thanks to her immersion in self-help therapy, Helen feels "reborn" (25) – a term that is loaded with connotations of Iraq's neoliberal 'rebirth'. The work on one's own body in the Western middle-class context is evidently based on the ideology of self-optimisation: Helen's professed aim is "making [her] life – As near perfect as any life can be" (27). All that Ravenhill's managerial state demands of its subjects, with the support of self-help guides, is to find their own "little ritual" (27) to pursue this agenda. In return, they obtain the quintessential neoliberal right of access "to pursue whatever means necessary to realize their own life projects inside a capitalist framework" (Featherstone et al. 170). Yet, as Helen's relapsing pain attacks evidence, the cure will only ever imperfectly address the 'ache'.

The biopolitical work of optimising the body (politic) serves, as the recurring motifs of pain and medication in *Crime and Punishment* suggest, as the model for the Iraq invasion. The playlet is set in "an occupied zone" and revolves around a "soldier interrogat[ing] a native woman" (front matter). Although it is not explicitly an Iraq war play, there are numerous allusions that associate the scene with the invasion: the soldier's questions about "the dictator" (83) and "the day the statue comes down" (84) are likely to be read as references to Hussein and the toppling of his statue – one of the most widely circulated "photo ops" in the image war (Mitchell 3). Similar to Moore's play *The Empire*, the structure of interrogation informs the internal communicative frame, which associates the dramatisation with the practices of state terror that Asad identifies at work "in interrogation centers where vital information is obtained" (28). The fact that *Crime and*

Punishment stages the application rather than the combating of terror is also implicit in Jenny Spencer's summary of the play as depicting "gradually escalating abuse" in the form of the soldier's torturing the woman "with insensitive, sadly inappropriate, and increasingly threatening language", leading to the "shocking, violent, and overdetermined end" of cutting out her tongue ("Terrorized" 73).

It is important in this regard that the interrogation scenario remains generic; neither the soldier nor the woman are named, unlike many of the other characters in the cycle. Prototypically and metonymically, the soldier stands for the invading country and the native woman for the occupied territory. As may be unsurprising in such a constellation, their interaction is extremely sexualised, and the threat of rape underlies the entire scene. The articulation of a dominant heteromasculine subject position against a 'native' female object position starkly illustrates the imaginative geographies of empire as a "penetrating phallic entity", whose advance guard consists in "male colonists [...] invited to inscribe their British authority on feminized overseas territories" (Gittings 2; see also Zine 31–32). This colonial power structure is given a neoliberal twist as it is filtered through the optimisation discourse. Helen's 'cure' for her stomach pain reappears here in the form of the mantra-like repetition of 'core values' as a remedy as well as concrete doses of medication. Thus, whereas the woman begins to position herself (and, by extension, the nation) in terms of a narrative of bereavement, as a "woman who was once a wife and mother and is now a widow", the soldier seems to proceed by the interrogation protocol by ascertaining: "You have been given coffee and a bread roll. You have received medication. You are feeling tranquil?" (83). Not once does the soldier respond to the woman's loss, as the language of interrogation does not provide a subjective position and affective sensibility for the interviewee. The more the woman seeks to express her grief, the more the soldier imposes his own emotional needs and sexual desires on her:

WOMAN. I've been a widow for five days. Your army ...
SOLDIER. I'm in a lot of pain here. I want you to love me. [...]
WOMAN. My husband was laid to rest yesterday. My son will be laid to rest tomorrow.
SOLDIER. Frigid bitch. [...] Sorry, sorry but ... look at me, I'm a person, I'm a human person, with a heart, I have so much love to give. (86)

The interviewee's attempts to establish her own subjectivity within the interrogation script are barred by the ever more erratic proceedings, determined by the soldier's selfish projection of his desires onto the woman. Early on in the dialogue, then, it becomes very obvious to what extent the measures designed to 'liberate' Iraq fail to apprehend the subjects who inhabit Iraqi society. The interrogator's inability to register the woman's enunciations stands metonymically for the invading army's profound "incomprehension of the situation and nation it seeks to transform" (Feldman, "Actuarial Gaze" 217).

There is a parallel here to the other interrogation play *Twilight of the Gods*, where the "report" (156) that Jane is working on can never adequately transcribe the testimony of Susan, the inhabitant of the occupied country.[26] Susan's repeated assertions that there is "no food in our zone" (156) are systematically (dis)qualified by translating them into the terms of the technocratic military operation: "Food supplies unsatisfactory" (157). What is more, the interviewee is, again, not endowed with a speaking position that is imbued with the authority to adequately describe the state of affairs: "Susan feels there's no food in Zone Eight" (157). The interrogator's tacit but systematic dismissal of the interviewee's statements points to the invading forces' exertion not only of military dominance but also of discursive control over the occupied territory and its subjects. Jane's subtle manipulations appear all the more insidious, for her pretension to be empathetic sustains Susan's erroneous belief that her – and the population's – pain and suffering could be registered: "you write it down, you write it down and put it in your report" (156); "You've got to let them know what's happening" (157). As Susan's increasingly desperate attempts to influence the reporting of the war indicate, there can be no assertion of subjectivity outside the correlative positions distributed within the discursive formation of the 'war on terror'. The only speaking position whose utterances can be documented is one that affirms a predetermined truth, according to which the invaders "were compelled to intervene, because of the terrible things that were happening in your country" (163). Only so long as the interviewee sticks to this game of truth can her voice be heard and transcribed.

Similarly, instead of recognising the woman's pain, the soldier in *Crime and Punishment* can only proceed by 'ticking the boxes' seemingly specified by the interrogation script. These stipulate that the interrogated has to appear 'tranquil'. The choice of this descriptor, repeated twice in his opening remarks ("You are feeling tranquil? [...] And almost tranquil" [83]), is probably not incidental. The soldier goes on to tell the woman: "I've fought my way through the desert. My tranquilisers were lost. My girl texted me to say she's got together with this – sorry – fuckwit" (84). The reference to tranquilisers, in combination with the soldier's repeated enquiries after the woman's tranquillity, reinforces

---

26 Again, there are various allusions that associate the dramatised conflict with the Iraq war; yet there is also a parallel to Israel's blockade of Gaza, evoked by references to the occupied zone and the fact that "the insurgents stop us getting the food through" (158). The blurring of geopolitical boundaries is, as is the case with the play cycle at large, deliberate and leads to a pervasive sense of a globalised state of emergency.

the analogy to the 'shocked and awed' body politic. Klein's analysis of the shock-therapy programme outlines the tactics of inducing a stupor in the populace, creating a "window of opportunity" to slip in the neoliberal shock treatment (48). Insofar as the interrogator in Ravenhill's piece remains an archetypal soldier figure, the reference to losing his tranquilisers could also be read as an allusion to Tim O'Brien's frequently anthologised Vietnam war short story "The Things They Carried" (1986). The soldier's speech echoes O'Brien's line, "Ted Lavender, who was scared, carried tranquilizers" (2). That Ravenhill's soldier admits to having been attracted to the Iraqi woman when he saw her in a news broadcast about the toppling of the statue, finding her "mouth [...] pornographic" (84), is also reminiscent of a passage in "The Things They Carried", where Jimmy Cross contemplates photographs of Martha, "her lips slightly open as she stared straight-on at the camera" (4). Just as Martha remains "flat and uninvolved" (11), the soldier's anger and arousal increase in proportion to the woman's refusals to requite his love.

As a meta-comment on the invasion, the soldier's repeated questions, "How do I make you fall in love with me?" (86), echo the official concerns with why 'they' hate/bomb 'us', reiterated especially in the choral scenes. His crude attempts exemplify the paradoxical expectation that a bereaved woman/country would greet the occupying forces with open arms. The woman's rejection of the soldier recalls utterances about the ungratefulness of Iraqi civilians, as captured by Ali's description of the early phase of the invasion:

> Already the lack of any spontaneous welcome from Shi'ites and the fierce resistance of armed irregulars have prompted the theory that the Iraqis are a 'sick people' who will need protracted treatment before they can be entrusted with their own fate (if ever). (162)

Beyond mimicking the conviction that there should be a 'spontaneous welcome' from the 'liberated' people, the soldier's attempts at love-making also reveal the inappropriateness of the 'cure' chosen in the shock therapy. The archetypal male soldier is only able to relate to the invaded people in terms of heterosexual desires: "Maybe there is love in another place, maybe if we invade again then a woman will say ..." (94). Reading the scene against the Vietnam war (short) story reveals the normative gender relations that structure every war, to varying degrees. The interrogation scene of *Crime and Punishment* exemplifies the discrepancy between, to stay within the terms of the market, supply and demand: a singular formula to win 'hearts and minds' is not going to work if the desires, needs, and suffering of those invaded cannot appear within established discursive frames.

The interrogation scene in *Crime and Punishment* can, on the whole, be seen as allegorical of the shock-therapy treatment. It exemplifies Klein's definition of disaster capitalism as "orchestrated raids on the public sphere in the wake of catastrophic events" (6). The raiding of the public sphere is implicit in the invading army's shooting of the woman's husband, who was a lecturer at university. Although the "husband was not allowed to teach" (84) under the dictator, the political alternative imposed by the invaders is even less desirable. As a result of reducing the previous socioeconomic system to 'scorched earth', the megalomaniac soldier-invader has paved the way, or created the market, for Western corporations: "They want supermarkets, they want garden centres, they want Xboxes, they want Starbucks. They got it. It's coming" (91). The shooting of the university lecturer is echoed by other front-line playlets in the cycle; Susan, for instance, "used to be an important person. I taught in the university. I was respected by my students", but the occupation diminished her to "this pathetic [person]" (157). The repeated references to the loss of lives and livelihoods of university lecturers and "civil servants" (159) could be read in analogy to the systematic dismantling of the public sector in the early phase of the Iraq invasion, in which half a million state workers were fired under the cover of "De-Baathification" (Klein 351).

Ravenhill's dramatisation of the shock treatment also reflects the televised spectacle of the Iraq invasion. As much as the soldier's comments on his own operating procedure suggest an implicit recording of the interrogation ("9.43 a.m. I have shot detainee in the foot" [91]), they persistently point to his awareness of an audience. These, strictly speaking, superfluous comments recall not only the torturers' reckless posing for the cameras in the Abu Ghraib photographs (e.g. Lynndie England's infamous thumbs-up sign, which has become known as "Doing a Lynndie") but also position theatregoers in an uneasy relationship to the representation. Audience members become spectators to their own experience of watching terror. "Shock and awe", as Feldman insists, "is more than a military tactic; it is simultaneously an exercise in war as visual culture for the consumption of the televisual audience, a technology of mass spectatorship" ("Actuarial Gaze" 217). The staging of the soldier's violation of the body (politic) in front of an audience whose presence is implicitly acknowledged becomes a disturbing spectacle, which works as a visceral demonstration and concomitant refusal of the brutal excesses of war.

Another play in the cycle, *Birth of a Nation*, adds a different dimension to Ravenhill's critique of the forcible extension of globalisation, showing that it is not only about the spread of universal – that is, Western – values, brands, and lifestyles but also about the recreation of a culture in the West's own image, to recall Mirzoeff. The piece is one of the few that was not staged in the form of double or triple bills in the London run; it received an exclusive staging at the Royal Court Downstairs. The production context forms diverse associations with the dramatic cosmos. The play is about a team of "Artist-Facilitators" (189) who "come to work with the local people after a foreign power has withdrawn" (front matter). It inserts itself more explicitly into UK-based contexts than the other plays, with the artists professing that "we all marched against [...] this war" (190). Especially in the Royal Court production, the association with the London anti-war protests must have been unmistakeable. It is particularly noteworthy in this respect that the production was directed by Ramin Gray, who had also directed Stephens's *Motortown* at the same venue in 2006, a play which similarly seeks to unmask the liberal hypocrisies surrounding the anti-Iraq war rallies: "they march against the war and think they're being radical. They're lying" (Stephens, *Motortown* 259). In the year of *Motortown*'s premiere, Dominic Cooke was appointed artistic director of the Royal Court Theatre. As was reported in the media at the time, Cooke deliberately set out to satirise his audience by looking at "what it means to be middle class", that is, by commissioning plays with "characters [that] represent the values of many of the theatregoers" (qtd. in Brown and Kennedy 9).

This stated goal seems to resonate particularly well with Ravenhill's approach in *Shoot/Get Treasure/Repeat*. Indeed, *Birth of a Nation* appears to speak specifically to a liberal audience. The artist-facilitators initially articulate a pronounced anti-war stance: "we called out to stop this bloody war but [...] still our so-called elected so-called democratically elected so-called representatives still they went ahead and pursued their horrible bloody little war" (191). The speakers' strategies of disassociation from the war story are reminiscent of the widespread use of the "Not in My Name" banners in the London protests. To reiterate Hutnyk's comment, "the slogan 'Not in My Name' was [...] itself indicative of responsibilities shirked, disavowed and ignored, and thereby deeply damaging" (138). The artist-facilitators clearly disavow their own responsibilities by disengaging from their 'so-called representatives', the "Butchers" (191). This rhetoric invokes the ubiquitous images of Blair with blood-stained hands, used at protest events and circulated widely on the internet. It is the 'Butchers' who reduced the foreign city, possibly alluding to Baghdad, to 'scorched earth': "a city with every building shattered and the people shattered and the dead littering the streets" (190). Presumably countering the 'blank slate' narrative, the artists declare their appreciation for the pre-existing civilisation:

> I've been looking you up [...] and – wow! – what a culture you used to have, what a culture, what an amazing culture you used to have. Before we had a culture [...] – you had your own

stories, beautiful huge really long epic stories, your alphabet, sculpting, dancing – you really – you had a culture here thousands of years ago. (191)

The use of repetition and the exaggerated expressions of fascination betray the insincerity of the sentiment. Despite the acknowledgement of the ancient civilisation of a country that could well be Iraq, the speakers reproduce the imagined geography of the 'blank slate' by endorsing the ideology of 'rebirth', which is also implicit in the title *Birth of a Nation*: "Here is ... a time to rebuild, a time to heal, [...] a new forward" (192). Significantly, the speakers fall back onto hegemonic geopolitical constructions of Iraq by promoting a 'new forward' that, eventually, completely overrides the 'amazing culture' previously lauded.

This is where an additional aspect of the imposition of globalisation becomes apparent, namely that which Eva Illouz has insightfully described as the export of a therapeutic model of subjectivity:

> not only have psychological models of selfhood given rise to a new habitus – which we may characterize as a 'global' therapeutic habitus – but [...] this habitus is characteristic of a social group of managers and cultural specialists most involved in the process of globalization. (220)

The therapeutic habitus clearly informs the speaking position developed by the 'cultural specialists' in Ravenhill's play. They approach the 'shattered' nation like a patient amenable to their therapeutic efforts: "We come to a place where everyone's been hurting and we start the healing process by working through, by working with art" (192). The phrase 'everyone's been hurting' sounds like a conventional Western truism, which carries diverse pop-cultural associations, most prominently with the R.E.M. hit "Everybody Hurts" (1992). This mindless application of an essentialising formula reveals the workings of what Illouz calls *emotional style*, in reference to "the ways a culture becomes 'preoccupied' with certain emotions and devises specific 'techniques' – linguistic, scientific, and ritual – to apprehend them" (14). The speakers position themselves in terms of the therapeutic self-narratives cultivated in the emotional style of the Western middle class: "For me it was abuse. The terrible abuse I'd suffered as a child. My father had ... I couldn't see any way of moving forward but [...] then I saw the sign: 'Heal Through Art'" (194). The art-therapeutic approach is applied to the foreign country in reliance on the idiom of neoliberal self-optimisation: "There is so much work to do here. There is so much pain to heal. [...] But you must sign up for the dance or the writing or the painting or the performance installation workshops" (196–197). The previously expressed admiration for the ancient culture is now exposed as a mere ploy to appeal to the 'native' subject and entice it to embrace what is essentially a form of cultural imperialism: instead of working with the traditional cultural forms, the 'epic stories, alphabet, sculpting, dancing', the people are supposed to 'sign up' for the new artefacts exported to the country.

The strategies of persuasion employed by the speakers increasingly resort to the rhetoric of the neoliberal 'reconstruction' programme explored in *Stovepipe*: "You want investment? You want tourism? You want civilisation? [...] – you want all that then [...] let some culture into the ruins of this shattered city" (197). This equivalential articulation discloses the circulation of 'culture' and 'civilisation' as commodities in a forcibly globalised free market. The artist-facilitators are thus exposed as the neoliberal agents of "New Labour's 'creative industries' paradigm", which Jen Harvie delineates as follows:

> Fundamentally, this model's economic emphasis prioritises commercial value over social value and fashions culture as marketable commodities [...]. The term [*creative industries*] potentially disempowers people by transforming them from collective audiences and makers into individual and alienated consumers. (23)

New Labour's creative-industries model of quantifying, commodifying, and capitalising on cultural items appears as a resource from which the speakers draw their language of advertising. They appropriate the marketing strategies of such campaigns as the European City of Culture scheme: "Wouldn't it be great in a few years' time if this was a city of culture, if this city had a festival like ... other cities" (197). By becoming enlisted in the transnational programmes of a project-based economy, the foreign city is forcefully opened up for the influx of Western cultural products. Contrary to their previous efforts to disidentify with the military mission, the artists are thus unmasked as the agents of a culture war that is only ostensibly "devoid of the violences of capital's imperialisms" (Alexander 185).

Birth of a Nation could be seen to inculpate a liberal middle-class audience by revealing the contradictions that underwrite a pronounced anti-war stance. It does so, especially, by establishing explicit connections between Western, particularly British, neoliberal systems and subjectivities and the workings of disaster capitalism abroad. The one speaker most firmly grounded in a British context is the miner-turned-dancer. His therapeutic self-narrative begins with the pit closures in the 1980s: "I was a miner. I was born a miner. There'd been mines in my region for centuries. [...] Then one day, we came through the town to find a sign: 'Pit closed'. [...] You just ... your world is gone" (193). What is especially remarkable is that his 'healing' process is connected not to the collective action of the miners' strike, which he briefly glosses, but stems from an eventual embrace of the pit closures as an opportunity for economic and personal advancement:

> we were fighting for the right to be shut away in the dark, shut down in the pit and have the coal on our lungs and the right to die an early death and that was […] totally fucking stupid. […] The mine wasn't going to open, really I shouldn't even want it to open – in a sane world – but still, when you can't see a way forward … (193–194)

The miner's development is paradigmatic of the shift towards the privatised citizen subject (see chapter three); his abandoning of solidarity with the miners epitomises "the emptiness of the modern self severed from communal relationships" (Illouz 1). The speaker's rejection of the miners' struggle points to an endorsement of Margaret Thatcher's conservative economic programme. The brutality of the policies that brought massive unemployment and loss of a whole way of life to entire communities and regions in the UK has been erased from the miner's self-narrative. Therapeutic insight here means the acceptance that the pit closures resulted in 'a way forward', towards (self-)optimisation.

Despite their liberal intentions, the outcome of the artists' cultural intervention is similar to the devastation caused by the military assault. At the end of *Birth of a Nation*, the contortions of a "woman [who] has lost her tongue and […] her eyes" (198) are misinterpreted as artistic expressions of the therapeutic self: "That's it, be brave. Express. Create. Be bold" (199). The scene closes as "*the* BLIND WOMAN *spasms*" and "*the* CHORUS *applaud*" (199). This ending raises compelling questions as to the audience's involvement: could their own applause during the curtain call be seen as mimicking the chorus, and thus as an endorsement of the violent imposition of the therapeutic habitus? In what ways are Western attempts, however benign, to understand or to 'help' the Iraqi population, inherently thwarted by cultural imperialism and a sense of superiority? Is there, within and beyond the cycle written by a British playwright, any way to see, hear, and apprehend the suffering of Iraqis outside of what Illouz sees as emotional capitalism or what Mark Fisher defines as "capitalist realism", that is, the "widespread sense that not only is capitalism the only viable […] system, but also that it is now impossible to even *imagine* a coherent alternative to it" (2)? If Ravenhill's critique is accurate, there is no way for British citizens, or the Royal Court audience of this particular production, to relate to the Iraq war outside the frames of emotional capitalism. *Birth of a Nation* cynically discloses the only response available to those neoliberal subjects who would occupy an anti-war position: disengage from a war launched by 'their' elected representatives. This ties in with the other choral scenes, which similarly outline the erosion of public spheres that might provide subjects with a powerful collective voice to speak out against (state) terror, corroborating Alan Read's view on the failure of the anti-war movement: "When we say 'Not in my name', our words cannot be heard too clearly because we gave up any right to speak in our own name some time ago" (243).

Stovepipe ties in with this critique of the neoliberal civic contract, whereby 'our so-called representatives' wage a war from which 'we' readily disengage. It illustrates the privatised reworking of the "Military Covenant between the nation, the Army and each individual soldier" that is traditionally construed as "an unbreakable common bond of [...] responsibility" (qtd. in Forster 1044). In place of the symbolic agreement that soldiers forfeit their civilian rights in exchange for support by the community of citizens,[27] there is solely an economic-legal contract regulating the deployment of neoliberal war agents who act in the interests of transnationally operating companies (or creative industries). The lack of an emotional or ethical link between contractors and the Western publics on whose behalf the war is waged conveniently divests citizens of complicity in the violence whose monopoly is relinquished by the managerial state. In staging the failure of various kinds of neoliberal war agents to bring 'relief' to Iraq, the plays discussed here derive their resistant potential from accentuating the "multiple and interlocking forms of 'terror'" that are summarily obliterated by the abstract concept against which the 'war on terror' is waged, namely, "the terror of neo-imperialism and global militarism, the terror of global corporate capitalism, the terror of poverty and starvation" (Zine 44).

4.4 Reporting Front-Line Deaths

It is significant that, at the end of Ravenhill's *Birth of a Nation*, it is a mute woman whom the artists call on to "tell us of your pain and struggle so the art can be made and the healing can begin" (198). For obvious reasons, the woman is unable to 'tell' her own version of the war story; her attempts at articulation are (mis)interpreted by the artist-facilitators: "This woman has lost her family. [...] We can only imagine how deeply your pain must run" (198). If seen as standing in for the Iraqi body politic, the woman becomes the generic victim of war whose story cannot be heard but is nevertheless appropriated for the sake of validating the schemes of the (cultural) imperialists. The final

---

27 As Anthony Forster summarises the doctrine of the military covenant, "army personnel are called upon to make personal sacrifices and in return are guaranteed fair treatment by the state" (1044).

image of the convulsing woman on stage, surrounded by cheering artists, potentially has a more drastic effect than Bean's final scene about manipulating the photograph of the Afghan schoolgirl in order to 'sell' the humanitarian invasion. With their respective endings, both plays raise the question of whose (war) stories get told, and by whom, and problematise the restrictive ways in which only certain subjects are endowed with a legitimate speaking position to report on the war.

Butler takes modes of storytelling as a point of departure for her enquiry into the politics of mourning and violence in *Precarious Life*. Writing about 9/11, she notes how, "[i]n the United States, we begin the story by invoking a first-person narrative point of view, and telling what happened on September 11" (*Precarious Life* 5). She assumes that the first-person narrative is particularly appealing in this context "because it resituates agency in terms of a subject, something we can understand, something that accords with our idea of personal responsibility" (5). The bereaved, mourning 'self' of the West is fully intelligible as a subject according to the norms that govern grievability and injurability; hence, this narrating subject is imbued with the authority to tell its own (9/11) story, from its own point of view. In contrast to the Western narrative of grief, 'other' subjects will always fall outside the 'frames of war' like "discarded negatives" (Butler, *Frames* xiii). Neither can their lives and losses be apprehended or mourned, nor could they acquire an enunciatory position to tell their own war stories. From the communities of bereaved on the home front, this chapter moves on to the differential allocation of grievability on the front line, examining Iraq war drama's complex relationship to the exclusionary norms of human intelligibility.

Once more, the apparent dichotomy of home versus front is at stake here. The juxtaposition of plays revolving around issues of mourning is designed to trace the various transgressions of this binary. Having said that, there is undeniably a perceptible line of demarcation that corresponds to the differential allocation of grievability. Joseph Pugliese, in his discussion of the "electronic morgue" built through the "Iraq Body Count" website, which offers a record of civilian and combatant deaths since the 2003 invasion, observes how the "rituals of mourning and the pain of loss can only be enacted in the civic spaces of the western metropolis"; in contrast, deaths occurring in Iraq are "reduced to the seriality of a body count or to the economical enumeration of a single bar graph" (12, 29). The differential valuation of lives ties in with the imaginative geographies charted throughout this chapter. The configuration of 'their' spaces as abstract targets for military intervention legitimises, and might partly be constitutive of, the elision of Iraqi/Afghan lives. To quote again from Graham's analysis of the virtualised representations of Arab cities: "Verticalized web and newspaper maps in the US and UK [...] have routinely displayed Iraqi cities as [...] impact points, where [...] bombs and missiles are either envisaged to land or have landed, grouped along flat, cartographic surfaces" ("Cities" 263). These 'flat' surfaces convey the impression of an uninhabited land, dotted with mere 'impact points' that can be targeted in precise, clean military operations. The lives and deaths of civilians have no place within this frame of war.

This is not the same as claiming that there are no visuals showing their suffering and losses – which is manifestly not so, as Iraqi civilian casualties have been depicted in the British media to an unprecedented degree (Fahmy and Kim 455). The point here is that these deaths remain "undetailed", as Feldman suggests; the "[a]nonymous victims of collateral damage" circulate outside the frames of an "antiseptic digitized [...] war" ("Actuarial Gaze" 214). In tune with the logic of collateral damage, the images of dead civilians are disseminated in ways that banalise them. Rancière argues that this is the case precisely not because we see too few images of horror but because "we [...] see too many nameless bodies"; visualisation, thus, serves as "simple superfluous illustration" (*Emancipated Spectator* 96). In order to avoid banalising massacres and victims, Rancière emphasises the necessity of "overturning the dominant logic that makes the visual the lot of multitudes and the verbal the privilege of a few" (97) – which returns us to the question of the distribution of speaking positions in the discursive field of war. In light of these considerations, I approach the plays in this section by asking whether or not they do any spatial work to remap Iraq as a three-dimensional space, populated by people whose lives and deaths matter, by recognisable persons who 'have a say' in the way their suffering is reported and apprehended.

Where, in the context of home-front plays, the issue of mourning is primarily focalised through (un)grieving femininities, the investigation of front-line negotiations of grievability brings another border-crossing figure into focus: "the subject or subjugated position crafted for war's sanctioned meaning maker, the embedded journalist" (Pratt 1516). Embedding reporters with American and British military units was turned into a common practice in the Iraq invasion and, to a slightly smaller extent, in the Afghan conflict, with the result that it became extremely difficult, though not impossible, for correspondents to report "from outside the embrace of the military" (Cockburn 13). As Pratt's comment on the 'sanctioned meaning maker' suggests, embeds are overwhelmingly perceived to be co-opted into the official war agenda. Butler goes as far as calling embedded journalism "a speech act in the service of the military operations" (*Precarious Life* 36–37). Although justifiably critical, this view of embedded reporters appears somewhat reductive. There certainly is some leverage for war correspondents to navigate the contradictory expectations that come with their responsibilities towards the media audience at home, who demand a style of reporting imbued with the authenticity that supposedly comes with proximity to the front line, towards the troops, who protect embedded journalists and confide in them, and towards the strategists of the military campaign, who expect conformity with mission objectives. The subject position of the embedded journalist is thus situated at the intersection of conflicting interests, desires, and political motivations. This already recalls the divergent forms of positioning available to the (un)grieving femininities analysed in the previous chapter.

While a number of photographs, films, and reports that have come forth from embeds in Iraq and Afghanistan doubtlessly confirm the impression of bias, there are cultural responses which foreground the agency that reporters retain. That the embedded perspective somewhat inevitably replicates the troops' viewpoint can be clearly discerned in Tim Hetherington and Sebastian Junger's award-winning documentary *Restrepo* (2010). The fact that the film has been named after a fallen soldier from the US army unit which hosted the British and American documentary makers already points to the reinforcement of the globalised hierarchy of grief. Without exception, all the events depicted in *Restrepo* are focalised through the anxieties of the US soldiers, whereas dead Afghan insurgents and civilians are visually registered, if at all, according to the logic of 'simple superfluous illustration'. This can be contrasted with an artwork that implicitly challenges Butler's claim about the "soldier-reporter who visually consecrates the destructive acts of war" (*Frames* xi), which was on view in the exhibition *Conflict, Time, Photography* at the Tate Modern in 2014–2015. Adam Broomberg and Oliver Chanarin, who travelled to Afghanistan as embeds with the British military in 2008, developed a strategy to manifest their refusal of co-optation. Instead of recording British fatalities as expected of them, the artists exposed a roll of photographic paper to the sun. The resulting artwork shows an abstracted spectrum of colours. The piece is, ironically, entitled *The Press Conference, June 9, 2008, The Day Nobody Died*, for a documentation of the press conference is precisely not what is offered. Broomberg and Chanarin's refusal to report on British front-line deaths, perpetuated over the course of a series of artworks consisting of exposed photographic paper, makes a powerful statement about the politics of (in)visibility at stake in artistic approaches to and mediations of deaths in the 'war on terror'.

I suggest that it is precisely the close entanglement of the subject/subjugated position of the embedded journalist with the frames of war that explains the heightened interest in this figure in contemporary drama. Prominent examples from the American and European theatre scenes include Tim Robbins's satire *Embedded* (2003), which premiered in Los Angeles and had a run at the Riverside Studio in London in 2004, and Elfriede Jelinek's *Bambiland* (Burgtheater

Wien, 2003), which offers an equally scathing critique of "the ruse of 'embedded journalism' and the sensationalism attached to the coverage of war" (Boll 127). In British war plays, embedded journalists make a minor appearance in Gregory Burke's *Black Watch* (2006), and home-front plays such as *Guardians* by Peter Morris (2005) deal with the motivations and fabrications of UK-based journalists who are anything but impartial observers. This section turns to two plays which feature embedded reporters as their protagonists and centre upon the ethical questions of war reporting, Colin Teevan's *How Many Miles to Basra?* (2006) and Jonathan Holmes's *Fallujah* (2007). Potentially, approaching the war through the lens of embedded journalists fosters an awareness not only of what the frames of war include but also of the 'discarded negatives'. This chapter excavates the theatrical traces and obliterations of wasted, ungrievable lives in the war zone.

Three Frames of Grievability: Colin Teevan's *How Many Miles to Basra?*

How Many Miles to Basra? by Colin Teevan was originally developed as a radio play for BBC Radio Three in 2004 and first produced for the stage at West Yorkshire Playhouse in Leeds in 2006. The modalities of war reporting are a central concern of the play, which frames the front-line action with scenes set at the BBC offices. The link between the different spatial and temporal frames is provided by protagonist Ursula, a radio journalist who is embedded with the fictional Third Royal Fusiliers regiment near Basra in Iraq. Even before the first front-line scene takes place, the expository scene set in the news editor's office self-reflexively cautions audiences against seeing any version of the war, including the one offered in this play, as authoritative. The editor's assistant, Sophie, informs Ursula, freshly returned from Iraq, that the news corporation has been "under pressure" since BBC journalist Andrew Gilligan reported that "the Government asked Intelligence to sex up the dossier on Saddam's weapon capabilities" (Teevan 11). The play is thus, first of all, positioned in relation to the discourse surrounding the early stages of the Iraq invasion. The highly publicised debate over inaccurate intelligence versus flawed reporting, which audiences are more than likely to have followed in the media at the time, is reflected on the level of dramatic discourse when Sophie explains that, due to the pressure exerted on the newsmakers, the editor has asked her to sort Ursula's recordings from Iraq:

URSULA. But I have a record of them. [...]
SOPHIE. He wanted an official record. [...]
URSULA. Show me this log of yours. [...] What kind of order's this?
SOPHIE. Chronological. From April 13th –

URSULA. But that's not the right order. You can't tell the story like that. That's not how it happened. [...] No, I should start with the VCP [vehicle checkpoint].
SOPHIE. That's where the United helped out the Bedouin?
URSULA. Helped out? Is that what the MoD said? [...] You shouldn't believe everything you hear. (9–11)

Their exchange calls attention to the competing versions of truth in the reporting of war: the 'official', chronological record does not correspond to what Ursula, immediately involved in events, perceives as the 'right order'. Her rejection of Sophie's log points to both the agency and the responsibility of reporters; there is an element of choice regarding the manner in which they 'tell the story', but also a duty to represent events as truthfully as possible.

The subsequent flashback scene, set on "*the Jalibah Road, Southern Iraq*" (11), unfolds the events in question in front of the audience. It soon becomes apparent that both Ursula's account and the 'official' version are flawed. Although the unit manning the vehicle checkpoint initially bemoan being posted to a remote supply route, they soon become involved in action as a car with three Iraqi Bedouins approaches. The sequence of events – similar to the scene at the building site in *Stovepipe*, the soldiers issue three warnings and then shoot the Bedouins, who turn out to be unarmed – appears intricately connected to Ursula's involvement (see also Lonergan 61). This is suggested by the way the satphone conversation with her editor shifts into a teichoscopic report to relay the spatially hidden action. Just as Ursula protests to Tariq, who wants her out of Iraq at the next opportunity, "I want to stay on until I do have a story", Geordie warns her that "there's a car coming full pelt", and she rejoices that "there might actually be something kicking off here" (15). She goes on to speak into the satphone "*in broadcast tone*" (15), describing events simultaneously within the internal communication system (for the editor/the prospective radio listeners) and the theatre audience. On a formal level, the conventional use of a teichoscopic perspective on the battle emphasises both the limits of representing armed combat in the theatre and the limitations of war reporting. Just as the car's approach to the checkpoint has to be conveyed verbally, Western audiences have to rely on mediated versions of front-line events.

The play's meta-discussion of the frames of war crucially extends to its representation of front-line deaths. At first glance, *How Many Miles to Basra?* seems to undercut the differential allocation of grievability, for the Bedouins' deaths ostensibly provide the central plot device. One Bedouin passes on a duty to the troops: he was carrying "blood money" to a sheikh who has taken his wife and son hostage, and his last words stipulate – crucially, it is Ursula who translates them – "you have killed me so the debt is yours" (22–23). Three ways, or frames, to make sense of the Iraqis' deaths compete in the play, which will, in the following, serve to structure my analysis. The first frame offers a critical reflection of the discursive derealisation of the life of the 'other'. The reduction of Iraqi subjecthood to the object position of the "shadow-life" (Butler, *Frames* xxix) is performatively enacted through the soldiers' speech acts. "*Readying himself*" for battle as the Bedouins' car is approaching, one of the soldiers, nicknamed after the cartoon character Dangermouse, adapts the traditional "Humpty Dumpty" nursery rhyme:

> One brown raghead, shitting on the wall – [...]
> One brown raghead, shitting on the wall – [...]
> And if one brown raghead should accidentally fall – [...]
> It's bang-bang you're dead, fifty bullets in your head. (14)

While the appropriation of the English nursery rhyme positions the speaker in terms of national belonging, the racist epithet *raghead* deprives the enemy of precisely that. As Benedict Anderson points out with regard to the circulation of the epithet *slant* in the context of the Vietnam war, such a term "erases nation-ness by reducing the adversary to his biological physiognomy" (148). Similarly, the universalising image of (presumably) Muslim men that relies on the turban as the mark "of a terrorist masculinity" (Puar 175) functions via an Orientalist reduction, as religious, social, cultural, and regional factors determining types of Muslim dress are effaced. The resulting stereotype of the turban-wearing male does not conform to "the norm of human life already established", but rather represents "a threat to life as we know it" (Butler, *Frames* xxix).

Possibly, the performative reiteration of the object position of the enemy 'other' from a speaking position of the culturally/nationally situated 'self' elicits an awareness of these ontological frames. As Dangermouse describes his response in one of the interspersed interview statements that were addressed *ad spectatores* in the original production (Walker 20), giving them a confessional aspect:

> I don't look, that's how I deal with it. [...] I mean, he's the enemy, isn't he? I don't feel anything for him. I hate him, his ugly face, his dirty clothes – [...] at least I know what it is to be clean – how can you live like that? That's what I tell myself. How can you live like that, you animal? [...] It's not like I really hate him, it's like if I looked, I might, might begin to feel something, how fucking miserable his life, all their lives, are. (23–24)

The soldier's utterance lays bare to what extent the dehumanisation of the 'other', whose life is always already unlivable, is instrumental in being able to wage war against 'him'. Dangermouse has to reiterate this rhetoric in preparation for battle; he even displays some awareness of the fictitiousness and functionality of the construct ('That's what I tell myself'). Significantly, the abjection of the 'other' has to be reiterated blindly, as the merest glimpse of the enemy might begin to destabilise it ('if I looked'). As Dangermouse seems to intuit, allowing "[t]hose who remain faceless" into view might enable "an apprehension of [...] the precarious life of the Other" (Butler, *Precarious Life* xvii–xviii), starting from the sense perception of 'how fucking miserable' this life is.

The first frame, operating at the level of the soldiers' utterances throughout the play, reveals that all lives do not count the same in the 'war on terror'. As they "*approach the bodies of the shot Bedouins tentatively*" (17), Dangermouse and Freddie rejoice: "we got them all [...]. Three nil to the Third Royals" (18). The dead bodies of the Iraqis count like points in a sports match; yet the discursive practice of adding these deaths to a score that could potentially become even disguises the differential scales of counting 'their' and 'our' bodies. Asad outlines how increased public distaste for troop deaths in liberal democracies has destabilised "the conventional understanding of war as an activity in which human dying and killing are exchanged" (35). The figure 'Three nil' connotes a match for players with equal chances and stakes, whereas modern wars, as Asad notes, are in fact characterised by "unequal killing": when 'we' are "fighting against militarily and ethnically inferior peoples [...] it is proper that the latter die in much larger numbers" (35). This becomes more explicit as Freddie defends himself against Stewart, the sergeant of the squad: "Hearts and minds is all very well [...], but if it's him or me, it's him" (19). The fact that the soldiers' search for "*booby trap devices*" (19) does not uncover any weapons – and, by extension, the larger failure to find WMD in Iraq – evidences the *a priori* construction of the non-life that has to be eliminated so that 'we' can live, regardless of whether 'our' life is factually at stake in the encounter. Interestingly, Dangermouse supports this line of defence by adding: "Freddie warned them, boss, three times. I counted" (19). As Stewart's rebuke, "but in what language?" (19), makes clear, 'our' scales are completely maladjusted to 'their' cultural/linguistic system. This reflects Butler's argument that, "[a]lthough numbers cannot tell us precisely whose lives count, and whose deaths count, we can note how numbers are framed and unframed to find out how norms that differentiate livable and grievable lives are at work" (*Frames* xx). Modes of counting the war dead, in other words, are deeply invested in the logic that structures the visual and discursive fields of war.

The second frame of approaching the Bedouins' deaths initially appears to make these lives (and deaths) count. In marked contrast to the squaddies' response, Stewart decides that they will make an effort to hand over the ransom in order to save "the wife and son of that poor bastard Sayed" (25). The dead Bedouin is named and his family is deemed worth protecting. The sergeant is perfectly aware that the official rules of engagement would not allow for this manoeuvre; he cannot have the mission authorised by his superiors because "the woman and her child [...] are not important [...]. Intertribal stuff, that's all" (45–46). On one level, then, Stewart's decision seems to evidence a moral responsibility that transcends the rules and regulations of the war system. In this regard, Stewart's decision seems to challenge the differential currency that diminishes 'their' lives. However, it becomes increasingly apparent that the sergeant is in fact motivated by a personal trauma, rather than an ethical imperative. It is revealed as the play moves on that Stewart is impelled less by his responsibility for the Bedouins' deaths than by his shooting of an unarmed girl during the Troubles in Northern Ireland – he keeps a photo of the dead girl in his tobacco tin and keeps reverting to the incident. His decision and the attendant rescue plot line do not restore the Iraqis' subjecthood; instead, their lives only count as ploys for Stewart to atone for an earlier mistake. The only reason why these lives are made to matter is linked to the personal history of a Western subject; the quest to deliver the ransom reveals his memories and mental images ("I see her still" [27]), whereas the Iraqi woman and child remain nameless and faceless objects. After the operation eventually leaves all of the soldiers dead, the play's resolution does not consist in the rescue of the Iraqi family but in Ursula passing over Stewart's story (and legacy) to his widow.

On a larger level, this second frame is reflective of discursive moves that instrumentalise the life of the 'other' without, in fact, recognising it. Following Butler's terminology, one could state that Stewart's scheme is predicated, at best, on an apprehension of Iraqi lives, if apprehension implies "marking, registering, acknowledging without full cognition" (*Frames* 5). But there is not the least modification of the conditions which craft the intersubjective scene of recognition. The act of withholding recognisability, while operating on a spurious registration of lives deemed worth protecting, connects the plot to the larger context of the Iraq invasion. Teevan said in an interview that, for him, the play "tells the story of a British sergeant who leads his troops into a suicidal misadventure on false pretences, in an attempt to 'do the right thing' as he sees it, much as I feel Tony Blair did in Iraq in 2003" (qtd. in Dewhurst 250). The Iraqi woman and child are not to be protected for their own sake, but to achieve absolution; in the play, Stewart suggests "it is the right thing to do" because the soldiers have "made a mistake" (45) that they need to redress. This logic is, indeed, somewhat reminiscent of Blair's post-9/11 speech, which reviewed previous humanitarian disasters: remarking on how the UK intervened in the Kosovo crisis in 1999 and the civil war in Sierra Leone in 2000, he claimed that, "if Rwanda happened again today as it did in 1993 [sic], when a million people were slaughtered in cold blood, we would have a moral duty to act there also" (Blair, "Labour Conference"). Within the discourse of humanitarian interventionism, the suffering of the 'other' is ascertained as a matter of legitimation. This is particularly evident in the case of the Iraq war. In his pre-invasion speech, Blair invoked the plight of the Iraqis, a majority of whom were "dependent on Food Aid" or "die[d] needlessly every year from lack of food and medicine" or were "in exile" ("Iraq Debate Speech" 244) in order to justify a military operation which would, in fact, aggravate rather than alleviate these problems (Jeffrey 62).

In consequence, the second frame works with an apparent valuation of Iraqi lives only to reveal the underlying contradictions of such a discursive position: the "sanctity [...] of human life" (Blair, "Statement" 215) is heralded to justify intervention, but the large-scale killing of civilian populations is condoned, or shrouded in the term *collateral damage*. Essentially, this frame is built on the same ideology as the first frame: instrumentalising 'their' lives for strategic purposes only works because of the previously agreed-upon notion that these lives have no intrinsic value. This becomes evident when the squad come to travel with Malek, an Iraqi translator who has lost his daughter in the invasion. Malek provides a back story to his daughter's life in an attempt to render it valuable: "The day the bomb came was my daughter's birthday. I had saved. [...] She had set her heart on a white silk dress. [...] She wanted to look like an angel" (67). Reminiscent of the type of narrative associated with the 9/11 story, Malek appropriates a first-person point of view that is not normally awarded to the suffering 'other'. This is why Ursula and Stewart cannot receive his narrative as an affirmation of the Iraqi child's grievability but try to extract a utilitarian purpose from her death:

URSULA. Is that why you want to continue with us?
MALEK. What do you mean?
STEWART. For your daughter. To save the Bedouin's wife and child, as a kind of compensation.
MALEK. Compensation? Why do all your English words that are to do with the most important things like heart and soul come from the language of the shopkeeper? [...] Nothing could compensate me for the loss of that dress. (67–68)

From the point of view of the invaders, the life of the 'other' can only be made to matter 'as a kind of compensation', for it does not count as a life per se. Malek refutes the "perception that human life has differential exchange value in the marketplace of death" (Asad 94) by affirming the absolute, incontrovertible value of his daughter's life. It is striking that he makes this point by using the same mercantile language that he critiques. His synecdochic replacement of *daughter* with *dress* appears as an ironic strategy to code the life that does not matter in terms of the commodity that does. This logic of substitution critically inflects the discursive framing that discounts 'their' lives while it renders 'ours' beyond exchange rates. His appropriation of market-based vocabulary can thus be understood as an unsettling performance of mimicry, or "colonial imitation", in Bhabha's sense (86).

On the one hand, Malek's speech could be read as a potent challenge to the norms of recognisability. In overturning the logic 'that makes the visual the lot of multitudes and the verbal the privilege of a few', to recall Rancière's remark, the play provides a speaking position to articulate the pain and suffering of the Iraqis, muted in official discourse:

> To remove this monster Saddam, whom you made to keep us in our place, you have bombed us, impoverished us, stood by and let our children die of the most preventable illnesses, starved us physically and intellectually, and then bombed us some more. [...] You reduce a country to rags, and then you call us ragheads. (50)

Not only does Malek's speech refute the rationale behind the 'humanitarian' intervention and the dehumanising enemy image, but it is also a powerful demand to recognise the vulnerability of Iraqi lives. Butler stipulates that, in the process of asking for recognition, "we have already become something new", since the petition "is to solicit a becoming, to instigate a transformation" (*Precarious Life* 44). On these terms, the play could be seen to reanimate the human waste that is shut out by the frames of war and endow precarious lives with a claim to grievability and subjecthood.

On the other hand, the play reinscribes a reductive typology of victimhood through its recurrence to the "ideograph 'women-and-children'" (von der Lippe and Väyrynen 23), a term that has been coined by Cynthia Enloe and is frequently used in feminist critiques to denounce the co-optation of women's and children's lives into the war effort as passive victims within a melodramatic structure. The lives of the Iraqi "mother and child" (92) are always and uncritically invoked in the form of this familiar collocation. As the prototypical victim of war, Malek's daughter is semantically linked to the girl that Stewart shot in Ireland: Malek's memory of his daughter, who "looked like an angel" in her new dress (67), interacts with Stewart's recollection of the girl being propelled from the car's windscreen, "like an avenging angel, still smiling even though there [is] this hole in her head" (72). In light of the Christian terminology used in Blair's justifications of the Iraq invasion, the play's mythical coding of child war victims appears somewhat incongruous with its criticism. Even though the play strongly refutes the notion that the mistakes made during British involvement in Northern

Ireland could be redressed in the Iraq campaign, it homogenises the fatalities that have occurred in these distinct contexts.

The self-reflexive negotiation of differential grievability that is implicit in the second frame turns into an explicit meta-discussion in the third frame, which is primarily associated with the subject position of the embedded journalist. When the Bedouins are shot dead, Ursula senses that this is the exclusive story she can offer to her listeners. Yet her editor, still connected to her via sat phone, apparently rejects its newsworthiness: "Three dead Iraqis is old news? [...] But three dead Brits and I can have top spot, I suppose" (25). Ursula's discussion with Tariq is directly reflective of the operation of war frames and their strategies of containment. While the deaths of British troops would "fit [the] agenda" (25), Iraqi civilian casualties have to be shut out, for alternative versions of the war are always delegitimised. Ursula's immediate commitment to nevertheless push the discarded incident into the discursive field of war – "I'm going to find that mother and child even if no one else does" (27) – could be read as indicative of performance's turn to wasted life. Again, it appears that an individual's agency and sense of responsibility can work against the impositions of official war frames. It is only due to Ursula's obstinate persistence, even after she has formally been withdrawn as an embed, that the story of the kidnapped Iraqis is (at least potentially) brought into the view of UK radio listeners (and the theatre audience). With the range of thoughts, feelings, and motivations given to Ursula as a dramatic character, she is constructed as a far more layered subject than the well-established critical view of embedded journalists would suggest. In fact, she comes into constant conflict with the squad and starts to act independently of them.

As was the case with the second frame, however, it turns out that her interest in the Iraqi woman-and-child is not ultimately grounded in an ethical position, and the full (hi)story of the wasted lives never unfolds in this frame either. Ursula does not succeed in moving the discarded negatives back into the frame; despite being the only survivor of the final incident of handing over the ransom, she can offer neither to her radio listeners in the diegesis nor to the external theatre audience an account that renders the Iraqi lives real, valuable, and grievable. Eventually, the hierarchy of grief remains firmly in place as Ursula realises, at the end of the play, that the only way to 'sell' her story is by subscribing to sanctioned framing devices: "The true story of Alpha Unit. [...] Sergeant McDonald's story as the main story. He made the decisions. The most interesting character" (85). The meta-theatrical overtones are unmistakable. The home-front scenes retrospectively frame the front-line flashbacks in terms of the conventional dramatic structure: there is a protagonist whose desires and decisions drive the plot. After the dictum 'three dead Brits and I can have top spot' has been accepted, the discussion merely revolves around the question of the appropriate response to the soldiers' deaths, as Patrick Lonergan notes (60–61). The responsible and recognisable human subject, at the end of the play, is invariably a Western one, whereas the lives and deaths of the Iraqis encountered in the war zone eventually vanish between and beyond the frames of the dramatic discourse.

Ultimately, one could claim that *How Many Miles to Basra?* remains just as vulnerable to the charge of derealising the life of the 'other' as the discursive mechanisms it seeks to expose. And yet what distinguishes the play from other approaches to war through the lens of embedded journalists is the high level of reflexivity it achieves concerning processes of selection and representation. Even if the Iraqi woman-and-child are discarded from the final version, this is done in a conspicuous and self-reflexive manner. Ursula and Tariq's negotiation of the modes of war reporting throws into sharp relief what Butler calls the "iterable structure" of the frame (*Frames* 24). Butler specifically suggests that it is the constant repetition, reproduction, and circulation of the frame that can call its normalising function into question. The play lays bare the iterability of the war story as providing a set of fixed positions – heroes, villains, victims – into which protagonists are inserted depending on circumstances. As these frames do not provide a viable subject position to the 'other', 'our' soldiers inevitably emerge as the protagonists: as Ursula puts it, they are "heroes, but –" (87). Consequently, even if the story the embedded reporter decides to make public does not break with the frames, the merit of staging this figure in war drama seems to consist in the fact that the mediation of war reporting is foregrounded. This stands in marked contrast to the fusing of the reporters' perspective with that of the troops in cultural responses such as *Restrepo*, where the embeds disappear entirely behind the lens that frames a highly engineered version of war.

Unembedding Perspectives, Extending Protection: Jonathan Holmes's *Fallujah*

Jonathan Holmes's play *Fallujah* seeks to move the vanishing and vanished lives and deaths of Iraqis centre stage. The play is largely built on verbatim testimony about US forces' 2004 siege of and subsequent assaults on the Iraqi city of Fallujah; it was staged as a promenade production around an art installation by Lucy and Jorge Orta and set to a sound installation by Nitin Sawhney, with both the design and the music supposed to act as stand-alone artworks. The piece was shown at London's disused Truman Brewery off Brick Lane in 2007, a space regularly hosting such popular events as the London Tattoo Convention or exhibitions like Gunther von Hagens's *Body Worlds* display (2002). To pick up on the consideration of the site-specificity of performance, *Fallujah* is clearly a production that, though taking place outside traditional theatre buildings, does not enter into any kind of dialogue with the spatial qualities or the sociopolitical significance of the place of performance. In adapting McKinnie's notion of "rent-seeking" performance, which appropriates place to increase its experiential value (26–27), one could conceive of the production as 'renting' a place that has already become firmly established as a site of entertainment.

Based almost entirely on documentary materials, *Fallujah* is intended to (re)present authentic testimony, primarily eyewitness accounts and original interviews, surrounding the assaults on the Iraqi city, which left a majority of the inhabitants displaced, injured, or dead and destroyed most of the infrastructure (Elworthy 21–24). The play focalises many of these events through a journalist who has to become a civilian witness for the sake of entering Fallujah. The journey of American reporter Sasha – a "composite figure", based on different real-life people, including several journalists (Holmes, "Introduction" 143) – from war correspondent to independent witness provides the linkage between the loosely associated scenes and stands exemplarily for the move outside the officially sanctioned frames of war. The first scene in which Sasha appears, set at a press briefing in Baghdad on 3 April 2004, as screens inform the audience, exposes her authorised speaking position as one that takes over the chronology suggested by the official version of events. The origin point of this version is the "discovery of the burned, brutalized and mutilated bodies of four American civilian contractors, working for Blackwater Security", as Sasha reports "*to camera*" (Holmes, *Fallujah* 160). The production space at Truman Brewery was saturated with TV screens, which replicated "*a situation familiar to us from broadcast news*" (160).

Initially, the audience are thus invited to approach the dramatised version of events in Fallujah from the same subject position made available to them in media representations: as televisual spectators of the violent conflict 'over there', they are encouraged to bring their perception in synch with official frames. It is the brutal death of grievable subjects, the mutilation of four 'civilian contractors', that necessitates an 'adequate' response, as a US general informs the media/theatre audience: "We are going to hunt down the people responsible for this bestial act. [...] It will be deliberate, it will be precise, and it will be overwhelming" (161). The analogies to the framing of 9/11 are evident: the attack displaces 'First World' subjects from their perceived safety, enables them to situate themselves as first-person speakers of a narrative that begins with 'our' loss, and justifies a violent 'counter'-attack on the presumed perpetrators. At first, it seems that Sasha partly complies with the subjugated position made available to her within this frame. Speaking about her experience as an embedded reporter outside Baghdad, she confesses to a British cleric that she has "developed a strange relationship with the sight of dead Iraqis. I feel safer when I see them. [...] They won't be trying to kill me today" (172). Hence, in the beginning, Sasha's position appears commensurate with official frames which stipulate that the perceived threat to 'our' lives justifies killing 'them'.

It is only when she disengages from her embedded position that her subject position also becomes unembedded from the exclusionary norms that govern grievability. In order to enter Fallujah, Sasha has to leave her journalistic credentials behind, for "[n]o press" is allowed to pass the checkpoint. Sasha's transformation from reporter to civilian witness constitutes a significant rite of passage. After scenes that seek to convey the assault on the city by means of "*the aural gamut of a bombardment [...] [that] goes on for several minutes*" (193), Sasha re-emerges to the audience as an eyewitness. She begins her narrative in a "*clearly very shaken*" manner, which jars with her previous, authoritative broadcasting mode: "This is what I found in Fallujah" (193). Sasha's direct audience address, where previously she had been seen to engage with interviewees or speaking to cameras, brokers a new frame. Having left her position as an embed, she negotiates a testimonial mode of enunciation:

> The Iraqi National Guard used loudspeakers to call on people to get out of the houses carrying white flags, bringing all their belongings with them. [...] Eight members of Eyad Naji Latif's family [...] gathered their belongings and walked in single file, as instructed, to the mosque. (193)

As the stage directions indicate, Sasha's testimony is underscored by the soundscape ("*We hear this taking place, but the stage remains bare*" [193]), which imputes authenticity to her account and incites audiences to imagine the scene taking place. Another witness, a doctor, takes over from Sasha and continues the testimony:

> Then [...] US soldiers [...] opened fire. [...] Survivors made desperate appeals to stop firing. But whenever one of them tried to raise a white flag they were shot. After several hours Eyad tried to raise his arm with the flag. But they shot him in the arm. Finally he tried to raise his hand. So they shot him in the hand. (193–194)

Sasha concludes the narrative by adding that the "US military at first refused to hand over bodies of fighters to be buried, and when they did, many were half-eaten by dogs" (194). The act of giving testimony provides a different mode of (story)telling: where embedded reporting is restricted by at least some selection mechanisms – e.g. as the Study Centre for Human Rights and Democracy in Fallujah reported, "embedded journalists refrained from photographing those shot in the head or any other evidence of deliberate killing of civilians" (qtd. in Elworthy 21) – the eyewitness can testify to atrocities outside of the strictures of war frames. Seen in contrast with her first appearance, becoming a witness to human rights violations in Fallujah provides Sasha with a different speaking subjectivity, one that comes into enunciation by articulating 'their' losses. This reverses the invocation of 9/11 as origin point. The Iraqi casualties are named and personalised: Eyad's loss of his parents, two brothers, sister-in-law, and nephew (193–194) cannot be measured against the primacy of 'our' loss or be subsumed under the seriality of a body count. Rather than starting from the mutilated bodies of the Blackwater contractors, the testimony zooms in on brutalised Iraqi corpses, 'half-eaten by dogs'. In consequence, Sasha's movement from embed to witness illustrates the need for brokering new frames of war coverage, which can work to foster an awareness of 'their' lives and losses.

While the dramatisation of eyewitness accounts from the besieged city arguably overturns the logic whereby the verbal remains the privilege of authorised speakers and the victims of mass violence are visually banalised, it is questionable to what extent it achieves political efficacy in performance. Even though the testimonial evidence is doubtlessly shocking, it is not clear whether the delivery triggers "politically consequential affective dispositions" (Butler, *Frames* 24). The merit of the testimonial format doubtlessly lies in (ac)counting (for) otherwise undetailed, anonymous lives; yet the epistemological certainty with which the speakers are endowed – which is somewhat inevitable, given the dramatisation of written, factual accounts – undercuts the affective potential that is usually associated with (the theatre of) testimony. To recur to Amanda Stuart Fisher's conception of testimonial theatre as allowing for unknowingness and fragmentation (see chapter three), the dramatised witnesses in *Fallujah* might appear to retain a conspicuously firm control over what they will have known as the truth about Fallujah. As Rancière explains, the "virtue of testimony" is conventionally seen precisely in its incompleteness; "not saying everything; showing that not everything can be said", and the "true witness" is conceived of as "one who does not want to witness" (*Emancipated Spectator* 90–91). Seen in light of these theorisations, the deliberation behind Sasha's becoming unembedded and the urge with which the theatre event conveys the eyewitness accounts might make the testimonies appear somewhat enforced. Performers could be seen to nudge audiences into certain spectatorial positions by means of 'assailing' them with graphic descriptions from various locations in the promenade production, speaking as they *"mingle with the audience"* (195). In this regard, McKinnie rightly points out that the "impressive spatial choreography" of site-specific performance sometimes signals an effort "to do spectators' interpretive work for them" (31).

If one nevertheless presumes that audiences do not assume an oppositional position towards the performance, the testimonies might work towards destabilising the frames that dictate whose lives and deaths count. The verbal presentation of eyewitness accounts can be read against Feldman's insightful note on the "doctrine of collateral damage" as "a calculated discounting of the wounded, the tortured, and the dead; [...] a systematic (de)archivization, deactualization, and virtualization of violence and its consequences" ("Structuring Enemy" 1712). By seeking to re-count the discounted bodies, *Fallujah* reinscribes 'the wounded, the tortured, and the dead' into the archive of the Iraq invasion. What is at stake here is an attempt to actively impact on processes of inclusion and exclusion in what Mitchell calls "the memory archive of the war" (68). This brings to the fore how *Fallujah* in particular, and performance in general, "might operate, metaphorically, as an archive, accreting or storing traces of traumatic violence" (Silverstone 3). The well-known harrowing images of the Blackwater contractors hanging from a bridge in Fallujah are gradually complemented by images that find no correspondence in the visual Iraq war archive: "pictures of maggots on tongues, babies with their heads on the ground, men with their heads halfway off", of "burned bodies", bodies that are "baking in the sun" or "bloated three times" (197), bodies "with a green colour" (170). These testimonial extracts are designed to counter the virtualisation of violence that Feldman describes or the containment of Iraqi deaths in the body count graph that Pugliese contests. The suggestion is that a frame which posits 'our' losses as the origin point and reference value will not hold for understanding what happened in Fallujah.

A central question about archiving the siege of Fallujah that the performance seeks to navigate concerns the use of napalm-type bombs by the US military. The eyewitness statement about the 'green' body, for instance, is juxtaposed with a screened statement by a Pentagon spokesman, claiming that "[n]apalm has not been used in Iraq. We use Mark 77 incendiary" (170). Over the course of the play, the connection between images of disfigured and maimed bodies and use of these bombs is established several times. When an activist explains that the firebombs are "chemical weapons" that "burnt peoples' skin even when water was dumped on their bodies" and a US spokeswoman affirms on screen that "Mark 77 does the job better" (188), the hypocrisy underlying the war story is unmasked. The same population whom Blair professed to save from Hussein's biological weapons ("Iraq Debate Speech" 232) was attacked with chemical bombs by the invading armies. By accentuating this profound contradiction, *Fallujah* potentially exerts a formative impact on the Iraq war archive. There is a clear gesture here towards the insurrection of minor knowledges about the invasion. It has to be noted, however, that the role of UK institutions is barely explicitly addressed in Holmes's play. Even if the play's disclosures might be seen to indict the Blair government, the blame for the atrocities is squarely laid on the US administration.

Within the play's laudable rebuilding of the war archive thus emerges its own blind spot, that of the UK's complicity in the siege and the war crimes committed in Fallujah. There is no hint, for instance, at the involvement of 850 British troops and specialists, mainly from the Black Watch regiment, in the offensive (Harnden and Harrison 16), despite that fact being well documented at the time of the production. Holmes's play (re)instates a somewhat naive binary between the brutal comportment of US forces in Fallujah and the more considerate approach pursued by their UK counterparts. As a British major informs Sasha (and, more importantly, the audience):

> the British aren't involved in this one. It's an American cock-up. My view is that the Americans' use of violence is not proportionate [...]. They don't see the Iraqi people the way we see them. They view them as *untermenschen*. They are not concerned about the Iraqi loss of life. (167)

The construction of Iraqi lives as unlivable, inferior, inhuman is fully ascribed to an ideology the British are supposed to have overcome, ironically, through their own (neo-)imperial entanglements: "The solution to law and order is simple – we did it in Northern Ireland – joint patrols with the local police" (166). The explications offered by the British major are nowhere contradicted in the play.[28] Disowning British complicity in the assault is problematic insofar as the play posits the incidents it uncovers as paradigmatic. As Sasha reports to camera about the situation in 2005: "Most people in the city continue to live in tents, or amid the rubble of their homes. Fallujah has become Iraq, and Iraq now is Fallujah" (212–213). The case expounded in the play is thus to be seen as an exemplary event in the Iraq war, as an extremely brutal manifestation of the shock offensive that reduced the city, and the country at large, to rubble. If responsibility for the situation is attributed to US forces, and if 'Fallujah has become Iraq', then UK forces, by implication, are not to be blamed for the descent of the Iraq campaign into a humanitarian disaster. Thus, the piece may well be designed to induce audiences to apprehend the violent loss of Iraqi lives, but it ultimately lets them off the hook as citizens of the UK, the more 'reasonable' coalition part-

---

[28] In an article published alongside the playtext, Holmes does concede that "the UK is not blameless in its behaviour in Iraq", yet he nevertheless repeats after the British officer cited in the play, claiming that the British army is "significantly more [...] responsible as an entity than the US military" ("Siege" 129).

ner. As several reviewers have noted, the play thus seems to harbour "a bias against the United States" (Fisher, "*Fallujah*").

The play's negotiation of a specifically British subject position with regard to the humanitarian catastrophe in Fallujah centrally hinges on the figure of Jo, modelled after British human rights activist Jo Wilding, who enters the performance space acting as a human shield to escort an ambulance trying to pick up injured Iraqis. The reason she can do so is revealed to be directly related to the hegemonic norms that constitute the intelligible human subject. "Hold your fire! [...] I'm English!", she shouts out to the American snipers (169). Later on in the play, Jo reflects on how she "hate[s] that a medic can't travel in the ambulance but I can, just because I look like the sniper's sister" (208). It is because she can be racially profiled as one of 'us' that Jo can be of particular help to 'them'. She explains that she is always positioned at the window of the ambulance, "the visible foreigner, the passport" (204). The passport, here, functions as a crucial signifier of human intelligibility. The emphasis on the sign that awards/withholds grievability is reinforced by Jo's hiding her valuable passport in her bra when her team is captured by Iraqi insurgents (180). This is later contrasted with the punitive system of registering subjects for the sake of detention, when Sasha reports that Fallujan citizens "were allowed to return to the city after undergoing biometric identification, provided they wear their ID cards all the time" (213). Due to her possession of both the visual appearance and official documentation that identify her with a nation-state whose subjects are deemed recognisable, Jo can deploy her own rights-bearing body as protection to those who are positioned as abject.

The pertinent question is how British audiences relate to her outcry, 'Hold your fire! ... I'm English'. Does it work as a powerful reminder of the responsibility that comes with belonging to a group of privileged national subjects? Are spectators likely to recognise the British activist's resistance to colonial governance in the war zone as pointing to their own civic and ethical involvements in the 'war on terror'? Reviews would suggest that the figure fails to trigger a heightened ethical awareness. While most critics applauded the star performance of Imogen Stubbs, the segment they invariably seized on is one where the British subject is herself in danger: "The scene in which she and a local woman are picked up by militia men and seem destined to die, shows actress Imogen Stubbs at her very best, as fear literally makes her shake" (Fisher, "*Fallujah*"). Significantly, then, the dramatic moment that seems to engage audiences most effectively and affectively is one where they identify with the vulnerability of a Western life in the war zone. Wilding's published testimony about her temporary captivity, in contrast, makes no such appeal to the readers' sympathy. Wilding cites one of her kidnappers: "If people oppose the occupation, he says, how is it that the government could carry on and do it. He's genuinely interested but also sarcastic: surely the great liberators must be truly democratic, truly governing by the will of the people?" (54). The insurgent's challenge to the Western version of democracy crucially problematises any attempts of UK citizens, be they as committed to the anti-war cause as Wilding, to disengage from the larger war effort. And yet no such consideration of the complicity of liberal subjects is included in the play. The production misses the opportunity of putting to the audience the question, raised by the insurgent and discussed by Asad: "If the vast majority of the citizens of these democratic countries support the destructive policies of their elected governments, are they in some sense also its partial agents?" (94).

In light of the themes concerned in this chapter, it appears unlikely that the theatre event radically rebuilds the frames of grievability. In the end, the humanitarian effort depicted through Jo is dependent on the privileged signifier of the passport and could thus be seen to condone, rather than challenge, the exclusionary norms of human intelligibility. I would concur with Paul Bond's criticism that "*Fallujah* has value in its representation of the horrors of the invasion, but [...] holds out as the de facto alternative those [...] who are involved in 'conflict resolution'", and it thus accepts the parameters of the invasion "as an *accomplished fact*" (Bond). In consequence, even though *Fallujah* doubtlessly turns to waste and wasted life, its critical potential may not necessarily be realised in each performance encounter with the audience. Although theatregoers are encouraged to 'unembed' themselves, alongside the travels of Sasha and Jo, from their spectatorial position as media consumers of the sanitised spectacle of 'shock and awe' and become witnesses to atrocities that have been redacted from the war archive, the decoding position audiences are likely to occupy does not necessarily reconfigure their ethical stance. Despite immersing audiences sonically and visually in the dramatised siege of Fallujah, the theatre event does not ask them to "consider the ways in which our lives are profoundly implicated in the lives of others", which, for Butler, is indispensable for an ethics of "'common' corporeal vulnerability" (*Precarious Life* 7, 42). If it does not reconfigure the frames of grievability, *Fallujah* nevertheless manifests an emphatic rejection of them. This is, perhaps, more than can be said of *How Many Miles to Basra?*, which – despite achieving a high level of critical reflexivity about the coverage of 'their' deaths – eventually recedes into 'our' perspective and storylines. *Fallujah*, in contrast, gradually shifts the origin point from 'our' to 'their' hurt and thus invites audiences to occupy a subject position that would seem uninhabitable to the narrator of the 9/11 story – although this interpellative invitation may not work to unsettle each individual audience member.

On the whole, with their interest in the modalities of reporting ungrievable deaths, the plays contest the derealisation of the 'other' that sits at the heart of the formation of communities of bereaved on the home front, as seen in Gilroy's *Motherland*, for example. Moreover, their assumption of the perspective of Western reporters and activists in their confrontation with Iraqi subjects in the war zone can be seen to work against the "inhuman geographies" perpetuated by the military representation of targets, which "remove[s] humans and other living beings from view" (Dalby 295). *Fallujah*, especially, manages to do so by opening up the war archive for the inclusion of images of Iraqi bodies that were burnt and maimed by the 'shock and awe' campaign of Western forces, whose claims to precision (bombing) are thereby refuted. Consequently, although narratives of grief may variously cross the boundaries between home and front, the front-line plays are more sensitive to the traces of the discarded negatives, ruins, and wasted lives that are shut out by most versions of war offered up to 'First World' viewers and theatre audiences.

4.5 Military Masculinities

The previous sections have traced war drama's continuation and contestation of a number of gendered, topographical, and ideological binaries: 'First World' versus 'Third World' femininities, 'safe' versus 'dangerous' spaces, 'us' versus the enemy 'other'. The recurrent focus on such dualisms may appear somewhat surprising in an era of "postmodern war" (Schott 21), which might be seen to connote uncertainties, fluidities, and flexible identities. Yet, as the preceding analyses have shown, the plays distinctly engage with the binary pairs that structure the discursive and visual fields of the 'war on terror', which Maryam Khalid has summarised as "the dichotomy between the benevolent, civilised and moral masculinity of the West and the backward, barbaric, oppressive, deviant masculinity of the 'brown man', the 'free' Western woman and the oppressed, subjugated Muslim woman" (20). As this brief sketch indicates, gender functions as a predominant structuring principle to encode the locations of 'self' and 'other'. The assumption that binary gender patterns bear no relevance to postmodern wars would, as Robin May Schott concedes, risk "overlooking [...] that gender may not be primarily fluid" and "undervalue the way in which gender hierarchies remain entrenched in meanings, institutions, and interactions" (22, 28).

After the discussions of (un)grieving femininities and traumatised masculinities on the home front and the analysis of appropriations of Afghan femininities in front-line plays, this final subchapter moves a position situated at the higher end of wartime hierarchies into view. In her analysis of the discourses and practices of protecting and proving identity in the 'war on terror',[29] Kim Rygiel has shown that "the privileged identity (and way of life) being secured is that of the white, 'western', wealthy male" (147). This particular subject position is not only privileged by citizenship policies on the Western home front – most of Rygiel's examples are drawn from Canadian (bio)politics – but has also been a dominant factor in the perception of the war:

> the war has largely been fought in the public eye, through images of male politicians and soldiers waging war in defense of their nations and on behalf of the 'civilized world'. Here the citizen has been constructed around highly masculinized representations of the largely white, male 'citizen-warrior' [...] [which are] based largely on an Anglo-American hegemonic masculinity. (147)

Over the course of the previous front-line sections, the white, male citizen-warrior has become an intensely familiar figure, from the British soldiers that rehearse the derealisation of the enemy 'other' to the neoliberal war agents that labour for the extension of globalisation. A sustained analysis of the role masculinity plays in the theatrical construction of such subjects and the way in which drama responds to, celebrates, or challenges hegemonic types of masculinity is therefore highly warranted.

The concept of hegemonic masculinities is most commonly associated with the work of R.W. Connell and the rise of masculinity studies in the 1980s. The term was coined to define "how particular groups of men inhabit positions of power and wealth, and how they legitimate and reproduce the social relationships that generate their dominance" (Carrigan et al. 592). According to this model, hegemony is achieved primarily through dominance over women and subordinated masculinities (in particular homosexual ones) and the institutionalisation thereof. In response to sustained critiques, Connell later qualified the concept by considering, at least in part, the multidimensionality of gendered hierarchies, specifically the role played by local, regional, and global factors (Connell and Messerschmidt 848–851). These qualifications are important when seeking to adapt the notion of hegemonic masculinities to the global 'war on terror' project, where hegemonic white masculinities are (re)produced locally in ways that interact with globalised heteronormative frames, for instance, against

---

[29] Rygiel defines these as follows: "Protecting identity refers to the need to make a certain privileged identity more secure. [...] Proving identity [...] has to do with policies and practices aimed at making populations more knowable and manageable" (146).

the construction of the subordinate, pathologised, 'failed' masculinity of the terrorist.

It bears emphasising that there is no monolithic bloc of privileged Anglo-American citizen-warriors, but the subjects that would make up this group are among themselves differentiated and hierarchised by national, regional, class, sexual, and other factors. For one thing, there are the gendered tropes that position the UK as "'riding pillion' on the American government's metaphorical motorcycle" (Enloe, Foreword vii). Such images of the 'special' US-UK relationship have framed British masculinities in line with the "growing perception [...] that Great Britain has become a submissive, feminized partner acquiescing to the will of an assertive, masculine one" (Carpenter 144).[30] In contradistinction to constructions of the US as a dominant, aggressive, masculine power, British or European citizen-soldiers are more commonly seen to inhabit a comparatively moderate masculinity that corresponds to the notion of a "'soft' and 'feminized' European Union" (Braidotti, *Transpositions* 46). Moreover, hegemonic masculinity crucially correlates with factors of class. As Illouz's work on the impact of the therapeutic narrative on contemporary models of subjectivity has shown, middle-class men in late-capitalist societies are more likely to position themselves within "'feminine' models of selfhood", for the "strong, self-reliant, unemotional" brand of hegemonic masculinity is becoming increasingly incompatible with the therapeutic ethos (231). This is why Illouz concludes that "working-class men are more likely to conform to models of hegemonic masculinity" (235).

As these deliberations indicate, the type of masculinity encountered most frequently in British front-line plays productively interacts with the hegemonic model. In slightly amending Rygiel's finding, cited above, one might suggest that the privileged subject position in front-line drama – in terms of stage time, at least – is that of the white, Western, working-class male. Although many of the plays are set in a military context, where ranks and regiments supposedly supplant class structures, most protagonists are positioned within lower-class backgrounds, and many of the plays tap into the tradition of "working-class realism" (Stephen Lacey qtd. in Sierz, *Rewriting* 17).[31] New writing in the first decade of the 21st century, as Ken Urban proposes, has often taken the form

---

30 A host of emasculating images of Blair has pervaded popular culture; apart from the common jibe that he was no more than Bush's 'poodle', the examples given by Rebecca Carpenter include a 2002 music video by George Michael that showed Blair as Bush's female dance partner (145–146).

31 As Sierz elaborates, these plays "depict working-class or lower-class life in an unglamorous – and often deliberately dirty – way, while stressing the truth or authenticity of this experience" (*Rewriting* 17).

of "naturalistic plays set in council flats and working-class pubs" (51) – an observation which some of the home-front plays reviewed in this study corroborate. When it comes to front-line plays, I would add to Suman Gupta's observation that, "[i]rrespective of whether the conflict is implicitly denounced or accepted [...], these are plays *about* soldiers" (102) the fact that these are almost invariably plays about working-class soldiers. Beyond the productions discussed so far and the case studies approached in this final section, Gregory Burke's *Black Watch* (2006) and Morgan Lloyd Malcolm's *Belongings* (2011), one could point to Simon Stephens's *Canopy of Stars* (2009) or to plays which stage one of the most iconic 'white trash' figures in the 'war on terror', Lynndie England, such as Peter Morris's *Guardians* (2005) or Beth Steel's *Lynndie England* (2011), by way of example.

Just as working-class masculinities appear particularly amenable to the hegemonic features of strength and self-reliance, military masculinities have often been described as exemplary hegemonic forms. As Christopher Gittings's thoughts on imperial masculinity suggest, it "is constructed as a definitive and hierarchical gender identity, one that feminizes what it reads as inferior formations of masculinity [...] [and] abrogates the homosexual subject's male gender identity" (4). The dominance over women and subordinate masculinities that is so crucial to Connell's model is, accordingly, especially pronounced in a military context. Following John Munder Ross, Nigel Edley and Margaret Wetherell define "martial masculinity" in terms of an "exaggerated masculine performance, characterised by tyrannical and aggressive behaviour, misogyny, and a rigid and artificial valorisation of all things masculine" (56). This raises the question whether, or to what extent, military masculinities have come under pressure due to the increase in female recruits and minority ethnic personnel and the opening of the armed forces to openly gay soldiers. The period of the 'war on terror' has been marked by extensive debates about the participation of women and homosexuals in military roles. If one dates the start of the conflict to 2001, it comes shortly after the lifting of the ban on the participation of homosexual service members in 2000. Situated at the other bookend of the period reviewed in this study, the withdrawal of British troops from Afghanistan in 2014, is the major decision to open front-line combat roles to women – the last bastion of male privilege in the military. These developments notwithstanding, Victoria Basham's evaluation of social diversity in the British forces has proven that "the salience of the archetype of 'the soldier' as a white, heterosexual man is [still] significant" – despite their de-facto inclusion in the military, the range of subjectivities available to female, gay, and minority ethnic personnel remains orientated towards the preservation of white, heteromasculine privilege (412, 417–421).

An enquiry into the figuration of military masculinities in front-line plays must not stop short of more covert, implicit forms of positioning. As Enloe has pointed out with regard to the comparative absence of gendered war stories in the wake of the 7/7 bombings, such a lack may just as well point to a host of gendered assumptions that goes unchallenged (Foreword vii–viii). More generally, Andrea Nachtigall has observed that 'war on terror' discourses repeatedly highlight the (failed or excessive) masculinity of the 'other', whereas the masculinities ascribed to the 'self' are rarely the subject of explicit negotiation (311). This chapter aims at tracing theatre's relationship to the hegemonic military masculinities privileged by 'war on terror' discourses as well as the ways in which dramatised subjects fall outside or resist such a model. After all, hegemonic attempts at suturing subject positions at privileged nodal points can never fully succeed in fixing their relations to an essentially unstable and shifting discursive field.

('Our') Boys Will Be Boys: Gregory Burke's *Black Watch*

Alongside *Stuff Happens* and *Guantanamo*, *Black Watch* is doubtlessly among the playtexts in the British 'war on terror' corpus that have been the most widely discussed. This is, on the one hand, to do with its extensive touring history and video recording of performances, which allowed for the piece to be seen by a substantial number of audiences. *Black Watch* was first performed in a disused drill hall at the Edinburgh Fringe Festival in 2006. The production was filmed by BBC Scotland during its 2007 Scottish tour, broadcast both on television and as a radio play in the same year (and released on DVD in 2008); the play also toured the US in 2007, Australia and New Zealand, the UK, and Ireland in 2008, and was launched in another international touring production with a new cast in 2010 (Burke xx–xxi). Beyond the show's considerable international appeal and critical acclaim, another, and perhaps more salient, reason why it has attracted so much scholarly attention is its exemplary status as one of the first productions staged in the inaugural season of the newly launched National Theatre of Scotland.

As Trish Reid summarises scholarly consensus on *Black Watch*, the play "is now widely acknowledged as the most important Scottish post-devolutionary theatrical event" (194). David Archibald comments that, as the National Theatre's "flagship production", Burke's piece "bears its own burden of representation: it is not simply *a* Scottish play about Iraq; it is *the* Scottish play about Iraq" (8). Unsurprisingly, then, much of the research into the production has coalesced around issues of national identity and nationalism: Reid discusses "the version of Scottish identity" heralded by the production (196); Marcia Blumberg analyses its function "both as a patriotic vehicle and as a counter-play that performs patriotic dissent" (79); Rebecca Robinson examines its "representations of nationhood, identity and belonging" (393); Joanne Zerdy excavates the production's "banal theatrical nationalism" (184). Although many of these studies comment on aspects of masculinity – the performance's "definite macho dynamic" (Blumberg 82) rarely goes unnoticed – their interest is ultimately in how gender and sexuality tie back with the discussion of Scottishness and nationhood. There has, to date, been no sustained analysis of the role military masculinity plays in the "deeply problematic" politics of the production, which Archibald ascribes to its erasure of the Black Watch's imperial past (8).

I would argue that the central contradiction unearthed by Archibald, the play's criticism of the Iraq war and simultaneous "celebration of empire (or at least [...] wilful forgetting)" (12), is intricately connected to its figuration of masculinity. Of particular relevance here is the way in which the history of the Black Watch is interleaved with the personal narratives of the soldiers represented. Archibald notes that "the two are fused together as the soldiers' stories are collected, ordered and placed within a broader historical narrative – 'The Golden Thread'" (8), that is, the teleological through-line that "connects the past, the present, the future" of the regiment, as protagonist Cammy explains (25). The script of the production, which is loosely based on interviews with Black Watch recruits, negotiates the soldiers' subject positions against this historical canvas. When Cammy is asked by the writer (Burke's fictionalised representative in the play) if the 'Golden Thread' is "why [...] [his] granddad joined", Cammy simply responds, "I dinnay ken", and Rossco and Granty add that "[h]e was probably just a fucking idiot tay"; "He's fay a long line ay idiots" (25). Archibald identifies these as "moments when the soldiers do undercut the monumentalising narrative", but he holds that "the general thrust is one that is at ease with the official Golden Thread mythology" (8).

Yet Cammy's refusal to position himself within the 'monumentalising narrative' is, I would suggest, no exception to the 'general thrust' of the play. The dynamics of positioning are such that the 'Golden Thread' runs through the production so as to constantly reinsert the soldiers, who largely refuse to appropriate that heroising narrative for themselves, squarely back within this glorious history. In this manner, their own reflexive strategies of positioning remain deliberately modest, which is clearly a more palatable strategy of subjectivation, given the controversial Iraq campaign in which the soldiers are involved. Precisely because the squaddies appear to make no claims to heroism, it becomes easier for spectators to grant it to them. That the regiment's "proud history is juxtaposed with their lack of autonomy as Britain's contribution to the

American forces in Iraq" (Blumberg 79) is less of a contradiction than would appear at first sight. Since the soldiers continuously construct themselves as ignorant, unknowing agents without access to the power/knowledge nexus that underlies the war, they bear no responsibility for the "aberration" of the Iraq invasion (Archibald 10). The soldiers' class position is of immense significance in this regard, for their lack of socioeconomic privilege seems to carry a "sense of the powerlessness of the [working-class] individual, unquestioningly carrying out command" (Hurley 275). The fact that the soldiers' apparent disengagement from the glorious thread of history enables the script (and spectators) to reinsert them firmly into it is important, for it works to occlude their complicity in imperial violence. "The effect is one that allows for audiences to "go 'over the top' in solidarity with 'our boys'", as Archibald rightly notes (12). This effect can only be realised, in performance, by eliding the soldiers' – and the regiment's, and Scotland's – participation in empire.

A similar occlusion applies to the connection between the particular brand of working-class masculinity negotiated for and by the soldier subjects and the structures of masculinism that are, apparently, critiqued in the play. This can be seen already in the opening moments. As Blumberg describes, the play begins with the ostensibly patriotic display of "moving beams of light in the shape of the St. Andrew's cross" as "the blaring music of bagpipes and drums builds to a climax" (82). As most critics agree, this opening references the sensational nature of the Edinburgh Military Tattoo. Initial associations with the spectacular parading of soldiers, and the attendant fetishisation of trained, uniformed, choreographed, and mostly male bodies,[32] are, however, "immediately subverted by the slightly comic, uncertain and embarrassed entrance of Cammy" (Robinson 395). In marked contrast to the cited spectacle, the protagonist enters "*dressed in civvies*" (Burke 3) and speaks to the audience with his arms hidden behind his back, in a nervous tone of voice, anxiously licking his lips and constantly swallowing an apparent lump in his throat.[33] Cammy greets audiences by admitting, "At first, I didnay want tay day this. [...] I think people's minds are usually made up about you if you were in the army" (3). By means of these opening lines, audiences are challenged to dispense with the image of strong, self-possessed, hardened fighters conjured up by the initial Tattoo reference, for, as Cam-

---

[32] A cursory survey of photographs of the Tattoo on the internet seems to suggest that the parading soldiers are predominantly male; incidentally, female soldiers sometimes appear to perform in tartan mini-skirts, which, in turn, heightens the sexualised appearance of the uniformed female bodies.

[33] All observations are based on the BBC Two Scotland recording of the performance at Highland Football Academy, Dingwall, broadcast on 27 August 2007.

my's diminished address would suggest, a more honest, moderate version of soldierly masculinity will be offered.

Paradoxically, it is the apparent disavowal of the spectacle of military masculinity that allows for the production to stage its own glorification of the uniformed body of the male soldier in the dance, fight, and movement scenes that are included in the show's peculiar mix of "a realist mode with heightened drama, stylised choreography, surreal images [...] and popular theatre forms" (Heddon 141). Just after the initial retraction of the sensational opening, spectators come to be positioned with regard to the heteronormative and masculinist frames through which the soldiers' narratives are focalised. Cammy explains that he and his "pals" (5) only agreed to tell their story because "this tasty researcher lassie phoned us up" (4). The audience laugh with the soldiers as they admit that they believed that the researcher "was gagging for a line up from some battle-hardened Black Watch toby" and "going to buy us drink all day and suck our cocks" (5). Again, an apparent contrast is established between the stereotypical warrior image of the Black Watch recruit and these 'ordinary' young men, dressed in jeans and tracksuits. They make no explicit claim to the hyper-masculinity of the 'battle-hardened' soldier, a label that can only be invoked in an ironic manner, yet audiences are made complicit with a 'boys will be boys' attitude through their laughter at the men's 'naive' sexism. As evident from the discourse surrounding the play, "Burke really did use an attractive female TV researcher to make the initial contact with Black Watch veterans" (Cull, *Gregory Burke's* Black Watch 4); there is no reflection on these sexist dynamics, either in the production or its attendant documentation. The suggestion is that spectators who want to hear "the 'real' stories of the soldiers in their own words", as promised by director John Tiffany (qtd. in Burke x), need to let themselves in for a bit of sexist banter. And "bantering dialogue", as David Pattie notes, is the "default conversational setting" (34). Despite the assertion that the play dramatises the 'real' soldiers, not the warriors paraded in military spectacles, this first scene does not negotiate any subject position for the characters outside the scripts of hegemonic masculinity. Instead, the "significance of 'birds, booze and brawling' to the culture of the military's white, (assumed to be) heterosexual men" (Basham 423–424) is fully endorsed: after their disappointment that the "bird" (5) never materialises, the soldiers only agree to tell their stories to the writer after he offers to pay for the 'booze' (6), and the latently aggressive atmosphere between the men signals that 'brawling' could erupt any minute – as it does, in fact, in a later scene (65).

The normative masculine rituals of 'birds, booze and brawling' – or, as the soldiers explain, "Sunday sesh", "Watch the football", "Blether pish" (7) – are set not only against the notion of military spectacle, but also against the masculinist sphere of politics and policy-making. They become the markers of a stereotypical working-class masculinity, characterised by "drinking, occasional fighting, womanizing" (Horrocks 126), which is authenticated by the play's sympathetic portrayal of the men. These practices are rendered innocuous precisely because the soldiers' disadvantaged location on vectors of class deprives them of autonomy in the larger scheme of things. The play's emphasis on the regiment's roots, recruiting from Scottish working-class communities "that had been used, over and over again, as fodder, for factories, for the mines, and for the forces" (Pattie 33) strikes an important critical note. The soldiers' disadvantaged class positions are, however, activated in a way that naturalises their performance of hegemonic masculinity. In other words, while their classed positionalities are openly negotiated in the production, there is no consideration of the ways these interact with their privileged gendered and sexual positions, nor of the equivalential articulations between martial masculinities and a highly masculinised political culture. These alliances are shrouded by a range of juxtapositions, which I will track in the following.

The transition from the civilian home-front to the military front-line setting takes place as "*the pool table splits open*" and two soldiers appear "*dressed in desert combats, berets and red hackles*" (8). While they seem to patrol the area by moving slowly on the pool table, each providing cover and protection for the other, a re-enacted news programme comes up on the screens in the performance space. The regiment's deployment to Iraq is contextualised as presenter John Humphrys reports that "news leaked out [...] that the soldiers of the Black Watch were to be sent north to help out the Americans in Iraq" (8). The vulnerability of the Scottish soldiers is underlined by reference to the deaths of three soldiers in an explosion, which foreshadows an event later to be staged. The exposure of the men's bodies to risk, viscerally evoked by the dense use of signifiers such as "triangle of death", "blown up", "suicide car-bomber", "ambush", "mortar bombs", and "insurgents" in the brief news extract (8), is contrasted with the slow and careful movement of the two soldiers in the space of the stage, who continuously keep their bodies close to each other, literally guarding each other's back. The broader theme that emerges from this juxtaposition, and which is endorsed by the play at large, is the notion that the male leaders who make the policy decisions – Scottish National Party leader Alex Salmond and Defence Secretary Geoff Hoon are represented on screen – carelessly dispose of the lives of these 'ordinary' men. In consequence, the soldiers depend on their solidarity and loyalty with each other, which is affirmed by the staging of homosocial bonding rituals. Significantly, in the re-enacted TV appearance, Salmond condemns the "duplicity and chicanery of the politicians who sent them into this deployment" (8). Hoon, in turn, denounces Salmond's exploitation of the occasion in order to "take political advantage about the tragic deaths of three brave men" (8). It seems that both male leaders appropriate the values of bravery and integrity ascribed to the Black Watch regiment, "the finest infantry soldiers in the world" (9), for the sake of attaining their own policy goals.

The sphere of political decision-making is abandoned as the next scene cuts to the soldiers' arrival at the military camp in Iraq, which sets the performance of soldierly masculinity against the masculinised culture of conventional politics. The oppositional structure works to conceal the close contiguity between the "current rise of militarism" and "a globalizing patriarchy that purveys a conquest-driven masculinist stance" (Zine 31). The performance thereby elides the deep entrenchment of military masculinities in a patriarchal public sphere. Akin to the suggestion that the soldiers, who do not even know "why the fuck we're here" (9), cannot be held responsible for the Iraq offensive, it is implied that they are performing a type of masculinity that is always already oppositional to the one inscribed at the policy level. The coding of their gendered subject position as resistant is what makes "their sexist, racist and homophobic language and attitudes" (Robinson 398) palatable and ensures that audiences nevertheless identify with the protagonists. The soldiers' articulations of sexism, racism, homophobia as well as transphobia become naturalised components of military masculinity and endow the representation with authenticity (these are, after all, the 'real' soldiers).[34]

Indicative of an ostensibly resistant masculinity is the officer's email, read out on an elevated platform on stage, which, again, contrasts the policy level with the 'boots on the ground'. In the email sent to his "darling" at home (12) – which recalls Carol Acton's comment on the heteronormative trope of letter-writing on the front – the officer admits: "I hope the government knows what it has got us into. I am not sure they fully understand the risks. The jocks are well and are coming at it with their usual gallows humour" (12). Again, a dichotomy between the mindless masculine militarism of the government, which has placed the soldiers into an unnecessarily risky situation, and the subjectivities of the ordinary Scottish soldiers ('jocks') emerges. The way in which the term 'gallows humour' naturalises the soldiers' sexist banter exemplarily illustrates the dramaturgical strategies that continuously place their performances of military masculinity in opposition to 'globalizing patriarchy'. Just as the "lions led by donkeys" theme, carried over from the First World War, works towards "absolving individual soldiers of responsibility" (Reid 195), the performance's affective

---

34 Next to various homophobic insinuations, a transphobic attitude is implicit in a joke about one of the squaddies being "a pre-op transsexual" (57).

investment in the national identity of the 'lions' is intricately connected to an unspoken affirmation of their gender and sexual identity. Michael Kimmel's discussion of the popular masculinist retreats of the 1990s, designed for men who wanted to reclaim their 'warrior within' (136), can serve to elucidate this point. A conventional image deployed in this context was that of the chauffeur: he is wearing the uniform and driving, but he only appears to be in charge, while he is given orders by someone else. As Kimmel remarks: "there is a missing piece to the image", namely, the fact "that the person who is giving the orders is also a man. Now we have a relationship *between* men" (137). The exclusive focus on the individual experience of the emasculated chauffeur – or the 'real' stories of the Black Watch soldiers – forecloses a wider view of patriarchal power relations.

The front-line scenes are characterised by the same heteromasculine rituals glimpsed in the home-front routines: the soldiers sit around with "*their trousers rolled down over their boots*" (13) in front of a wagon plastered with pin-up posters; they play "toby tig", a game where you "get your cock out and whack [other soldiers] on the puss way it" (24); they "*are watching porn*" (34); wonder whether they "get loads ay fanny after" their deployment (50); constantly express their impatience to be involved in "fucking fighting" (40) or "tay shoot some cunt" (51); and they regularly engage in rounds of ten-second fights with each other (55 – 56). They blatantly derive their gendered subject positions from stereotypically masculine domains and practices, their virility (emphasised by a noticeable obsession with their crotches), excessive swearing (there is barely an utterance not qualified by *fuck*, *cunt*, or *fucking*), and a latent aggression that is cultivated in the ritual of the ten-second fights but also erupts uncontrollably. The soldiers' practices cite the common military bonding rituals that are familiar, for example, from Anthony Swofford's memoir *Jarhead* (popularised through the 2005 Sam Mendes film of the same name), which details the soldiers' participation in such routines as the 'field-fuck', or from leaked images of contractors "dancing naked around a fire in the guard-force compound" in the Kabul hazing incident (Higate, "Drinking" 456). In *Black Watch*, the men's participation in these norm-bound rituals is staged in a way that naturalises the homosocial culture of the military. Lindsey Feitz and Joane Nagel's reading of "wars as sites of homosocial masculine solidarity, arenas of male sexual aggression, [...] stages where gender and sexual scripts are enacted and reinforced" (217) bears particular relevance here.

What is staged in *Black Watch* is, essentially, a reiterative performance of gender in Butler's sense. The production's use of choreography and physical theatre, especially, reveals that "performativity is not a singular act, but a repetition and ritual, which achieves its effects through its naturalization in the context of a body" (Butler, *Gender Trouble* xv). Significantly, however, the aestheticisation of military masculinity serves to naturalise the performative processes of its construction. In other words, there is nothing in the performance that lays bare, as Butler has formulated the subversive potential of drag, *"the imitative structure of gender itself – as well as its contingency"* (187). The naturalisation of military masculinity, again, works in conjunction with the show's elision of imperial culpability. "The spectacular and sentimental staging conventions" may not only "distract viewers from the nationalism enfolded within the production" (Zerdy 190) but also deflect scrutiny of its reification of hegemonic masculinity. The crucial point here is that music, light, sound, costume, gesture, bodies, and movement cohere and converge in such a way as to position audiences on a primarily affective register towards the spectacle of military masculinity, initially disavowed but now fully endorsed in performance segments such as the play's final parade scene, which aestheticises the muscular male fighting body. This undercuts the play's anti-war tendencies in much the same way that Swofford professes soldiers' admiration for films that are critical of war, like Stanley Kubrick's *Full Metal Jacket* (1987), "because the magic brutality of the films celebrates the terrible and despicable beauty of their fighting skills" (qtd. in Peebles 1664).

The staging of young, well-built, physically apt performers fighting with each other, guarding each other's backs, or marching to the sound of pipes and drums amounts to an alluring theatrical spectacle. In this sense, the performance stays fully in tune with the hegemonic "configuration of the sensible" that Rancière connects – via Deleuze/Guattari – to "the 'right' relationship between what a body 'can' do and what it cannot" (*Emancipated Spectator* 71). The theatrical codes provide a synthesis of homogeneous elements that, together, instate the subject form of the 'archetypal' male warrior as a coherent affective and corporeal (dis)position. There is nothing disparate in this conglomeration of signs; rather, the staged "acts, gestures, and desire produce the effect of an internal core or substance" (Butler, *Gender Trouble* 185). Key, here, is the lack of the parodic repetition operative in drag, for instance, which might cause a disturbance to the heteromasculine order of signs, reveal the gendered body as performative, and martial masculinity as a contingent construct. Instead, this type of gender identity is articulated as "a static cultural marker, […] rather [than] as an incessant and repeated action of some sort", to invert Butler's famous dictum (152).

To underscore this point, it may be insightful to look at the play's ending, which, in many ways, mirrors the opening move of replacing military spectacle with 'real' soldierly masculinity:

CAMMY. That's what we joined the army tay day.
ROSSCO. Fight.

CAMMY.	No for our government.
MACCA.	No for Britain.
NABSY.	No even for Scotland.
CAMMY.	I fought for my regiment.
ROSSCO.	I fought for my company.
GRANTY.	I fought for my platoon.
NABSY.	I fought for my section.
STEWARTY.	I fought for my mates. (72)

The 'mates' are represented as the climax, the smallest and most significant homosocial unit on which the entire military structure and the larger system of the nation-state rest. The construction of the homosocial team as discursive rallying point echoes "discourses of military masculinity seen in popular culture, of the 'band of brothers' where trust, loyalty, and mutual support ensure that 'no man is left behind'" (Woodward and Winter 292). The soldiers, ultimately, articulate their subjectivity towards each other, rather than a more abstract national collectivity. Neither the text substratum nor the performance contains any sign that calls the valuation of these bonds into question. As a consequence, *Black Watch* cements the self-image of the British forces as "dependent on tight-knit bonding to maintain effectiveness", with "the most [...] operationally effective groups [...] comprised of (presumed to be) heterosexual men" (Basham 421).

It is my suggestion that, by positioning audiences in an essentially empathetic relationship towards 'our boys', spectators are gently cajoled into an endorsement of the Iraq campaign, despite the play's critical attitude towards the invasion. At issue here is what John Kelly calls "the ease with which 'supporting the troops' becomes 'supporting the policy'" (732). The type of military masculinity heralded by the production is key to the "reactionary" politics of the play that Archibald ascribes solely to its elision of empire (12). If the success of the British military depends on 'operationally effective' homosocial units, and if *Black Watch* ultimately affirms the validity and appeal of male bonds, then the type of gendered subjectivity endorsed by the production is one that is conducive to the war effort. The missing link here is between the subjection of young working-class men to sexist, militarist, and imperial codes and the "socialization and training" that warriors require "in order to fight effectively" (Goldstein 252). Consequently, the gendered and classed subject position negotiated for and by the Black Watch soldiers in the production can be comfortably reinserted into the Iraq war story, despite its claims to being oppositional to it.

Women at Camp Bastion: Morgan Lloyd Malcolm's *Belongings*

Whereas, in the homosocial frame of *Black Watch*, there is nothing to challenge the soldiers' performance of military masculinity, Morgan Lloyd Malcolm's *Belongings* provokes a confrontation between hegemonic masculinity and its 'others': femininity and homosexuality. Both 'othered' subject positions converge in the figure of Deb, a lesbian soldier whose subjectivity is asserted against the archetype of the white, male, heterosexual soldier, represented by the character Sarko. Malcolm's choice of dramatis personae is remarkable, given not only the absence of female soldiers from most of the front-line plays discussed so far but also the relative dearth of lesbian characters and representations of lesbian subculture in contemporary British drama more generally (Pankratz 206). The play, which was first produced in 2011 as part of the Hampstead Theatre Downstairs programme and transferred to the West End venue Trafalgar Studios in the same year, intercuts front-line scenes set in the "*sleeping quarters*" of the "*desert*" camp where Deb and Sarko are stationed in Afghanistan (Malcolm 16) – quite possibly representative of the British army's largest desert base Camp Bastion – with home-front scenes of the kitchen-sink type, where Deb adjusts her 'belonging(s)' to an altered home. Inevitably, the focus here will be on the front-line scenes, although the production does not draw a neat separation between the two spaces and temporalities; the set merges the scenographic elements indicating the Afghan camp and the Chippenham kitchen, and the dialogues set in the two spaces increasingly intersect with each other.

Belongings speaks to the debates sketched at the outset of this section, surrounding the inclusion of homosexual personnel in the British army and the opening of combat roles to women. The latter issue was often promoted by reference to the asymmetrical nature of the conflicts in Iraq and Afghanistan, whose blurred front lines made it extremely difficult to keep female soldiers in a safe distance to action (Feitz and Nagel 203). When it comes to televisual representations of the Afghan war, popular BBC series such as *Our Girl* (2013–), which centres on a female medic's experience of military operations in Afghanistan, or *Bluestone 42* (2013–2015), whose team of bomb-disposal experts posted in Afghanistan includes a female specialist, have pointed to the close involvement of female soldiers in enemy contact. In these TV series, the female service personnel slot easily into the heteromasculine culture of the military, which is, essentially, affirmed by the representations. The way in which the female characters participate in the chauvinistic banter, games, and jokes and engage in sexual affairs with the male soldiers points to the provisional inclusion of women soldiers on condition that they perform their gender and sexuality in such a way as to ultimately protect the military's privileged identity. This works, for instance, so long as women conform to their symbolic (and often also enacted) role as sexual objects in male bonding rituals (see also Basham 422).

The opening of the first front-line scene of *Belongings* immediately conveys the sexualised dynamics of which Deb seeks to partake as a privileged member:

SARKO *is holding a bottle of shower gel that has had a cock and balls drawn on it.* [...]
DEB. Someone got 'cocked'? [...]
SARKO *grabs a plastic box of his stuff and holds up, one by one, his belongings that have been 'cocked'.*
SARKO. Shampoo! Hair gel! Face cream!
DEB. Vain bastard. You've got more toiletries than me.
SARKO. Oh this is one I aint seen before. My toothbrush? You twat! [...]
DEB. I'm a fuckin' genius! [...] It's like you're sucking a nob!
SARKO. Yeh yeh. Laugh it up. So glad to know we've got you protecting our country.
DEB. Oh like you're so pure.
She holds up her hairbrush which has also been cocked and brushes her hair with it.
DEB. (*Playacting.*) Oh I wanted to brush my hair but someone keeps poking me with their hard-on. (16–17)

As the scene establishes, Deb's participation in the games, rituals, and banter cultivated in the army facilitates her apparently seamless performance of military masculinity. There are innumerable examples in the play that confirm Goldstein's observation of how, "[i]n a traditionally male environment (the military), women look and act professionally by acting like men – for example, by performing physically demanding tasks, controlling emotions, using raw language or a command voice" (379). Indeed, Deb proves her equal physical strength at "*lifting weights*" (44), reproaches herself for appearing too "fuckin' soft" (48), uses even rawer language than her male comrade, and playfully issues orders to him: "Shut up your whining and make me a brew" (34). Most obviously, then, Deb's gender performance exemplifies how "there are genders, ways of culturally interpreting the sexed body, that are in no way restricted by the apparent duality of sex", as Butler has established (*Gender Trouble* 152).

Sex may not delimit gender, in this case, but Deb's sexed identity still provides an obstacle, or at least an incentive, in the sense that she has to out-perform other male soldiers in the typical emasculating practices used to denigrate the other's and enhance one's own sense of masculinity. This corroborates Melisa Brittain's basic observation that "a woman soldier's need to prove she is as tough as the boys [is] a matter of great urgency" (90), which is evident from Deb's fiercer dedication to the game of 'cocking' each other's belongings. Deb achieves a more durable sense of masculinity only by continuously rendering her male comrade effeminate; for instance, she employs female epithets to address Sarko, as in "[m]an up princess" (21), to challenge his tenuously acquired manhood. Deb and Sarko's game also reveals how military masculinity relegates male homosexuality to the constitutive outside against which it defines itself. That the ultimate triumph consists in positioning the male soldier as homosexual ('It's like you're sucking a nob') reverberates throughout the play, with Deb depriving Sarko of masculinity, and enhancing her own, by invoking homoerotic scenarios of Sarko "and the Major tied up in a dungeon and fucking each other free" (32), for example. On the whole, then, despite her position as sexed 'other' in the army, Deb is fully complicit with the "domination-submission relationships" established in military culture (Goldstein 333).

And yet her performance of gender goes beyond a mere imitation and reinforcement of military masculinity. Basically, Deb's performance could be read in terms of what Jack Halberstam has theorised as "female masculinity", which he defines as "a queer subject position that can successfully challenge hegemonic models of gender conformity" (9). Deb can exploit her contradictory positioning for the sake of enlarging the repertoire of intelligible gendered/sexed subject codes. She not only mimics heteromasculine soldiers but also 'playacts' hegemonic versions of femininity, as her imitation of the ignorant and vain female, brushing her hair with a 'cocked' hairbrush, exemplifies. Orna Sasson-Levy's study of the identity practices of Israeli women soldiers has shown that their gender performance neither adheres to a submissive femininity nor an entirely masculine model but merges aspects of both in order to forge a 'third way' of 'doing' gender (83–89). For Sasson-Levy, one way of reading women's appropriation of men's chauvinistic sense of humour and practices is to see it, analogous to the workings of drag, as destabilising essentialist conceptions of gender (85–86). In this sense, Deb's reiteration of gendered acts could be seen as displaying elements of both female-male and female-female drag, as exploiting the dualistic scripts of hegemonic gender performances to render both masculinity and femininity contingent. On the other hand, as Sasson-Levy concedes, women soldiers' appropriation of masculine identity practices is not only, or not necessarily, subversive, because it can be read as submission to the androcentric discourse of the military (82). Problematically, female soldiers who appropriate masculine forms of behaviour often (have to) exhibit a patriarchal and misogynist viewpoint; they start deriding women as essentially inferior and identify with anti-feminist attitudes in order to retain their privileges in a masculinist culture (89).

This second aspect has particular resonance in the play because Deb also identifies as a lesbian. Paradoxically, her queer positionality initially helps her adapt to the masculinised military culture insofar as she can easily exploit the discourses that reduce females to sexual objects. To the extent that Deb's sexual desires are orientated towards women, her subjectivity chimes with the heterosexist culture of the military, which is scenically conveyed by the posters of "*several topless women*" (16). This enables Deb to join in with Sarko's heterosexual banter, revolving around the discussion of female celebrities' suitability as sexual objects: "Lindsay Lohan?"; "She'd be too eager to please"; "Give me Maggie [Gyllenhaal] any day"; "Not enough tits for me" (18). Deb's contradictory location as both queer and heteronormative subject is indicative of what Jin Haritaworn, building on Jasbir Puar's approach, discusses as "the (symbolic) entry of (some) gay subjects into the national project", which is "inseparable from the wars on Afghanistan and Iraq"; this tenuous inclusion results in iterations of "a heteronormative masculinity among white gay men" (2) – and, as can be seen in this case, women. Haritaworn's central and intriguing point is that the queer "performance of military masculinity, once a subversive, parodic repetition of a violently heterosexual masculinity [...] has become a loyal repetition to the nation" (2). Similarly, one would have to read Deb's gender performance as affirmative of nationalist and heteronormative power relations. Her apparent insertion into a privileged subject position testifies to the extension of citizenship in the 'war on terror' to '(some) gay subjects' on the basis of the concomitant exclusion of the terrorist 'other'.

This type of homonationalism is illustrated in *Belongings*, for instance, as all patriotic speeches are given to Deb. She is the one who counters Sarko's frustration about giving up his life "for a fuckin' country who barely even knows we're out here" (20) with the unequivocal assertion: "We're the best army in the world mate. [...] I'm proud of being part of it" (21). More importantly, she positions herself as a patriotic British soldier against the one-dimensional enemy image of the "Taliban. The fuckin' evil ones. The bad guys" (38). Deb's access to military masculinity seems, indeed, tied to her participation in a nationalist project. The way in which this builds on a "redefinition of the West as sexually progressive" (Haritaworn 2) is reflected as Deb begins to wonder about Afghan women's sexuality underneath the burqa:

> I'm looking at this woman and thinkin' it must be pretty shit livin' under all that cloth all the time. I'm thinkin' her husband must be keepin' her under lock and key. That their sex must be horrible. But have I got it wrong? Is it actually fuckin' sensual? [...] Or am I assumin' right? Is [it] cold, mechanical, brutal? (49)

The correlation operative in the discursive formation of the 'war on terror', whereby a fixed opposition is established between Western equality, connoted by images of 'emancipated' female soldiers (see Brittain 73), and Oriental oppression, epitomised by iconic representations of burqa-clad Afghan women, is, however, disrupted in the play at large. Deb's liberal oscillation between heteronormative/homosexual and masculine/feminine scripts is increasingly obstructed as Sarko comes to deny Deb's subjectivation in terms of a female masculinity. Sarko's mounting resistance testifies to the efforts of the prototypical white, male, heterosexual British soldier to secure his privileged position against incursions of the 'other'. It is because she is, after all, "not a man" (31) that Deb's subject position can never become fully sutured at the upper end of military hierarchies. An increasing tension derives from the fact that her sexed identity precludes a stable positioning in terms of the hegemonic masculinity she aspires to, for Sarko starts to reposition her as a female sexed object. Deb's struggle to assert her masculinity against this refusal is another pertinent example of failed attempts at subjectivation in relation to the 'war on terror' discourse, and the homosexual woman soldier can be read alongside the many dramatised subjects whose attempts at becoming intelligible are rejected by those endowed with state power and/or privileged speaking positions within the discursive formation.

It appears that the fluid gender performances that Deb navigates are, ultimately, incompatible with the essentialised gender/sex binaries that undergird the structures of militarism. Putting up posters from *"new lads mags"*, Sarko muses about "a mate who's on the subs – fuckin' easy life that. The girlfriends and wives have nothing to worry about as no women allowed on board" (29). He comes to yearn for the gendered compartmentalisation of combat that had been, and still is, in place in some areas of the forces – such as the Royal Navy Submarine Service alluded to here – whereby male soldiers could rely on the separation of masculinised war zones from feminised domestic environments.[35] Evidently, the integration of female soldiers such as Deb places the symbolic gendered order of the military under pressure. Sarko's comment is illustrative of the gender-normative assumptions that feed into the line of argument of those opposing female soldiers' involvement in combat: "Women [...] must be denied access to 'the front', to 'combat' so that men can claim a uniqueness and superiority that will justify their dominant position in the social order" (Enloe, *Does* 15). Since the presence of women on the Afghan front line makes Sarko feel that he is "in the wrong place" (30), he starts to forcefully reposition Deb within her 'proper' gendered location. He refeminises her by drawing on a biologistic discourse and essentialised sexual dichotomies: "lesbians are fakin'. You've got boobs and a fanny. You're a threat" (30); "Women need men. For reproduction. It's programmed into your brains" (33). The conflict culminates in

---

35 Incidentally, the first deployment of female submariners with the Royal Navy took place in 2014, which, again, coincides with the year of troop withdrawal from Afghanistan.

Sarko's violent attempt to re-establish (sexual) domination over the female subject: eventually, he *"uses his strength to overpower* DEB. *[...] He pulls her trousers and knickers down and fucks her aggressively from behind"* (33).

The rape scene critically inflects hegemonic articulations of military masculinity, on at least two levels. First of all, it drastically reveals the rigidly dichotomised gender structures of militarism and war. The rape puts a brutal end to Deb's attempts at asserting fluid, multiple subject positions by reinserting her into the binary structures of sexual domination. Sarko's rape of Deb 'from behind' draws on the ancient trope of "feminizing enemy soldiers" by means of "anal rape, with the victor in the dominant/active position and the vanquished in the subordinate/passive one" (Goldstein 359). There is thus a homoerotic subtext to the rape scene that points to the 'haunting' force of repressed homosexuality in military culture (see Butler, *Bodies* 111), while it clearly remains legible as a desperate attempt to control Deb's femininity. The scene brings to the fore persisting gender inequalities by demonstrating how women in "entrenched masculinist spaces [...] remain vulnerable to sexual exploitation", while "their ability to control [...] their role is limited" (Feitz and Nagel 218). In other words, Deb can ultimately only negotiate a narrowly prescribed range of gendered/sexed positions. If female sex, gender, and sexuality serve to encode structures of dominance in the military, women soldiers can only play along with the games and rituals to an extent that may at times seem subversive yet finally reinforces existing hierarchies. Against the reading proposed here, critic Michael Billington has ascribed to the rape scene itself a delimiting view of gender identity; he takes issue with the portrayal of Sarko for confirming "the all-men-are-rapists theory" ("Multifaceted Women" 40). In my view, the play offers no such bland generalisations, but rather illustrates Susan Brownmiller's argument, summarised by Edley and Wetherell, that "rape is [...] used by a dominant group as the last resort [...]: rapists are simply an 'advance guard' doing the 'dirty work' from which all men benefit indirectly" (187).

Secondly, the rape scene rescripts specific narrative strands of the larger war story. Set against the prevalent discursive move of pitting 'our' women's freedom against 'their' women's oppression, the scene crucially inverts the "stereotype of the dark rapist" and the "trope of interracial rape" that was revitalised in the 'war on terror' context, as Brittain has pointed out (81). She analyses the infamous rescue narrative according to which US soldier Jessica Lynch was saved from her Iraqi captors as an echo of "imperialist narratives that constructed Indian men, particularly Muslims, as rapists of English 'ladies'" (80). In the context of debates surrounding women's involvement in combat, "the specter of [interracial] rape provides one of the strongest nationalist objections regarding women's alleged vulnerability" (Cohler 252). *Belongings* inflects these neo-imperial discourses by resituating the spectre of rape within the culture of the British military. Concerns about 'brown' men's violation of 'white' women are unmasked as bogus arguments used to camouflage the prevalence of rape and sexual harassment of women (soldiers) within Western military and social structures.[36] In this manner, the play shifts attention to British patriarchy, emphasising that diversity and equality in institutions like the army cannot be achieved if their "heteronormative culture [...] also remains intact" (Basham 414). Against official interpretations of the Abu Ghraib scandal, for instance, *Belongings* raises a question about the systematic, rather than singular, use of sexual violence in militarised culture.

To recur to the questions formulated at the outset, *Belongings* stages self-reflexive performances of military masculinity, whereas *Black Watch* is more representative of Enloe's remark on the naturalisation of gendered hierarchies. The equivalential relation between reiterations of soldierly masculinity and the militarisation of foreign policy is obscured by the framing of the Black Watch soldiers in terms of a resistant, honest, and loyal version of masculinity. The absence of an overt engagement with the soldiers' gendered/sexual positionalities betrays what Enloe has called a "stunning lack of curiosity about masculinities", resulting in the construal of men as "just naturally those who wield violence" (Foreword vii–viii). Malcolm's piece, in contrast, offers a more obvious reflection on the interrelations between performances of gender/sexuality and military/social structures. With the character of Sarko, it stages the prototypical white, male, heterosexual soldier as the guardian of one of the last bastions of male privilege, against whose defence mechanisms Deb's articulation of a fluid subject position ultimately fails.

The divergent politics of naturalisation or illustration of (the sociopolitical effects of) hegemonic masculinity in *Black Watch* and *Belongings*, respectively, map onto the two home-front plays' different modes of 'working through' male trauma. The endorsement of military masculinity as an identitarian mode to counter the loss of self-control in *The Two Worlds of Charlie F.* corresponds to the affirmation of a 'resistant' masculinity in the face of the manipulations of a masculinist foreign policy in *Black Watch*. Burke's and Sheers's plays consolidate the correlation of masculinity and victimhood in the discursive field of the 'war on terror', which operates to absolve individual soldiers of responsibility. Conversely, the reflection on men's complicity in patriarchal modes of violence in *Men in the Cities* echoes back with the illustration of the nexus of male priv-

---

36 In this context, Hunt and Rygiel discuss how the claim "that the war on terror is being waged in order to protect women's rights" deflects attention from the violence against women perpetrated by the Western invaders themselves, evident from "emerging reports that Coalition forces have sexually assaulted [...] female coalition soldiers in Afghanistan and Iraq" (9–10).

ilege and violent practices of exclusion in *Belongings*. Just as Goode resituates a culpable subject as perpetrator within the trauma paradigm, Malcolm does not make a victimised subjectivity available to any of her characters, for the position of victim is intrinsically incompatible with female soldiers' efforts at proving their 'belonging'. Whereas audiences of the latter set of plays, then, may be encouraged to reflect on the mutual constitution of gender hierarchies and the war system, the former pair of productions positions audiences primarily in an affective and affirmative (dis)position towards the 'regiment of the wounded' or 'our boys', who will, essentially and inevitably, be boys.

5 Conclusion

The scenic space in British theatre productions that engage with the 'war on terror' is a site where subject positions are tenuously achieved, violently imposed, jointly occupied, refused, negated, appropriated, and challenged. Figures on stage position themselves and each other in constant relation to the discursive outside; figures off stage are withheld from view and audibility such that their absence enters into discursive circulation – as dialogic tool, spectral entity, silent prop, or discarded negative. The subject who (dis)appears in 'war on terror' drama is invariably a positioned one, situated in complex constellations of racial, gendered, sexual, religious, and class hierarchies and at the intersecting grids of the discursive field. And yet the dramatic cartographies of subject locations do not amount to a clear map.

The first insight that emerges from this analysis of British post-9/11 drama is that the home and the front of the 'war on terror' are, indeed, staged as the "co-constituted operative centres of a never-ending battle" (Hutnyk 159). Many of the plays explored in this study trace the trajectory of border-crossing subjectivities. The military, humanitarian, and economic interventions abroad serve as a constant frame of reference for the figuration of subject positions in home-front drama: from the hapless housing-estate inhabitant who is subjected to the exceptional logic of the "carnival of torture" (Puar 100), tried and tested in the prisons of Abu Ghraib, Guantánamo, and a number of undisclosed black sites, via the neoliberal citizens who situate their lifestyle and consumer choices against the mass-mediated images of ruin and destruction, to the traumatised veterans, carrying the visible wounds and haunting flashbacks of the war zone into the therapeutic (and theatrical) apparatus designed to reintegrate them. In turn, the citizen-soldiers, aid workers, and neoliberal war agents sent to bring 'freedom and democracy' to Iraq and Afghanistan not only impose a set of cultural conventions and products onto distant populations but are also variously confronted with an 'other' who is uncannily similar. A recurring motif in front-line plays is thus a moment of (mis)recognition, or a struggle over recognition, in which the ostensible 'other' reclaims a precarious life, the identity of the 'same', and/or fails to resist the optics of detection and hermeneutics of suspicion that lead to their being incarcerated or killed. In bringing the theatres of war into the playhouses of the UK, the front-line plays more often than not relocate the fissures implied by the 'clash of civilisations' thesis within the signifying space of the British nation.

If critical mimesis "makes and unmakes bodies and worlds" (Hughes, *Performance* 14), the plays discussed in this study variously (re-)enact the becoming and unbecoming of subjects. Because spectators are inevitably implicated as the ones who confer or deny subjectivity, the theatre is a particularly potent site to explore the modalities and boundaries of subject formation in the 'war on terror' context. What the analysis of the plays has continuously brought to the fore is the delimitation of permissible subjectivation conditioned by (counter-)terrorism discourses. Subjects who fail to police their statements or who become liable to suspicion purely because of their racial, ethnic, and classed positioning are confronted with the violent rejection of their attempts at becoming (a professional terrorist, a 'cool' black Muslim, an innocent traveller). Suspicious subjects perpetually fail to realise Foucauldian techniques of the self, such as the confessional speech or the playful fashioning of a hybrid, pop-culturally inspired cultural identity, against the 'founding interpellation' as terrorist. Seen against the practice of racial profiling or the campaigns that cue the extended police family to identify the 'next terrorist', theatre events situate audiences in an ambivalent relationship to established visual and interpretive schemes. On the one hand, spectators are asked to resist inculcated modes of reading the 'other' as a threat to the 'self'. On the other hand, the (suspected) terrorists that figure in drama also often elicit an uneasy response; their complacent and incoherent narratives speak to a destructive sense of rage. In any case, with its embrace of unreliability and ambiguity, post-9/11 drama persistently unlooses the point of suture that produces the Muslim-as-terrorist.

In terms of the argument developed here, one can detect in the frequently encountered invisibility paradigm an imperative to protect subjects who are exploited, paraded, or fetishised in the iconography of the 'war on terror'. Especially those subject forms that are already highly overdetermined are not easily brought to the stage without reproducing the surveying gaze trained to detect their deviance; apart from the Islamic terrorist, the veiled Muslim woman clearly comes into view here. The socially conditioned modes of looking at the 'other' objectify them according to the discursive dividing practices that situate Western citizens (or spectators) as liberal, rational, reasonable. In these cases, the marked absence, or unmarked presence, of subjects on stage can work to highlight the constructedness of the items that circulate in the war of images and expose the mechanisms whereby these are 'photoshopped', commodified, and instrumentalised.

When it comes to those faceless 'shadow lives' that cannot be apprehended within the hegemonic frames of war, however, the politics of invisibility may cede some of this progressive impetus. In light of scholars' repeated emphasis on war drama's capacity to reanimate wasted life, its function of "[i]nvoking the other, encouraging empathy for the one not quite like you" (Malpede xxvii), of having "bare life [...] piled up on stage" (Boll 61), there are remarkably few attempts in the corpus under consideration to render precarious subjects intelligible and recognisable. Although some productions give a voice and a body to those whose lives and losses otherwise remain undetailed, the events related to the 'war on terror' are almost invariably approached through 'our' perspective. While deliberately leaving a subject invisible has proved to be a fruitful dramaturgical manoeuvre to unsettle the visual and discursive regimes of suspectification and Orientalism, absenting the local inhabitants and victims of war (zones) abroad from British theatre stages does not seem to further debate or promote an ethical sensibility. The findings of this book thus encourage the adoption of a more sceptical stance towards post-9/11 drama's potential to reposition the 'other'.

Despite heeding the imperative to avoid appropriating 'their' voices and subjectivities, the persistent focalisation of the distant theatres of war through 'our' soldiers largely works to reproduce the spectatorial position of "first-world viewers who seek to understand 'what happened over there'" (Butler, *Frames* 78). Given the intense privatisation of war and blurring of front lines, the frequent decision by playwrights to represent the Iraq and Afghan campaigns through the eyes of British troops appears almost stubbornly conventional. While there is something highly suggestive about the staging of uniformed 'boots on the ground' against a spectral enemy entity that fails to materialise, the plethora of representations of soldiers also raises concerns about the slippery divide between "supporting the troops" and "supporting the policy" (J. Kelly 732). With few exceptions, audiences are placed into an affirmative relationship towards 'our boys' (and sometimes 'girls'). Especially since the lower-class position of the soldiers is frequently implied or explicitly activated, many plays approach the interventions through the lens of a subject that lacks access to power/knowledge. The British squaddie becomes the most likely representative of a confused public in the war zone: bound to the formless 'war on terror' campaigns in ways they cannot fully penetrate or prefer not to scrutinise, they are desperately holding on to the civilisational values that define 'us' and the established enemy profile that helps identify 'them' but gradually see these certainties disintegrate.

With respect to the subject positions made available to the audience, those plays that are critically mimetic of efforts at dissociation appear to be the most challenging. These productions variously refract and reject the positioning encapsulated by the "Not in My Name" protest slogan. In this regard, it seems that the verbatim plays are especially cautious, at times allocating blame to the pitiful politicians who make momentous wrong decisions, at other times assuring citizens of the functioning of a liberal democratic order into which those who veer from the path of 'freedom and democracy' or are falsely imprisoned in legal 'black holes' (and thus placed beyond the reach of these values) can be smoothly reintegrated. In contrast, some of the fictional plays convey a profound sense of a globalised state of emergency, or "crisis ordinariness" (Berlant 8), which calls neoliberal culture as well as the system of political representation more severely into question. A number of plays crucially problematise the notion that UK citizens could disavow their own complicity in the war system simply by disengaging from their "so-called democratically elected so-called representatives" (Ravenhill 191). If their interpellative invitation is realised in the performance encounter, these plays potentially implicate – or even inculpate – audiences in a critique that excavates the formation of a neoliberal consensus which ties citizenship to the market and to militarism. The shared speaking position from which to denounce acts of (state) terror had, as is suggested, already been fractured before the Iraq invasion was launched, rendering the act of collective enunciation suspect.

On the whole, the relationship between the subject positions articulated in drama and the system of dispersion that characterises the discursive formation of the 'war on terror' is highly politicised and complex. In part, the order, correlations, positions, and divisions that Foucault identifies as constitutive of discourse are dramatically negotiated in ways that sustain the discursive regime. Especially where the gendered/sexual structuring of the war story is concerned, few plays radically reconfigure the heteronormative culture and power relations of militarism and war. Throughout the playtexts, the appeal of heterosexual narratives surrounding men's departure for war and women's holding down the home front is starkly apparent, even if it provides a set of subject positions that the plays subtly undermine. If they do so, there is rarely an alternative gendered storyline that is spun around the question of why and how 'we' go to war. The somewhat archaic associations between fighting men and weeping women are only slowly beginning to be eroded.

There is, in contrast, a marked destabilisation of the corresponding positions that are specific to the current 'war on terror' context. Not only do virtually all the plays divest the antagonistic opposition between the terrorist and the patriot of validity, but they also resolutely disrupt the dividing practices of the liberating and civilising missions. The front-line plays detach, or even invert, the correlative positions of the white rescuer and the 'brown woman' in need of saving, of the neoliberal war agents and the economically or culturally 'starved' population in need of some superior, prepacked, mass-produced culture or therapeutic shock treatment. The home-front plays rescript the differential logic that demarcates 'freedom and democracy' from the constitutive outside represented by fundamentalism and dictatorship in terms of a logic of equivalence, showing that 'our' liberal and democratic values are entirely encoded in – or even commensurate with – the terms of the free market.

5 Conclusion

As this book has demonstrated, the discursive formation of the 'war on terror' provides a rich context of subject construction in contemporary British drama. The ways in which subjects are (dis)appearing, (un)becoming, and (dis)positioning themselves and each other in the scenic space consistently interact and intercede with the subject codes, norms, and schemes of intelligibility operative in the system of dispersion. From the Afghan tribal chief claiming that he is blissfully 'enduring freedom', via the young British Muslims seeking to sever their ties to the travelling terrorist assemblage, to the disenchanted soldier's sweetheart caught between a dissenting and a supportive femininity – these are subjects to whom the wars invariably matter and subjects who come to matter through their positions in the field of war. In spite of the doubtlessly accurate characterisation of the corpus of post-9/11 drama as issue-based, or fact-based, the findings of this book suggest that these plays navigate the complexities of the discourse – rather than the empirical or consensual reality – of the 'war on terror'. The type of theatre analysed here is not counter-discursive, but it negotiates, inflects, and participates in the discursive circulation of stories, idioms, controversies, testimonies, and pieces of (mis)information in the face of global insecurities. Between the beginnings of the Iraq war in 2003 and troop withdrawal from Afghanistan in 2014, British drama has made a vital contribution to attempts at building and rebuilding the archive of the 'war on terror' and the viable forms of subjectivity lodged in and dislodged by it.

Works Cited

Primary Literature

Adam, Henry. *The People Next Door*. Nick Hern Books, 2003.
Bano, Alia. *Shades*. Methuen Drama, 2009.
Bean, Richard. *On the Side of the Angels*. *The Great Game: Afghanistan*, Oberon Books, 2009, pp. 213–227.
Brace, Adam. *Stovepipe*. Faber and Faber, 2009.
Brittain, Victoria, and Gillian Slovo. *Guantanamo: 'Honor Bound to Defend Freedom'*. Oberon Books, 2004.
Burke, Gregory. *Black Watch*. Faber and Faber, 2010.
Crouch, Tim. *The Author*. Oberon Books, 2009.
Edgar, David. *Testing the Echo*. Nick Hern Books, 2008.
Gilroy, Steve. *Motherland*. Oberon Books, 2009.
Goode, Chris. *Men in the Cities*. Oberon Books, 2014.
Hare, David. *Stuff Happens*. Faber and Faber, 2006.
Holmes, Jonathan. *Fallujah: Eyewitness Testimony from Iraq's Besieged City*. Constable and Robinson, 2007.
Jones, Cat. *Glory Dazed*. Nick Hern Books, 2013.
Kelly, Dennis. *Osama the Hero*. *Plays One*, Oberon Books, 2008, pp. 47–120.
Malcolm, Morgan Lloyd. *Belongings*. Oberon Books, 2011.
Moore, DC. *The Empire*. Methuen Drama, 2010.
Morgan, Abi. *The Night Is Darkest Before the Dawn*. *The Great Game: Afghanistan*, Oberon Books, 2009, pp. 191–212.
O'Brien, Tim. "The Things They Carried." *The Things They Carried*, Mariner Books, 2009, pp. 1–25.
Patel, Vinay. *True Brits*. Bloomsbury Methuen Drama, 2014.
Ravenhill, Mark. *Shoot/Get Treasure/Repeat: An Epic Cycle of Short Plays*. Methuen Drama, 2009.
Sen Gupta, Atiha. *What Fatima Did...* Oberon Books, 2009.
Shakespeare, William. *As You Like It*. Edited by Michael Hattaway, Cambridge UP, 2000.
Sheers, Owen. *The Two Worlds of Charlie F*. Faber and Faber, 2012.
Soans, Robin. *Talking to Terrorists*. Oberon Books, 2005.
Stephens, Simon. *Motortown*. *Royal Court Plays 2000–2010*, edited by Ruth Little, Methuen, 2010, pp. 207–280.
Stephens, Simon. *Plays: 2*. Methuen Drama, 2009.
Stephens, Simon. *Pornography*. Methuen Drama, 2014.
Teevan, Colin. *How Many Miles to Basra?* Oberon Books, 2006.
Williams, Roy. *Days of Significance*. Methuen Drama, 2009.

Secondary Literature

Abu-Lughod, Lila. "Do Muslim Women Really Need Saving? Anthropological Reflections on Cultural Relativism and Its Others." *American Anthropologist*, vol. 104, no. 3, 2002, pp. 783–790.
Acton, Carol. *Grief in Wartime: Private Pain, Public Discourse*. Palgrave Macmillan, 2007.
Agamben, Giorgio. *Homo Sacer: Sovereign Power and Bare Life*. Translated by Daniel Heller-Roazen, Stanford UP, 1998.
Agamben, Giorgio. *State of Exception*. Translated by Kevin Attell, U of Chicago P, 2005.
Ahmed, Rehana. "British Muslim Masculinities and Cultural Resistance: Kenny Glenaan and Simon Beaufoy's *Yasmin*." *Journal of Postcolonial Writing*, vol. 45, no. 3, 2009, pp. 285–296.
Ahmed, Sara. *The Cultural Politics of Emotion*. Edinburgh UP, 2004.
Ahmed, Sara. *The Promise of Happiness*. Duke UP, 2010.
Akhtar, Parveen. "'(Re)Turn to Religion' and Radical Islam." *Muslim Britain: Communities under Pressure*, edited by Tahir Abbas, Zed Books, 2005, pp. 164–176.
Alcoff, Linda Martín. "Cultural Feminism versus Post-Structuralism: The Identity Crisis in Feminist Theory." *Signs*, vol. 13, no. 3, 1988, pp. 405–436.
Alcoff, Linda Martín. "The Problem of Speaking for Others." *Cultural Critique*, no. 20, 1991–1992, pp. 5–32.
Alexander, M. Jacqui. *Pedagogies of Crossing: Meditations on Feminism, Sexual Politics, Memory, and the Sacred*. Duke UP, 2005.
Ali, Tariq. *Bush in Babylon: The Recolonisation of Iraq*. Verso, 2003.
Althusser, Louis. "Ideology and Ideological State Apparatuses (Notes towards an Investigation)." *Lenin and Philosophy and Other Essays*, translated by Ben Brewster, Monthly Review Press, 2001, pp. 85–126.
Anderson, Benedict. *Imagined Communities: Reflections on the Origin and Spread of Nationalism*. Verso, 1991.
Angermüller, Johannes. "From the Many Voices to the Subject Positions in Anti-Globalization Discourse: Enunciative Pragmatics and the Polyphonic Organization of Subjectivity." *Journal of Pragmatics*, vol. 43, no. 12, 2011, pp. 2992–3000.
Anthias, Floya. "Where Do I Belong? Narrating Collective Identity and Translocational Positionality." *Ethnicities*, vol. 2, no. 4, 2002, pp. 491–514.
Archibald, David. "'We're Just Big Bullies ...': Gregory Burke's *Black Watch*." *The Drouth*, no. 26, 2008, pp. 8–13.
Asad, Talal. *On Suicide Bombing*. Columbia UP, 2007.
Auslander, Philip. *Presence and Resistance: Postmodernism and Cultural Politics in Contemporary American Performance*. U of Michigan P, 1994.
Back, Les. *The Art of Listening*. Berg, 2007.
Bahramitash, Roksana. "The War on Terror, Feminist Orientalism and Orientalist Feminism: Case Studies of Two North American Bestsellers." *Critique: Critical Middle Eastern Studies*, vol. 14, no. 2, 2005, pp. 221–235.
Basham, Victoria Marie. "Harnessing Social Diversity in the British Armed Forces: The Limitations of 'Management' Approaches." *Commonwealth and Comparative Politics*, vol. 47, no. 4, 2009, pp. 411–429.
Baudrillard, Jean. *The Spirit of Terrorism and Requiem for the Twin Towers*. Translated by Chris Turner, Verso, 2002.

Bauman, Zygmunt. *Liquid Times: Living in an Age of Uncertainty*. Polity Press, 2007.
BBC News. "London Bomber: Text in Full." 1 Sept. 2005, http://news.bbc.co.uk/2/hi/uk/4206800.stm.
BBC News. "Police Begin Counter-Terror Publicity Campaign." 13 Dec. 2010, www.bbc.com/news/uk-11978812/.
Bean, Hamilton, et al. "'This Is London': Cosmopolitan Nationalism and the Discourse of Resilience in the Case of the 7/7 Terrorist Attacks." *Rhetoric and Public Affairs*, vol. 14, no. 3, 2011, pp. 427–464.
Behdad, Ali. *Belated Travelers: Orientalism in the Age of Colonial Dissolution*. Duke UP, 1994.
Bell, John. "Performance Studies in an Age of Terror." *The Drama Review*, vol. 47, no. 2, 2003, pp. 6–8.
Bennett, Catherine. "Women Lose When the West Weighs In." *Guardian Weekly*, 8 Apr. 2011, p. 20.
Berg, Sebastian. "Multiculturalism and Racism in Blair's Britain." *Britain under Blair*, edited by Merle Tönnies, Universitätsverlag Winter, 2003, pp. 33–48.
Berlant, Lauren. *Cruel Optimism*. Duke UP, 2011.
Berlant, Lauren, and Michael Warner. "Sex in Public." *The Routledge Queer Studies Reader*, edited by Donald E. Hall and Annamarie Jagose, Routledge, 2013, pp. 165–179.
Berton, Danièle. "Norme et marginalité: De la bonne ou de la mauvaise réputation dans *The People Next Door* de Henry Adam." *Études écossaises*, no. 10, 2005, pp. 159–173.
Bhabha, Homi K. *The Location of Culture*. Routledge, 1994.
Bharucha, Rustom. *Terror and Performance*. Routledge, 2014.
Bhattacharyya, Gargi. *Dangerous Brown Men: Exploiting Sex, Violence and Feminism in the War on Terror*. Zed Books, 2008.
Biesecker, Barbara. "No Time for Mourning: The Rhetorical Production of the Melancholic Citizen-Subject in the War on Terror." *Philosophy and Rhetoric*, vol. 40, no. 1, 2007, pp. 147–169.
Billington, Michael. "Multifaceted Women Grapple with One-Dimensional Men." Review of *Belongings*, *Guardian*, 23 June 2011, p. 40.
Billington, Michael. *State of the Nation: British Theatre since 1945*. Faber and Faber, 2007.
Blair, Tony. "'Britain Has Never Been a Nation to Hide at the Back'." *Guardian*, 21 Mar. 2003, www.theguardian.com/politics/2003/mar/21/uk.iraq/.
Blair, Tony. "Full Text: Blair Speech on Terror." *BBC News*, 16 July 2005, http://news.bbc.co.uk/2/hi/uk_news/4689363.stm.
Blair, Tony. "Iraq Debate Speech to the House of Commons." *Tony Blair in His Own Words*, edited by Paul Richards, Politico's Publishing, 2004, pp. 231–246.
Blair, Tony. "Labour Conference: Full Text; Tony Blair's Speech." *Guardian*, 2 Oct. 2001, www.theguardian.com/politics/2001/oct/02/labourconference.labour6/.
Blair, Tony. "Speech to the US Congress." *Tony Blair in His Own Words*, edited by Paul Richards, Politico's Publishing, 2004, pp. 247–257.
Blair, Tony. "Statement on Military Action in Afghanistan." *Tony Blair in His Own Words*, edited by Paul Richards, Politico's Publishing, 2004, pp. 216–220.
Bleeker, Maaike, and Isis Germano. "Perceiving and Believing: An Enactive Approach to Spectatorship." *Theatre Journal*, vol. 66, no. 3, 2014, pp. 363–383.
Blumberg, Marcia. "Unraveling the 'Golden Thread': Performing the Politics of *Black Watch*." *Political and Protest Theater after 9/11: Patriotic Dissent*, edited by Jenny Spencer, Routledge, 2012, pp. 79–92.

Boll, Julia. *The New War Plays: From Kane to Harris*. Palgrave Macmillan, 2013.

Bolton, Jacqueline. Commentary. *Pornography*, by Simon Stephens, Bloomsbury Methuen Drama, 2014, pp. xxi–lxxi.

Bond, Paul. "*Fallujah*: Sympathy Alone Is Not Enough." *World Socialist Website*, 1 June 2007, http://www.wsws.org/en/articles/2007/06/fall-j01.html.

Borradori, Giovanna. "Autoimmunity: Real and Symbolic Suicides; A Dialogue with Jacques Derrida." *Philosophy in a Time of Terror: Dialogues with Jürgen Habermas and Jacques Derrida*, edited by Giovanna Borradori, translated by Pascale-Anne Brault and Michael Naas, U of Chicago P, 2003, pp. 85–136.

Bottoms, Stephen. "Putting the Document into Documentary: An Unwelcome Corrective?" *The Drama Review*, vol. 50, no. 3, 2006, pp. 56–68.

Boucher, Geoff. "The Politics of Performativity: A Critique of Judith Butler." *Parrhesia*, no. 1, 2006, pp. 112–141.

Brady, Sara. *Performance, Politics, and the War on Terror: 'Whatever It Takes'*. Palgrave Macmillan, 2012.

Braidotti, Rosi. "Identity, Subjectivity and Difference." *Thinking Differently: A Reader in European Women's Studies*, edited by Rosi Braidotti and Gabriele Griffin, Zed Books, 2002, pp. 158–180.

Braidotti, Rosi. *Transpositions: On Nomadic Ethics*. Polity Press, 2006.

Brittain, Melisa. "Benevolent Invaders, Heroic Victims and Depraved Villains: White Femininity in Media Coverage of the Invasion of Iraq." *(En)Gendering the War on Terror: War Stories and Camouflaged Politics*, edited by Krista Hunt and Kim Rygiel, Ashgate, 2006, pp. 73–96.

Brown, Mark, and Maev Kennedy. "New Director to Satirise Audience." *Guardian*, 7 Feb. 2007, p. 9.

Brubaker, Rogers, and Frederick Cooper. "Beyond 'Identity'." *Theory and Society*, vol. 29, no. 1, 2000, pp. 1–47.

Brummett, Barry, and Detine L. Bowers. "Subject Positions as a Site of Rhetorical Struggle: Representing African Americans." *At the Intersection: Cultural Studies and Rhetorical Studies*, edited by Thomas Rosteck, Guilford Press, 1999, pp. 117–136.

Bulley, Dan. "'Foreign' Terror? London Bombings, Resistance and the Failing State." *British Journal of Politics and International Relations*, vol. 10, no. 3, 2008, pp. 379–394.

Burke, Jason. *The 9/11 Wars*. Penguin Books, 2011.

Burnett, Jonathan. "Community, Cohesion and the State." *Race and Class*, vol. 45, no. 3, 2004, pp. 1–18.

Burnett, Jonny, and Dave Whyte. "Embedded Expertise and the New Terrorism." *Journal for Crime, Conflict and the Media*, vol. 1, no. 4, 2005, pp. 1–18.

Buse, Peter. *Drama + Theory: Critical Approaches to Modern British Drama*. Manchester UP, 2001.

Butler, Judith. *Bodies That Matter: On the Discursive Limits of 'Sex'*. Routledge, 1993.

Butler, Judith. *Frames of War: When Is Life Grievable?* Verso, 2009.

Butler, Judith. *Gender Trouble: Feminism and the Subversion of Identity*. Routledge, 2006.

Butler, Judith. *Precarious Life: The Power of Mourning and Violence*. Verso, 2004.

Butler, Judith. *The Psychic Life of Power: Theories in Subjection*. Stanford UP, 1997.

Canton, Ursula. "*Guantanamo*: Documenting a Real Space?" *Mapping Uncertain Territories: Space and Place in Contemporary Theatre and Drama*, edited by Thomas Rommel and Mark Schreiber, Wissenschaftlicher Verlag Trier, 2006, pp. 87–100.

Carpenter, Rebecca. "'We're Not a Friggin' Girl Band': September 11, Masculinity, and the British-American Relationship in David Hare's *Stuff Happens* and Ian McEwan's *Saturday*." *Literature after 9/11*, edited by Ann Keniston and Jeanne Follansbee Quinn, Routledge, 2008, pp. 143–160.

Carrigan, Tim, et al. "Toward a New Sociology of Masculinity." *Theory and Society*, vol. 14, no. 5, 1985, pp. 551–604.

Carroll, Rory. "Cola Wars as Coke Moves on Baghdad." *Guardian*, 5 July 2005, p. 14.

Caruth, Cathy. "Recapturing the Past: Introduction." *Trauma: Explorations in Memory*, edited by Cathy Caruth, Johns Hopkins UP, 1995, pp. 151–157.

Caruth, Cathy. *Unclaimed Experience: Trauma, Narrative, and History*. Johns Hopkins UP, 1996.

Causey, Matthew, and Fintan Walsh. "Introduction: Performance, Identity, and the Neo-Political Subject." *Performance, Identity, and the Neo-Political Subject*, edited by Matthew Causey and Fintan Walsh, Routledge, 2013, pp. 1–17.

Cavendish, Dominic. "A Nation's Soul." Review of *Days of Significance*, *Telegraph*, 20 Mar. 2008, http://www.telegraph.co.uk/culture/theatre/drama/3671963/Days-of-Significance-A-nations-soul.html.

Chadderton, David. "*Motherland*." *British Theatre Guide*, 2009, www.britishtheatreguide.info/reviews/motherlandDC-rev/.

Chalabi, Munir. "Political Observations on Sectarianism in Iraq." *ZNet*, 24 Jan. 2007, zcomm.org/znetarticle/political-observations-on-sectarianism-in-iraq-by-munir-chalabi/.

Chamberlin, Sheena M. Eagan. "Emasculated by Trauma: A Social History of Post-Traumatic Stress Disorder, Stigma, and Masculinity." *The Journal of American Culture*, vol. 35, no. 4, 2012, pp. 358–365.

Chang, Robert S. "The End of Innocence or Politics after the Fall of the Essential Subject." *The American University Law Review*, vol. 45, no. 3, 1996, pp. 687–694.

Chaudhuri, Una. *Staging Place: The Geography of Modern Drama*. U of Michigan P, 1997.

Cixous, Hélène. "The Towers: Les tours." *Signs*, vol. 28, no. 1, 2002, pp. 431–433.

Clark, Timothy. "Derangements of Scale." *Telemorphosis: Theory in the Era of Climate Change*, vol. 1, edited by Tom Cohen, 2012, dx.doi.org/10.3998/ohp.10539563.0001.001.

Cockburn, Patrick. "A Distorted View of War." *Independent*, 23 Nov. 2010, Viewspaper, pp. 12–13.

Cohler, Deborah. "Keeping the Home Front Burning: Renegotiating Gender and Sexuality in US Mass Media after September 11." *Feminist Media Studies*, vol. 6, no. 3, 2006, pp. 245–261.

Colleran, Jeanne. *Theatre and War: Theatrical Responses since 1991*. Palgrave Macmillan, 2012.

Connell, R.W., and James W. Messerschmidt. "Hegemonic Masculinity: Rethinking the Concept." *Gender & Society*, vol. 19, no. 6, 2005, pp. 829–859.

Contractor, Sariya. *Muslim Women in Britain: De-mystifying the Muslimah*. Routledge, 2012.

Cooke, Miriam. "Saving Brown Women." *Signs*, vol. 28, no. 1, 2002, pp. 468–470.

Crenshaw, Kimberlé. "Demarginalizing the Intersection of Race and Sex: A Black Feminist Critique of Antidiscrimination Doctrine, Feminist Theory and Antiracist Politics." *Feminist Legal Theory: Foundations*, edited by D. Kelly Weisberg, Temple UP, 1993, pp. 383–398.

Croggon, Alison. "Review: Osama the Hero / Ying Tong / Circus Oz." *Theatre Notes*, 25 June 2007, http://theatrenotes.blogspot.co.at/2007/06/review-osama-heroying-tongcircus-oz.html.

Cull, Nicholas J. *Gregory Burke's* Black Watch: *Theatre as Cultural Diplomacy*. USC Center on Public Diplomacy, 2007.
Cull, Nicholas J. "Staging the Catastrophe: The Tricycle Theatre's *The Great Game: Afghanistan* and Its Diplomatic Journey from London to the Pentagon, 2010–11." *Theatre Topics*, vol. 21, no. 2, 2011, pp. 125–137.
Dahl, Mary Karen. "State Terror and Dramatic Countermeasures." *Terrorism and Modern Drama*, edited by John Orr and Dragan Klaić, Edinburgh UP, 1990, pp. 109–122.
Dalby, Simon. "The Pentagon's New Imperial Cartography." *Violent Geographies: Fear, Terror, and Political Violence*, edited by Derek Gregory and Allan Pred, Routledge, 2007, pp. 295–308.
Davies, Bronwyn, and Rom Harré. "Positioning: The Discursive Production of Selves." *Journal for the Theory of Social Behaviour*, vol. 20, no. 1, 1990, pp. 43–63.
Davis, Walter A. *Art and Politics: Psychoanalysis, Ideology, Theatre*. Pluto Press, 2007.
Dawson, Graham. *Soldier Heroes: British Adventure, Empire and the Imagining of Masculinities*. Routledge, 1994.
Deleuze, Gilles, and Félix Guattari. *A Thousand Plateaus: Capitalism and Schizophrenia*. Translated by Brian Massumi, Athlone Press, 1988.
Delgado, Maria M., and Caridad Svich. "Theatre in Crisis? Performance Manifestos for a New Century: Snapshots of a Time." *Theatre in Crisis? Performance Manifestos for a New Century*, edited by Maria M. Delgado and Caridad Svich, Manchester UP, 2002, pp. 1–14.
Delgado-García, Cristina. *Rethinking Character in Contemporary British Theatre: Aesthetics, Politics, Subjectivity*. De Gruyter, 2015.
Der Derian, James. "War as Game." *The Brown Journal of World Affairs*, vol. 10, no. 1, 2003, pp. 37–48.
de Waal, Ariane. "'Do Not Run on the Platforms … If You Look a Bit Foreign': De/Constructing the Travelling Terrorist Assemblage." *Liminalities: A Journal of Performance Studies*, vol. 12, no. 5, 2016, pp. 1–17.
de Waal, Ariane. "Staging Wounded Soldiers: The Affects and Effects of Post-Traumatic Theatre." *Performance Paradigm*, no. 11, 2015, pp. 16–31.
Dewhurst, Madeline. "'Theatre and the Impossible'. An Interview with Colin Teevan." *Contemporary Theatre Review*, vol. 15, no. 2, 2005, pp. 246–251.
Diamond, Elin. "The Violence of 'We': Politicizing Identification." *Critical Theory and Performance*, edited by Janelle G. Reinelt and Joseph R. Roach, U of Michigan P, 2007, pp. 403–412.
Diken, Bülent, and Carsten Bagge Laustsen. "Zones of Indistinction: Security, Terror, and Bare Life." *Space & Culture*, vol. 5, no. 3, 2002, pp. 290–307.
Drake, Michael S. "Commemorating Fatalities of War and National Identity in the Twenty-First Century." *Corporeality: The Body and Society*, edited by Cassandra A. Ogden and Stephen Wakeman, U of Chester P, 2013, pp. 121–132.
Edgar, David. "Too True? The Achievements and Limitations of Fact-Based Theatre." *Anglistentag 2007 Münster: Proceedings of the Conference of the German Association of University Teachers of English*, edited by Klaus Stierstorfer, Wissenschaftlicher Verlag Trier, 2008, pp. 103–114.
Edley, Nigel. "Analysing Masculinity: Interpretative Repertoires, Ideological Dilemmas and Subject Positions." *Discourse as Data: A Guide for Analysis*, edited by Margaret Wetherell et al., Sage Publications, 2001, pp. 189–228.

Edley, Nigel, and Margaret Wetherell. *Men in Perspective: Practice, Power and Identity.* Prentice Hall / Harvester Wheatsheaf, 1995.

Edwards, Aaron. *The Northern Ireland Troubles: Operation* Banner *1969–2007.* Osprey Publishing, 2011.

Eisenstein, Zillah. *Global Obscenities: Patriarchy, Capitalism, and the Lure of Cyberfantasy.* New York UP, 1998.

Elliott, Anthony. *Subject to Ourselves: Social Theory, Psychoanalysis and Postmodernity.* Paradigm Publishers, 2004.

Elshtain, Jean Bethke. *Women and War.* U of Chicago P, 1995.

Elworthy, Scilla. "Background: The Situation in Fallujah." *Fallujah: Eyewitness Testimony from Iraq's Besieged City*, edited by Jonathan Holmes, Constable and Robinson, 2007, pp. 1–25.

Enloe, Cynthia. *Does Khaki Become You? The Militarization of Women's Lives.* Pandora Press, 1988.

Enloe, Cynthia. Foreword. *(En)Gendering the War on Terror: War Stories and Camouflaged Politics*, edited by Krista Hunt and Kim Rygiel, Ashgate, 2006, pp. vii–ix.

Fahmy, Shahira, and Daekyung Kim. "Picturing the Iraq War: Constructing the Image of War in the British and US Press." *International Communication Gazette*, vol. 70, no. 6, 2008, pp. 443–462.

Fanon, Frantz. "Algeria Unveiled." *The New Left Reader*, edited by Carl Oglesby, Grove Press, 1969, pp. 161–185.

Farrell, Kirby. *Post-Traumatic Culture: Injury and Interpretation in the Nineties.* Johns Hopkins UP, 1998.

Featherstone, Mark, et al. "Discourses of the War on Terror: Constructions of the Islamic Other after 7/7." *International Journal of Media and Cultural Politics*, vol. 6, no. 2, 2010, pp. 169–186.

Feitz, Lindsey, and Joane Nagel. "The Militarization of Gender and Sexuality in the Iraq War." *Women in the Military and in Armed Conflict*, edited by Helena Carreiras and Gerhard Kümmel, Verlag für Sozialwissenschaften, 2008, pp. 201–225.

Fekete, Liz. "Anti-Muslim Racism and the European Security State." *Race and Class*, vol. 46, no. 1, 2004, pp. 3–29.

Feldman, Allen. "On the Actuarial Gaze: From 9/11 to Abu Ghraib." *Cultural Studies*, vol. 19, no. 2, 2005, pp. 203–226.

Feldman, Allen. "The Structuring Enemy and Archival War." *PMLA*, vol. 124, no. 5, pp. 1704–1713.

Fernandez, Sonya. "The Crusade over the Bodies of Women." *Patterns of Prejudice*, vol. 43, no. 3–4, 2009, pp. 269–286.

Finburgh, Clare. "Watching War: Spectacles of Conflict on the Twenty-First Century Stage; The Fear and Function of Terrorism." Performance Research Seminar, Goldsmiths, University of London, 12 November 2014.

Fischer-Lichte, Erika. *History of European Drama and Theatre.* Translated by Jo Riley, Routledge, 2002.

Fischer-Lichte, Erika. *The Transformative Power of Performance: A New Aesthetics.* Translated by Saskya Iris Jain, Routledge, 2008.

Fisher, Amanda Stuart. "Trauma, Authenticity and the Limits of Verbatim." *Performance Research*, vol. 16, no. 1, 2011, pp. 112–122.

Fisher, Mark. *Capitalist Realism: Is There No Alternative?* O Books, 2009.

Fisher, Philip. "*Fallujah.*" *British Theatre Guide*, 2007, www.britishtheatreguide.info/reviews/fallujah-rev/.
Fisher, Philip. "*Stovepipe.*" *British Theatre Guide*, 2009, www.britishtheatreguide.info/reviews/stovepipe-rev/.
Fletcher, Jackie. "*The People Next Door.*" *British Theatre Guide*, 2003, www.britishtheatreguide.info/reviews/peoplenextdoor-rev/.
Forster, Anthony. "Breaking the Covenant: Governance of the British Army in the Twenty-First Century." *International Affairs*, vol. 82, no. 6, 2006, pp. 1043–1057.
Foucault, Michel. "About the Beginning of the Hermeneutics of the Self: Two Lectures at Dartmouth." Transcribed and edited by Mark Blasius and Thomas Keenan, *Political Theory*, vol. 2, no. 2, 1993, pp. 198–227.
Foucault, Michel. "About the Concept of the 'Dangerous Individual' in 19th Century Legal Psychiatry." Translated by Alain Baudot and Jane Couchman, *International Journal of Law and Psychiatry*, vol. 1, no. 1, 1978, pp. 1–18.
Foucault, Michel. *Archaeology of Knowledge*. Translated by A.M. Sheridan Smith, Routledge, 2002.
Foucault, Michel. *Discipline and Punish: The Birth of the Prison*. Translated by Alan Sheridan, Vintage Books, 1979.
Foucault, Michel. "The Ethics of the Concern of the Self as a Practice of Freedom." *Ethics: Subjectivity and Truth*, edited by Paul Rabinow, The New Press, 1997, pp. 281–301.
Foucault, Michel. *The History of Sexuality*. Vol. 1, *An Introduction*. Translated by Robert Hurley, Pantheon Books, 1978.
Foucault, Michel. *The History of Sexuality*. Vol. 2, *The Use of Pleasure*. Vintage Books, 1990.
Foucault, Michel. "The Order of Discourse: Inaugural Lecture at the Collège the France, Given 2 December 1970." Translated by Ian McLeod. *Untying the Text: A Post-Structuralist Reader*, edited by Robert Young, Routledge and Kegan Paul, 1981, pp. 51–78.
Foucault, Michel. *The Order of Things: An Archaeology of the Human Sciences*. Tavistock Publications, 1970.
Foucault, Michel. *'Society Must Be Defended': Lectures at the Collège de France 1975–76*. Edited by Mauro Bertani and Alessandro Fontana, translated by David Macey, Penguin Books, 2003.
Foucault, Michel. "The Subject and Power." *Critical Inquiry*, vol. 8, no. 4, 1982, pp. 777–795.
Foucault, Michel. "Truth and Power: Interview with Alessandro Fontana and Pasquale Pasquino." *Power/Knowledge: Selected Interviews and Writings 1972–1977*, edited by Colin Gordon, translated by Colin Gordon et al., Pantheon Books, 1980, pp. 109–133.
Foucault, Michel. "What Is an Author?" *Aesthetics, Method, and Epistemology*, edited by James D. Faubion, The New Press, 1998, pp. 205–222.
Foucault, Michel. "The Will to Knowledge." *Ethics: Subjectivity and Truth*, edited by Paul Rabinow, The New Press, 1997, pp. 11–16.
Fragkou, Marissia, and Philip Hager. "Staging London: Participation and Citizenship on the Way to the 2012 Olympic Games." *Contemporary Theatre Review*, vol. 23, no. 4, 2013, pp. 532–541.
Franks, Mary Anne. "Obscene Undersides: Women and Evil between the Taliban and the United States." *Hypatia*, vol. 18, no. 1, 2003, pp. 135–156.
Fuchs, Elinor. *The Death of Character: Perspectives on Theater after Modernism*. Indiana UP, 1996.

Galli, Carlo. "On War and on the Enemy." Translated by Amanda Minervini and Adam Sitze, *The New Centennial Review*, vol. 9, no. 2, 2009, pp. 195–220.
Gardner, Lyn. "*The People Next Door.*" *Guardian*, 1 Aug. 2003, p. 28.
Gardner, Lyn. "A Powerful Vision of Despair." Review of *Men in the Cities*, *Guardian*, 2 Aug. 2014, p. 5.
Garner, Steve. *Racisms: An Introduction*. Sage Publications, 2010.
Geaves, Ron. "Negotiating British Citizenship and Muslim Identity." *Muslim Britain: Communities under Pressure*, edited by Tahir Abbas, Zed Books, 2005, pp. 66–77.
Gilbert, Helen, and Jacqueline Lo. *Performance and Cosmopolitics: Crosscultural Transactions in Australasia*. Palgrave Macmillan, 2007.
Gilliat-Ray, Sophie. *Muslims in Britain: An Introduction*. Cambridge UP, 2010.
Gilmore, Leigh. "Limit-Cases: Trauma, Self-Representation, and the Jurisdictions of Identity." *Biography*, vol. 24, no. 1, 2001, pp. 128–139.
Gilroy, Paul. "Multiculture, Double Consciousness and the 'War on Terror'." *Patterns of Prejudice*, vol. 39, no. 4, 2005, pp. 431–443.
Gilroy, Paul. "'Where Ignorant Armies Clash by Night': Homogeneous Community and the Planetary Aspect." *International Journal of Cultural Studies*, vol. 6, no. 3, 2003, pp. 261–276.
Gittings, Christopher E. Introduction. *Imperialism and Gender: Constructions of Masculinity*, edited by Christopher E. Gittings, Dangaroo Press, 1996, pp. 1–8.
Goldstein, Joshua S. *War and Gender: How Gender Shapes the War System and Vice Versa*. Cambridge UP, 2001.
Gottschalk, Peter, and Gabriel Greenberg. *Islamophobia: Making Muslims the Enemy*. Rowman and Littlefield Publishers, 2008.
Graham, Stephen. "Cities and the 'War on Terror'." *International Journal of Urban and Regional Research*, vol. 30, no. 2, 2006, pp. 255–276.
Graham, Stephen. "Demodernizing by Design: Everyday Infrastructure and Political Violence." *Violent Geographies: Fear, Terror, and Political Violence*, edited by Derek Gregory and Allan Pred, Routledge, 2007, pp. 309–328.
Gray, Mitchell, and Elvin Wyly. "The Terror City Hypothesis." *Violent Geographies: Fear, Terror, and Political Violence*, edited by Derek Gregory and Allan Pred, Routledge, 2007, pp. 329–348.
Gregory, Derek. "Defiled Cities." *Singapore Journal of Tropical Geography*, vol. 24, no. 3, 2003, pp. 307–326.
Gregory, Derek. "Vanishing Points: Law, Violence, and Exception in the Global War Prison." *Violent Geographies: Fear, Terror, and Political Violence*, edited by Derek Gregory and Allan Pred, Routledge, 2007, pp. 205–236.
Gregory, Derek. "Who's Responsible?" *ZNet*, 3 May 2004, zcomm.org/znetarticle/whos-responsible-by-derek-gregory/.
Gregory, Derek, and Allan Pred, editors. *Violent Geographies: Fear, Terror, and Political Violence*. Routledge, 2007.
Grice, Elizabeth. "'In My Darkest Hours, I Question the Wisdom of What We Did. Afghanistan Was Our Vietnam'." *Telegraph*, 5 Apr. 2014, p. 23.
Grice, Elizabeth. "'We Were Inseparable – Best Friends'." *Telegraph*, 19 Nov. 2009, p. 31.
Gupta, Suman. *Imagining Iraq: Literature in English and the Iraq Invasion*. Palgrave Macmillan, 2011.

Haaken, Janice. "Cultural Amnesia: Memory, Trauma, and War." *Signs*, vol. 28, no. 1, 2002, pp. 455–457.
Halberstam, Judith [Jack]. *Female Masculinity*. Duke UP, 1998.
Hall, Stuart. "Encoding, Decoding." *The Cultural Studies Reader*, edited by Simon During, Routledge, 1993, pp. 90–103.
Hall, Stuart. "Introduction: Who Needs 'Identity'?" *Questions of Cultural Identity*, edited by Stuart Hall and Paul Du Gay, Sage Publications, 1996, pp. 1–17.
Hall, Stuart. "New Ethnicities." *Stuart Hall: Critical Dialogues in Cultural Studies*, edited by David Morley and Kuan-Hsing Chen, Routledge, 1996, pp. 441–449.
Hall, Stuart. "The Question of Cultural Identity." *Modernity and Its Futures*, edited by Stuart Hall et al., Polity Press, 1992, pp. 273–316.
Hall, Stuart. "The Work of Representation." *Representation: Cultural Representations and Signifying Practices*, edited by Stuart Hall, Sage Publications, 1997, pp. 13–74.
Hammond, Philip. "Introduction: Screening the War on Terror." *Screens of Terror: Representations of War and Terrorism in Film and Television since 9/11*, edited by Philip Hammond, Arima Publishing, 2011, pp. 7–18.
Han, Béatrice. *Foucault's Critical Project: Between the Transcendental and the Historical*. Translated by Edward Pile, Stanford UP, 2002.
Haque, M. Shamsul. "Global Rise of Neoliberal State and Its Impact on Citizenship: Experiences in Developing Nations." *Asian Journal of Social Science*, vol. 36, no. 1, 2008, pp. 11–34.
Harding, James M. "Counterbalancing the Pendulum Effect: Politics and the Discourse of Post-9/11 Theatre." *Theatre Survey*, vol. 48, no. 1, 2007, pp. 19–25.
Haritaworn, Jin. "Loyal Repetitions of the Nation: Gay Assimilation and the 'War on Terror'." *Darkmatter*, no. 3, 2008, www.darkmatter101.org/site/2008/05/02/loyal-repetitions-of-the-nation-gay-assimilation-and-the-war-on-terror/.
Harnden, Toby, and David Harrison. "Black Watch Troops Chase Fallujah Fugitives." *Telegraph*, 24 Nov. 2004, p. 16.
Harvie, Jen. *Staging the UK*. Manchester UP, 2005.
Haschemi Yekani, Elahe. "The Politics of (Social) Death and Rebirth in *The Road to Guantánamo* and *Taxi to the Dark Side*." *Birth and Death in British Culture: Liminality, Power, and Performance*, edited by Anette Pankratz et al., Cambridge Scholars Publishing, 2012, pp. 67–80.
Haß, Ulrike. "Vom Sprechen, das nicht aus einem Mund kommt: Chor und Geografie bei Heiner Müller." *Aufbrüche: Theaterarbeit zwischen Text und Situation*, edited by Patrick Primavesi and Olaf A. Schmitt, Theater der Zeit, 2004, pp. 237–246.
Heddon, Deirdre. *Autobiography and Performance*. Palgrave Macmillan, 2008.
Herman, Vimala. *Dramatic Discourse: Dialogue as Interaction in Plays*. Routledge, 1995.
Hesford, Wendy S. "Staging Terror." *The Drama Review*, vol. 50, no. 3, 2006, pp. 29–41.
Hewitt, Steve. *The British War on Terror: Terrorism and Counter-Terrorism on the Home Front since 9/11*. Continuum, 2008.
Hickman, Mary J., et al. *'Suspect Communities'? Counter-Terrorism Policy, the Press, and the Impact on Irish and Muslim Communities in Britain*. London Metropolitan University, 2011.
Hickson, Ella. "Motherland." *Fest*, 6 Aug. 2008, www.festmag.co.uk/archive/2008/93551-motherland/.

Higate, Paul. *Critical Impact Report: The Politics of Profile and the Private Military and Security Contractor*. Global Insecurities Centre, 2013.

Higate, Paul. "Drinking Vodka from the 'Butt-Crack': Men, Masculinities and Fratriarchy in the Private Militarized Security Company." *International Feminist Journal of Politics*, vol. 14, no. 4, 2012, pp. 450–469.

Ho, Christina. "Responding to Orientalist Feminism: Women's Rights and the War on Terror." *Australian Feminist Studies*, vol. 25, no. 66, 2010, pp. 433–439.

Hodges, Adam. *The 'War on Terror' Narrative: Discourse and Intertextuality in the Construction and Contestation of Sociopolitical Reality*. Oxford UP, 2011.

Holmes, Jonathan. "Introduction to the Play." *Fallujah: Eyewitness Testimony from Iraq's Besieged City*, edited by Jonathan Holmes, Constable and Robinson, 2007, pp. 141–145.

Holmes, Jonathan. "The Siege of Fallujah and the Geneva Conventions." *Fallujah: Eyewitness Testimony from Iraq's Besieged City*, edited by Jonathan Holmes, Constable and Robinson, 2007, pp. 113–137.

Hopkins, Steven. "7/7 Bombings: How London Bravely Carried On after a Harrowing Day of Trauma." *Huffington Post*, 7 July 2015, http://www.huffingtonpost.co.uk/2015/07/07/77-bombings-london-victims-what-happened_n_7612010.html/.

Horrocks, Roger. *Masculinity in Crisis*. St Martin's Press, 1994.

Hughes, Jenny. *Performance in a Time of Terror: Critical Mimesis and the Age of Uncertainty*. Manchester UP, 2011.

Hughes, Jenny. "Theatre, Performance and the 'War on Terror': Ethical and Political Questions Arising from British Theatrical Responses to War and Terrorism." *Contemporary Theatre Review*, vol. 17, no. 2, 2007, pp. 149–164.

Hunt, Krista, and Kim Rygiel. "(En)Gendered War Stories and Camouflaged Politics." *(En)Gendering the War on Terror: War Stories and Camouflaged Politics*, edited by Krista Hunt and Kim Rygiel, Ashgate, 2006, pp. 1–24.

Hurley, Kieran. "Uncomfortably Spectacular." *Contemporary Theatre Review*, vol. 18, no. 2, 2008, p. 275.

Hutnyk, John. *Pantomime Terror: Music and Politics*. Zero Books, 2014.

Illouz, Eva. *Saving the Modern Soul: Therapy, Emotions, and the Culture of Self-Help*. U of California P, 2008.

Ingram, Alan, and Klaus Dodds, "Spaces of Security and Insecurity: Geographies of the War on Terror." *Spaces of Security and Insecurity: Geographies of the War on Terror*, edited by Alan Ingram and Klaus Dodds, Ashgate, 2009, pp. 1–18.

Innes, Christopher. "Towards a Post-Millennial Mainstream? Documents of the Times." *Modern Drama*, vol. 50, no. 3, 2007, pp. 435–452.

Isin, Engin F. "The Neurotic Citizen." *Citizenship Studies*, vol. 8, no. 3, 2004, pp. 217–235.

Issacharoff, Michael. *Discourse as Performance*. Stanford UP, 1989.

Jackson, Richard. *Writing the War on Terrorism: Language, Politics and Counter-Terrorism*. Manchester UP, 2005.

Jamison, Matthew. "Humanitarian Intervention since 1990 and 'Liberal Interventionism'." *Humanitarian Intervention: A History*, edited by Brendan Simms and D.J.B. Trim, Cambridge UP, 2011, pp. 365–380.

Jardine, Cassandra, and Richard Savill. "A Very British Way of Mourning." *Telegraph*, 8 July 2009, p. 15.

Jeffrey, Alex. "Containers of Fate: Problematic States and Paradoxical Sovereignty." *Spaces of Security and Insecurity: Geographies of the War on Terror*, edited by Alan Ingram and Klaus Dodds, Ashgate, 2009, pp. 43–63.

Jones, Matt. "After Kandahar: Canadian Theatre's Engagement with the War in Afghanistan." *Canadian Theatre Review*, vol. 157, Winter 2014, pp. 26–29.

Kaplan, E. Ann. *Trauma Culture: The Politics of Terror and Loss in Media and Literature*. Rutgers UP, 2005.

Katz, Cindi. "Banal Terrorism: Spatial Fetishism and Everyday Insecurity." *Violent Geographies: Fear, Terror, and Political Violence*, edited by Derek Gregory and Allan Pred, Routledge, 2007, pp. 349–361.

Kellaway, Kate. "Theatre of War." *Observer*, 29 Aug. 2004, p. 5.

Kelly, John. "Popular Culture, Sport and the 'Hero'-fication of British Militarism." *Sociology*, vol. 47, no. 4, 2013, pp. 722–738.

Kelly, Mark G.E. *The Political Philosophy of Michel Foucault*. Routledge, 2009.

Kent, Nicolas. Introduction. *The Great Game: Afghanistan*, Oberon Books, 2009, pp. 7–8.

Kerr, Rachel. "A Force for Good? War, Crime and Legitimacy: The British Army in Iraq." *Defense and Security Analysis*, vol. 24, no. 4, 2008, pp. 401–419.

Kershaw, Baz. *The Politics of Performance: Radical Theatre as Cultural Intervention*. Routledge, 1992.

Kershaw, Baz. *The Radical in Performance: Between Brecht and Baudrillard*. Routledge, 1999.

Khalid, Maryam. "Gender, Orientalism and Representations of the 'Other' in the War on Terror." *Global Change, Peace and Security*, vol. 23, no. 1, 2011, pp. 15–29.

Kilcullen, David. "The New War Zone." *Guardian*, 28 Sept. 2013, pp. 38–39.

Kimmel, Michael S. "Masculinity as Homophobia." *Theorizing Masculinities*, edited by Harry Brod and Michael Kaufman, Sage Publications, 1994, pp. 119–141.

King, Anthony. "Understanding the Helmand Campaign: British Military Operations in Afghanistan." *International Affairs*, vol. 86, no. 2, 2010, pp. 311–332.

Kintz, Linda. *The Subject's Tragedy: Political Poetics, Feminist Theory, and Drama*. U of Michigan P, 1992.

Klein, Naomi. *The Shock Doctrine: The Rise of Disaster Capitalism*. Penguin, 2008.

Kreuder, Friedemann, et al. Vorwort. *Theater und Subjektkonstitution: Theatrale Praktiken zwischen Affirmation und Subversion*, edited by Friedemann Kreuder et al., Transcript Verlag, 2012, pp. 11–18.

Kritzer, Amelia Howe. *Political Theatre in Post-Thatcher Britain: New Writing 1995–2005*. Palgrave Macmillan, 2008.

Kumar, Sanjay. "An Afghan Feminist Movement?" *The Diplomat*, 22 May 2012, thediplomat.com/2012/05/an-afghan-feminist-movement/.

Kundnani, Arun. "Integrationism: The Politics of Anti-Muslim Racism." *Race and Class*, vol. 48, no. 4, 2007, pp. 24–44.

Kuti, Elizabeth. "Tragic Plots from Bootle to Baghdad." *Contemporary Theatre Review*, vol. 18, no. 4, 2008, pp. 457–469.

Laclau, Ernesto, and Chantal Mouffe. *Hegemony and Socialist Strategy: Towards a Radical Democratic Politics*. Verso, 2001.

Laera, Margherita. "Mark Ravenhill's *Shoot/Get Treasure/Repeat*: A Treasure Hunt in London." *TheatreForum*, no. 35, 2009, pp. 3–9.

Laing, David. "War and Conflict: Theatre of War." *The List*, 31 July 2008, https://edinburghfestival.list.co.uk/article/10667-war-and-conflict/.

Lane, David. *Contemporary British Drama*. Edinburgh UP, 2010.
Lathan, Peter. "*Motherland.*" *British Theatre Guide*, 2007, www.britishtheatreguide.info/reviews/motherland-rev/.
Ledent, Bénédicte. "A Play of Significance: Roy Williams's *Days of Significance* and the Question of Labels." *Engaging with Literature of Containment*. Vol. 2, *The Worldly Scholar*, edited by Gordon Collier et al., Rodopi, 2012, pp. 295–307.
Lehmann, Hans-Thies. *Postdramatic Theatre*. Translated by Karen Jürs-Munby, Routledge, 2006.
Lemke, Thomas. "'The Birth of Bio-Politics': Michel Foucault's Lecture at the Collège de France on Neo-Liberal Governmentality." *Economy and Society*, vol. 30, no. 2, 2001, pp. 190–207.
Lentin, Alana, and Gavan Titley. *The Crises of Multiculturalism: Racism in a Neoliberal Age*. Zed Books, 2011.
Lewis, Jeff. *Language Wars: The Role of Media and Culture in Global Terror and Political Violence*. Pluto Press, 2005.
Lewis, Philip. *Young, British and Muslim*. Continuum, 2007.
Linenthal, Edward T. *The Unfinished Bombing: Oklahoma City in American Memory*. Oxford UP, 2001.
Lo, Jacqueline. "Tracing *Emily of Emerald Hill*: Subject Positioning in Performance." *Myths, Heroes and Anti-Heroes: Essays on the Literature and Culture of the Asia-Pacific Region*, edited by Bruce Bennett and Dennis Haskell, Centre for Studies in Australian Literature, 1992, pp. 120–131.
Lonergan, Patrick. "Re-imagining Ireland, Occupying Iraq: Colin Teevan's *How Many Miles to Basra?*" *The Binding Strength of Irish Studies: Festschrift in Honour of Csilla Bertha and Donald E. Morse*, edited by Marianna Gula et al., Debreceni Egyetemi Kiadó, 2011, pp. 58–65.
Loveridge, Lizzie. "A *CurtainUp* London Review: *The Great Game*." *CurtainUp*, 2009, http://www.curtainup.com/greatgame09.html/.
Loveridge, Lizzie. "*The People Next Door*." *CurtainUp*, 2003, http://www.curtainup.com/peoplenextdoor.html/.
Luckhurst, Mary. "Verbatim Theatre, Media Relations and Ethics." *A Concise Companion to Contemporary British and Irish Drama*, edited by Nadine Holdsworth and Mary Luckhurst, Wiley-Blackwell, 2013, pp. 200–222.
Luckhurst, Mary. "A Wounded Stage: Drama and World War I." *A Companion to Modern British and Irish Drama: 1880–2005*, edited by Mary Luckhurst, Blackwell, 2006, pp. 301–315.
Luckhurst, Roger. "Traumaculture." *New Formations*, no. 50, 2003, pp. 28–47.
Luckhurst, Roger. *The Trauma Question*. Routledge, 2008.
Macalister, Terry. "BP 'Has Stranglehold over Iraq'." *Guardian Weekly*, 5 Aug. 2011, p. 10.
Malpede, Karen. Introduction. *Acts of War: Iraq and Afghanistan in Seven Plays*, edited by Karen Malpede et al., Northwestern UP, 2011, pp. xv–xxxii.
Mamdani, Mahmood. *Good Muslim, Bad Muslim: America, the Cold War, and the Roots of Terror*. Pantheon Books, 2004.
Mamdani, Mahmood. "Good Muslim, Bad Muslim: A Political Perspective on Culture and Terrorism." *American Anthropologist*, no. 104, 2003, pp. 766–775.
Martin, Brian. "From Balzac to Iraq: Soldiers, Veterans, and Military Adaptation." *The Comparatist*, vol. 30, no. 1, 2006, pp. 68–80.

Martin, Carol. *Theatre of the Real*. Palgrave Macmillan, 2013.
McCartney, Helen. "Hero, Victim or Villain? The Public Image of the British Soldier and Its Implications for Defense Policy." *Defense and Security Analysis*, vol. 27, no. 1, 2011, pp. 43–54.
McClintock, Anne. "Paranoid Empire: Specters from Guantánamo and Abu Ghraib." *Small Axe*, vol. 13, no. 1, 2009, pp. 50–74.
McKenzie, Jon. "Democracy's Performance." *The Drama Review*, vol. 47, no. 2, 2003, pp. 117–128.
McKinnie, Michael. "Rethinking Site-Specificity: Monopoly, Urban Space, and the Cultural Economics of Site-Specific Performance." *Performing Site-Specific Theatre: Politics, Place, Practice*, edited by Joanne Tompkins and Anna Birch, Palgrave Macmillan, 2012, pp. 21–33.
Megson, Chris. 2005. "'This Is All Theatre': Iraq Centre Stage." *Contemporary Theatre Review*, vol. 15, no. 3, pp. 369–371.
Mirzoeff, Nicholas. "War Is Culture: Global Counterinsurgency, Visuality, and the Petraeus Doctrine." *PMLA*, vol. 124, no. 5, 2009, pp. 1737–1746.
Mitchell, W.J.T. *Cloning Terror: The War of Images, 9/11 to the Present*. U of Chicago P, 2011.
Modood, Tariq. *Multicultural Politics: Racism, Ethnicity and Muslims in Britain*. Edinburgh UP, 2005.
Mohanty, Chandra Talpade. "US Empire and the Project of Women's Studies: Stories of Citizenship, Complicity and Dissent." *Gender, Place and Culture*, vol. 13, no. 1, 2006, pp. 7–20.
Montag, Warren. "'The Soul Is the Prison of the Body': Althusser and Foucault, 1970–1975." *Yale French Studies*, no. 88, 1995, pp. 53–77.
Moran, Jon. "Politics, Security, Intelligence and Liberty after 9/11." *Intelligence, Security and Policing Post-9/11: The UK's Response to the 'War on Terror'*, edited by Jon Moran and Mark Phythian, Palgrave Macmillan, 2008, pp. 11–31.
Morey, Peter, and Amina Yaqin. *Framing Muslims: Stereotyping and Representation after 9/11*. Harvard UP, 2011.
Morgan, Abi. "My Afghan Marathon." *Guardian*, 9 Apr. 2009, Arts, p. 24.
Mouffe, Chantal. "Agonistic Public Spaces, Democratic Politics, and the Dynamic of Passions." *Thinking Worlds: The Moscow Conference on Philosophy, Politics, and Art*, edited by Joseph Backstein et al., Sternberg Press, 2008, pp. 95–104.
Mouffe, Chantal. "Hegemony and New Political Subjects: Toward a New Concept of Democracy." *Marxism and the Interpretation of Culture*, edited by Cary Nelson and Lawrence Grossberg, U of Illinois P, 1988, pp. 89–101.
Mouffe, Chantal. *The Return of the Political*. Verso, 1993.
Musavi, Sayed Arif. "10-Year-Old Girl Exchanged in Marriage in Balkh Province, Man Slices Wife's Neck in Herat Province." *RAWA News*, 15 Feb. 2015, goo.gl/a6Bi4S.
Nachtigall, Andrea. *Gendering 9/11: Medien, Macht und Geschlecht im Kontext des 'War on Terror'*. Transcript Verlag, 2012.
Nash, Geoffrey. *Writing Muslim Identity*. Continuum, 2012.
Nash, Jennifer C. "Re-thinking Intersectionality." *Feminist Review*, vol. 89, no. 1, 2008, pp. 1–15.
Neal, Andrew W. *Exceptionalism and the Politics of Counter-Terrorism: Liberty, Security and the War on Terror*. Routledge, 2010.

Orr, John, and Dragan Klaić. "Terrorism and Drama: Introduction." *Terrorism and Modern Drama*, edited by John Orr and Dragan Klaić, Edinburgh UP, 1990, pp. 1–12.

Pakis, Elisavet. "Julie Tolentino's Queer Mestiza: Unsettling a White Western Order of Subjectivity and Belonging." *Contemporary Theatre Review*, vol. 24, no. 1, 2014, pp. 21–39.

Pankratz, Anette. "*Queer Drama*: Mark Ravenhill." *Das englische Drama der Gegenwart: Kategorien – Entwicklungen – Modellinterpretationen*, edited by Merle Tönnies, Wissenschaftlicher Verlag Trier, 2010, pp. 193–209.

Pantazis, Christina, and Simon Pemberton. "From the 'Old' to the 'New' Suspect Community: Examining the Impacts of Recent UK Counter-Terrorist Legislation." *British Journal of Criminology*, vol. 49, no. 5, 2009, pp. 646–666.

Parekh, Bhikhu. "Europe, Liberalism and the 'Muslim Question'." *Multiculturalism, Muslims and Citizenship: A European Approach*, edited by Tariq Modood et al., Routledge, 2006, pp. 179–203.

Pattie, David. "Gregory Burke." *The Methuen Drama Guide to Contemporary British Playwrights*, edited by Martin Middeke et al., Methuen Drama, 2011, pp. 22–41.

Pavis, Patrice. *Dictionary of the Theatre: Terms, Concepts, and Analysis*. U of Toronto P, 1998.

Peebles, Stacey. "Lines of Sight: Watching War in *Jarhead* and *My War: Killing Time in Iraq*." *PMLA*, vol. 124, no. 5, 2009, pp. 1662–1676.

Pfister, Manfred. *The Theory and Analysis of Drama*. Translated by John Halliday, Cambridge UP, 1988.

Phelan, Peggy. *Unmarked: The Politics of Performance*. Routledge, 1993.

Phoenix, Aisha. "Somali Young Women and Hierarchies of Belonging." *Young*, vol. 19, no. 3, 2011, pp. 313–331.

Pollock, Griselda. "Art/Trauma/Representation." *Parallax*, vol. 15, no. 1, 2009, pp. 40–54.

Poole, Elizabeth. "The Effects of September 11 and the War in Iraq on British Newspaper Coverage." *Muslims and the News Media*, edited by Elizabeth Poole and John E. Richardson, I.B. Tauris, 2006, pp. 89–102.

Pratt, Mary Louise. "Harm's Way: Language and the Contemporary Arts of War." *PMLA*, vol. 124, no. 5, 2009, pp. 1515–1531.

Pred, Allan. "Situated Ignorance and State Terrorism: Silences, W.M.D., Collective Amnesia, and the Manufacture of Fear." *Violent Geographies: Fear, Terror, and Political Violence*, edited by Derek Gregory and Allan Pred, Routledge, 2007, pp. 363–384.

Puar, Jasbir K. *Terrorist Assemblages: Homonationalism in Queer Times*. Duke UP, 2007.

Puar, Jasbir K., and Amit S. Rai. 2002. "Monster, Terrorist, Fag: The War on Terrorism and the Production of Docile Patriots." *Social Text*, vol. 20, no. 3, 2002, pp. 117–148.

Pugliese, Joseph. "Asymmetries of Terror: Visual Regimes of Racial Profiling and the Shooting of Jean Charles de Menezes in the Context of the War in Iraq." *Borderlands E-journal*, vol. 5, no. 1, 2006, www.borderlands.net.au/vol5no1_2006/pugliese.htm/.

Radstone, Susannah. "The War of the Fathers: Trauma, Fantasy, and September 11." *Signs*, vol. 28, no. 1, 2002, pp. 457–459.

Rancière, Jacques. *Chronicles of Consensual Times*. Translated by Steven Corcoran, Continuum, 2010.

Rancière, Jacques. *The Emancipated Spectator*. Translated by Gregory Elliott, Verso, 2011.

Rancière, Jacques. *The Politics of Aesthetics: The Distribution of the Sensible*. Edited and translated by Gabriel Rockhill, Bloomsbury, 2013.

Rashid, Ahmed. "Prospects for Peace in Afghanistan." *Asian Affairs*, vol. 41, no. 3, 2010, pp. 355–366.
Rayner, Timothy. *Foucault's Heidegger: Philosophy and Transformative Experience*. Continuum, 2007.
Read, Alan. *Theatre, Intimacy and Engagement: The Last Human Venue*. Palgrave Macmillan, 2008.
Reckwitz, Andreas. *Das hybride Subjekt: Eine Theorie der Subjektkulturen von der bürgerlichen Moderne zur Postmoderne*. Velbrück Wissenschaft, 2006.
Redling, Ellen. "New Plays of Ideas and an Aesthetics of Reflection and Debate in Contemporary British Political Drama." *Journal of Contemporary Drama in English*, vol. 2, no. 1, 2014, pp. 159–169.
Rees, Jasper. "Theatre Leads the Way on the War on Terror." *Telegraph*, 22 June 2004, p. 17.
Reid, Trish. "Post-Devolutionary Drama." *The Edinburgh Companion to Scottish Drama*, edited by Ian Brown, Edinburgh UP, 2011, pp. 188–199.
Reinelt, Janelle G. "Selective Affinities: British Playwrights at Work." *Modern Drama*, vol. 50, no. 3, 2007, pp. 305–324.
Reinelt, Janelle G. "Toward a Poetics of Theatre and Public Events: In the Case of Stephen Lawrence." *The Drama Review*, vol. 50, no. 3, 2006, pp. 69–87.
Reisigl, Martin. "Sprachkritische Beobachtungen zu Foucaults Diskursanalyse." *Foucault: Diskursanalyse der Politik; Eine Einführung*, edited by Brigitte Kerchner and Silke Schneider, Verlag für Sozialwissenschaften, 2006, pp. 85–103.
Reuter, Christoph. *My Life Is a Weapon: A Modern History of Suicide Bombing*. Translated by Helena Ragg-Kirkby, Princeton UP, 2004.
Richardson, John E. *(Mis)Representing Islam: The Racism and Rhetoric of British Broadsheet Newspapers*. John Benjamins Publishing, 2004.
Ridout, Nicholas. "Full English." Keynote Lecture at the Annual Conference of the German Society for Contemporary Theatre and Drama in English, University of Barcelona, 6 June 2015.
Robinson, Rebecca. "The National Theatre of Scotland's *Black Watch*." *Contemporary Theatre Review*, vol. 22, no. 3, 2012, pp. 392–399.
Rostek, Joanna. "(Un)Othering the Terrorist: Responses to Terrorism in Two Contemporary British Plays." *Deconstructing Terrorism: 9/11, 7/7 and Contemporary Culture*, edited by Jürgen Kamm et al., Verlag Karl Stutz, 2013, pp. 95–116.
Rubik, Margarete. "Fragmented Biographies: Restoring a Voice to Guantanamo Prisoners: Brittain and Slovo's *Guantanamo: 'Honor Bound to Defend Freedom'*." *Narrative in Drama*, edited by Merle Tönnies and Christina Flotmann, Wissenschaftlicher Verlag Trier, 2011, pp. 53–61.
Rubin, G. James, et al. "Enduring Consequences of Terrorism: 7-Month Follow-Up Survey of Reactions to the Bombings in London on 7 July 2005." *British Journal of Psychiatry*, vol. 190, no. 4, 2007, pp. 350–356.
Rutherford, Jonathan. "At War." *Cultural Studies*, vol. 19, no. 5, 2005, pp. 622–642.
Rygiel, Kim. "Protecting and Proving Identity: The Biopolitics of Waging War through Citizenship in the Post-9/11 Era." *(En)Gendering the War on Terror: War Stories and Camouflaged Politics*, edited by Krista Hunt and Kim Rygiel, Ashgate, 2006, pp. 145–167.
Saal, Ilka. "'It's about Us!': Violence and Narrative Memory in Post 9/11 American Theater." *Arcadia*, vol. 45, no. 2, 2010, pp. 353–373.

Saha, Anamik. "Locating MIA: 'Race', Commodification and the Politics of Production." *European Journal of Cultural Studies*, vol. 15, no. 6, 2012, pp. 736–752.
Said, Edward W. *Orientalism*. Penguin Books, 2003.
Sasson-Levy, Orna. "Frauen als Grenzgängerinnen im israelischen Militär: Identitätsstrategien und -praktiken weiblicher Soldaten in 'männlichen' Rollen." *Gender und Militär: Internationale Erfahrungen mit Frauen und Männern in Streitkräften*, edited by Ruth Seifert and Christine Eifler, Ulrike Helmer Verlag, 2003, pp. 74–100.
Schlensag, Stefan. "The Myth of the Classless Society: Politics of Identity and Hegemony in *Bridget Jones's Diary*." *Cases of Intervention: The Great Variety of British Cultural Studies*, edited by Marie Hologa et al., Cambridge Scholars Publishing, 2013, pp. 145–163.
Schlote, Christiane. "A Different Theatre of War: Humanitarian Aid on British Stages." *Ethical Debates in Contemporary Theatre and Drama*, edited by Mark Berninger and Bernhard Reitz, Wissenschaftlicher Verlag Trier, 2012, pp. 121–135.
Schott, Robin May. "Gender and 'Postmodern War'." *Hypatia*, vol. 11, no. 4, 1996, pp. 19–29.
Scott, Catherine V. "Rescue in the Age of Empire: Children, Masculinity, and the War on Terror." *(En)Gendering the War on Terror: War Stories and Camouflaged Politics*, edited by Krista Hunt and Kim Rygiel, Ashgate, 2006, pp. 97–117.
Seidler, Victor J. *Urban Fears and Global Terrors: Citizenship, Multicultures and Belongings after 7/7*. Routledge, 2007.
Sharma, Nandita. "White Nationalism, Illegality and Imperialism: Border Controls as Ideology." *(En)Gendering the War on Terror: War Stories and Camouflaged Politics*, edited by Krista Hunt and Kim Rygiel, Ashgate, 2006, pp. 121–143.
Shaw, Marc E. "Unpacking the *Pinteresque* in *The Dumb Waiter* and Beyond." *Harold Pinter's The Dumb Waiter*, edited by Mary F. Brewer, Rodopi, 2009, pp. 211–229.
Shivani, Anis. "Good Muslims versus Bad Muslims in Contemporary Literature." *The Antioch Review*, vol. 71, no. 1, 2013, pp. 40–58.
Shotter, John. *Cultural Politics of Everyday Life: Social Constructionism, Rhetoric and Knowing of the Third Kind*. Open UP, 1993.
Sierz, Aleks. "Playwright Adam Brace on *Stovepipe*." *Theatrevoice*, 13 Mar. 2009, www.theatrevoice.com/audio/playwright-adam-brace-on-stovepipe/.
Sierz, Aleks. *Rewriting the Nation: British Theatre Today*. Methuen, 2011.
Silverstone, Catherine. *Shakespeare, Trauma and Contemporary Performance*. Routledge, 2011.
Smith, Paul. *Discerning the Subject*. U of Minnesota P, 1988.
Soto-Morettini, Donna. "Trouble in the House: David Hare's *Stuff Happens*." *Contemporary Theatre Review*, vol. 15, no. 3, 2005, pp. 309–319.
Sparke, Matthew B. "A Neoliberal Nexus: Economy, Security and the Biopolitics of Citizenship on the Border." *Political Geography*, vol. 25, no. 2, 2006, pp. 151–180.
Spencer, Charles. "It's Funny, Romantic – and Islamic." Review of *Shades*, *Telegraph*, 10 Feb. 2009, p. 27.
Spencer, Charles. "Lives in the Time of Terror." Review of *Pornography*, *Telegraph*, 7 Aug. 2009, p. 24.
Spencer, Charles. "The Most Thrilling Drama in Town." Review of *Stovepipe*, *Telegraph*, 11 Mar. 2009, p. 25.
Spencer, Charles. "Upsetting – and Unforgettable." Review of *Osama the Hero*, *Telegraph*, 12 May 2005, p. 18.

Spencer, Jenny. Editor's Introduction. *Political and Protest Theater after 9/11: Patriotic Dissent*, edited by Jenny Spencer, Routledge, 2012, pp. 1–15.
Spencer, Jenny. "Terrorized by the War on Terror: Mark Ravenhill's *Shoot/Get Treasure/Repeat*." *Political and Protest Theater after 9/11: Patriotic Dissent*, edited by Jenny Spencer, Routledge, 2012, pp. 63–78.
Spivak, Gayatri Chakravorty. "Can the Subaltern Speak?" *Colonial Discourse and Post-Colonial Theory: A Reader*, edited by Patrick Williams and Laura Chrisman, Harvester Wheatsheaf, 1994, pp. 66–111.
Spivak, Gayatri Chakravorty. "Terror: A Speech after 9/11." *Boundary*, vol. 31, no. 2, 2004, pp. 81–111.
Stabile, Carol, and Deepa Kumar. "Unveiling Imperialism: Media, Gender and the War on Afghanistan." *Media, Culture & Society*, vol. 27, no. 5, 2005, pp. 765–782.
Starck, Kathleen. "Current Global Conflict and the Invasion of the Private in *The Pull of Negative Gravity* and *When the Bulbul Stopped Singing*." *Mapping Uncertain Territories: Space and Place in Contemporary Theatre and Drama*, edited by Thomas Rommel and Mark Schreiber, Wissenschaftlicher Verlag Trier, 2006, pp. 61–72.
Stephens, Angharad Closs. "'Seven Million Londoners, One London': National and Urban Ideas of Community in the Aftermath of the 7 July 2005 Bombings in London." *Alternatives*, vol. 32, no. 2, 2007, pp. 155–176.
Südkamp, Holger. "*Among Unbroken People Next Door (In the Time of the Messiah)*: Henry Adam's Drama of Interculturality." *Staging Interculturality*, edited by Werner Huber et al., Wissenschaftlicher Verlag Trier, 2010, pp. 161–175.
Sun. "Don't Back Benn." 17 Apr. 2007, p. 8.
Tarlo, Emma. "Islamic Cosmopolitanism: The Sartorial Biographies of Three Muslim Women in London." *Fashion Theory*, vol. 11, no. 2–3, pp. 143–172.
Taylor, Alastair, and Gary O'Shea. "Suffer Little Children …" *Sun*, 19 Aug. 2009, pp. 4–5.
Taylor, Diana. "Afterword: War Play." *PMLA*, vol. 124, no. 5, 2009, pp. 1886–1895.
Taylor, Paul. "*The Empire*." *Independent*, 20 Apr. 2010, Viewspaper, p. 15.
Terrill, Chris, director. *Theatre of War*. Uppercut Films, 2012.
Tomlin, Liz. *Acts and Apparitions: Discourses on the Real in Performance Practice and Theory, 1990–2010*. Manchester UP, 2013.
Tompkins, Joanne. "Breaching the Body's Boundaries: Abjected Subject Positions in Postcolonial Drama." *Modern Drama*, vol. 40, no. 4, 1997, pp. 502–513.
Tönnies, Merle. "The Codes of 'Self' and 'Other' and the Manipulation of Audience Sympathy: Conflicts between the West and the Islamic World in Contemporary British and Irish Drama." *Race and Religion in Contemporary Drama in English*, edited by Bernhard Reitz, Wissenschaftlicher Verlag Trier, 1999, pp. 77–84.
Tosh, John. "Hegemonic Masculinity and the History of Gender." *Masculinities in Politics and War: Gendering Modern History*, edited by Stefan Dudink et al., Manchester UP, 2004, pp. 41–58.
Tyler, Imogen. *Revolting Subjects: Social Abjection and Resistance in Neoliberal Britain*. Zed Books, 2013.
Upstone, Sara. "9/11, British Muslims, and Popular Literary Fiction." *Reframing 9/11: Film, Popular Culture and the 'War on Terror'*, edited by Jeff Birkenstein et al., Continuum, 2010, pp. 35–44.
Urban, Ken. "Cruel Britannia." *Cool Britannia? British Political Drama in the 1990s*, edited by Rebecca D'Monté and Graham Saunders, Palgrave Macmillan, 2008, pp. 38–55.

Vale, Allison. "*Days of Significance.*" *British Theatre Guide*, 2009, www.britishtheatreguide.info/reviews/RSCdayssignif-rev/.
van Houdt, Friso, et al. "Neoliberal Communitarian Citizenship: Current Trends towards 'Earned Citizenship' in the United Kingdom, France and the Netherlands." *International Sociology*, vol. 26, no. 3, 2011, pp. 408–432.
Viner, Katharine. "Feminism as Imperialism." *Guardian*, 21 Sept. 2002, p. 26.
Voigts-Virchow, Eckart. "Richard Bean." *The Methuen Drama Guide to Contemporary British Playwrights*, edited by Martin Middeke et al., Methuen Drama, 2011, pp. 1–21.
von der Lippe, Berit, and Tarja Väyrynen. "Co-opting Feminist Voices for the War on Terror: Laura Bush Meets Nordic Feminism." *European Journal of Women's Studies*, vol. 18, no. 1, 2011, pp. 19–33.
Wald, Christina. *Hysteria, Trauma and Melancholia: Performative Maladies in Contemporary Anglophone Drama*. Palgrave Macmillan, 2007.
Walgenbach, Katharina. "Gender *als* interdependente Kategorie." *Gender als interdependente Kategorie: Neue Perspektiven auf Intersektionalität, Diversität und Heterogenität*, edited by Katharina Walgenbach et al., Barbara Budrich, 2007, pp. 23–64.
Walker, Lynne. "Murky Morals in Desert Drama." Review of *How Many Miles to Basra?*, *Independent*, 2 Oct. 2006, Extra, p. 20.
Walklate, Sandra, et al. "Witnessing Wootton Bassett: An Exploration in Cultural Victimology." *Crime Media Culture*, vol. 7, no. 2, 2011, pp. 149–165.
Walter, Tony. *On Bereavement: The Culture of Grief*. Open UP, 1999.
Weidle, Roland. "Mimetic Narration: Documentary Theatre and the Staging of Truth." *Narrative in Drama*, edited by Merle Tönnies and Christina Flotmann, Wissenschaftlicher Verlag Trier, 2011, pp. 63–79.
Weiss, Thomas G. *Humanitarian Intervention: An Introduction*. Polity Press, 2007.
Westgate, Chris. "David Hare's *Stuff Happens* in Seattle: Taking a Sober Account." *New Theatre Quarterly*, vol. 25, no. 4, 2009, pp. 402–418.
Whitaker, Raymond. "Cycle of Violence." Review of *The Great Game: Afghanistan*, *New Statesman*, 7 May 2009, www.newstatesman.com/theatre/2009/05/afghanistan-british-plays/.
Wierzoch, Janina. "Time and Temporalities in Contemporary British War Plays: Roy Williams's *Days of Significance* and Owen Sheers's *The Two Worlds of Charlie F.*" *Journal of Contemporary Drama in English*, vol. 3, no. 1, 2015, pp. 110–126.
Wilding, Jo. "Testimonies." *Fallujah: Eyewitness Testimony from Iraq's Besieged City*, edited by Jonathan Holmes, Constable and Robinson, 2007, pp. 29–64.
Wilkie, Fiona. "The Production of 'Site': Site-Specific Theatre." *A Concise Companion to Contemporary British and Irish Drama*, edited by Nadine Holdsworth and Mary Luckhurst, Wiley-Blackwell, 2013, pp. 87–106.
Wintour, Patrick. "David Cameron Tells UK Troops Their Work in Afghanistan 'Will Live Forever'." *Guardian*, 3 Oct. 2014, goo.gl/Ke4Du4.
Woodward, Rachel, and Patricia Winter. "Discourses of Gender in the Contemporary British Army." *Armed Forces and Society*, vol. 30, no. 2, 2004, pp. 279–301.
Woodward, Rachel, et al. "Heroic Anxieties: The Figure of the British Soldier in Contemporary Print Media." *Journal of War and Culture Studies*, vol. 2, no. 2, 2009, pp. 211–223.
Youngs, Gillian. "The 'New Home Front' and the War on Terror: Ethical and Political Reframing of National and International Politics." *International Affairs*, vol. 86, no. 4, 2010, pp. 925–937.

Yuval-Davis, Nira. "Intersectionality and Feminist Politics." *European Journal of Women's Studies*, vol. 13, no. 3, 2006, pp. 193–209.
Yuval-Davis, Nira. "Intersectionality, Citizenship and Contemporary Politics of Belonging." *Critical Review of International Social and Political Philosophy*, vol. 10, no. 4, 2007, pp. 561–574.
Zabcı, Filiz. "Private Military Companies: 'Shadow Soldiers' of Neo-Colonialism." *Capital and Class*, vol. 31, no. 2, 2007, pp. 1–10.
Zerdy, Joanne. "Fashioning a Scottish Operative: *Black Watch* and Banal Theatrical Nationalism on Tour in the US." *Theatre Research International*, vol. 38, no. 3, pp. 181–195.
Zine, Jasmin. "Between Orientalism and Fundamentalism: Muslim Women and Feminist Engagement." *(En)Gendering the War on Terror: War Stories and Camouflaged Politics*, edited by Krista Hunt and Kim Rygiel, Ashgate, 2006, pp. 27–49.
Žižek, Slavoj. *Welcome to the Desert of the Real! Five Essays on September 11 and Related Dates*. Verso, 2002.

General Index

7/7 9, 15, 29, 48, 64, 69, 74, 87–88, 93, 96, 99, 104–112, 117, 119, 138–140, 248

9/11 1–10, 15–18, 29, 37, 51–54, 57–58, 61, 68, 74–79, 84, 87, 90–95, 97, 99, 109–110, 114, 117, 140, 155, 159, 162–165, 179, 225, 232–233, 237, 239, 243

Abu Ghraib prison 1, 15–16, 51, 66–67, 69, 134, 219, 263, 265
Afghan war 74–75, 120–122, 125, 141, 146, 161–165, 167–168, 172, 174–175, 177–178, 186–190, 199–200, 226–227, 257, 263, 267
Agamben, Giorgio 48, 95, 182–186
Ahmed, Sara 58–59, 74, 86, 101, 141
al-Qaeda 60, 164–165
Althusser, Louis 25–26, 31, 36, 175
anti-war protest 3, 58, 118, 125, 154, 186, 220, 223–224, 243, 267
anxiety 48–50, 57–59, 61, 64–65, 73, 102–103, 140
archive 1, 23, 240–241, 243–244, 269
articulation 37–38, 41
Auslander, Philip 21–22, 45

Baudrillard, Jean 110, 114
Bhabha, Homi K. 171, 178, 234
Bharucha, Rustom 1, 5, 7, 51, 85, 190
bin Laden, Osama 51, 62–64, 165
Blair, Tony 18, 74, 88, 93–94, 99, 114–118, 139, 186, 204–205, 213, 220, 232–234, 240–241, 246
Bluestone 42 146, 257
Bottoms, Stephen 1, 4, 71, 113, 123
Brady, Sara 5, 18, 113, 171
Braidotti, Rosi 39, 84, 188
British Armed Forces 150, 247
Britz 75, 84
burqa 186, 189–192, 203, 260
Bush, George W. 17–18, 68, 99, 114–115, 204, 246
Butler, Judith 20, 25–26, 30–34, 125, 128–130, 139, 165, 173, 176, 185, 198, 225–227, 231–232, 234, 236, 243, 254–255, 258

Cameron, David 164–165
capitalism (*see also* neoliberalism) 84, 94, 100, 108, 204, 206, 215, 219, 222–224
Caruth, Cathy 143, 145
casting 43, 202
character 41–46
Charlie Hebdo attack 29
Chaudhuri, Una 13, 43, 63, 90
chorus 98–101
Christianity 158, 189, 234
citizenship 9, 48–53, 56–57, 59, 66, 76, 87–88, 92–96, 98, 100–103, 106–107, 109–113, 115–117, 224, 243, 245, 260, 268
– ceremony 87–88
– collective 95, 100–102, 268
– loss of 51
– neoliberal 98, 100–103, 106, 112
– test 76, 94
clash of civilisations thesis 17, 162, 164, 172, 265
class 8, 36–37, 56, 83, 92, 132–134, 178, 214–215, 220–221, 246–247, 250, 252, 267
Cold War 94, 163–165
Colleran, Jeanne 5, 9, 116, 124, 156
colonialism 89, 163, 165, 187–189, 196, 202, 216, 234
cosmopolitanism 78, 81–83, 92
counter-terrorism 52, 59–60, 88
critical mimesis 22–23, 32, 53, 61, 66, 90, 99, 101, 103, 110, 116, 136, 181, 265, 267

Deleuze, Gilles 14, 23, 33, 40, 85, 112, 255
democracy 4, 17, 28, 37, 66, 72–73, 93–94, 110, 115–116, 164, 185, 243, 267–268
Derrida, Jacques 18, 30, 109–110, 164, 166

292 — General Index

discourse   3, 12, 15–21, 23–24, 26–27, 29–30, 32–37, 39–40, 45–47, 53–54, 64, 70, 101, 104, 112, 129, 138, 156, 176, 180, 268–269
discursive formation   2–3, 12, 15–24, 33–34, 36, 38, 40–41, 43–44, 50, 67–68, 92–93, 125, 180, 200, 217, 260–261, 268–269
drama   3–8, 21, 24, 26, 41–46, 90, 116, 161, 166, 181, 210, 235–236, 266
– form semantics of   4, 46
– post-9/11   1–8, 10, 12, 22, 70, 76, 86, 92, 95, 117, 121, 140–141, 161, 166, 265–269

embedded journalism   226–228, 235–239
enemy   1, 52, 59–60, 64–65, 67–68, 94, 147, 162–173, 176, 178, 180–182, 184–185, 199, 214, 230–231, 260, 262, 267
– spectral   1, 166, 168–169, 173, 180–182, 267
– structuring   166, 168, 178
– within   52, 58–59, 69
England, Lynndie   219, 247

falling man   155–156
feminism   8, 33, 119, 156, 186, 188–190, 194–195, 198, 201, 234
First World War   120, 139, 181, 253
Fischer-Lichte, Erika   11, 13, 44, 145
Foucault, Michel   2–3, 15–21, 23, 26–29, 33–35, 68, 177, 266, 268
fundamentalism   37, 74–75, 78–80, 92, 109, 268

gender   30, 32, 51, 77, 83, 119–121, 126–127, 130, 135–138, 149–150, 189, 201, 218, 244–248, 254–264, 268
– performativity   31–32, 254–255
– wartime constructions of   118–121, 126, 134–137, 149–150, 234, 261–262, 268
Gilroy, Paul   9, 53, 94, 172
globalisation   113–114, 180, 205, 213, 219, 221–222, 245, 253, 268
Greenham Common   201
Green Zone   171, 210

grief   102, 107, 118–122, 124–126, 128–131, 137–138, 155–157, 225–227
grievability   30, 128–130, 146, 195–196, 225–226, 231, 234–235, 238, 242–243
Guantánamo Bay detention camp   1, 15, 67, 178, 181–186, 265
Guattari, Félix   14, 33, 40, 85, 255
Gulf War   135, 162

Hall, Stuart   29, 35–38, 75–76, 92
Hampstead Theatre   62, 64, 76, 84, 257
heteronormativity   51, 79–80, 121, 150, 251, 260, 268
hijab   78–79, 84, 88–91
home, the   49–50, 64
home front   49–50, 73, 97–98, 118, 126, 265, 268
homonationalism   51, 260
Hughes, Jenny   5, 8, 10, 22, 61, 72, 90, 96, 101
humanitarian intervention   186, 196–198, 200–202, 232–234, 242–243
Hurt Locker, The   146, 171, 210
Hussein, Saddam   10, 165, 171–172, 186, 215, 240

identity   11, 24, 32, 37–38, 41, 85, 161, 163, 245
– cultural   61, 79, 84, 178, 266
– national   61, 79, 117, 120, 170, 248
– politics of   8, 11, 38, 141
Illouz, Eva   102, 139, 150, 221, 223, 246
imaginative geography   48, 69, 97, 100, 111, 162, 168, 172, 189, 193, 204–205, 212, 216
imperialism   89, 163, 209, 213, 222–224, 262
improvised explosive device (*see also* weapon)   146–147
indefinite detention   1, 184–185
interpellation   25–26, 31, 48, 53, 55–57, 93, 95, 175–178, 180, 266
intersectionality   12–13, 38–39, 76
invisibility   166, 173, 266
Iraq war   1, 4, 7, 11, 58, 69, 74–75, 113–121, 124–125, 131, 138, 161–163, 165, 167–169, 171–172, 186, 203–214,

217–220, 223, 225–226, 228, 232–237, 240–241, 249, 256–257, 262–263, 267–268
Islam (*see also* Muslims)   74–81, 83, 91–92, 109, 164, 194, 198
Islamic State   28
Islamophobia   75, 85, 92

Jarhead   135, 254

Kent, Nicolas   181, 190–191
Kershaw, Baz   2, 7, 21–22
Klein, Naomi   204, 206, 208, 210, 212, 214, 218–219

Lacan, Jacques   36–37, 55
Laclau, Ernesto   2, 18, 30, 36–38, 45
Lehmann, Hans-Thies (*see also* postdramatic theatre)   4, 41, 46, 98, 101, 116, 142
liberation   163, 186–190, 197, 200–201, 203
Live 8   110–112
London bombings (*see* 7/7)
Longo, Robert
– *Men in the Cities*   154–155
Luckhurst, Roger   139–141, 156

masculinity   2, 51, 92, 119, 126, 134–136, 147–151, 158, 200–201, 216, 244–263
– hegemonic   148, 160, 245–248, 251–252, 255, 257, 262–263
– military   119, 126, 134–136, 148–150, 244–249, 251–263
– traumatised   148–150, 156–160
McClintock, Anne   69, 165, 173, 182
military culture   134, 148, 209, 247, 251, 254, 257–262
motherhood   127, 129–131
Mouffe, Chantal   2, 7, 18, 30, 36–38, 45, 164
mourning   (*see* grief)
multiculturalism   9, 37, 61, 82, 84, 90–92, 170
Muslims (*see also* Islam)   6, 9, 28, 37, 52, 56–57, 74–85, 87–92, 104–106, 108–109, 184, 188, 203, 230, 266

nation   49, 56, 67, 113, 120, 130–131, 170–171, 260
National Theatre London   113, 116, 215
National Theatre of Scotland   248
neoliberalism (*see also* capitalism)   81, 93, 98, 100–103, 112, 117, 204–207, 213–216, 221–224, 268
New Labour   57, 60–61, 76, 88, 94–95, 222
new writing   8, 10, 54, 64, 246
Northern Ireland conflict   52, 72, 164, 234–235, 241

O'Brien, Tim
– "The Things They Carried"   218
Olympics   110–112
Orientalism   51, 89, 187–191, 193–196, 201–203, 230, 260
Our Girl   257
overdetermination   36–37, 41, 45–46, 50, 59, 64, 71, 76, 80, 87, 89, 100, 266

paranoia   60, 165, 171, 173, 177
patriarchy   89, 154, 156, 253–254, 263
patriotism   50–54, 56–58, 60, 64–70, 73–74, 260
performance studies   5–6, 11, 42
Phelan, Peggy   23, 44, 83, 89–90
Pinter, Harold   173–174
political theatre   1–2, 6–8, 19, 21–23, 46
postdramatic theatre   41–42, 100, 142, 152
poststructuralism   2, 11, 13, 24–26, 29, 33–34, 38–39, 41–42
post-traumatic stress disorder   (*see* trauma)

private security industry   206, 209–211, 224
Puar, Jasbir   51–52, 54, 61, 66, 118, 260
Pugliese, Joseph   1, 48, 86, 109, 225

queer   51, 66–67, 259–260

race   48, 51, 56–57, 59, 85–88, 170, 178, 180, 185, 205, 262
racial profiling   48, 57, 85, 87, 266
racism   38, 57, 85, 87–88, 170, 230, 253

Rancière, Jacques   7, 93, 99, 101, 107, 117, 155, 226, 234, 239, 255
rape   156, 216, 262–263
Reckwitz, Andreas   29–30, 35, 40
recognition   25, 30–33, 53, 86–88, 147, 171, 175–177, 232, 234, 265
Reinelt, Janelle   8, 12, 117, 134
Restrepo   227, 236
Revolutionary Association of the Women of Afghanistan   189, 197
Road to Guantánamo, The   178–179, 181, 185
Route Irish   210
Royal Court Theatre   70, 76–77, 83, 151, 173, 220, 223

Second World War   104, 134
securitisation   6, 9, 61, 67, 97, 185
shock and awe   203–205, 212, 219, 243–244
site-specific performance   13, 207–208, 236–237, 239
soldiers   19, 135, 146, 161, 167–168, 180–181, 210, 224, 246–247, 257–259, 267
– death of   118, 120, 122, 124, 128–129, 252
– wounded   139, 141–151
space   48–50, 65, 86, 95–97, 111, 113, 126, 133, 161–162, 168, 172, 181–183, 185–186, 204, 207–208, 225–226
– of exception   48, 182–183
– public   100–101
– urban   48–49, 69, 73, 82, 86–87, 95–98, 110
spectatorship   26, 35–36, 44–45, 47, 59, 66, 86–87, 90, 98, 116, 127–128, 130–131, 143, 147–148, 150–151, 155–156, 182, 208, 219, 237, 239, 256, 266–267
Spencer, Jenny   5–6, 8–9, 216
Spivak, Gayatri Chakravorty   34, 187, 189, 195–196
storytelling   152, 196, 225, 238
subject   11, 13, 19, 24–35, 39, 41–43, 46, 53
subjection   25, 27–29, 33–34, 53, 56, 68, 137, 176, 256

subjectivation   27–29, 32, 34, 44, 55–56, 64, 68, 73, 98, 103, 111, 176–177, 180, 249, 261, 266
subject position   2–3, 11–14, 24, 26, 29, 33–48, 50, 54, 61, 64–65, 67, 70, 89, 91–92, 94, 119–121, 137, 154, 156, 172–173, 180, 193, 202, 227, 236–237, 243, 245–246, 265, 268
suspicion   9, 48, 53, 58–59, 62, 70, 78, 177, 180, 184, 265–266

Taliban   147, 174–175, 186–194, 198–199
technology of the self   26–29, 34, 40, 128, 177
terror city   48, 54, 95, 97, 110, 112
terrorism   1, 5–6, 9, 48, 52, 54, 60, 64, 68, 70–71, 73, 92, 103, 109, 164, 166, 173, 180
testimony   29, 73, 144–145, 182–185, 236–240
Thatcher, Margaret   37, 223
therapeutic ethos   147, 221, 223, 246
torture   1, 51, 65–66, 68–69, 165, 219, 265
tragedy   115, 167, 171
trauma   138–146, 148–153, 156–160, 240
Traverse Theatre   54, 59, 104, 151
Tricycle Theatre   10, 104, 107, 116, 131–133, 181, 190, 199

United 93   179

verbatim theatre   2–4, 8, 45, 70, 122–124, 128, 267
Vietnam War   120, 156, 218, 230
visuality   5, 85, 90, 166, 185

'war on terror'   1, 8–9, 15, 28–29, 46, 48, 50, 56, 60, 69–70, 94, 97, 112, 118, 129, 140, 156, 163–166, 180, 183, 185, 204, 224, 244–245, 266
– discourse   2–3, 12, 15–21, 23–24, 28–29, 31, 46, 64, 67–68, 74, 93, 101, 109, 137–138, 159, 200, 217, 260–261, 268–269
– iconography   91, 116, 118, 168, 266

weapon   117, 135–136, 146–147, 240
– and phallic imagery   135–136
– of mass destruction   117, 186, 231, 240
witnessing   18, 139–140, 182, 237–239, 240, 243
Woolwich murder   152–154, 156, 159
Wootton Bassett   118, 120–122, 125, 129, 138, 140

xenophobia (*see* racism; *see also* Islamophobia)

Yasmin   75, 84
Yuval-Davis, Nira   9, 39

Žižek, Slavoj   82, 93, 115, 168–169, 173

Index of Plays

Adam, Henry
– *The People Next Door*   54–62, 64, 68–70, 73–74, 179–180

Bano, Alia
– *Shades*   6, 76–85, 92, 203
Bartlett, Mike
– *Artefacts*   205
Bean, Richard
– *England People Very Nice*   84, 202
– *On the Side of the Angels*   197–203, 225
Brace, Adam
– *Stovepipe*   6, 206–214, 222, 224, 229
Brittain, Victoria, and Gillian Slovo
– *Guantanamo: 'Honor Bound to Defend Freedom'*   8, 181–186, 248
Burke, Gregory
– *Black Watch*   228, 247–257, 263–264

Crome, Karla
– *Mush and Me*   76
Crouch, Tim
– *The Author*   3

Edgar, David
– *Testing the Echo*   76

Gilroy, Steve
– *Motherland*   121–134, 137–138, 149, 244
Goode, Chris
– *Men in the Cities*   142, 151–160, 263–264
Great Game: Afghanistan, The   190–193, 195–199, 202–203
Gupta, Tanika
– *White Boy*   76

Hare, David
– *Stuff Happens*   8, 113–118, 248
Holmes, Jonathan
– *Fallujah*   6, 228, 236–244

Jones, Cat
– *Glory Dazed*   121, 141

Kelly, Dennis
– *After the End*   54
– *Osama the Hero*   54, 62–70, 73–74, 103, 177, 180

Lichtenstein, Jonathan
– *The Pull of Negative Gravity*   141

Malcolm, Morgan Lloyd
– *Belongings*   6, 141, 247, 257–264
Moore, DC
– *The Empire*   6, 167, 173–181, 184–185, 215
Morgan, Abi
– *The Night Is Darkest Before the Dawn*   191–197, 200, 202–203
Morris, Peter
– *Guardians*   228, 247

Norton-Taylor, Richard
– *Called to Account*   116

Patel, Vinay
– *True Brits*   86–87

Ravenhill, Mark
– *Shoot/Get Treasure/Repeat*   95–103, 105, 111–113, 115, 117–118, 206, 214–225

Sen Gupta, Atiha
– *What Fatima Did...*   6, 76, 84–92, 203
Shakespeare, William
– *As You Like It*   105
– *Much Ado about Nothing*   131–132
Sheers, Owen
– *The Two Worlds of Charlie F.*   142–151, 160, 263–264
Soans, Robin
– *Talking to Terrorists*   8, 70–74
Steel, Beth
– *Lynndie England*   247
Stephens, Simon
– *Canopy of Stars*   121, 247

– *Motortown*   121, 141, 220
– *Pornography*   10, 95, 104–113, 115, 118, 152, 159

Taylor, Ali
– *Overspill*   53

Teevan, Colin
– *How Many Miles to Basra?*   228–236, 243

Williams, Roy
– *Days of Significance*   121, 131–138, 166–174, 180–181, 185, 214
– *Sing Yer Heart Out for the Lads*   171

www.ingramcontent.com/pod-product-compliance
Lightning Source LLC
Chambersburg PA
CBHW030609230426
43661CB00053B/1908